"In *Interaction for Designers*, Brian has given designers with every level of experience—from students to seasoned professionals—a helpful, practicable, and comprehensive playbook of methods, techniques, and strategies for the thoughtful crafting connected products, services, and interactive experiences. Brian's refreshing approach gives clear advice while eschewing a dogmatic process, and is an indispensable addition to the canon of interaction design literature."

Jason Brush, Global EVP, Experiences & Innovation, POSSIBLE

Interaction for Designers

Interaction for Designers shows you how to connect a product with its users, whether it's a simple toaster, a complex ecosystem of intelligent devices, or a single app on your smartphone. This book covers the entire design process so you can start with an idea and carry it through to an engaging final design. It carefully leads you step by step and richly illustrates each stage with examples drawn from business communication, social media and the social economy, consumer electronics, architecture and environments, health care, psychology, art and culture, education, athletics, automotive design, entertainment, fashion, the family home, and a wealth of others. You'll learn how to brainstorm ideas, research them, explore them, evolve them into finished designs, pitch them, all with the goal of helping you make things that people love. Includes over 200 color images, a glossary, and links to web resources highlighting design concepts and designer interviews.

Brian L. M. Boyl is a professor at Art Center College of Design, and Director of the Visual Interaction Area of Emphasis in the Department of Graphic Design.

Interaction for Designers

How to Make Things People Love

Brian L. M. Boyl

Routledge
Taylor & Francis Group
NEW YORK AND LONDON

First published 2019
by Routledge
52 Vanderbilt Avenue, New York, NY 10017

and by Routledge
2 Park Square, Milton Park, Abingdon, Oxon, OX14 4RN

Routledge is an imprint of the Taylor & Francis Group, an informa business

Library of Congress Cataloging-in-Publication Data
Names: Boyl, Brian, author.
Title: Interaction for designers : how to make things people love / Brian Boyl.
Description: New York, NY : Routledge, 2019. | Includes bibliographical references and index.
Identifiers: LCCN 2018050048| ISBN 9780415787246 (hbk : alk. paper) | ISBN 9780415787253 (pbk : alk. paper) | ISBN 9781315226224 (ebk)
Subjects: LCSH: Product design.
Classification: LCC TS171 .B689 2019 | DDC 658.5/752—dc23
LC record available at https://lccn.loc.gov/2018050048

ISBN: 9780415787246 (hbk)
ISBN: 9780415787253 (pbk)
ISBN: 9781315226224 (ebk)

Typeset in Avenir
by Apex CoVantage, LLC

To Krystina, who has dedicated so much to others and deserves a little dedication in return.

Contents

Acknowledgements

I'd like to acknowledge the collaboration I've had with my esteemed colleague, Jeff Higashi. His professionalism, insight, and creativity are boundless and my understanding of design would be a mere shadow of what it is without him. I would also like to applaud the help of Lucia Zezza, whose illustrations and imaging work appears throughout this entire book.

But most of all, I'd like to acknowledge the amazing designers I've had the pleasure to work with who have contributed so critically to this book. They are some of the best designers in the world and celebrating their talent was one of the central motives for writing this. They've all been incredibly supportive and I'm grateful for the experience we've had together.

DESIGNERS OF INDIVIDUAL PROJECTS

Johnathan Abarbanel, Sherlan Abesamis, Tanya Chang, Aska Cheung, Diana Choung, Angela Chu, James Chu, Sana Desai, Katy Dill, Chufan Huang, Jae Hee Jang, Radhika Kashyap, Alex Kasper, Nairi Khachikian, Gabe la O', Christine Lai, Frida Lau, Jae Lee, Bessy Liang, Audrey Liu, Oliver Lo, Mary Louise McGraw, Chase Morrison, Jonathan Nishida, Sophie Tang, Avis Tao, Elbert Tao, Tash Ushiyama, William Van Skaik, Amber Wang, Kiki Wang, Schei Wang, Steve Wang, Chris Wu, Hui Ye, Hanna Yi, Zhihan Ying.

DESIGNERS ON TEAM-BASED PROJECTS

Team ABC: Ofir Atia, Calvin Lien, Serena Jorif, Alice Yu
Team Aura: Margo Dunlap, Vanessa Gu
Team Brown: Justin Babakian, Dennis Dang, Ben Kasum, Joe Tsao
Team Cheeseburger: James Chu, Chloe Kim, Juno Park, Yidan Zhang
Team Cora: Christina Hsu, Andy Cooper, Rachel Goldinger
Team CTX: Lars Fiva, Emily Harrington, Tammy Hsieh, Michele Lee
Team Culina Metra: Katrina Hercules, Neal Smith
Team Delta: Angela Dong, Jenny Kim, Devin Montes, Naomi Tirronen, Joshua Woo
Team Effi: Amiarli Java, Quinton Larson, Wendy Wang
Team Face It: Leah Demeter, Yenju Lai, Fred Tsai
Team Frank: Justin Babikian, April Cheung, Kelsey Chow, India Hillis, Joe Tsao
Team Ha: Yuni Choi, David Huang, Kristy Lee, Vincent Zhang
Team HA+CH: Yuni Choi, David Huang, Kristy Lee, Vincent Zhang
Team Hakuna Matata: Rosalia Hosseinzadeh, Suguru Ogata, Tina Tsung
Team Inyerface: Daniela Cardona, Leah Demeter, Emin Demirci, Jeff Smith
Team IX: Angela Chu, Andy Park, Kelly Weldon, Alfred Yoo
Team Kairos: Tanya Chang, Jon Hsiung
Team Laundry: Asli Akdemir, Lynn Lei, Nathan Lu, Yozei Wu
Team Lechee: Jenny Chen, Sara Ferris, Wenzhou Liang, Karim Merchant
Team My Favorite: Busarin Chumnong, Elly Nam, Mariko Sanchez, Xiaoyi Xie
Team Nudge: Martin Francisco, Michael Noh, Sean Whelan
Team O2: Sam Giambalvo, Charlie Hodges, Gen Hur, Ryan Van Noy

Team Porkbun: Justin Nam, Daniel Smitasin, Shirley Van
Team Provision: Joey Cheng, Albert King
Team Remora: Shane Li, Victoria Lin, Peter Santos, Kuan Yu
Team Respire: Kasia Burzynska, Wendy Wang
Team Rytm: Sherry Chen, Kim Chow, Kenneth Tay
Team Seamrippers: Matthew Benkert, Derling Chen, Ian Liao, Mike Rito
Team WeeFee: Trevor Cheney, Caitlin Conlen, Cindy Hu, Michelle Lee, Chase Morrison
Team Wolf Pack: Judy Chu, Tina Ou, Jane Park, Jade Tsao
Team Xmen: Michelle Kim, Refaeli Ma, Kiki Wang, Mindy Wang

Preface

This book is inspired by courses I've taught at the graduate and undergraduate level for the past twenty-five years. During that time, the discipline of designing for interactive media and devices was largely invented and has been reinvented several times. While the lucky designers entering the field today can do so directly through many well-established programs, many of us who've been around since the dark ages traveled a circuitous route to get here. While I came from data analysis, programming, game design, and film, colleagues of mine came from disciplines as diverse as music, information architecture, human computer interaction, product design, biology, theater, psychology, and sociology. These varied roots resulted in a multifaceted discipline that is equal parts brain and heart.

The discipline we know as Interaction Design came into its own after the dot-com bust of the early 2000s, although its genesis was established long before that. This time was also when the digital behemoths that we have today rose like phoenixes from the ashes of that bust: The Googles, the Amazons, the Facebooks, and even Apple resurrected itself from its near-death experience into being one of the most valuable corporations in the world. That bust and subsequent rise of the digital economy are tightly interconnected: As this nascent sector began to grow, those who were tasked with the responsibility of designing for it recognized that a new approach was needed. We had to wipe away our past baggage in the quantitative analysis of human–computer interaction, the data-centric approach of systems' analysis, the media focus of interactive multimedia, and realign our sights squarely on the user and their experience.

We needed to create a discipline that placed not only a user's satisfaction, but even their delight, as the central concern. If we can arrange bits and pixels any way we want, why can't we make that arrangement enjoyable? Corporate culture noticed this as well, and the converging interest between those with means and those who make created the right conditions for the new discipline of Interaction Design to emerge.

The dot-com bust obliterated almost every class I taught. Yet, the discipline quickly resurrected itself. I began to shepherd close to 100 projects per year, accumulating into the thousands over the past decade and a half. This volume of productivity stimulated the evolution of methodologies at a breakneck pace. Each term, my students and I would experiment with approaches, keeping those that were successful and throwing out those that were not. There was a great deal of collaboration across disciplines and with several corporate sponsors, so we would discover new processes term by term, even week by week. We worked with automotive designers, ad creatives, hardware developers, social scientists, technologists, doctors, futurists, and business executives. I felt as if the methodologies and processes in my classes were akin to an organism taking advantage of the DNA of every discipline injected into our great exploratory Petri dish, adapting the best traits and sloughing off the rest. It was a kind of methodological Darwinism.

These classes began to take on the flavor of a design studio themselves by being beacons for sponsored projects: educational and professional mash-ups where teams of designers work in tight collaboration with corporate clients to develop solutions for particularly thorny problems they faced. These explorations have allowed me and my designers to live on the cutting edge of design. For the student, they provided real-world experience. For the client, they got work outside the burden of their often-stifling corporate culture, allowing them to probe discoveries shaped more by what *should* happen rather than corporate politics. In this context, the methods you will learn in these pages have been brought to bear on challenges facing companies such as Google, Toyota, Microsoft, NASA, the United Nations, Dell, UCLA Medical Center, HTC, Honda, GM, and LG, among numerous others.

A testament to the success of the methods developed in this book is not only the consistent return of sponsors to our classes, but also that our graduates land top-level entry design positions. And the work they do sets the gold standard in the places where they go. Many of our past graduates advance to lead their respective design departments within the organizations they work for. With the acquisition of this book, you are now the beneficiary of the successful processes and methods that got them started.

My selfish objective for writing this book was to improve the quality of what I teach. I have gathered so much knowledge throughout my years with amazing designers—about what works and what doesn't—that it has become impossible to go over it all in my classes while also striving to provide quality feedback on their individual projects. I pointed things out as they came up in our critiques, but I never seemed to have time to cover them with any depth or breadth that did the topics justice. With this book added to the mix, I can do that. Because of this, while I've been writing I've had my designers—all several hundred of them throughout the years—at the forefront of my mind. At each stage in the process, for each detail I consider, I ask the question "What would I say to my designers?" This has been my guiding light.

Introduction

This book rests on the shoulders of giants. Most notably Alan Cooper and Dan Saffer, along with John Kolko, Morville and Rosenfeld, Jesse James Garrett, William Lidwell, Steve Krug, their associates, and a multitude of others cited in the bibliography. My work here would not be possible without their having carved a path through the thick dark forest of confusion inherent in any new discipline. Their trail has guided me countless times in my work, teachings, and, of central importance here, my writing of this book.

With such excellent literature, I have often been asked why the world needs yet another book on Interaction Design. After numerous attempts to integrate the work from these masters into my instruction, the results have been mixed at best. Eventually, I ended up abandoning these texts altogether, and it began to bother me as to why. It was not because these books were failures—far from it: They are packed with excellent content and are rich in their ability to establish a tradition of shared practice. They introduce us to the concepts and methodologies that form the basis of Interaction Design. But I came to realize they were more about establishing the definition of these concepts than doggedly laying out a clear program for the discipline. To teach my designers, I needed a guide that allowed them to start with nothing and led them to a detailed, well-considered, and inspiring something. That book really didn't exist.

This claim will most likely be met with a great deal of skepticism from those of you who are familiar with these works. Indeed, many of them are based on process: They begin with things that we should be doing first, and for the most part end with things we should be doing last. Yet if they were truly about the evolutionary process of design, they would not only introduce topics such as the all-important wireframe, for example, as they all do, or discuss how wireframes have many different fidelities, which some do; they would also clearly lay out how wireframes should be used throughout the design process, how their fidelities should evolve over its course, and they would present examples as to what each stage of wireframe should look like. None succeeded in this test enough to prompt me to continue to assign it as reading in my class.

This deficiency is not only about wireframes. It's also challenging to find works that do this consistently across a broad range of topics, methodologies, and frameworks such as scenarios, prototyping, behavior design, aesthetic development, ideation, iconography, and mock-ups, just to name a few. I yearned for a text that relied on generous examples that carefully guided the reader step by step to a well-considered design solution of an interactive system: A program for Interaction Design. That's why I wrote this. If that's what you want, this book is for you.

Laying out a program is my primary objective, but I'm fully aware of how risky this is: If we gather ten interaction designers in a room we would probably have ten different processes. In fact, I'd wager that if we gathered ten projects from one interaction designer, we'd see ten different processes as well. The point is that there is not one overarching process for this discipline. Mine is just one, but one that has been tested and refined numerous times through hundreds of projects and consistently produces excellent results. That being said, I'm the first to admit that even my process continually evolves. It was born from a methodological Darwinism and continues to be a living and changing thing. This is merely a snapshot of how it stands now, as well considered as I can muster at this point.

But take heart: Just because there are several processes and methods, Interaction Design is not haphazard. Although every project may have its unique process, there are traditions of practice. For example, research usually happens first; we focus on users and consider their feedback a great deal; through iteration, we explore, reflect, and refine; and we hold off on the minute details until last. I adhere to most of the traditions in the discipline, yet I take a few liberties for both pedagogical and philosophical reasons. These differences are most apparent when we look at the scope of the process that this book covers. You will encounter this immediately, in the first chapter, where I start from zero with an initial inciting idea that gets everything rolling.

Starting from zero is very rarely the case in the real world. For example, if you're a designer at Facebook, I sincerely doubt you will ever face the reality of throwing out the entire Facebook website and redesigning it from scratch. (Although one of my former students has come very close by working on the team that addressed Facebook's overall design.) Instead, you will most likely be tasked with refining a detail component through some form of agile process that iteratively releases bits of functionality and content over the course of several weeks or months. Conversely, in these pages, we do not start with the assumption that you're adding to something that already exists. Since our objective is to introduce and broadly cover the process of Interaction Design as a whole, we start from scratch and end with a complete design. Our approach is holistic.

Professionally, your immediate focus is more than likely not that broad. However, if you're involved in a startup or are on a small design team, you may be required to do it all. I do not know your specific responsibilities, but I do know that if I start from scratch and end with a finished product, at some point along the way I will have covered the singular problem you face. I address the entirety of the design process not because I am some proponent of waterfall vs. agile—for those of you who know the terminology—but that this perspective is pedagogically appropriate for an introductory work. Brain surgeons start their career learning general anatomy; consider this the general anatomy of Interaction Design.

This work is first and foremost about process. I introduce and discuss how to evolve several methods and frameworks that allow you to expose the current design problem you face to yourself and others on your team. Step by step, these frameworks externalize your application of design considerations and lead you to a finished design. They allow for feedback and discussion to ensure that your design effort is focusing on the right thing at the right time with the right level of fidelity, and is progressing in keeping with everyone's vision.

Our approach is holistic because it's the best way to introduce a subject, but pedagogy isn't the only rationale for the scope of this book; there is a philosophical rationale as well. It is common practice to assume that the Interaction Design process begins with user research and ends with detailed wireframes. I don't wholly subscribe to this. We do not have to arrive on a project after its concept has been formulated; we can be the source of the inciting idea itself. We don't have to be handed a project's strategic vision; we can participate in developing that as well. It's not good practice for us to spend time designing micro-interactions just so we can hand them to a developer who then assumes the full responsibility for the nuances of their behavior; interaction designers know *why* these should behave the way they are designed, so they should also be responsible for defining precisely *how* they behave as well. Finally, I believe the interaction designer's responsibility does not end with the wireframe, but with the thing our users sense, such as the arrangement of the pixels on a screen or the inflection of a voice in a natural language interface. Our philosophy is that interaction designers are responsible for the complete design of the system from structure, through behavior, to the execution of the interface. There is no stopping mid-way and handing things off to others to complete.

Many in the industry will agree with these points, except the last one: that the final aesthetic designs are part of Interaction Design as well. My position on this is born from my belief that if we end our work at the wireframe, we are not carrying through our understanding of importance and structure all the way to the final thing the user senses. We have abdicated our responsibility as a designer. Many disagree with this and point to the fact that the skills of an interaction designer are not always compatible with the skills of someone responsible for aesthetics. In response, I point to the role of a director on a film.

Cinema requires the input of several creatives: The writer, the storyboard artist, the actors, the set designer, the cinematographer, the editor, and the special effects artist, just to name a few. But when we consider the final work on the screen—the thing we detect with our senses—we assign that responsibility to the director. They are the auteur of the film. Likewise, depending on its size, an interactive project may have researchers, information architects, user experience designers, interface designers, and visual designers, but, in the end, it is the interaction designer who is responsible for the final impact the design has on its audience. Someone has to take responsibility for this final result or the project will fail. That someone is the interaction designer. Just as the director is the auteur of a film, the interaction designer should be the auteur of an interactive system. This broad design responsibility is what I mean by holistic design.

Books have a finite number of pages, and so writers are always faced with what to include and what to omit. You will find my focus is on breadth rather than any one topic in depth, so you may wish to further the discussions here with details from other sources. I not only encourage this, but have strived to make this a central point of the work through the substantial use of citations. If you would like a different take, or more in-depth look at a topic, I've provided you the means to do so.

We've also created a website to extend the content of this book that you can enjoy at InteractionForDesigners.com. The site is a way that we can address more detail than can be contained in a printed work and keep on top of the rapidly evolving nature of Interaction Design. It contains additional content that extends discussions of some of the chapters, provides social links where you can follow the most current and up to date topics revolving around the book, and finally, and probably most importantly, the site includes a detailed practicum: A set of assignments that I provide my class for each chapter in the book. You can use the practicum to guide you in the creation of your own project using this book as your primary reference.

I sincerely hope that these pages provide you with a broad understanding of the process of Interaction Design, and inspire you to dig deeper into topics that are of particular interest. Indeed, you may become an expert in aesthetic design or structural design, or may wish to remain more of a generalist whose expertise is the entire design process. Whatever goal you may have for your future in Interaction Design, we hope this work establishes a solid foundation to reach it.

Now, let the design begin!

1 Concept

As Rogers and Hammerstein suggest in *The Sound of Music*, when learning we should "Start at the very beginning, it's a very good place to start" (Hammerstein & Rodgers, 1965). So let's begin our Interaction Design journey at the beginning, with nothing: A new project entirely from scratch.

Starting entirely from scratch is rare. Most commonly, a fairly substantial "something" already exists and we designers are brought in to add, refine, or extend a feature set. If we're lucky enough to enter a project at ground zero, it's quite likely many of the features that form its foundation have been decided upon already. Rarely do we start from scratch.

But if we are to lay the foundation of a fundamental understanding of Interaction Design, we must look at the big picture. We need to start with nothing and arrive at a complete picture of the design. The particular problem you may face might not start from zero, but we don't know what you have and what you don't. If we start with the assumption of nothingness and provide you all the tools you need to complete a design, we are guaranteed, somewhere along the way, to address the stage you're in.

1.1 THE BRIEF

A well organized project usually begins with a brief which states—at the highest level—the goals of the project. It may be only a few sentences or may be several pages, but when we designers receive one we usually like to see that it provides not only an identification of the design problem to be solved, but also some context as to why solving the problem is important.

A brief includes:

1. An overview or description of the project.
2. The problem or challenge to be solved.
3. The scope.
4. Background and insight about the problem.
5. The criteria to be used to measure the project's success.

The project's challenge is the central component of the brief and should provide a clear statement of the project's primary goal, free from jargon that muddles clarity (Karjaluoto, 2014, p. 120). For example, one such statement could be "Design a product that operates in a 10 by 20 room that leverages our company's fiber optic display technology." Or, "Improve the visual interface for guiding the Mars Rover." Or, "Explore communication solutions to mitigate traffic jams on freeways." Each of these needs further clarification, and we would expect these statements to be followed by a presentation of why the goal is essential, what is the current state of the art, why that is insufficient, and why the effort of developing a solution is necessary.

It is usually not incumbent upon a designer to define the broad goals of a project. This is the role of the client in collaboration with the project's leadership. So, if the brief is created by the client and the management, why do we care about it? Because our designs need to deliver on these goals. They need to satisfy the project's success criteria, so it's crucial that these objectives inform us. If we embark on a design without knowing what the goals are, it will more than likely come back to haunt us later, and sometimes end disastrously (Unger & Chandler, 2009, p. 39).

There is one more element we look for in a well-formed brief: Proper scope. If it is too broad, it may not provide a design team with enough guidance, and they may flounder. However, if it's scoped too tightly, it won't allow the team enough room to explore, inhibiting their ability to arrive at a better design. Apologies if this description seems vague, but it's difficult to be more specific since every project is different and every team is different as well. Suffice it to say that a well-scoped project seems to hum along nicely, while ones that aren't are fraught with problems. The scope must simultaneously provide guidance and latitude that agree with the external expectations of the client, the company or organization, and the internal skills and motivations of the project's team. An appropriately scoped and balanced brief kicks the project off in the right direction.

Our design journey begins with the reception of this brief. And the first step we like to take is to brainstorm ideas revolving around it.

1.2 IDEATION AND PROPER JOURNALING

Ideas can come to us anytime, anywhere. The trick is not coming up with one, but determining if it's good. When ideas arrive, we need to be effective at capturing them and building a collection of them to compare against each other. This is where ideation comes in and being skilled at ideation is a hallmark of a good designer.

Ideation is, quite simply, the process of generating ideas (Karjaluoto, 2014, p. 132). As designers, everything we do in life is fodder for ideas, so the process of ideation should always be with us. We should engage in methods that not only allow us to explore ideas when we are working, but during the rest of our lives as well. Capturing ideas in a journal allows us to do this.

When designers dive down the research rabbit hole in the process of, for example, looking at trends or researching competitors, we may fall into the trap of forgetting that we are not researchers, but designers. A designer's goal is to come up with ideas and solutions, not scholarly articles. When we research, whether it be casual research, as in the conceptualization phase that we are engaged in now, or a more focused and determined effort, as in the research phases addressed in the following few chapters, the effort should expand our horizons, give us new insight, and stimulate ideas. For this reason, it's important to ideate while we research. Study a topic, let those ideas flow, and get it down on paper (Figure 1.1).

Designers ideate in many ways. Some are comfortable with drawing; others are more comfortable with writing and stories. Many of them mix both. Regardless of the approach, it's important to capture our ideas, and it's also important to avoid the computer. Use pen, pencil, and paper (Saffer, 2010, p. 115). But don't just scribble them down on a notepad that will never be seen again; become skilled at capturing them in ways that allow them to be reviewed in the future. Ideation properly journaled allows for better access later.

Proper journaling entails having a single place or notebook for those ideas. This can also help if at any time in the future you need to prove that it was indeed you that came up with an idea. This means a clean notebook, bound and possibly enumerated, without any pages torn out. Each page should be dated, and the book should be signed by you.

Although we all have various levels of skill when it comes to drawing or writing, strive to make your ideas clear. Use good separation between ideations so that they are easily reviewed. In the ideation examples, notice how simple yet precise the drawings are. Notice the clean lettering and the ample white space there is. These all add to the legibility of the drawings. There are several ideas per page,

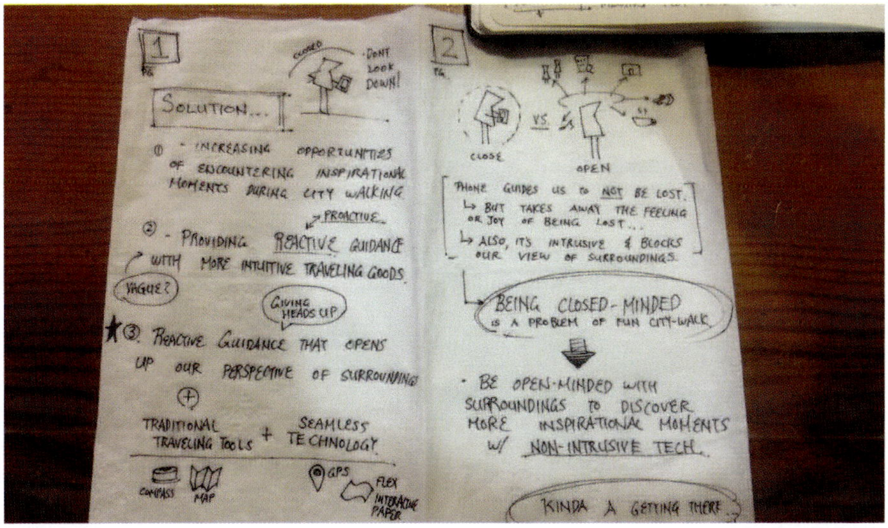

Figure 1.1
Capture your ideation (from Pingo, by Team Hakuna Matata, used by kind permission of Suguru Ogata, Tina Tsung, and Rosalia Hosseinzadeh).

and no idea is addressed in much detail. They are quick and precise sketches laid down for future reference. These form the core of your brainstorming. Cleanly rendered ideation leads to better understanding, but if any of these guidelines inhibit the capture of ideas in the first place, forget them. The most important thing is that the idea is captured. In the end, the only bad idea is the one that wasn't captured.

We've stressed the importance of rendering your ideation in a way that can be analyzed later, but that's all for naught if we don't review them. In fact, the act of ideation itself is rather useless unless we can chisel away a moment of time for ourselves every so often to consider our ideas. We should think of our journal as a bank of ideas, revisit them, and mark the ones that are special (Krause, 2015, p. 178). Your journal is not just a place to capture ideas, but a place to inspire creativity.

1.3 CONCEPT BRAINSTORM

Anyone can have a great idea, but to generate good ideas on command requires skill. To aid in the generation of ideas, we've found the following approaches useful: Intuition, scope change, observation, trends, scenarios, mind mapping, group creativity, creativity cards, exhaustion, and separation.

1.3.1 Intuition and Passion

A designer's intuition is a powerful thing. Concepting through intuition is a means by which we reflect on something that either inspires us or, contrarily, irks us, and we apply it to a design solution. It may be something small or something substantial, but it should be something that almost dumbfounds you that still happens today.

As an example, I can't stand it when I get on to a freeway just to be faced with traffic at a standstill. With today's advances in communication, it's ridiculous that this still happens. Before I commit to the onramp, I have ample means available to avoid that mess and become yet one more addition to the problem. If others were informed about the issue as well, I have a hunch this could significantly cut down on freeway congestion.

There should be signs before the onramp that indicate the traffic density or drive times to the next exit. I'm aware that it costs money, but so does burning gas. Freeway construction is not cheap either, and that happens all the time. Yes, mobile GPS systems can indicate traffic and be asked to reroute you but fiddling with navigation systems while driving is dangerous. Additionally, relying on apps or on-board navigation systems will leave many out in the cold because they do not use them.

Yes, there are many challenges to such a system, but it's a perfect example of an idea off the top of my head that I'm passionate about. You have them, too, and probably several of them. Brainstorming is the time to get them out of your head and onto paper.

1.3.2 Scope Change

The basic concept of changing scope to develop ideas, either in context or in time, is to switch our perception to see it as a different problem. For example, maybe we're tired of lugging our suitcases around an airport trying to get food before the next flight. What would we like to have happen? Probably just merely sit at the gate and have someone get us food. Let's change the scope: Maybe it's not about food, but a service that gets you things while you sit at the airport. This could work for purchasing earbuds, getting a magazine, or a coffee. Scope change again: Maybe it's not about airports, but this service can be anywhere. Maybe while we get a haircut at the mall, someone gets us a sandwich from the food court. Perhaps we could create a system that employs people to get things for other people: a crowd-sourced assistant. What started as an annoyance for one situation in one context was scope changed into something for many situations in many contexts.

1.3.3 Contextual Inquiry and Observation

A particular type of scope change is to change context to a specific type of individual or situation. These individuals or situations are your target market or target context. To gain insight into potential concepts, it's instructive to observe these people or situations. This is a process called contextual inquiry: observations in the field that allows us to understand better the design problem we face (Cooper, 2015, p. 44). For our purposes here, we will just refer to them as our target.

Do we think there is a potential need in a particular environment? If so, visit that environment. Engage with it (Figure 1.2). We should use ourselves to understand what our target may be going through or what the situation lacks. We use this heuristic approach to great effect later in our design process, but, for now, it helps us not only to understand the environmental factors that we may face in our design, but also helps us prepare appropriate questions and activities for our user research later.

In general, how do people behave in the situation we are considering for our design? What are their challenges or frustrations? What about the situation does not supply them with the goals they want? Are there devices or technologies that could better help them achieve those goals? Why is it that those technologies are not available in that situation? Are the appropriate tools available, but their mindset is not in the right place to use them? How can that change?

Observing people and their situations, becoming empathetic with them, their needs, their wants, and their desires is one of the most fruitful means of developing creative concepts. Place yourself in situations where you can observe them from a distance. See what they do or how they behave. Bring your journal, sketch their activities, and brainstorm possible solutions.

Figure 1.2
Contextual inquiry: Visit the environment and engage with it (from Tier X, by Schei Wang, used by kind permission of Schei Wang).

Contextual inquiry not only helps us consider possible concepts, but it also prepares us, the designers, for what is about to come: Research. When we enter the research process we will strive to gain an understanding of the competition. When we do so, we may begin to frame our opportunities from the point of view of our competition and begin to blind ourselves to different approaches that may be revolutionary. Conducting contextual inquiry prior to fully understanding how others solve it allows us to see things differently. Make use of your innocence at this stage. Capture your ideas in your journal and carry those ideas forward as you do your research. Use the learnings from contextual inquiry to allow yourself a level of skepticism when you analyze your competitors in the research process you will engage in shortly.

1.3.4 Underserved Populations

Another user-focused scope change is considering a group of people either locally or globally whose needs are not being met by the type of system you're designing. What are some ways these deficiencies can be solved? Looking at underserved populations can be a rich entry point for ideas. If the market is significant enough, it can be a windfall for any organization that can fulfill that need. But care needs to be taken here. How familiar are you with them? Are you one of them or do you know of someone who is of that group? We need to gain a great deal of understanding of, and empathy for, them, or we will end up being just another group that exploits their plight. Live there, be with them, talk to them, strive to be as close to them as possible. That way we will be able to think of solutions that benefit them as opposed to benefiting just us (Figure 1.3).

1.3.5 Trends

We often think of trends as things that are popular right now. And that's fine if you're a consumer, but designers make things that will take time to get to market, so we need a level of insight into things that will be hot sometime in the future. The best way to do this is to use our intuition as a means of considering what may be

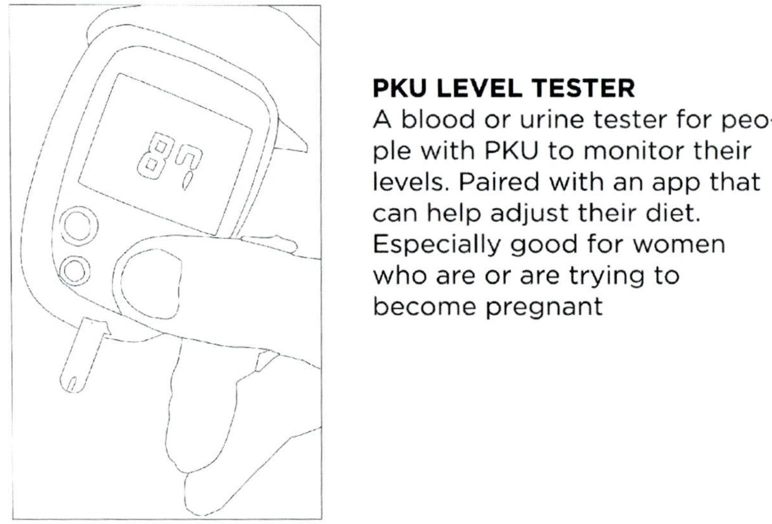

Figure 1.3
Underserved populations: A phenylketonuria (PKU) tester (from Culina Metra, by Team Culina Metra, used by kind permission of Katrina Hercules and Neal Smith).

"trending." Look around you. Be sensitive to the world and observe things that you think have a chance to become more popular over time.

Trends, more than anything, rely on intuition, so it's important to hone this sense. Practice it often and become sensitive to things around you. To lend focus, consider certain topics like technology trends, social trends, environmental trends, geopolitical trends, or simply trends that you see around you that others may not see at all (Figures 1.4 and 1.5).

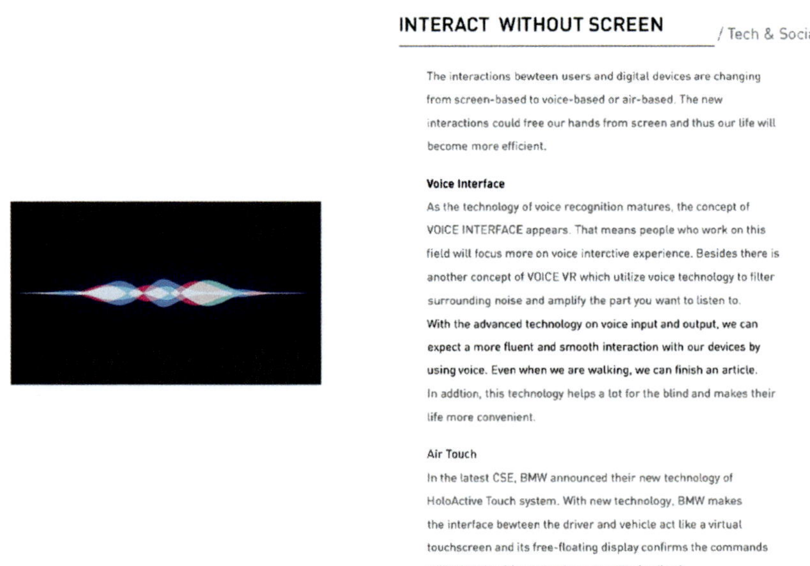

Figure 1.4
The technological trend of screenless interaction (from Odmo, by Hui Ye, used by kind permission of Hui Ye).

1.3.6 Future Casting

Once you've identified a trend, consider how it will evolve in the future, and the best way of doing so is to look at the past. In fact, if we want to have some insight into what may happen five years ahead, we should look at things five to ten years back. How much has changed since then? That's how much we should expect may

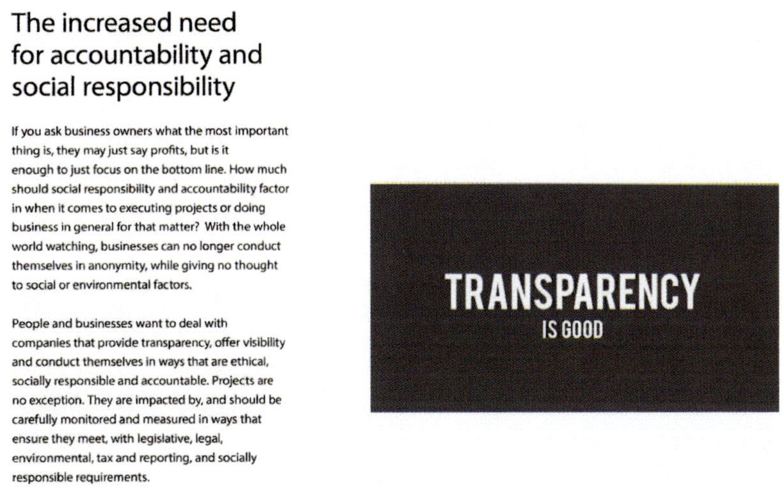

Figure 1.5
The social trends of accountability and responsibility (from Sourced, by Jonathan Nishida, used by kind permission of Jonathan Nishida).

change in the future. What changes have been gradual and what have been disruptive? Gradual changes are the incremental ones, such as slight variations of form or technology in a cell phone. Disruptive ones are revolutionary, like the advent of the iPhone or Google's ability to monetize the search engine: They changed paradigms and destroyed companies. Is the trend you're looking at experiencing a gradual change or is it in for a disruption? What do you foresee that disruption to be (Figure 1.6)?

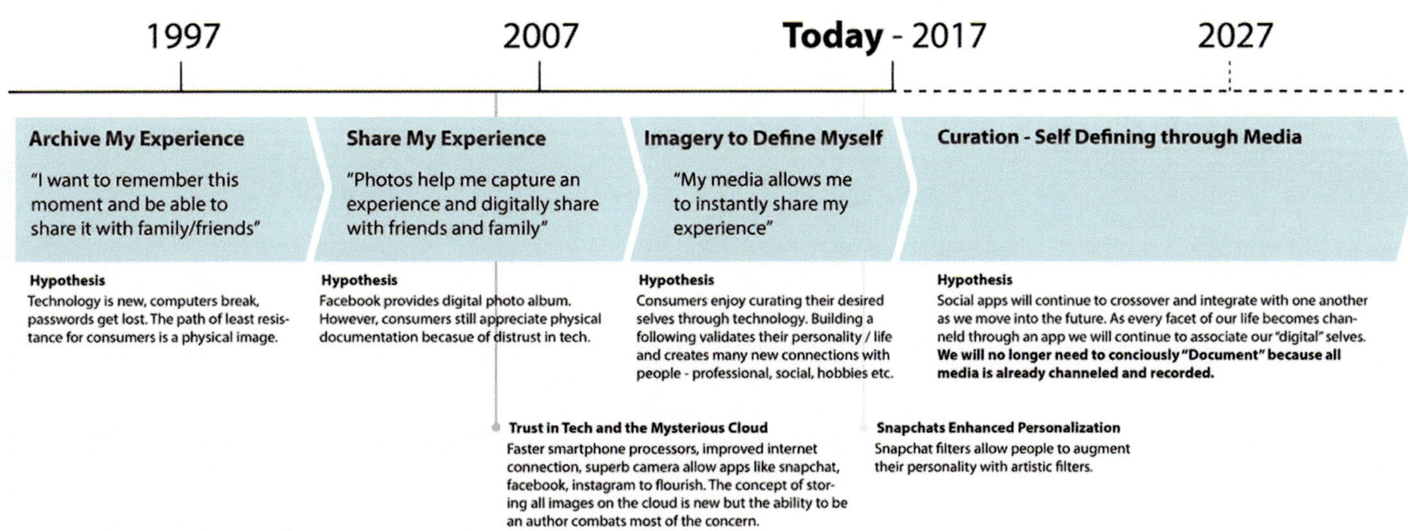

Figure 1.6
Future casting: Media and self (from Campfire, by Team Seamrippers, used by kind permission of Matthew Benkert, Derling Chen, Ian Liao, and Mike Rito).

1.3.7 Scenarios

Of all the design methodologies that appear in this book, scenarios are the most critical for the generation and clarification of our ideas. A scenario is a depiction of a user experience that conveys context, and, as such, we will be engaged in the process of creating and refining scenarios throughout the entire book. For the purposes of developing concepts, a useful scenario to look at is the experience that currently exists, or the "current scenario".

Refer to your target observations. What do they tell us about the current scenario our user experiences? We can create scenarios in a number of ways: We can storyboard them, photograph them, create them from a set of image pulls, play-act them, or rely on a combination of these (Figure 1.7). But in the end all these ways of depicting a scenario are simply the means of revealing what our user goes through in time.

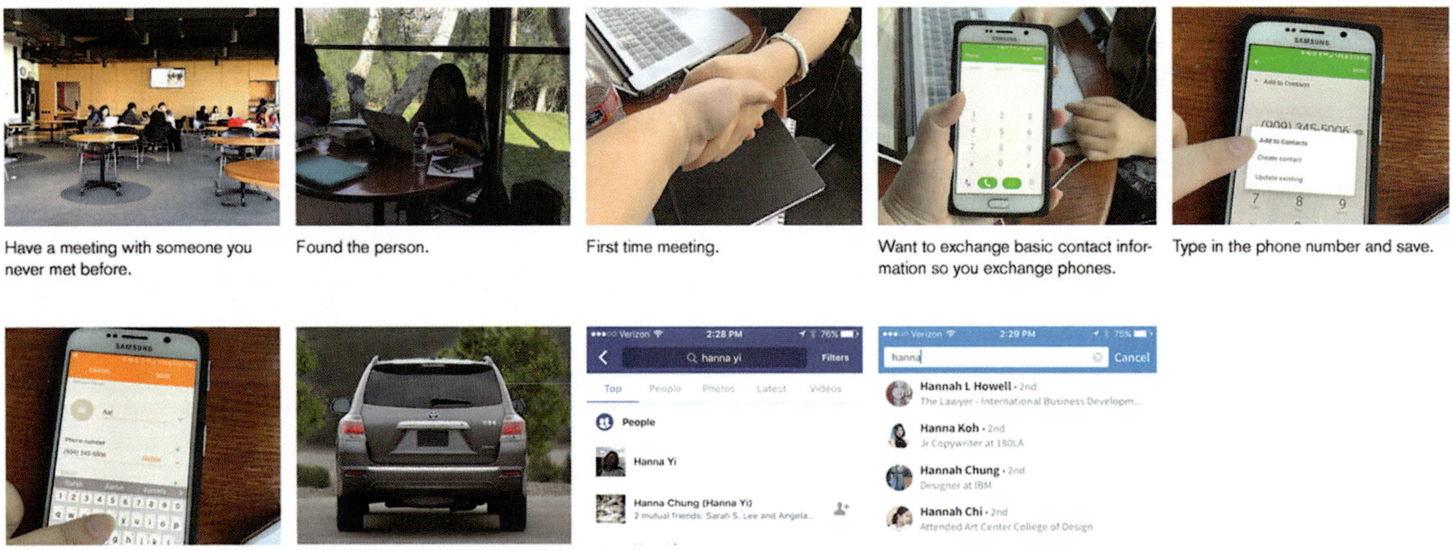

Have a meeting with someone you never met before. / Found the person. / First time meeting. / Want to exchange basic contact information so you exchange phones. / Type in the phone number and save. / Type in name and email. / Leaving after the meeting. / Try to add and search each other on facebook when at home. / Try to connect on LinkedIn.

Figure 1.7
A photographed current scenario (from Keepintouch, by Amber Wang, used by kind permission of Amber Wang).

What kind of problems do they encounter along the path of that scenario? These are called pain points, or points of friction, and they are the things that present us with opportunities ripe for design solutions.

1.3.8 Role Playing

We find role-playing, a form of discovering flow, to be one of the most effective and entertaining methods of generating ideas. The approach is to do as much as we can to become the user trying to achieve something in a specific context. If we are designing a system for the blind to use to cook, then blindfold yourself and cook. If we're designing for people with arthritis, we should tape up our knuckles. If we're designing something for teenagers, hang out with them and try to become one of them.

Become the user in a certain context. What do they want? What do they need? Configure an environment, create props with tape balls, and role play a scenario. Capture ideas in your journal as they come.

1.3.9 Magic Moments

While current scenarios are a depiction of the present user experience, magic moments are a brief moment that solves a problem or point of friction. We've found the best way to create magic moments is to use our intuition, or consider the pain points along the current scenario and ask: "Wouldn't it be wonderful if . . .?"

Magic moments are like little scenarios that focus on solutions. They can be depicted as a single image or a few. Take care, however, that they are less about exact solutions and more about providing a feeling as to how wonderful it would be if such a solution existed. We are not designing anything yet. We are just expressing a possibility (Figure 1.8). In fact, ambiguity is an advantage at this stage: We want to leave ourselves a great deal of room to develop myriad design solutions that balance the various aspects fundamental to our goals. If things are too prescribed, our creativity will be suppressed.

Figure 1.8
A magic moment: Connecting mom with her school age child (from Reset, by Team Lechee, used by kind permission of Sara Ferris, Wenzhou Liang, Karim Merchant, and Jenny Chen).

1.3.10 Mind Mapping

An affinity diagram is a presentation of concepts that reveals their association with each other. Mind maps represent one such affinity diagram (Kolko, 2011, p. 76), where we use a concept to generate other concepts. The mind map starts with one or a collection of ideas and expands from there (Lupton, 2011, p. 22). Start with ideas generated either from your brief or your intuition. On a big sheet of roll paper or a big wall and some sticky notes, ask questions related to the items you put down: "What could come of this one? What does this other one relate to? What does this remind me of?" (Figure 1.9). The goal of the mind map is to expand out through the idea space to exhaust our mind of anything lingering there.

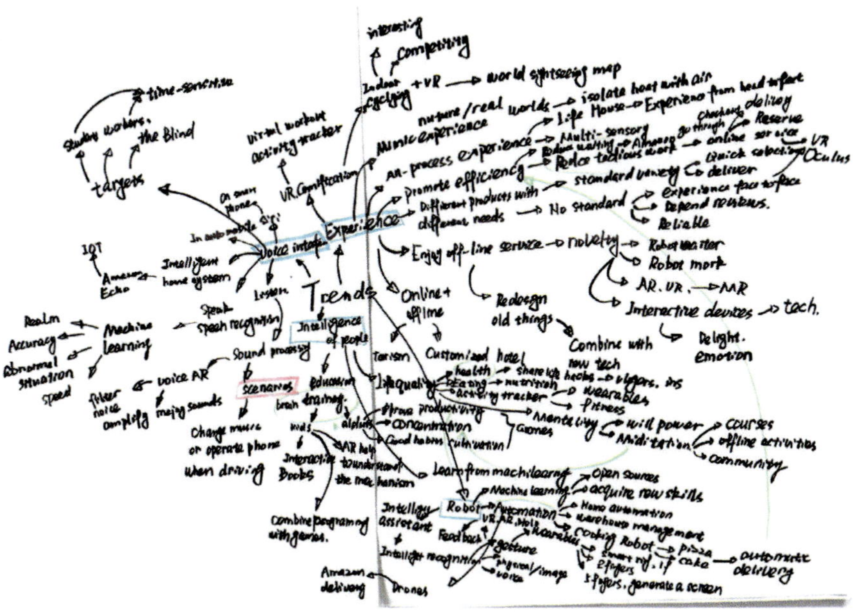

Figure 1.9
Mind map as a journal entry (from Odmo, by Hui Ye, used by kind permission of Hui Ye).

1.3.11 Group Creativity

Mind maps, either on sticky-note walls or on roll paper, are particularly effective in groups. This is because the information being considered is not locked up in our heads, but out in the open. The data has been made physical, enabling an entire group to work with it (Saffer, 2010, p. 94) (Figure 1.10). This allows the entire group to be involved in the creative process and facilitates bouncing ideas off each other.

We will be brainstorming a great deal in this book, and these activities are not just useful for generating concepts, but generating ideas in general. Make a point to refer to all the activities here (section 1.3) at any stage in the design process when you're tasked with coming up with ideas.

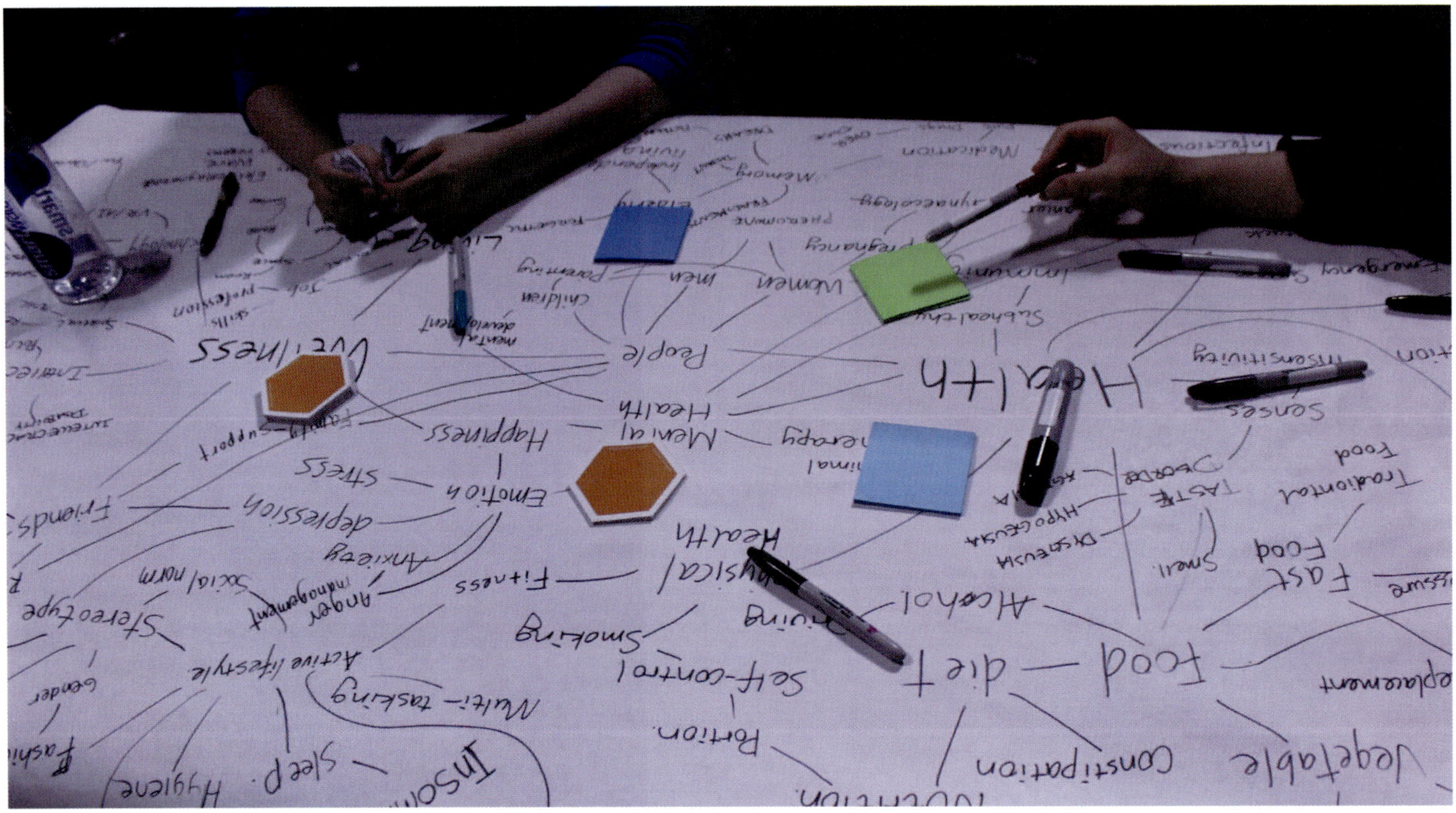

Figure 1.10
Mind mapping can foster group collaboration (from Mavis, by Team Xmen, used by kind permission of Michelle Kim, Refaeli Ma, Kiki Wang, and Mindy Wang).

1.3.12 Creativity Cards

Creativity cards, also called method or idea cards, are a hallmark of the design firm IDEO where various cards are used to direct the designer's focus (IDEO, 2003). A version of this activity is to have various stacks of cards: One stack could contain physical environments, another could be a type of person, a third could be a technology, and a fourth could be a pre-existing product. Others could contain things to try and questions to ask. A player draws cards then develops ideas around that focus. For example, a designer draws a kitchen, the internet of things, the vision impaired, and a music system. The team brainstorms design solutions considering these topics: How can we use the internet of things in the kitchen to allow the vision impaired to control their music system? We can see how this can stimulate ideas.

1.3.13 Beyond Low Hanging Fruit

Exhaustion and boredom are two highly underestimated stimulators of ideas. Early in the idea generation process, we may be able to think of several ideas. Several of these are good because we've been thinking about them for some time and now we have a chance to express them. After that stage is over, some ideas may be good, but most of them tend to be low hanging fruit: Ideas that many other people have come up with as well. When these are gone, we usually reach exhaustion.

Should we stop when we've reached this point? No. Reaching exhaustion is a critical part of the creative process because we may be entering the territory beyond the low hanging fruit; starting to consider things that may be unique. This is hard, and it should be, or else everyone would be doing it, so keep pushing. Sometimes the ideas that come out of this stage are stupid, but there may be a diamond in the rough that is genuinely original.

Be careful to establish limits, because this process can go on forever. Giving ourselves a fixed number of ideas to produce is often a good strategy—it forces us to reach exhaustion while placing a fixed limit on the effort. Is your goal 50 ideas? 100? 1,000? What number would take you beyond exhaustion? Another aspect you can limit is time, such as a few hours or so. Once the limit has been reached or the inspiration stops, give it a rest.

Put the effort aside for a day or so then come back to it again. We likely will see some new ideas that we haven't considered before. This is when things start to get interesting. These may begin to be ideas that are truly novel—that may have few competitors in the marketplace. In this round, we will probably reach exhaustion much more quickly because we've expended all the low hanging fruit yet again. Repeat the process of inspiration, exhaustion, and rest a few times until it becomes challenging to come up with new ideas even with rest.

1.3.14 Give it a Rest

Speaking of giving ourselves a break, when we put our brainstorming aside, we're not actually putting it aside. We are thinking about it in the back of our minds as we experience other aspects of our life: eating lunch, commuting, getting ready for our day, getting ready for bed, dealing with those close to us, et cetera. These events can cause us to think of different situations that can help the creative process. They can stimulate ideas we wouldn't necessarily have thought of by just sitting in a room and forcing ourselves to come up with ideas.

We can enhance this process in numerous ways: We can immerse ourselves in a situation that is relevant to the ideas being considered. For example, if we're trying to find improvements for the shopping experience, we should go shopping. Make sure we carry our journal to capture ideas while there. This is similar to role playing, but we are not playing out a fantasy scenario. We are merely going about our lives within a context relevant to the design problem we're trying to solve.

1.4 GATHERING THE BEST IDEAS

Having gone through the idea generation process, you should have a wealth of ideas logged into your journal. We usually suggest collecting 50 or more in order to get beyond the low hanging fruit. Put these ideas into a list, give things a rest for about a day or so, and then select your top ideas (Figure 1.11).

1.5 BIG IDEAS

Once we've used the methods above or others to generate a wealth of ideas, then comes the time to select the best. In the web resources for this book, I've included some guidance on how to identify those ideas that are good, and eliminate those

Figure 1.11
Listing brainstormed ideas, and identifying top selections (from Culina Metra, by Team Culina Metra, used by kind permission of Katrina Hercules and Neal Smith).

SWIM PACER HEART MONITOR A swim pacer that is based on your heart rate and adjusts to give you a custom workout.	**BIG FEET** Sensor near tip of shoes to let parents know when their kids outgrow their shoes.	**VIDEO GAME COGNITIVE TEST** Video games that measure the cognitive functions of athletes after head trauma.
HARMONICA BREATHALYZER A harmonic that keeps track of musician's blood alcohol level so they know when they approach the legal limit.	**TRI TRAINING WATCH** Simply measure time and distance of a swim, bike, and/or run workout with programmable goals.	**ALZHEIMER'S MEMORY GAME** A simple game designed to measure the memory of people who have or may have Alzheimer's.
SHOE SCALE Shoes that monitor your weight throughout the day, everyday to give a meaningful look at your progress.	**RELATIONSHIP BAROMETER** Input your emotional state after interacting with people to help you gain an understanding of how you respond to others. Helps pinpoint toxic and positive relationships.	**POSTURE SHOES** Shoes or insoles that measure your posture and recommend exercises to correct bad form.
SWEATBAND MONITOR A sweatband that measures nutrients lost during work out. Partnering app then recommends replenishing foods/drinks.	**PACIFIER THERMOMETER** A pacifier that measures your baby's temperature and can alert you if it is becoming sick.	**PURCHASE TRACKING FOR HEALTH** Rite Aid tracks your purchases through loyalty card and alerts you to possible health conditions based on your purchases. (ie, Anti acid purchases = prompt to check for acid reflux)
EARBUD BLOOD PRESSURE MONITOR Earbuds measure blood pressure in a none intrusive way.	**KEEP CONNECTIONS, BE HAPPY** An app where you make a list of "favorite" people in your life. Based on your contact history it will prompt you to reach out based on time, events, and emotions.	**NO BENDS SCUBA DIVING WATCH** A diving watch that tells you how fast to descend/ascend and how long you can stay at a certain depth before getting sick.
STD FINDING UNDERWEAR A special lining in your underwear can be easily tested to find STDs.	**MOOD MUSIC** A mood tracking app that also tracks the music you listen to. It will then suggest music to listen to based on your mood and judge your mood based on your music.	**PROTEIN TRACKER** An app that tracks protein amounts in meals and food items for people with PKU.
CRIB MATTRESS MONITOR A crib mattress that monitors baby's breathing, temperature, movement, and sleep and alerts parents to any abnormalities.	**COUCH-1650 YDS** Like the Couch - 5K app, this device provides a training regimen, encouragement, and music to get you swimming a mile.	**PKU LEVEL TESTER** A urine tester for people with PKU to monitor their levels. Paired with an app that can help adjust their diet.
SUCKLING SENSOR Special bottle nipple that analyzes how much your baby is drinking to help inform mom's pumping regimen.	**PROGRAMED LIGHTING** Set your house lights to an alarm. Based on your alarm and sleep patterns (that are measured), your lights will dim to give you natural light input before bed to help you sleep and wake.	**1 PACK - 0** An app for smokers that sets up a program and social network for people trying to quit smoking.

that aren't. You may wish to review that discussion before we proceed (look for "Good Ideas" in the Additional Content section of InteractionForDesigners.com).

Once our top selections have been made, we then would like to arrange them for our design team to review. This is where the concept of the "Big Idea" comes in. Advertising great David Ogilvy once said:

> You can do your homework from now until doomsday, but you will never win fame and fortune unless you also invent big ideas. It takes a big idea to attract the attention of consumers and get them to buy your product.
>
> (Ogilvy, 1985, p. 16)

We name this next step in the concepting process "The Big Idea" in honor of Oglivy because it's a method of presenting a wealth of ideas for rapid analysis common in advertising.

Big Ideas are a formatting approach more than anything else. In fact, they kind of look like a classic 1970s' Ogilvy ad with a big image, big header, and some descriptive text. This method is particularly well suited to a collaborative environment. I've often seen the walls of huge conference rooms at ad companies coated with hundreds of these, with executives quickly poring over them.

It starts with our set of "good" ideas we edited from our brainstorm list. We'll create a "Big Idea" from each of these. To make one, first, develop a consistent format that allows for the easy recognition of a title, image, and short description (Figure 1.12). Consistency is key here: it will enable people to very quickly assess the idea without being confused by the layout. Also critical is to choose our title and image cleverly so that they quickly convey the essence of the idea without the audience having to read the short description. The description should only be there to add detail.

Then, we lay out our Big Ideas on some large surface, be it a wall, floor, or table. I've seen ad agencies coat the walls of a room with thousands of these pages. The goal here is to allow reviewers the ability to compare numerous ideas against each other quickly (Figure 1.13).

Figure 1.12
The "Big Idea" format (from Tranquillo, by Team My Favorite, used by kind permission of Busarin Chumnong, Elly Nam, Mariko Sanchez, and Xiaoyi Xie).

Figure 1.13
Wall layout for brainstorms and big ideas (Kiki Wang, used by kind permission of Kiki Wang).

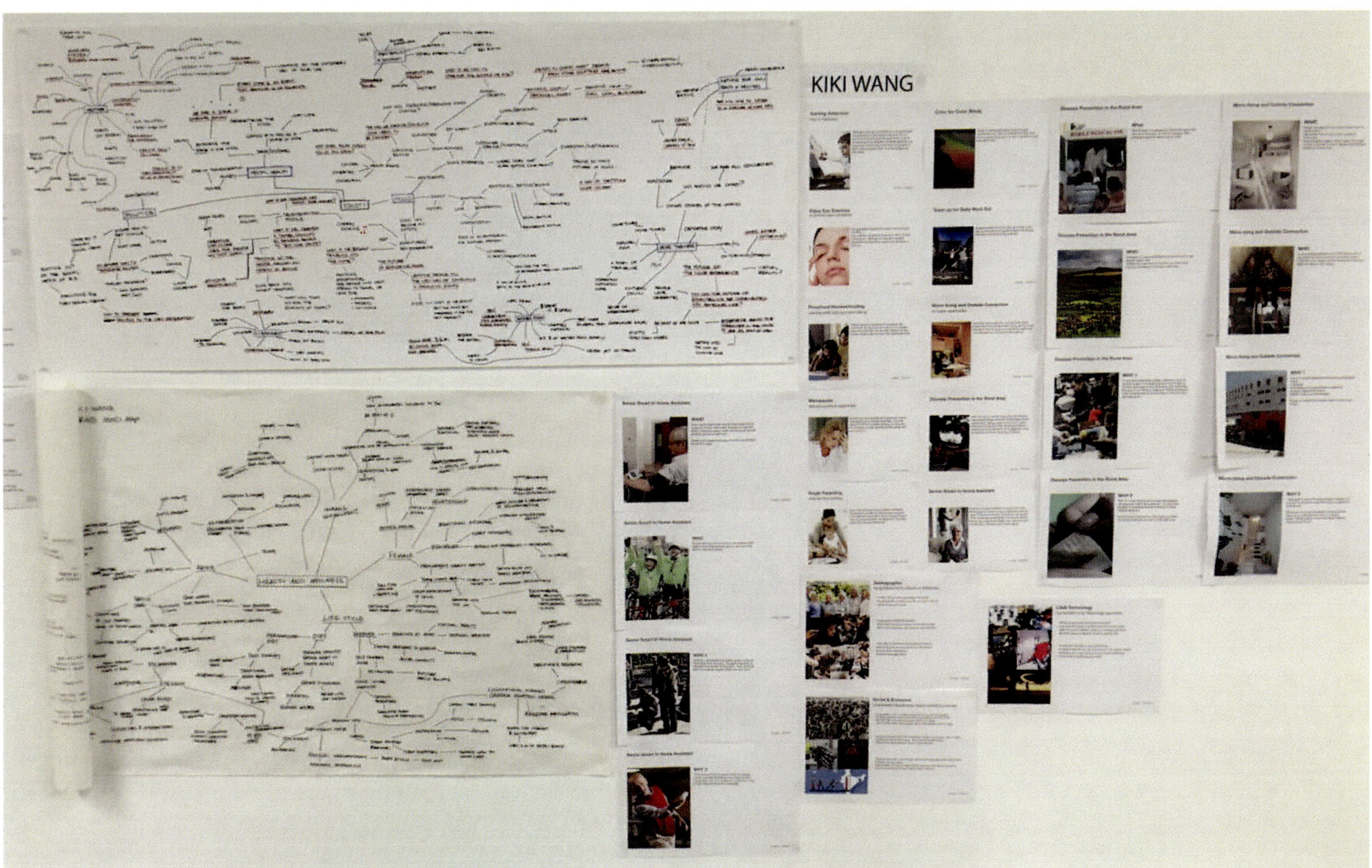

Consider the relationship between these ideas. Are there ones that stick out? Are there ones you'd love to be spending your time on? Are there others that, after looking at them for a while, you want nothing to do with? When you start to get a feeling as to the ones you're gravitating towards, mark them for the next step.

1.6 THE STRATEGIC PYRAMID

That next step is to dig a little more deeply into each of our most successful concepts, but before we do so, let's discuss a useful mnemonic to further clarify ideas: The Strategic Pyramid (Figure 1.14).

Figure 1.14
The strategic pyramid (from Artbug, by Radhika Kashyap, used by kind permission of Radhika Kashyap).

The pyramid identifies the fundamental questions that need to be asked for a given concept. For most design efforts, it's essential to establish the questions of what, who, why before we determine when and where something is used. The pyramid reflects this structure: What, who, and why form the pyramid's foundation—its bottom layer—while when and where rest on the middle layer, atop that foundation. When all those are answered, we can address the question of how. In this way, the pyramid signifies the approach we should take to solve our design problem.

1.6.1 The Foundation: What, Who, and Why

The first question that is usually addressed for a concept is "What is it?" What is the thing that is being designed? Is it a mobile system to find where nightlife is happening, a device to assist in remote surgery, or a tool to be used to explore planets? What do we intend the system to be? Admittedly, this may not always be the initial question, and that's why it resides at the same foundational level as the other two—who and why—but often it's what we think of first.

The next question we ask may not be the primary inspiration, but it is usually the most important. That is "who." Who is it for? Is it for 20-somethings trying to find something to do at night, is it for eye surgeons, or is it for interplanetary scientists at NASA? Different groups bring different desires, knowledge, and skills to the table that permeates every aspect of the design. It is so critical we may even start with this question. For example, if we've identified a underserved audience but don't quite know yet how to reach them, the "who" may be the initial question that challenges us to figure out what to make to satisfy their wants and needs. Therefore "what" and "who" share the foundation of the pyramid. They can play equal roles in defining the problem to be solved.

Knowing your target market helps your design, but, essentially, it's meaningless unless you know why they want to use your product. Why does our 20-something want to go out? Because they want to meet people. Why does the eye surgeon need to perform surgery remotely? Because the operation is rare and the patient and the surgeon are likely not in the same place. The question of why provides insight into our user's goals and motivations that drive the kind of information and control our system must deliver.

What, who, and why often come as a tightly intertwined package. The question of "what" may be the instigator, but it's considerably affected by who it's for and why they want to use it.

1.6.2 Context: When and Where

The next level up in the strategic pyramid is the question of where and when the system is used. This is the level where we consider context. Is the audience primarily using our product at the office, at home, outside, during their commute, or every week at 5 p.m. on Friday? It's quite common that the where/when question is a mixture of both where-ness and when-ness. For example, it could be used when someone is relaxing at home. When? When we are at home. Where are we? Home. Don't get too caught up in whether it's a when or a where, we just need to make sure that we're aware of the primary contexts in which our users engage the system.

1.6.3 The How

At the top of the strategic pyramid is "How." What is meant by this is "How should the system be designed" and is precisely the question that the design effort is intended to solve. Therefore, the "How" at this stage doesn't have an answer yet. It stands atop the pyramid to prompt us to contemplate and frame our approach to the design.

1.6.4 Applying the Pyramid

It's useful to create a strategic pyramid for each of our top ideas in the Big Idea stage and briefly answer the questions the pyramid poses. We've even engaged in processes where we establish the foundational questions of what, who, and why, and then embark on a brainstorming process to explore the contextual questions of where and when. Whatever the method, bear in mind that, in the big idea stage, the presentation needs to be quickly digestible so that several ideas can be considered at once, while, in the strategic pyramid phase, we're defining those ideas a step further (Figure 1.15).

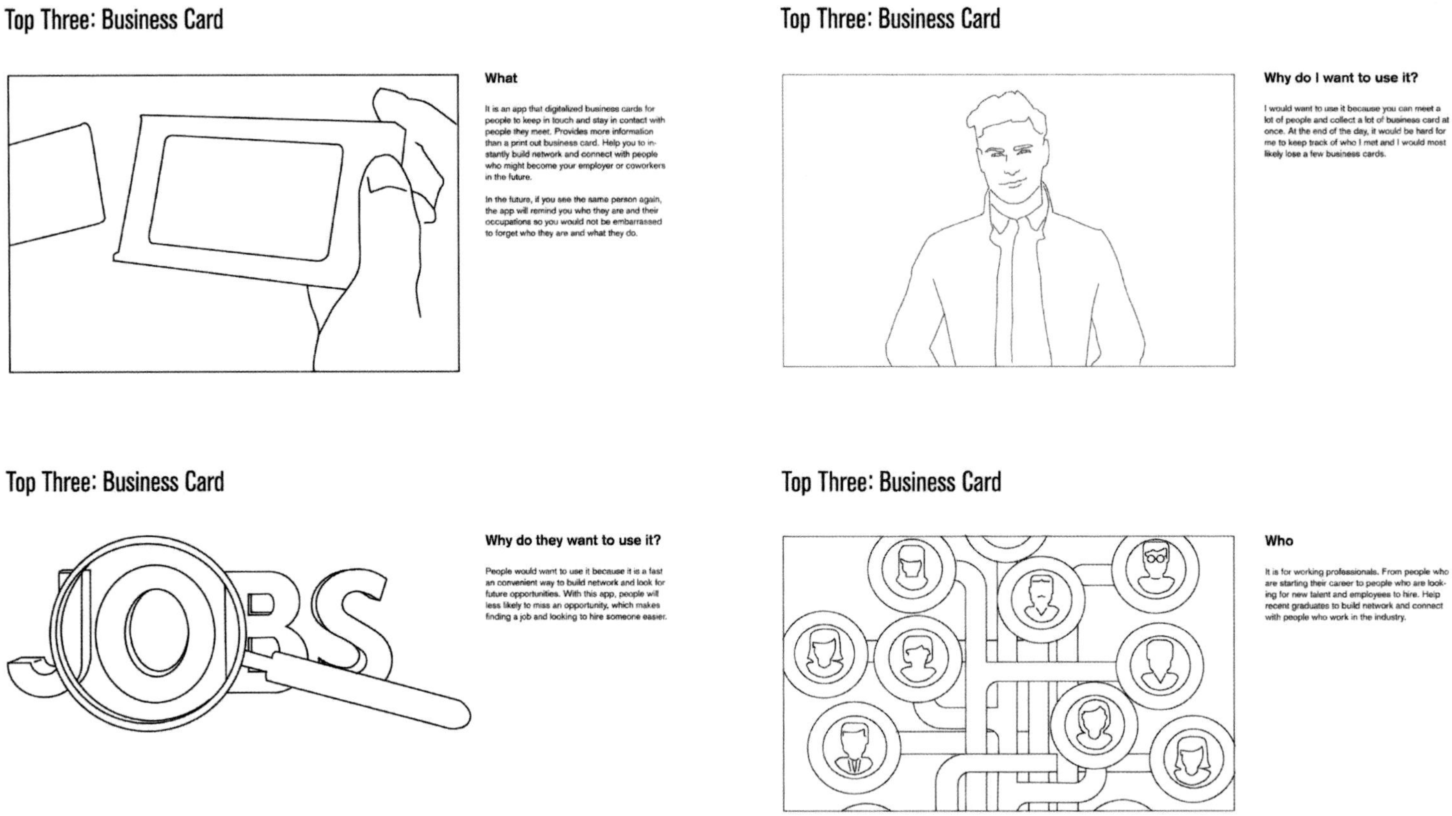

Figure 1.15
What is it? Who is it for? Why do they want to use it? Why do we want to do it? (from Keepintouch, by Amber Wang, used by kind permission of Amber Wang).

2 Opportunity

Once we've gone through the concept phase and have landed upon creative ideas that seem promising, it's time to assess them more deeply. We need to know enough about the design problem they pose to determine if they're viable and to identify a set of criteria that defines their success. Since we must uncover whether a hunch about a concept is valid, our considerations need to be as objective as possible. This is where the formal research process begins.

It's also a time to tweak our ideas based on discoveries we make. Just because we are no longer primarily focusing on concepts doesn't mean we have left concepting behind. Quite the contrary: Designers research to stimulate ideas (Canaan, 2003, p. 235). We need to keep our ideas flowing and our journal active.

2.1 DESIGN HYPOTHESES

Good research starts with good design hypotheses. A well directed research challenge starts with a hypothesis that can be tested. If we don't know to some degree what we want to discover, we will be all over the place with our research. We should have the genesis of that hypothesis from our concepting phase: The what, who, and why that form the foundation of our Strategic Pyramid. For our research, we need to assess the viability of what it is, who it is for, and why they want to use it.

Design hypotheses are similar in form to hypotheses in science. They state a problem or challenge and postulate a solution. In science, an effort is then made to determine whether the hypothesis is accurate. Design is certainly not science—it relies heavily on subjective considerations, not objectively verifiable truths—but the construction of a hypothesis is as useful to a designer as a scientist: It focuses our attention on what the problems are and how we propose to solve them. This, in turn, leads us into defining the requirements of the design that support our hypothesis. Considering an ecosystem to relieve freeway traffic congestion, a hypothesis could look something like this:

"Congestion is made worse on freeways because drivers have little knowledge that it is congested before they enter. We propose a system where drivers are clearly and safely informed of congestion before they enter a freeway. We believe this will reduce congestion, improve traffic flow, and make the driving experience less stressful because the driver will have the opportunity to avoid bad traffic, or at the very least will not be surprised by it."

As we can see in the example above, the design hypothesis states the assumptions that are being made that ground the project and then hypothesizes a design solution that can satisfy these claims. The challenges the user faces are at the essence of our design hypothesis. It's instructive to clarify what the hypothetical issues are so that our client and project team is on board with it (Figure 2.1).

Figure 2.1
Design hypothesis of expanding the classroom through technology (from Campfire, by Team Seamrippers, used by kind permission of Matthew Benkert, Derling Chen, Ian Liao, and Mike Rito).

Hypothesis

Field trips provide great first person experience; however, they require physical travel / chaperones, and are typically very structured.

Currently children are finding new more interactive methods to learn online and fuel their curiosity on different subjects.

There is an opportunity for students to travel anywhere in the world to explore **different locations under the guidance** of their teacher right from a classroom with the help of today's advanced tech.

2.2 SECONDARY VS. PRIMARY RESEARCH

Research can be divided into two types: Primary research and secondary. Primary research is the original study or observation itself, while secondary research interprets and draws conclusions from those observations (Crouch & Housden, 2003, p. 22). We will perform both primary and secondary research when we verify our intuitive hypotheses. Our secondary research will be mainly focused on how to design our idea to take advantage of opportunities we see and discover. Our primary research, on the other hand, will mostly be interviews and observations of our potential user base.

In reality, primary and secondary research often go hand in hand. We may come up with an idea by observing people from a distance, then conduct some secondary research by exploring the idea's competitive landscape (to be described below), and then continue our primary research further by observing a small set of people perform a set of tasks, and then return to secondary by discussing the concept with an expert or two in the field. We may continue this back and forth between primary and secondary until we get a sense of the problem at hand and the parameters of success. Each organization, each researcher, and each problem may pose a different mix of approaches, but, for the sake of clarity in these pages, we will separate the discussion between primary and secondary.

Somewhat non-intuitively, we suggest starting the process with secondary research. Why wouldn't we start with primary? Simply because we've found it useful to prepare for our primary research—our user studies—by understanding the problem better through our secondary research: We may as well rely on the work of others to better understand the issues before exposing ourselves to the possible delicate situation of confronting people. Also, we want to be efficient and respectful of our user's time, so we should start with some understanding of the problem before we meet with them. All that being said, we probably developed our design hypothesis through experiencing a problem ourselves or observing it to some degree in others. In other words, we have already performed a degree of heuristic primary research in the determination of our idea in the first place. Let's dig deeper into these ideas and see if they hold water.

2.3 CONCEPT IDEATION

As mentioned before, ideation does not stop when conceptualization ends. It simply changes focus. Now, instead of brainstorming unrelated ideas, we brainstorm possible solutions around single ideas (Figure 2.2). Beyond this, though, the ideation process and the task of good journaling hasn't changed.

To frame our research, we can fix certain aspects of the concept to dive more deeply into the others. Fix the who and why and explore the what. Fix the what and explore the where and when. Use the brainstorming techniques outlined in the previous chapter (section 1.3) to push your possible solutions around (Figure 2.3), but keep with the core idea.

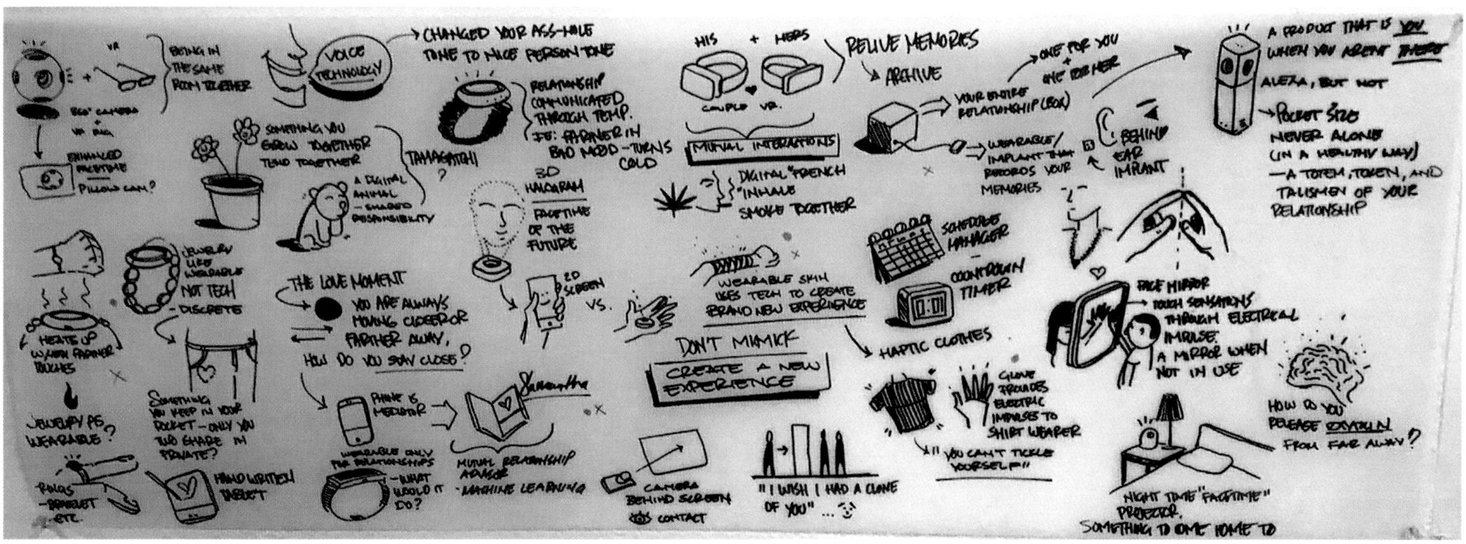

Figure 2.2
Brainstorming solutions around a single idea (from Sync and Harmony, by Team ABC, used by kind permission of Serena Jorif, Calvin Lien, Alice Yu, and Ofir Atia).

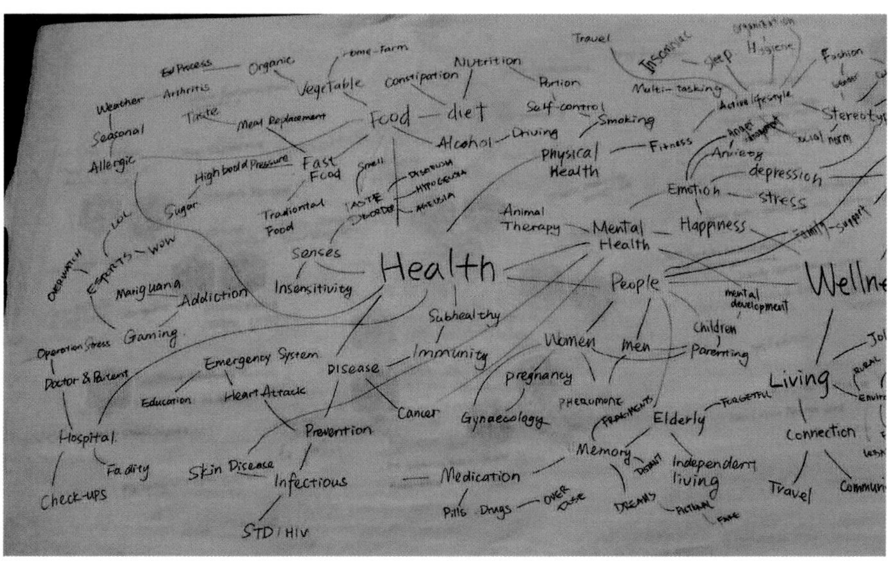

Figure 2.3
Use brainstorming techniques: mind map of project goals (from Mavis, by Team Xmen, used by kind permission of Michelle Kim, Refaeli Ma, Kiki Wang, and Mindy Wang).

2.4 GENERAL TREND ANALYSES

Our hypothetical idea may not currently be possible, but trends suggest that things are evolving into it becoming a reality. Emergent opportunities are probably the most fruitful source of viable concepts, especially in the realm of developing technology. Our hope would be that by the time our product is designed and built, the opportunity will be viable. Because of this, as a designer, it's advantageous to stay abreast of developing trends, wants, and needs. Having a futuristic perspective allows us to be sensitive to these emerging opportunities and positions us to design solutions for them (Figure 2.4). We introduced trends in the previous chapter, but let's consider them with a little more formality here, in order to provide further direction for our research. You may wish to review Figures 1.4 and 1.5 to recall our previous discussion.

Figure 2.4
Researching opportunities in emerging markets (from Campfire, by Team Seamrippers, used by kind permission of Matthew Benkert, Derling Chen, Ian Liao, and Mike Rito).

Let's start by realizing that inventions have a "ripeness." Have you ever had an idea, and a short time thereafter something appears that is either exactly your idea or something very close? This is the concept of synchronicity, where similar solutions often arise from different sources at the same time. This happens because the environment (could be technology, market, or social attitudes) has the components necessary for an idea to be realized. Because people share similar experiences and objectives, they come up with similar ideas.

Ripe ideas are where a great deal of inventiveness comes from. But if you aren't familiar with the state of the art and how things are evolving, you most likely won't be one of those people initially coming up with the new idea. Trend research can provide us with insight into ideas that have ripeness. It can point to a convergence where a product concept can become viable.

To analyze a trend, it's essential to have a clear understanding of the state of the art of that trend. What is the current situation? What trends are out there that are converging to make an idea possible? Let's consider, for example, augmented reality (AR). There are several components that have converged to make this concept feasible:

1. People need a device where they can see the AR layer. That could easily be supplied by a screen on a mobile phone.
2. The device has to "see" the scene. That's the mobile phone's camera.
3. There has to be technology that motion captures the image and "locks" the graphic layer onto the scene. That is done by many things on the phone: The phone's accelerometers, software that visually analyzes the motion, and a fast processor to compute it.

4. We need useful information to present. This could be content scraped from any number of mapping applications such as Google Maps or Apple Maps. Finally, we need
5. An audience enthusiastic about using it.

We have these things, so AR is now a fully realized possibility. Its emergence should have been foreseen a few years ago, and was by many, especially by those who were developing its fundamental technology.

We've had connected devices with cameras in our pocket for decades. That technology didn't need to evolve for AR to emerge. The film industry has used motion mapping technology for several years as well. But there are a few things that had to evolve simultaneously to make AR happen. Most notably, the processors in a mobile device had to become fast enough to crunch the numbers in real time. This didn't happen until recently. Also, there needed to be useful content to present. That's still evolving, but with the increased attention to detail in mapping software, that's emerging quickly. The audience also had to become comfortable with using AR. That's still evolving as well, but with more apps using AR, it's catching on.

Much like future casting, to analyze a trend we need to know not only the state of the art and what the limitations are, but the past as well. Regarding AR, by looking at how things evolved, we could see that processors were getting faster on mobile devices. Also, we could see that motion mapping software was improving its ability to analyze a scene and lock virtual items to the real ones in the shot. Trend analysis relies on future casting techniques: look back to see forward.

Trend analyses are largely qualitative but are more believable if they are substantiated through quantitative elements (Figure 2.5). A free and useful tool to aid the qualitative aspects of a trend analysis is Google Trends. With this, we can assess the relative importance of search words over time. For example, if I wanted to see how "trendy" the term "Augmented Reality" is, I'd simply plug that term into Google Trends, and I'd see if there was an increase in search interest of that term over time, where it was being searched, and related topics. We can also use it to compare topics to see if one is trending better than another. If we can pare our idea down to a set of search terms, we can develop some interesting data on the trends integral to our idea.

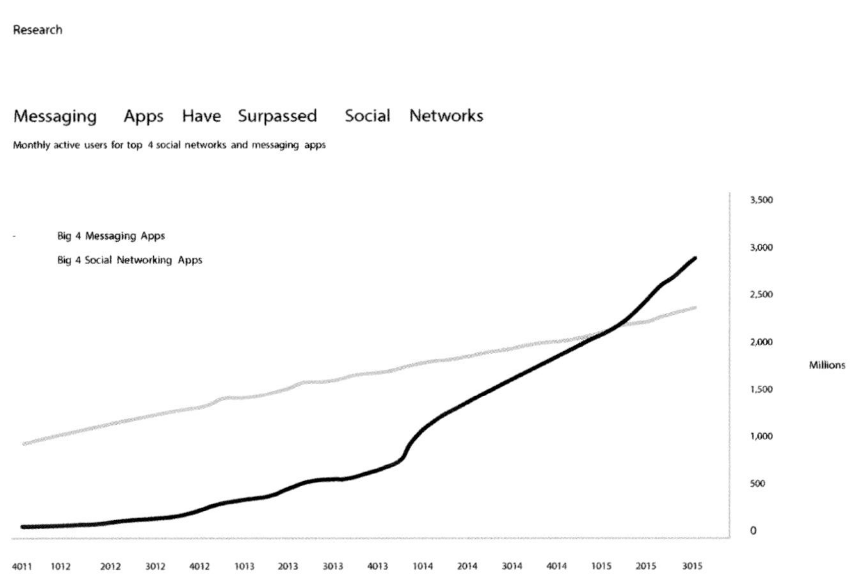

Figure 2.5
Quantitatively substantiating claims through market data (from Hungry, by Jae Lee, used by kind permission of Jae Lee).

2.5 COMPETITIVE LANDSCAPE

Trends allow us to divine the future, but what about the here and now? What is the current competition for our idea? Building a competitive landscape helps us assess this and allow us to get a sense of the market and ". . . a sense of the state of the art" (Cooper, 2015, p. 38).

We may have built a competitive landscape already in our concept phase, and, if so, let's give it more clarity and more objectivity. Flesh it out with real data. If we haven't created one yet, we start by considering the competitors specific to our idea. Search the web and see what comes up. Also, search keywords that may be associated with our idea. Does it employ specific technologies that can be searched? What comes up in the patent database? Who's using those technologies and for what purpose? Eventually, we'll keep seeing the same companies battling each other in the market. Begin listing them, identifying their competing products, and clarifying their advantages and disadvantages (Figures 2.6 and 2.7).

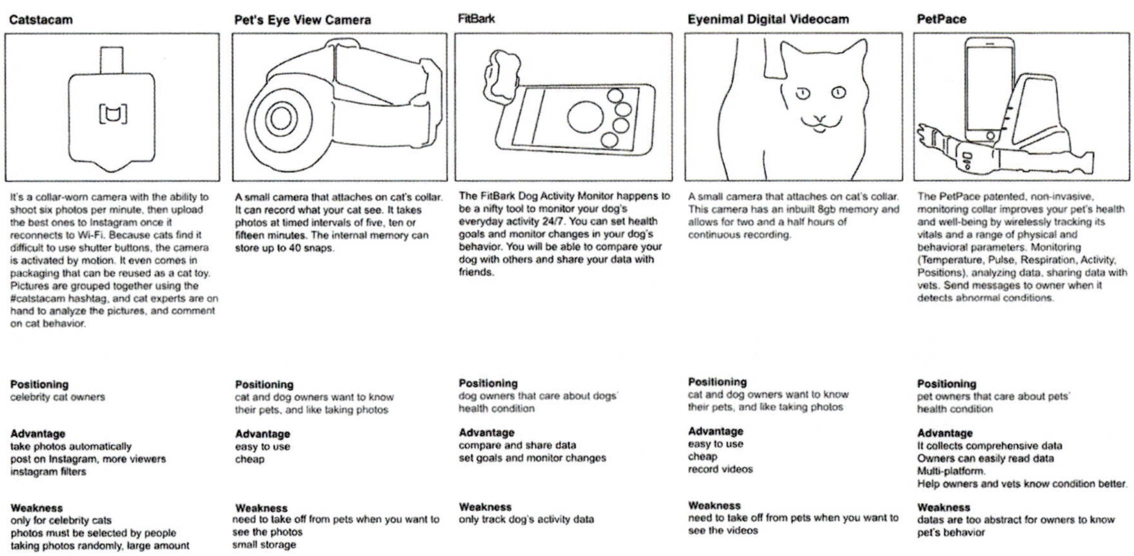

Figure 2.6
The competitive landscape of pet monitoring (from Snapcat, by Zhihan Ying, used by kind permission of Zhihan Ying).

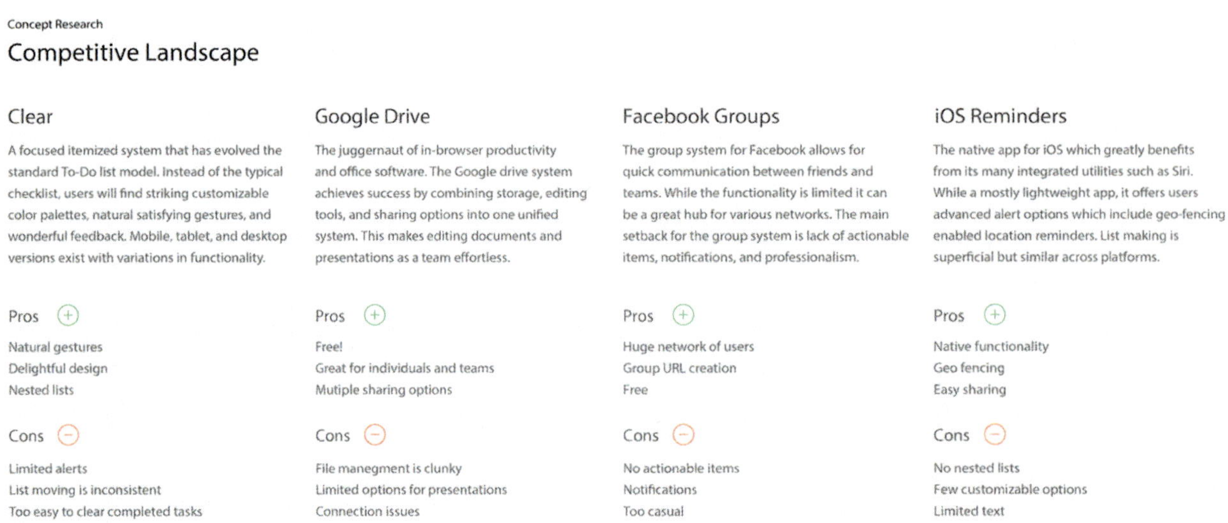

Figure 2.7
The competitive landscape of group connectivity (from Thread, by Chase Morrison, used by kind permission of Chase Morrison).

One common error in the development of a competitive landscape is the omission of a whole category of competitors. The most prevalent in this regard is the lack of consideration of analog solutions when we are considering those that are digital. The most significant competitor for taking notes on a digital device is not other digital devices, but paper and pencil. When considering solving their needs, people don't just seek out digital solutions, they look at everything. Your competitive analyses should, too. If we don't consider both analog and digital, our analyses will be flawed.

The advantages and disadvantages that we applied in our brainstormed competitive landscape will become our competitors' strengths and weaknesses. This may seem like a simple semantic change—and it very well may be if our pros and cons were reasonably objective and detailed—but let's spend a little more time and care to make sure that our intuition has a factual basis. What things can we specifically point to that demonstrate their strengths? Do we have any evidence of the success of those things, such as market data for a particular product? What evidence do we have of weaknesses? How are we verifying that?

It might be useful to debate this with a colleague where you play the role of a defender of a particular strength or weakness, and your interlocutor takes the other side. Then switch roles. What have you learned? Can you involve a judge to be objective and take notes? Whatever method you use, try to be as honest as possible. Again, it will not do you any favors later if you gloss over something that is a challenge to your idea now.

2.6 COMPETITION FEATURE ANALYSIS

As we probe deeper into the viability of our idea, we must become somewhat of an expert in the field, or at least the market. This effort requires that we know what each of our competitors does. Our work on our competitive landscape probably revealed a few close competitors, especially when we consider those attributes by which it is to be distinguished in the marketplace. We should learn a lot more about what makes them successful. What features do they offer their audience? What are the typical things provided by the products in that sector? Creating a feature analysis of the competition allows us to compare and contrast our competition specifically in terms of the features they offer.

To create a feature analysis, review the products of your competition. Itemize their features. What are the common ones? What are those that are unique? Create a grid that identifies competitive products along one axis and features along another (Figure 2.8). It's also instructive to identify not only if they contain a certain

Figure 2.8
Competition feature analysis of fitness trackers (from Tier X, by Schei Wang, used by kind permission of Schei Wang).

feature or not, but also how effectively the feature is offered. This can lead to insights such as the features consumers expect of a product in our segment, as well as what level of execution of these features leads to success.

2.7 EXPERT INTERVIEWS

Who do we know or can gain access to who are experts in the users, products, or services required by our design hypothesis? Often, we are working on something where we may have little to no expertise. In fact, it's good practice to assume that we don't have expertise, whether we think we do or not. Involving experts allows us to quickly gain a skilled opinion about our opportunity (Figures 2.9 and 2.10).

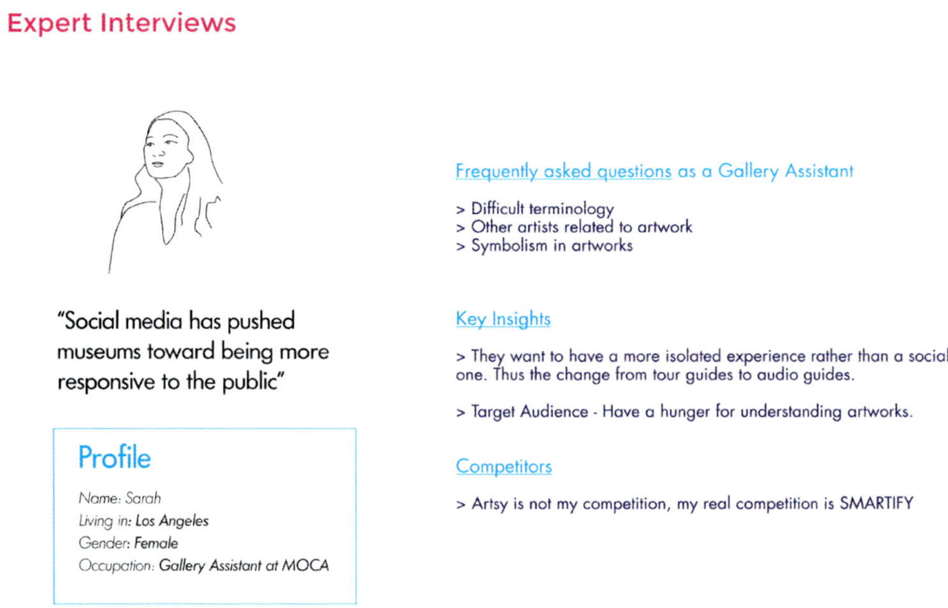

Figure 2.9
Information guides in museums: Expert interview synopsis (from Artbug, by Radhika Kashyap, used by kind permission of Radhika Kashyap).

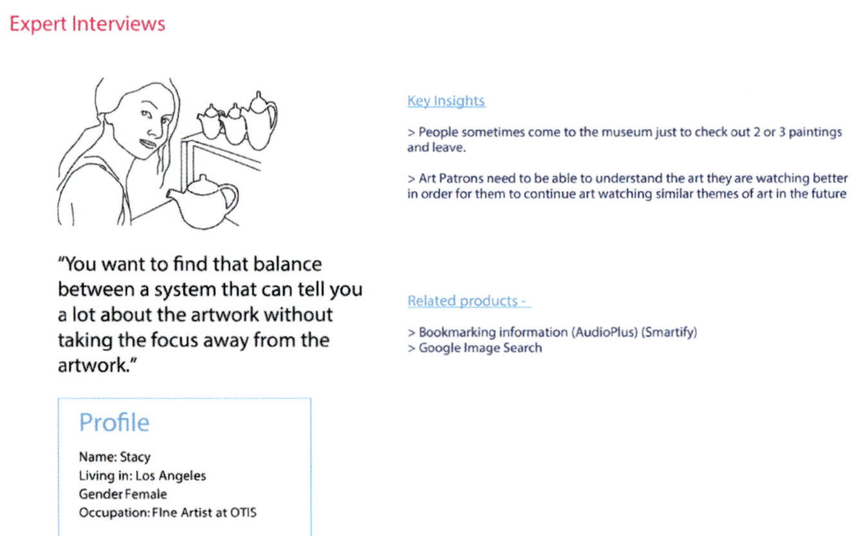

Figure 2.10
Information guides in museums: Expert interview synopsis (from Artbug, by Radhika Kashyap, used by kind permission of Radhika Kashyap).

Experts are usually not users themselves, but provide us insight into the product space, its users, and its stakeholders. We are not interviewing them and observing them in the same way we will be approaching our users. In fact, we place them in the secondary research phase precisely because they provide us with a better perspective on the problem and the people.

Who is an "expert" though? For a product designed to help recovering alcoholics, a psychiatrist who deals with those patients is a clear expert. It's a person who is not our user, but deals with them a great deal and can give us expert advice about our audience as a whole. But experts don't have to have advanced degrees from top-tier universities. If you're designing a system for grocery checkout, the cashier could be an expert. If you're designing an app for child safety at the park, your stay-at-home parent may be the expert.

Direct interview questions are often the best way to tease out pertinent information from our experts, but it is possible for them to give us excellent feedback if we also take them through the same process we would hope our users to go through in our hypothesized solution. Talk to them about our magic moments. Do they agree these moments would indeed be magical? Can they add anything to the idea? They may be able to point out things that neither our intuition nor our competitive analysis have revealed, and allow us to see trends we may not have been aware of (Figure 2.11).

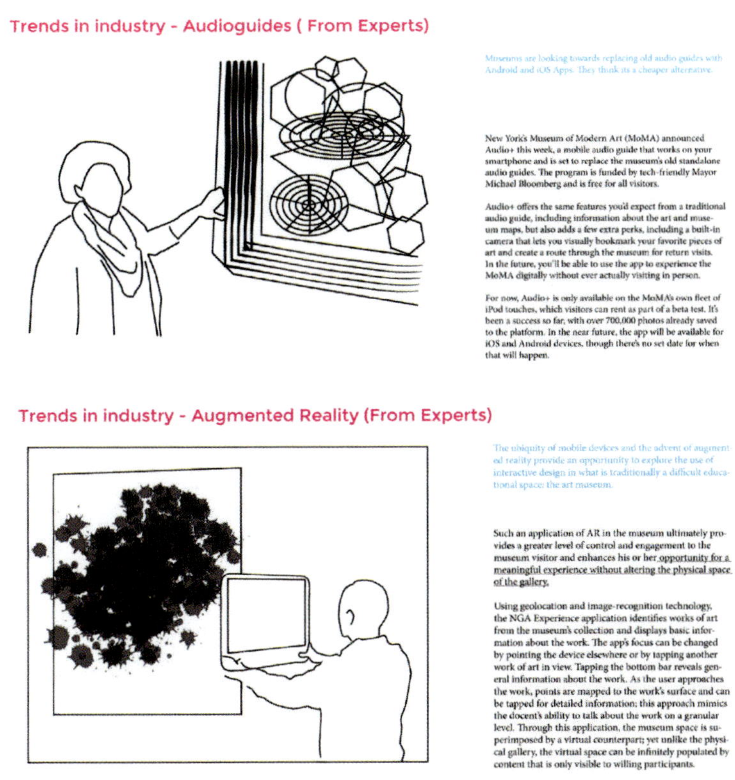

Figure 2.11
Information guides in museums: Concept specific trends (from Artbug, by Radhika Kashyap, used by kind permission of Radhika Kashyap).

2.8 COMPETITION DETAIL RESEARCH

Among other things, we can use our expert interviews to assess whether our competitive analyses were comprehensive. Did we consider all the competition out there? Who are our closest competitors? For those that are closest, we should become an expert on them. We should use them. Analyze them. Break them open and break them down. What is effective about them? What is problematic?

With our closest competitors we should go beyond just a feature analysis and break them into their component parts and see what makes them tick. Reverse engineer them. How are they put together? What kind of functionality do they have? How does that functionality work? How are they designed? What kind of parts are they designed with? Perform patent or copyright searches and see what intellectual property they own or contain. What is their overall structure? The more we know about them, the better we can identify and take advantage of opportunities (Figure 2.12).

Figure 2.12
Competition detail research: Deconstructing both virtual and physical products (top: REI Adventures, by Avis Tao; bottom: Kinect, by Tash Ushiyama, used by kind permission of Avis Tao and Tash Ushiyama).

2.9 PAIN POINTS

A word of warning: Although we should become an expert with respect to our competition, we shouldn't become too attached to how they do things. Looking only to them will lead us to an understanding of how they solved the problem, but may blind us to how the solution should be solved.

When assessing features, it's also critical to revisit our user's current scenario. Ask "how do people currently achieve the goals I would like my product to achieve?" Observe someone going through that process or go through it yourself. Provide insight into pain points as well as where things are done well (Figure 2.13). What are the points of friction in the current process? What are the opportunities to smooth out the experience? What are the magic moments?

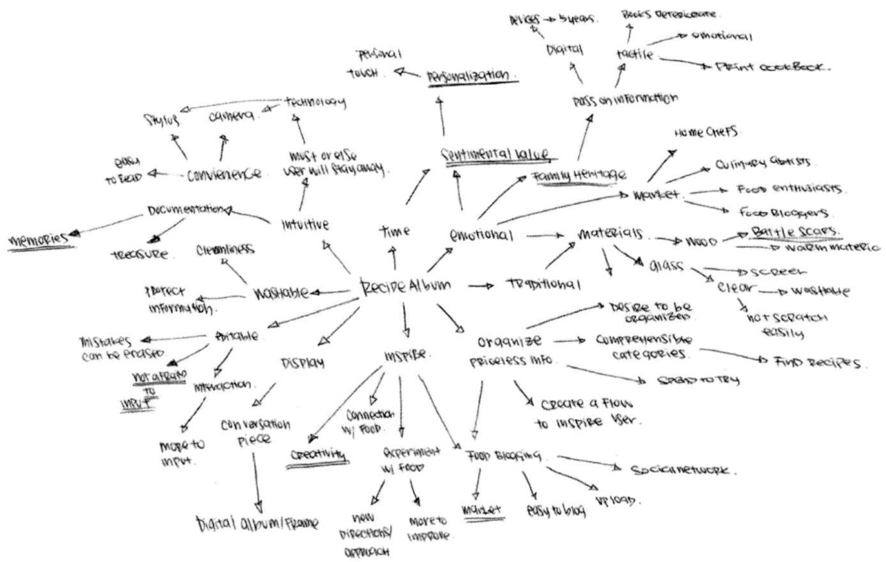

Figure 2.13
Feature brainstorming a recipe device (from Aroma, by Bessy Liang, used by kind permission of Bessy Liang).

2.10 STRATEGIC VISION

After reviewing our competition and further assessing the pain points in the current scenario, what opportunities do we see? How do we assess and present the opportunity we feel is out there? This is the role of frameworks that define the strategic vision of our idea and include SWOT analyses, positioning matrices, positioning statements, persona, and text scenarios. Let's begin discussing these frameworks with those that capture the opportunities we've discovered in our market research.

2.11 MARKET SWOT

A business research tool common for assessing a market opportunity is the SWOT analysis. The acronym stands for strengths, weaknesses, opportunities, and threats (Böhm 2009, pg. 1). Strengths and weaknesses are "inward facing" in the sense that they deal with the strengths and weaknesses of our particular idea. Opportunities and threats are outward facing in that they identify forces in the general marketplace: The opportunities and threats presented by our competition or other forces.

A SWOT analysis is based on the competitive analyses we've performed above. Through these, we're already in tune with our competition and are beginning to develop some insight into the opportunities that are out there. Let's try to list those opportunities we feel are most important. What are the biggest threats? List those, too. Now look inward, into our idea. What strengths do we hypothesize our solution should have in order to take advantage of the opportunities presented by the market? What are some weaknesses that we will most certainly face? This last one is often the most challenging because we are usually blind to our weaknesses. But they are there, and they're real, or else someone would have executed our idea already. We just need to discover them (Figure 2.14).

Clarifying the categories in a SWOT allows us to objectively look at requirements that we should achieve in realizing our idea. Certainly our idea is vague at this point—it's really only a hypothesis—so the "S" and "W" column of our SWOT is mostly conjecture, but it's good to contemplate these, especially the weaknesses. Is there a way that we can overcome our weaknesses? Can we develop solutions

Figure 2.14
A SWOT analysis of news aggregators (from Sourced, by Jonathan Nishida, used by kind permission of Jonathan Nishida).

News Aggregator:
SWOT Analysis

Opportunities	Threats	Strengths	Weaknesses
-News Aggregator and Fact Checkers exist within separate worlds. There's an opportunity for a coming together of the two.	-Google could apply social media aspects to their service and use their API to pull more fact checked content into its curation.	-Instead of publishing own media content (like Yahoo News), will hire Journalist and analyst to fact check published sources.	-People might want news sources that they agree and to not want to see news sources from the opposite side
-With recent events, young audi audiences are more focused on con temporary issues and current events	-Yahoo could make a less rigid platform to facilitate individual's interests.	-Specific event based organization rather than topic or tag	-People may still fall into the pitfalls of fake news if it is not strictly curated
-Media's blatant biases are becom ing more apparent to some and distrust in their writing having hidden agendas is turning readers away.		-Make the bias within certain news sources more obvious. Allow for easier moments of comparison between media sources.	-Not many platforms support social aspects because they may be avoiding arguments and heated threads
-Not many platforms have a commenting section or forum characteristics		-Allow commenting sections for dialogue and discussion	

whereby we can inoculate our ideas as much as possible from threats posed in the marketplace? What kind of features would allow us to overcome these issues? Armed with this knowledge now, as opposed to when we're deep into design, will enable us to bake those solutions into the foundation of our system rather than superficially tacking them on in the end.

2.12 POSITIONING MATRIX

Let's leverage our expert interviews, competitive analyses, and our SWOT to make our opportunities a little more objective. One effective way to do this is to build a positioning matrix for our competition that clearly presents a market opportunity (Karjaluoto, 2014, p. 91). A positioning matrix is a graph of the opportunity space of our idea. It maps our competition onto an *x–y* grid (Figure 2.15).

To create a positioning matrix, we begin by using our designerly insight into the market opportunity. There should be a reason or two why we think our idea is viable or innovative. Tap into that (Karjaluoto, 2014, p. 102). Study the claim, "I think my idea is different than anything out there because of *x* and *y*." If we can substantiate that, then most likely *x* and *y* are the axes of our positioning matrix. For example, when Google just started, its main competition was Yahoo search. It beat out Yahoo because Google was simple and provided more relevant results. In this case, Google's *x* was simplicity, and its *y* was relevancy.

But axes need a few other characteristics to make them work in a positioning matrix. One is that the ends of each axis should be mutually exclusive: A product or service that can be placed on one side of the axis cannot simultaneously exist on the other. Google searches cannot be both relevant and non-relevant, or visually complex in one sense and simplistic in another. If there is ambiguity about what an axis is or what the end extremes are, the axis needs better definition.

Another characteristic is to be positive with the extremes. We shouldn't have "simple" on the Google side, and "confused" or "cluttered" on the Yahoo side, even if that's what we may feel. Think of why Yahoo is that way. Someone made a conscious choice to position it like that. We could call the Yahoo side "content rich" or "browsable" or "multi-functional" as opposed to cluttered. In this way, we portray that we hold a certain amount of respect for those that reside on the opposite side. This approach tends to keep the discussion more objective because

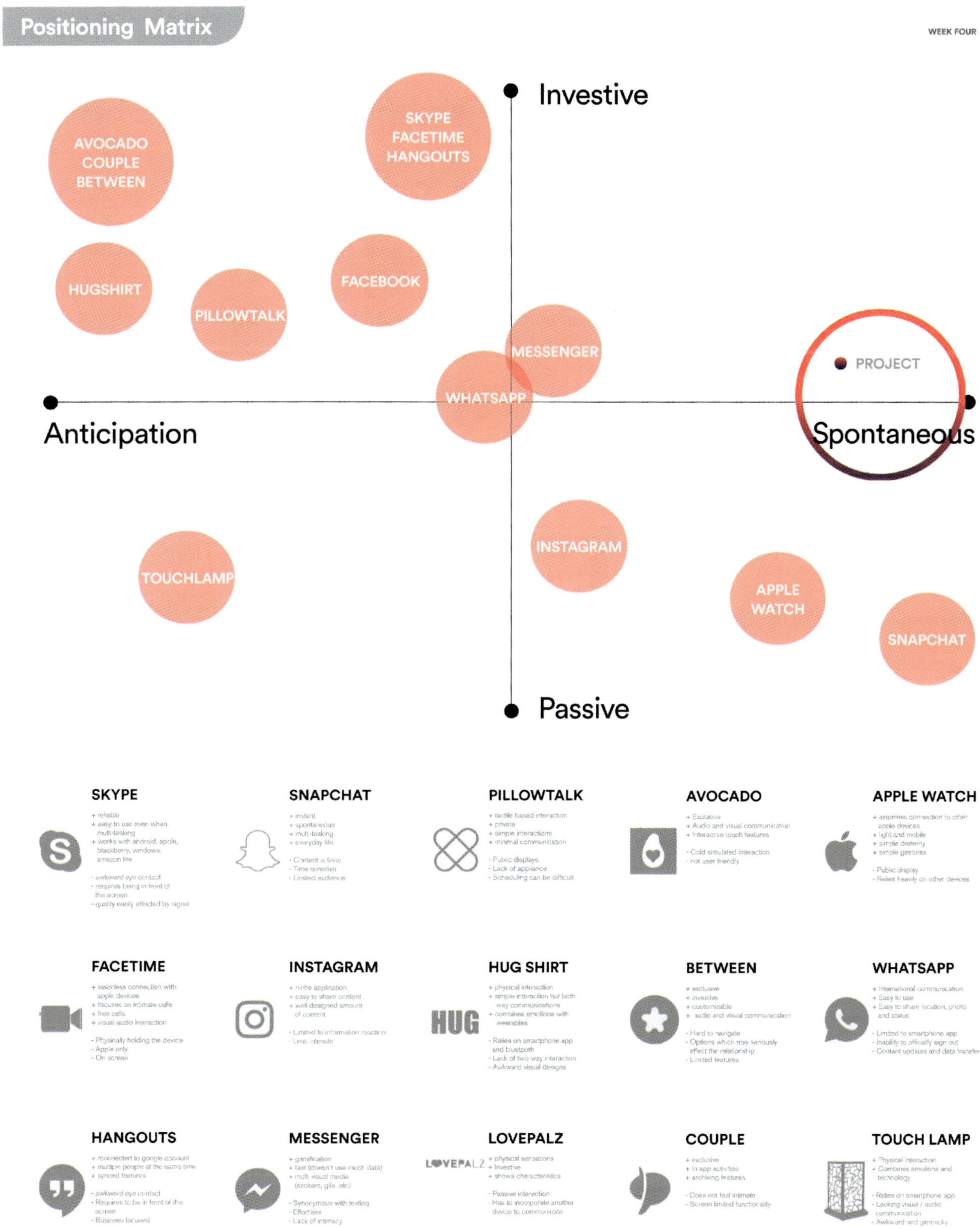

Figure 2.15
A positioning matrix of social apps (from Sync and Harmony, by Team ABC, used by kind permission of Serena Jorif, Calvin Lien, Alice Yu, and Ofir Atia).

we understand there are reasons why they are the way they are. Treat your negative axes with respect.

Another feature that makes for a proper axis is that it should represent a continuum. We should be able to say that Google's search results were "highly" relevant to the criteria, and maybe Yahoo's was "only moderately" relevant. There may have been another search engine out there that was "poor" or "extremely poor." This allows us to rank the competitors across this continuum, and see who our closest competition is.

Finally, we are conditioned that the horizontal axis (the *x* axis) travels from negative on the left to positive on the right. Likewise, the vertical axis goes from negative on the bottom to positive on the top. We want the opportunity we are targeting to be of the most positive nature; hence we should align our axes so that the opportunity we want to exploit is in the top right of the graph—the positive *x* and positive *y* quadrant. People will probably get it if we don't arrange it this way, but if we are in control of the image, why not arrange it to make the most positive impression we can?

Let's place each of our competitors onto this graph. If our insight is correct and our axes represent that insight accurately, we will see our market opportunity open up on the graph—ideally in the top right. If done correctly and honestly, the axes of our positioning matrix create a set of design criteria that we can use to define our design strategy. Positioning matrices present a market hole our solution can fill (Ries & Trout, 2001, p. 54).

A single positioning matrix presents only two opportunities to be taken advantage of. There is no reason why we should limit ourselves to just two: There may be more. We can create a positioning matrix for each, but also be keenly aware that we're trying to identify the most important criteria: The set that presents the most fruitful opportunity for our product. We should not be doing numerous positioning matrices or we will become confused.

2.13 GOALS, NOT FEATURES

Looking at pain points, magic moments, and the feature set of our competition often leads us to consider a preliminary feature set for our design, but users gravitate toward certain products not because of features, but because they fulfill certain needs. A reader is attracted to the *New York Times* app not necessarily because they like the way the navigation works, but because they want to be informed. And users may like the features provided by the navigation because they allow them to be better informed. The distinction may seem subtle at this point, but it's essential. We will not be starting our design with features. That often leads to an overabundance of features—called feature creep—because we have no means by which we can assess if one feature is more important than another. We need to look at a user's goals and determine the features necessary to satisfy those goals, not the other way around.

When we are analyzing a competitor's feature set, we don't have someone telling us what they expected their audience's goals to be. We are only able to see the features. However, those are the thumbprint of the user goals. Successful products understand what their audience wants—their goals—and provides them ways to achieve their goals through the features they offer. Assessing the features of our competitors in terms of the goals they provide is a way we can reverse engineer the process and get the information we want. From this, we can propose an improved set of goals and have our features follow from that. But it's challenging, if not impossible, to identify these goals unless we know a little more about our user.

2.14 THE TARGET

Who are we targeting as our primary user? If our answer is "everyone", think again: Designing for everyone is a difficult task verging on the impossible (Cooper, 2015, p. 62). It's often a recipe for disaster. The more narrowly we can define our target, the more we can know details about them. And the more we know about them, the better our design. Yes, maybe almost everyone can use it, but that's much different than specifying a target. The target is the most critical user in our range of users. If we design for that person and make the product broadly acceptable while still inspiring that person, the rest of our potential audience will follow.

Are there factors that limit our audience? Are there aspects of the project that allow specific users to gravitate towards it more than others? What does our target look like? How old are they? What is their living situation? What things do they appreciate? It's instructive to create a moodboard—a composite of images—that provides us with a feel of our target user. Be critical not only about who is in this collection, but who is not. Don't worry that we're leaving out entire market segments; we will be considering how to broaden things later. For now, it's best to be narrow and focused.

2.15 TARGET MARKET

Given our hypothesized user, what are some things we should know about them? If they're a baby boomer, what kind of life experiences have they most likely had? If they're a recovering alcoholic, what stages have they gone through and where are they now (Figure 2.16)?. If they are a child, what developmental stages are they in? If they hail from an underdeveloped locale, what's their relationship to things that we may take for granted? In what way does their situation make them more capable than us?

These will be generalizations based on our impression of who our target should be, so there's a great deal of subjectivity at the basis of this, but we are striving to become better acquainted with the realities of who our target is and what their concerns are (Figure 2.17), Additionally, we need to move beyond our intuition to

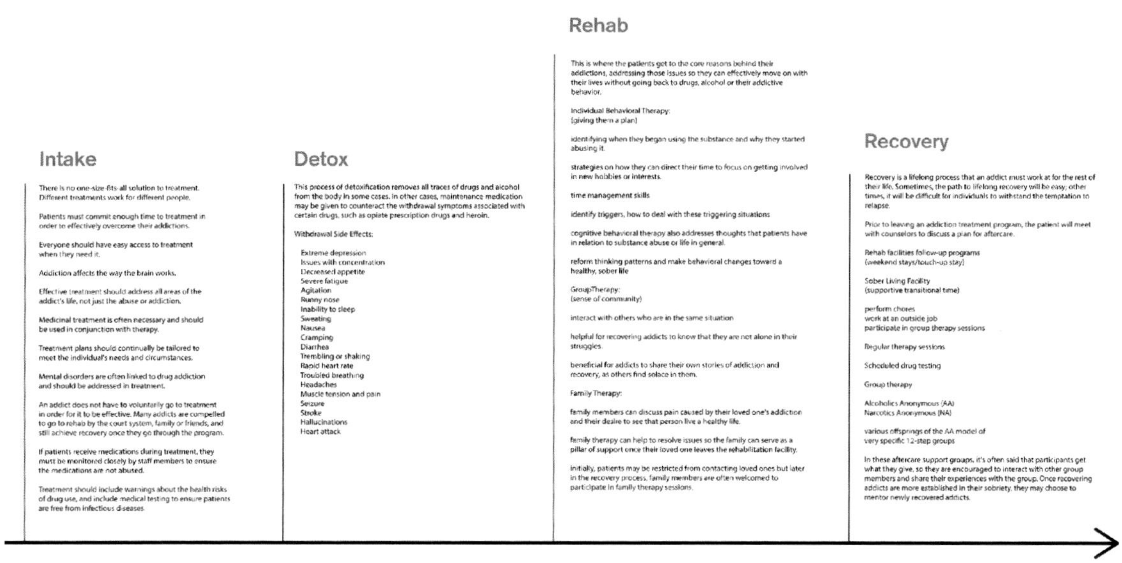

Figure 2.16
A general understanding of a target: The rehabilitation process for alcoholics (from Addmit, by Team CTX, used by kind permission of Emily Harrington, Tammy Hsieh, and Lars Fiva).

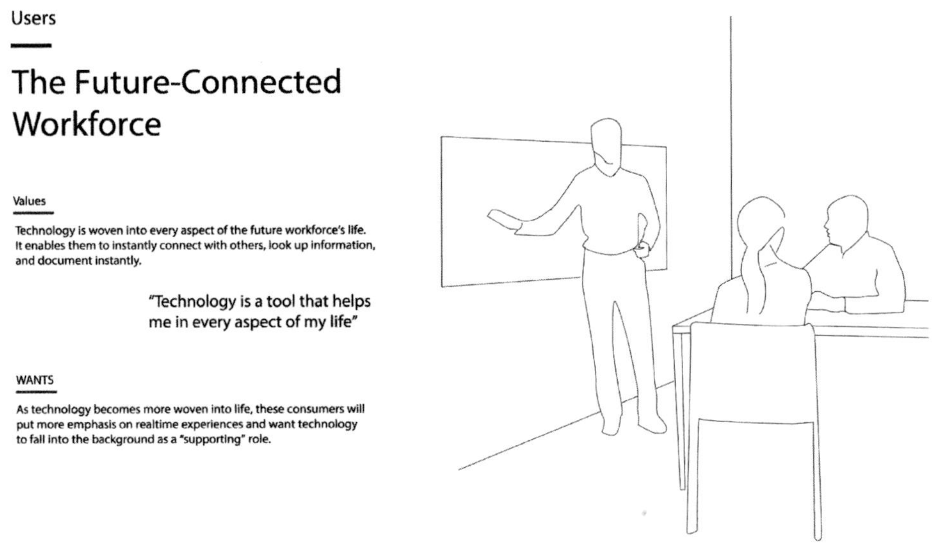

Figure 2.17
Who is your target? (from Campfire, by Team Seamrippers, used by kind permission of Matthew Benkert, Derling Chen, Ian Liao, and Mike Rito).

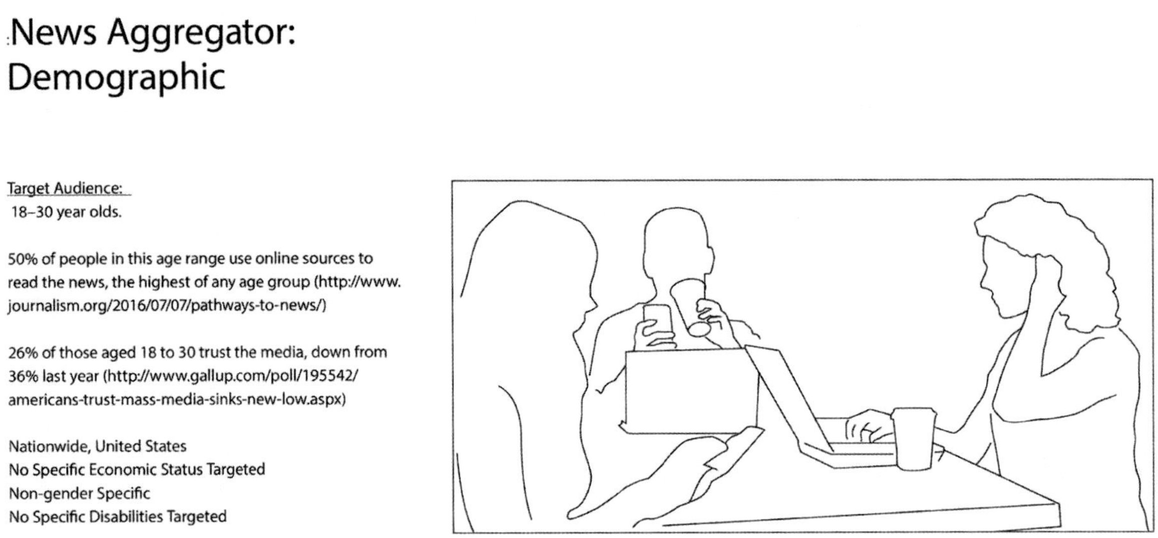

Figure 2.18
Establish market viability quantitatively (from Sourced, by Jonathan Nishida, used by kind permission of Jonathan Nishida).

perform some quantitative and objective secondary research (Figure 2.18). In the end, we should summarize our findings in a presentable manner.

2.16 PROVISIONAL PERSONA

We will dive more deeply into the concept of personas in following chapters, but, at this stage, it serves us to consolidate our perception of our target into a description of a person (Saffer, 2010, p. 106). That person may or may not exist, and, in fact, to be as truthful to our ideal as possible, the person may indeed have to be fictional.

This construct is called a persona. And at this stage we are still working with a hypothesis of who that person is, so we clarify it as a provisional persona simply because we haven't performed any primary research yet to determine if our hypothesized target is correct. It will be revised and updated based on what we will learn in our user research, but it's helpful to imagine who this person is based on our intuition. Name them, provide an image of them, describe who they are and what they do (Figure 2.19). What are their likes and dislikes?

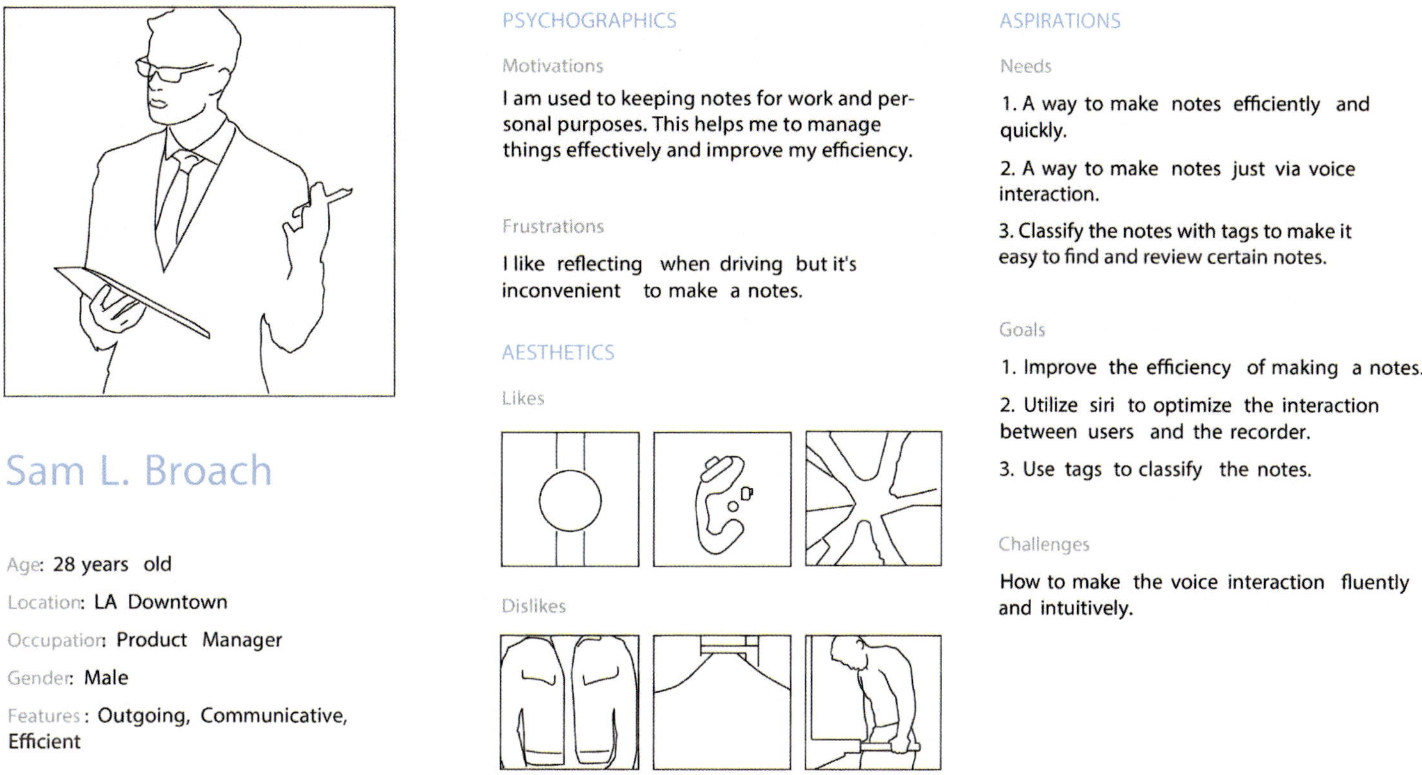

Figure 2.19
The structure of a provisional Persona (from Odmo, by Hui Ye, used by kind permission of Hui Ye).

We will be designing a system of artifacts and experiences that is intended to fit into our target's lives. It's instructive to consider those things that they already use and enjoy. These things are related products, not competitors, and it's important to understand that distinction. They do not provide the same services or achieve the same goals as our proposed system; they are the other things that we might expect to find in their lives. What kind of car would we expect them to have? What kind of clothes would they buy? What kind of foods do they enjoy? What kind of technology turns them on? What products and devices do they aspire to?

Collect a set of images of related products. Create an image board of those that you think your target would like and those they would not. You may use these later in the user research process to see if your perception of your user's likes and dislikes are correct.

As a means of understanding what is needed in this study, consider a friend or acquaintance who is a particularly outstanding character similar to your target. How would you describe them to another friend, given the terms above? That's the level of clarification your persona needs. Just to make sure I'm clear here: I'm not saying that your friend is the persona. A persona is often a fictitious person characterizing your intuition about your target. Your friend may be an introvert while the persona is an extrovert. Your friend may be female while your persona is male. The persona is not your friend; it's just that the description of your friend should provide you guidance on the level of specificity your persona requires. Finally, if there was one quote or anecdote that typifies our persona, what would that be?

2.17 USER GOALS

Our target market and provisional persona should have provided a more detailed clarification of our user. With these in hand, we are better armed to determine our user goals (Figure 2.20). User goals are the broad objectives that our users will be able to achieve with our system. They clarify the result of a set of interactions our users have with our system. For example, our ultimate goal could be to reduce traffic congestion on freeways. Through research, we've learned that one of the best ways to do this is by notifying drivers beforehand. This may have formed the essence of our design hypothesis. But now we need to translate this hypothesis into goals we want our users to achieve. For our freeway problem these may be:

1. To be informed early enough to be able to choose to enter the freeway or not.
2. To stay safe.
3. To be able to absorb the information quickly.
4. To be able to access the information regardless of what technology they have.
5. To be able to trust the information.

Figure 2.20
Design goal: Connecting with friends (from Campfire, by Team Seamrippers, used by kind permission of Matthew Benkert, Derling Chen, Ian Liao, and Mike Rito).

The goal of the user is to get information about lousy traffic before they commit to the freeway: in essence, item 1, above. They could choose to act on that information or not, but chances are that a significant population would (I would!). Therefore, if that user goal is satisfied, the project goal is satisfied, thereby satisfying the brief. This user goal becomes a requirement of the design, and if it's fulfilled, we've done our job.

2.18 POSITIONING STATEMENTS

We have a design hypothesis, an understanding of our competition, an idea of who our user may be, and the problem we are trying to solve. These components can come together in the form of a strategic vision called a positioning statement.

A positioning statement frames the product we are creating in terms of what it is, who it's for, what it is solving, what the competition is, and how it differentiates from that competition. It's a statement that is heavily derivative from our positioning matrix and rolls together aspects of our strategic pyramid with our competitive analysis, target market, and our design hypothesis. It clarifies how our product differentiates itself from the competition and how it derives value from that distinction. It specifies the product's position, which is not only helpful in understanding our target's wants and needs, but also provides us with a tool to sell the product to top management (Ries & Trout, 2001, p. 160).

A well-formed positioning statement considers five things (Skok, 2013):

1. Your target.
2. The alternatives.
3. The type of product you're designing.
4. Its key problem-solving capability.
5. Its differences with the current alternatives.

With these, the statement can be framed like this:

"For [your target], who would like [the differences from current alternatives], our product is [the type of product you're designing] that is [your key problem-solving capability] unlike [the alternatives]."

As an example of how to build one, let's look at one of my favorite systems, the endurance athletic tracker, Strava. When it emerged in 2011–2012 it could have had a positioning statement such as this:

"For endurance athletes—especially runners and cyclists—who wish to be part of a community of athletes, Strava is a performance tracking system that is highly social, easy to use, and challenges users to compete on specific routes, unlike Garmin Connect or Map My Ride."

This may not be accurate now (as of this writing, Garmin Connect and Map My Ride have evolved features similar to Strava), but this is a well-formed positioning statement as things stood in 2011. It clarifies what it is, who it's for, why the target audience would want to use it, and how it differs from the competition to make it valuable. It provides a vision for the project, hence its role as a vision statement. We will present other vision statements in the chapters to come, but for now the positioning statement clarifies those opportunities that we have uncovered so far.

2.19 DESIGN CRITERIA

Design criteria are a set of principles that guide our design. They are intended not as explicit directives or requirements to be strictly adhered to, but as a set of guideposts that allow us as designers to have the freedom to interpret, yet keep us on track.

To develop design criteria, consider the findings we've discovered during our research and specified in our strategic frameworks. The criteria refine these down to a small set of goals that our product should achieve to be successful (Figure 2.21). They should agree with, and often stem from, the vision statements we've been considering such as our design hypothesis, positioning statement, and value proposition. One of the best research deliverables to help establish at least some of our criteria is our positioning matrix. If the matrix was done correctly, the axes where we positioned our product formulate at least two of our most critical criteria. More, if we were able to create more than one accurate positioning matrix.

For example, when we discussed positioning matrices earlier, we used the example of Google beating out Yahoo because of simplicity and relevancy. "Simple" and "relevant" would have been a set of design criteria for Google if we were able to teleport ourselves back in time. For the Strava example we used in creating our value proposition, above, it would have been the words "connected" and "competitive".

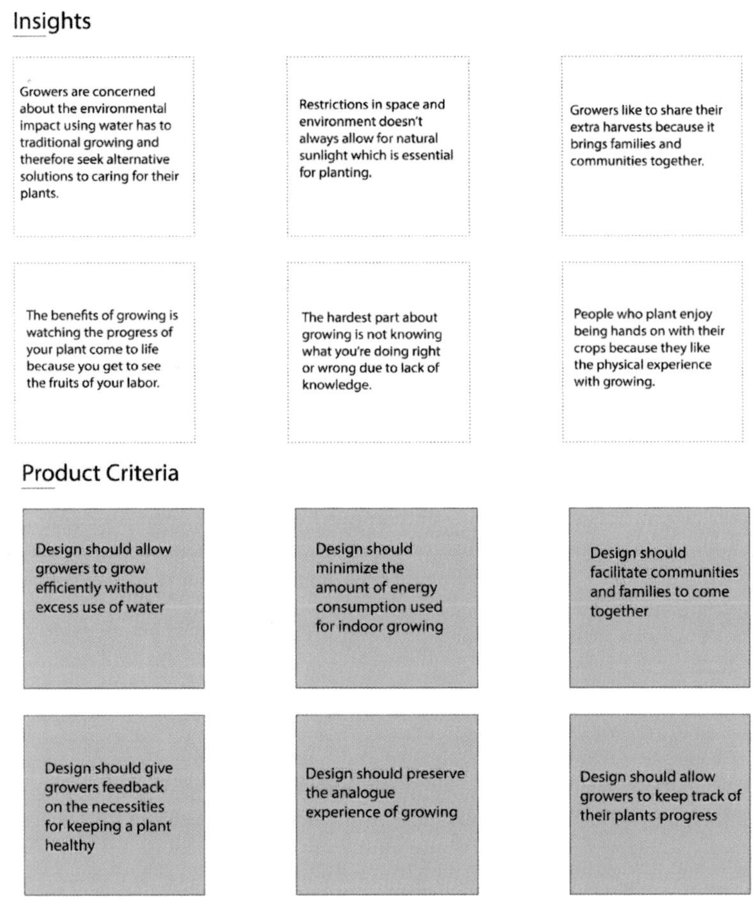

Figure 2.21
Indoor gardens: Translating research into design goals (from Berry, by Team Porkbun, used by kind permission of Justin Nam and Daniel Smitasin).

Design criteria will guide us in producing the things in our system: The features, the components, the content. Continuing the Strava example, if designers were to use the word "connected" as design criteria, it should have things in the system that allow users to be connected. And Strava does: We can follow people that inspire us, it has "kudos" which are akin to likes on Facebook, and each post of an activity can have comments. The connectedness is delivered upon by specific components and elements of content. The same is true with the criteria "competitive". In addition to our positioning matrix and vision statements, we should also review our SWOT for guidance on design criteria. All of these should give us a great deal of information about the criteria necessary for success.

The form of a criteria statement should not be overly complicated. Since it should provide guidance throughout the project, it should be clear and concise almost to the level of being glanceable. Numerous criteria undermine this "glanceability". And long descriptions ruin this as well. A form that we've found to be successful is something akin to the big ideas we used in the conceptualization phase: Supply an image, a clear and accurate title, and a short description. And restrict criteria to be between three to five items (Figure 2.22).

The image supplied is best to be iconographic, since, if well done, these are usually the most "glanceable" form of imagery. In the layout, the title should be distinct, and the body is only there to provide a brief insight into what it is. If you need or desire a further description, you may create one in a separate document outlining the design strategy. The expression of the top-level criteria should be something you and every designer on your team can pin to a wall and look at often.

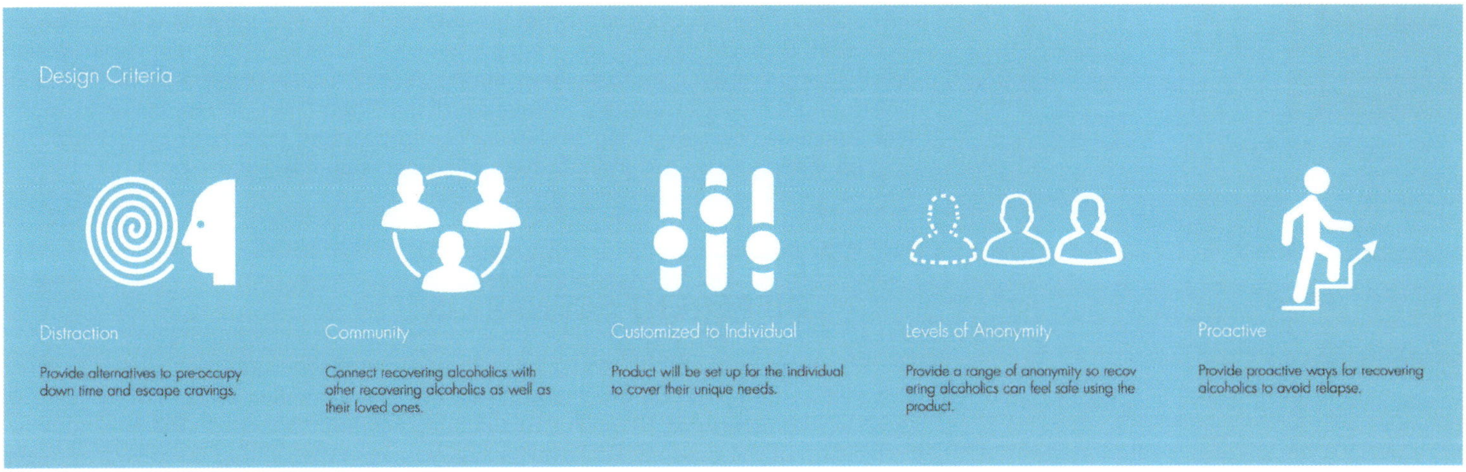

Figure 2.22
Design criteria for a project aiding alcoholism recovery (from Addmit, by Team CTX, used by kind permission of Emily Harrington, Tammy Hsieh, and Lars Fiva).

2.20 SCENARIOS

Our positioning statement presents a strategic vision, but designers usually don't operate in the realm of strategy. We are often more comfortable in the tactical realm of solutions. So, from a designer's point of view, what do we really mean by our positioning statement? What kind of solutions can we provide at this stage that exemplifies what we mean? To solve this, let's revisit our user's current scenario and our proposed magic moments. But let's take our magic moments a little further by turning them into brief scenarios of what we would eventually like our users to experience.

Scenarios provide a way of considering our audience's journey by casting us, the designers, into the role of the user. This allows us to become empathetic with our user to consider the important pathways they will be traveling throughout our system. "Designers, however well-meaning, aren't the users" (Saffer, 2010, p. 33). We aren't our users, but we should get into their heads as much as possible. Scenarios achieve this by allowing us to "interact intimately" (Carroll, 2000, p. 45) with the situation. But becoming empathetic with our users is not the only strength of a scenario. Scenarios are engaging (Quesenbery & Brooks, 2010, p. 22) and, as such, are effective in communicating our designs to, say, our team, our company leadership, or, most importantly, a group of investors (Cooper, 2015, p. 102).

Our exposure to books and movies has made us experts in understanding our world through stories. However, when designers begin speaking of their products, often they lapse into what I like to call "feature speak", where they itemize and describe features. This tends to numb our audience, causing them to lose interest in the discussion. People connect much better when listening to stories about people and their experiences rather than objects and what they do. In fact, the sharing of experiences is one of the easiest ways we learn (Johnson, 2010, p. 122). Focusing on a user's experience is a way to frame the features of our product to better engage our audience. We learn about it by seeing what someone does with it.

Essentially, this is what a polished product pitch video does, and even ad campaigns often use scenarios to sell a product. In the face of numerous trade-offs and dependencies in the design problem at hand, scenarios allow us to communicate our ideas effectively and keep a team on track and focused on the appropriate solution (Carroll, 2000, p 60).

One of the central approaches we rely upon is the process of scenario-based design. As such, you will see the application of scenarios throughout our design effort and I would dare to say they are the most critical tool in our arsenal for considering the user's experience. Because of this importance, it benefits us to spend a little time discussing them in detail. We introduce the topic here, but then dive in more deeply as we progress through the process outlined in this book.

2.21 DIFFERENT OBJECTIVES, DIFFERENT SCENARIOS

"Scenarios are stories—stories about people and their activities" (Carroll, 2000, p. 46) and they can be used throughout the entire creative process (Carroll, 2000, p. 15), from concept, through structural and aesthetic design, to the final communication of the product. However, not all scenarios throughout the design process are the same. It's important to know the objective of the particular scenario you're considering to embellish it with the proper scope and level of detail.

For example, a scenario used early in the design process needs to provide a vision for how the product could work in general, but if it gets too detailed it may unnecessarily restrict the development of ideas (Cooper, 2015, p. 106). However, scenarios in the design phase that reflect the key paths or use cases (Cooper, 2015, p. 106) need to be as detailed as possible to tease out all critical situations so that no stone is left unturned. But it is precisely this detail that, when used in the final pitch phase, will at best bore your audience and at worst make them believe that your product is so complex that it should be avoided at all costs.

2.22 TEXT SCENARIOS

One of the quickest ways to get a scenario going is to start with our magic moments, add a little context and detail, and use words instead of pictures. These are called user stories, or text scenarios. "Words are easy to conjure and quick to record, and . . . they very often explode into fireworks of ideas and imagery" (Krause, 2015, p. 176). Text scenarios use words to create a verbal story of a user's experience. To start, we need to set up the situation by describing the user, the situation, and what the user wants. Since we've put effort into all these things already, it makes perfect sense to use them. Your persona becomes the main character and your magic moments can be seen as excerpts of that story. Flesh out that story using your persona as the protagonist, and you have the beginnings of a user story or text scenario.

Any two readers of a novel come away with different impressions about the look of the characters, settings, and even the actions within the book. Likewise, text scenarios are inherently vague. This is bad for detailed design, but great for scenarios where we haven't yet determined what the interface is, or even the context or device that is being used.

The power of a text scenario is its inherent ambiguity. We refer to this as "strategic ambiguity" because it is an intentional ambiguity injected into our process that allows us to consider not only a single possible solution, but, as you will see as we proceed, a wealth of possible solutions that allow us to consider which is best.

We encourage this strategic ambiguity through the terminology that is used within the text scenario itself. To create a strategic ambiguity, whenever the user interacts with our system in our text scenario or user story, we use the word "the system" to intentionally make it vague. Does "the system" refer to a wearable or a mobile device? We don't know, and we shouldn't know until we explore the possibilities. Likewise, whenever we refer to interactions our user may have with the system, we put effort into making these ambiguous as well. A user doesn't "click on a field and type" they "input information". They don't "swipe the image left to throw it away", they "trash it". How do users "input"? How do they "trash"? We don't know and at this stage, we don't care. We use words precisely because of their ambiguity (Figure 2.23).

TEXT SCENARIO OF USER'S EXPERIENCE

Jessie comes home from work at the office on a Friday night. She takes a shower, reads a book for an hour and starts to get ready for dinner at 8:30 PM. She steps into the kitchen and opens her refrigerator. She slowly looks over what she has but can't think of anything to make on the fly. She uses "the system" by searching keywords, "rice cake, cheese, eggs" and "the system" automatically lists out the possible recipes. Jessie looks through them and finds a delicious-looking dish that says it originated from Korea. She looks through the ingredients and "the system" notifies her of one missing ingredient but she didn't want to go out of her way to get just one ingredient so she uses "the system's suggestions for substitutions." She begins to layout her ingredients on the island and "the system" begins to prompt her on each step of the recipe but before she began she wants to watch a video that will help her prepare so she stops "the system" and watches the related video. Afterwards, she prompts "the system" to start the voice once again but thought that she might have a breakthrough in her cooking skills, so she decides to record the entire process using "the system." When she finishes making her dinner, she takes a photo of her meal with her phone. She sits down in front of her TV, turns it on, begins to play the recording, and eats as she watches. As she finishes, she wants to save this recipe for future references and uses "the system" to save it in her personal, digital cookbook. She piles the dishes into the sink and gets ready for bed. The next day, before she starts her daily chores, she wants to plan out her meals for the following week of work. She uses "the system" for inspiration and looks at the diverse community of chefs' recipes. She bookmarks her favorites into her digital cookbook which automatically lists the missing ingredients into her grocery shopping list. After that, she begins to clean her house when she discovers her old cooking books in the shelves. She brings them out and uploads the recipes using "the system." She then begins a conversation about the uploads in the community of chefs using "the system." The conversation leads to point of changing the old recipes and adding new ingredients. Jessie decides to follow their advice and prompts "the system" to make the following changes to the recipe and the meal plan for the day. She gets ready to go to the market, and uses "the system" to get her grocery list. When she gets home from the market and steps into the kitchen, "the system" has her edited recipe ready to go.

Figure 2.23
A text scenario of a recipe system using strategic ambiguity (from The Making, by Hanna Yi, used by kind permission of Hanna Yi).

3 User Research

We've put a great deal of work into the strategic vision of our project through researching its opportunity, but, at this point, our idea is driven by a design hypothesis. A well-considered hypothesis, since it's grounded in market research, but a hypothesis nonetheless. To assess the viability of our idea, we need to test it against potential users. User research allows us to do just that, as well as allowing us to gather more information to refine further the approach to our design solution.

Who are we designing for anyway? We have several people who have some level of interest in it. The client, the project leadership, the developer, the design team, and the designer all have a stake in the successful design of the project. We are designing for all these entities, even us, the designer, ourselves. But in terms of the final manifestation of the product, we design for only one person: the consumer, the user. As Ries and Trout say in *Positioning: The Battle for Your Mind*: "Don't let corporate egos get in the way" (Ries & Trout, 2001, p. 193). If there is anything in the product that makes no sense to our user, it is not only superfluous and a wasted effort, but may inhibit success because it could undermine their acceptance of what we make.

We see this problem often in web design. For example, I am a member of a sports club. My most frequent use of their site is to look at their schedules or sign up for classes. I would hazard to guess that 90% of the site's traffic, if not more, is for just that purpose. Yet when I go there, I must slog through a landing page filled with all the good they are doing for the community, speaking of how great an organization they are. I must navigate through a menu where the first items have nothing to do with schedules or signups, but are "about us", "invest", "volunteer", and "join". These are not bad topics, it's just that they are not necessary for that 90% of traffic that visits the site. It isn't until the end of the menu where I see "register for classes" and "schedules". And when I make those selections the site takes me to yet another site that looks completely different, without the same design care as the rest.

The message is clear. This is a site designed to satisfy the ego of the client and their primary interests: Who they are, their role in the community, seeking outside investors, and new members. Offering what is needed by its main constituency is an afterthought. The impression I come away with is that the organization takes for granted its primary customer: those who form the community who pays the dues month after month to keep the club afloat.

By contrast, when I visit Nike or Apple, I face a rich display of the products that I can buy from them. Where is the about, community, or investor page? They're there, but way at the bottom of the footer. Their site cares about me, the customer, and what I want.

Designing for the interests of the user is tough. All the entities involved in the project's production face a litany of external pressures. The client has personal interests which may not align with the target audience, the project leadership wants to make the client happy, the developer has a code base that they want to leverage to make things work within a deadline, and we designers want to make impressive work. None of these serve the purpose of the user. Unfortunately, the user is not at the table, and they are not the ones with the purse strings. But it is not in the project's interest to design for the ego of the client, the project leadership, the developer, or the design team. To be successful, the project must be designed for the user. But if they're not there, who is their advocate?

Us.

The designer needs to be the user's champion. Since the success of the design is directly tied to how well it satisfies the interest of the user, we are the ones who are best suited to promote their interests within the production team. Hence, we need to know our audience intimately. A deep understanding of them will not only lead to better design, but will also help us to more easily detect if the project is veering off track and what to do to fix it. This is why the purpose of our primary research is to get to know our user.

3.1 ETHNOGRAPHY

What methodologies should we use for our user research? This is a rich subject, especially in the social sciences, that goes well beyond the scope of this book. But it serves our purpose here to outline a few of the most relevant issues with respect to conducting user research for design.

The approach that commonly produces the most fruitful insight has been through observing people and their situations, a discipline known as Ethnography: "The systematic and immersive study of human cultures" (Cooper, 2015, p. 45). Further, the form of ethnographic study we most commonly employ is the observation and inquisition of people, often and most usefully, in their environments. Because of this, it's instructive to consider some basic principles of ethnographic research (Brewer, 2000).

3.2 CONTEXTUAL INQUIRY AND OBSERVATION, REVISITED

When we were developing our concepts, we engaged in contextual inquiry to discover potentially viable ideas. It's instructive to revisit that effort before we meet with users and begin to ask them to devote time to us. But now, our contextual inquiry and our observations of our target market can take on a different quality: It can be informed by our opportunity research. As such we can be much more specific in our study.

In general, how do people behave in the contexts and use the possible devices we are considering to integrate into our design? What other ways can the content and control of our system be delivered? When we visit the environment, can we also see people using our competition? Do they use it elsewhere, and if so, where? What are they physically doing when they are using it? What are your thoughts as to why? Their physical behavior will eventually lead to a set of postures that will form the basis of a great deal of design effort later, so we should probe these questions now with a keen eye to detail (Figure 3.1).

Figure 3.1
Posture observations of how people use cameras (from Kinect, by Tash (Tatsuro) Ushiyama, used by kind permission of Tash (Tatsuro) Ushiyama).

Consider analogous postures and contexts. These may not be contexts and postures exhibited by our competition, but completely different possibilities. Analogs are not the normal use of the context we are considering but something different, yet possible. Can you think of other ways that people can use the context or device you're considering? What are those ways? Can you find examples of that type of use in the field, possibly with other devices or systems? What does that look like? What postures are those users in? How do they behave with the device when they're in those postures? Rethinking use can lead to revolutionary solutions and allow us to gain a foothold in the marketplace by being disruptive.

3.3 ETHICS

Potential users are a rich source of information. They can provide us with insight, solutions, and tell us if something is working for them or not. But when we start involving living things—and people especially—we need to be ethical about it. We should not get into the habit of exploiting them for only our gain but should approach the relationship from the perspective that we should give back to them as much as we get from them.

There are a few rules we need to live by when we deal with human subjects, even informally (Saffer, 2010, p. 83):

Get informed consent: Tell the subject what you are doing and how the information will be used. Tell them enough so that they know what it's all about, but not so much that you affect the integrity of the study.

Explain the risks and benefits: We may not be administering medical remedies (although we might!), but your research may carry some risks. Make sure your subjects know that. But also inform them of the benefits. What are you trying to solve? How could it eventually make their lives better?

Respect privacy: This does not mean that we should avoid entering their home or their lives in some way. To do proper ethnographic research we would like to get as close to our subjects as possible, and seeing what they surround themselves with can provide great insight, but you should take measures to respect their privacy; for instance, if your subject requests anonymity, then obscure information which could lead to your subject's identity. Black out names and provide generic images.

And finally, give back: When we perform user research, we are inserting ourselves into their personal lives, benefiting from how they live and what they know. We are asking them to devote their time and expertise to help us with our problem. What are we doing for them?

Pay subjects for their time or otherwise strive to give back, even though they may not ask or want it. What can you do for them that can enrich their lives? Can you help them with something? Can you offer them something like gifts or food? When you offer, don't expect anything in return—no *quid pro quo*—you are not buying them off. Go into the situation with the assumption that you may end up giving way more than you get.

For example, one of my designers wanted to learn how the elderly used mobile devices. She arranged with a senior living facility to visit. She could have easily brought her designs, scheduled a group of seniors to meet with her, and observed their interactions with her product. That would have been great for her, but how was she benefiting their lives? Maybe it was a source of entertainment for them, but it would have had very little lasting value.

Instead, she arranged to visit the facility once a week for a month, about an hour at a time, and held sessions where she taught them how to use their mobile devices. How to call their kids, how to text, how to discover and to download apps, and how to post on Facebook. Not once did she break out her prototypes, but the information she got about the challenges the elderly face when they interact with digital devices was invaluable, and changed her design drastically. But more importantly, she gave back to them something of lasting value.

What can you give back to your subjects? Challenge yourself to come up with possibilities beyond just pay, gifts, or food. They are providing you with valuable information; can you do the same for them?

3.4 SUBJECTS, SCREENING, AND SAMPLE SIZE

To research our user, we first need to identify who our user is. We did this already when we identified a target market and developed a provisional persona for them (see Figure 2.18). Since these were based on our intuition, they were only a hypothesis: Our best guess as to who the user is. We may realize throughout our user research that our hypothesized target isn't really our market, and that's fine, but don't let the fact that you don't quite know who they are inhibit you. We need to start somewhere, and our hypothesis is a good place to start.

We need to identify and contact a group of people who fit our target as closely as possible. But who are these people? This is where screening questions, or "screeners", come in. Screeners are a small set of questions we should ask potential subjects to determine if they are possible candidates for our research. For example, if we are designing a system where users can share meals with each other, we should be looking not only for people in the right age group, but those who would also like to share meals, but don't because it's too difficult. We could ask as a screening question if they enjoy being with people when they eat. If they say yes, they're in. If no, they're probably not our target market. Thank them and move on to your next candidate. Another group you should be interested in is not only the target themselves, but those people who may influence your target. We refer to these as consumer stakeholders: Those people who are not our consumer, but may greatly influence our consumer (Figure 3.2).

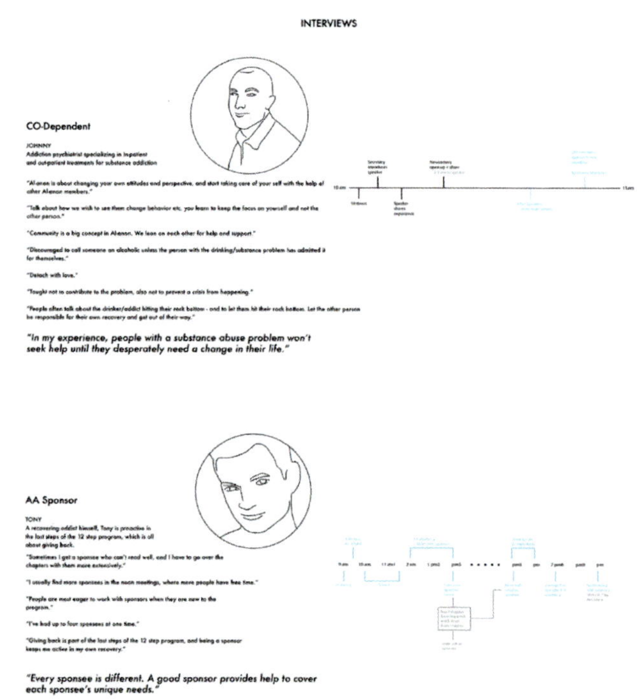

Figure 3.2
Stakeholder interviews for alcoholism recovery (from Addmit, by Team CTX, used by kind permission of Emily Harrington, Tammy Hsieh, Michele Lee, and Lars Fiva).

Another thing we should be considering is the size of the group we would like to research. The larger the size of the group, the more work it is, but the more accurately we will know about them as a collection. A sample size of one is easy but will give us little insight into whether the issues that arise are true for our target market, or true just for that individual. A sample size of thousands could potentially provide us with a great deal of insight about the group, but may be well beyond our resources. The size of the group should be large enough to provide valuable information, but small enough to be manageable within the resources at our disposal.

Since, as a designer, our end goal is not to develop a research paper, but to develop insight into how things should be designed, we have less of a need for large sample sizes than a social scientist. We need a sample size large enough to determine if an issue is relevant to the group, or to just an individual. For preliminary design purposes, we've experienced that between five to ten individuals is sufficient to determine if results are true in general for the group, or anecdotal to an individual.

3.5 ASPIRATIONAL VS. ACTUAL TARGET

When we are considering who to include in our user group, keep in mind we are designing for two people: The actual target and the aspirational target. The actual target is the real person we are designing for. The aspirational target is the person they want to be. Sometimes the aspirational target and the actual target are one in the same; sometimes they're not.

To elucidate, when Scion developed its mini truck, the xB, it's aspirational target was the 22-year-old male: Fresh out of college, making their own living, newly free of mom and dad. The car was framed as hip and zippy, able to carry a massive subwoofer in the back. But the actual target was the 35-year-old male. They needed a practical car that could carry things—most importantly a young family. It needed to fit their tight family budget but, because of its youthful character, it provided its owner that sense that they were still young and sporty. While the ad campaign was aspirational, the car itself was practical. The ad campaign got them to the dealership, the practicality of the car closed the deal[1].

This is not unusual. Ad campaigns are usually directed at the aspirational target because that's what inspires the actual target. It gets them excited. But ads do not make the car run, do not allow us to put groceries in the back, do not allow us to shift into fourth gear. Ads are superficial, often about feel and style and are less about substance. This is important to note in the sense that when we design our functionality—how things operate and how our product behaves—it had better work well for the actual target: The person for whom we are building it. But its style and feel, its surface details, can be aspirational. Utility is actual; style is aspirational.

The promotion, the style, the onboarding experience all should be for the aspirational target, since these are intended to attract users. However, the structure and the functionality need to be deeply baked in the comfort zone of the actual user, or the product will be quickly rejected. Are your aspirational target and actual target the same? If not, when considering questions of a presentation nature, probe the aspirational. When considering questions of functionality, consider your actual target.

When we're doing our initial user research, it's best to consider our actual target, and then use those subjects to find out information about their aspirations. Those aspirations will be used to define our persona, which we will discuss at the end of this chapter.

3.6 WHAT WE'D LIKE TO KNOW

After we've identified an individual to interview, what are we trying to find from them? What will be useful for our design? Every project is different, and every interview may yield unique results, but there are some things that we should be looking for in general.

3.6.1 A Typical Day

What does our subject do throughout a typical day? This provides us insight into possible times and places where our system can connect with its audience (Figure 3.3). A typical day in our user's life not only allows us to see opportunities for interaction, but it also builds within us a better understanding of our subject and, hence, our target. Since empathy for our target will be one of the most important tools in our arsenal, it's important for us to know how they spend their time. What do they do during the week? What do they do on weekends? What are their aspirations: What would they like to do?

Figure 3.3
A typical day of an elderly woman (from Emma, by Team Delta, used by kind permission of Devin Montes, Naomi Tirronen, Joshua Woo, Angela Dong, and Jenny Kim).

The typical day may be good to know, but other time frames may be relevant as well. Are they experiencing a phase of a disease? What are the aspects of that phase and what are the other phases? (See Figure 2.15.) Maybe what is more pertinent to our product is not a broader scope than a day, but a smaller one. Perhaps we're designing something to train sprinters, and we need to know what the athlete does in a 20-second time span. Whatever the scope that makes sense to our product, it's also good to look at a typical day as well.

3.6.2 Goals and the Current Scenario

The system we will be designing is intended to achieve certain goals for our user. Use the work we did in the previous chapter, where we itemized potential user goals. Do these goals make sense for our interviewee? How do they currently achieve these goals today? Can they show you? Strive to document what they do. What do they like and dislike about the process?

We may be considering activities that are achievable today, but with difficulty. Or we may be proposing something that is entirely new and novel. Even if it doesn't exist today, there is most likely an activity that is the closest to achieving the same goals. That's what we should be investigating.

Pay attention to points of friction along the way. The interviewee may be perfectly happy with the way things are, but we may see subtle points of friction. Note these, as well as when things are working well.

3.6.3 Related Products

When we were building our provisional persona, we considered a list of related products: things they would either be likely to own or aspire to that were not competitors to our idea. Related, but not competitive. Now is the time to test those assumptions. As you observe your interviewees, observe things that they own. What do they wear? What do they carry? What do they drive? What would they like to drive? Ask them about things they'd like to have but maybe can't afford. Why do they like them? What do they dislike and would like to see improved?

Across all our interviewees, if similar items keep cropping up they can be considered related products. These can give us insight into how our product should be designed. If it's an actual product they have, they use, and enjoy, try to figure out why. Find out why they purchased it in the first place. What inspired them to get it and what would they be willing to pay for products like it? Finally, explore aspirational products they'd like to have, but can't. These things can tip us off to how our product should look and feel. What adjectives do they use when they describe these things?

3.6.4 Aspirational Adjectives

A strategy we will be employing to great effect will be to use words to guide our design. We call these guidewords and start this process here, with our interviews. Ask your interviewee to describe those artifacts and experiences they enjoy. How do those things make them feel? Remember, we are trying to find words they use that connect more with their wants and dreams than their current reality.

Listen carefully to the adjectives they use. If they say something vague, such as "I liked visiting Barcelona because it was cool," push them further. "Cool" is vague. What do they mean by that word? Can they be more descriptive? Collect these words, record them, and indicate what our subject is referring to when they use them. These are aspirational adjectives and they provide us insight into the guidewords that will lay the foundation for our aesthetic design.

Do these words lead us into any insight about how our system should feel? If our system were a car, what kind of car would it be? Is it a Porsche or a Humvee or a Bentley? Strive to make these aspirational, but keep them honest by not making them too unrealistic. How does our interviewee imagine that choice will feel when it's used? What does it look like and sound like? Start creating a list of words that convey the aspirational adjectives they use to describe these feelings.

3.6.5 User Inspiration

But what is really meant by these aspirational adjectives anyway? Things that look "sophisticated" to our target may not be "sophisticated" to us. It's instructive not only to have your target identify aspirational adjectives, but also provide some example of those words as well.

The user research process is critical to establishing these references because we do not design for ourselves, but for our target. They may have quite a different set of tastes than we do and we need to become sensitive to those tastes. But we must admit we bring our sensibilities into the equation as well, and we should—we are designers, are we not? So, the trick is to find things that inspire them that inspire us, too.

Are there inspirations that we can begin to see across all our subjects? Can we clarify or define what those similarities are? Can we find things on our own that may fit and extend that aesthetic? At this stage, these references don't have to be specific products or interfaces, although eliciting their feedback on these is always useful. They can be photographs of nature, or architecture, or art.

Of importance is the media and imagery with which our users surround themselves. What kind of feelings do these things convey for them? What do they like? What do they dislike? What things do they use that achieves the same goals as your system? How do they feel about them? What would make them feel better about those things? How could they become more aspirational?

3.6.6 General Pain Points

On the other side of the spectrum, what do our users dislike? What frustrates them in various products or services? What difficulties do they encounter when they are dealing with the competition and what would they like to see fixed (Figure 3.4)? These moments are rich for solution brainstorming, as we will see later (Saffer, 2010, p. 104).

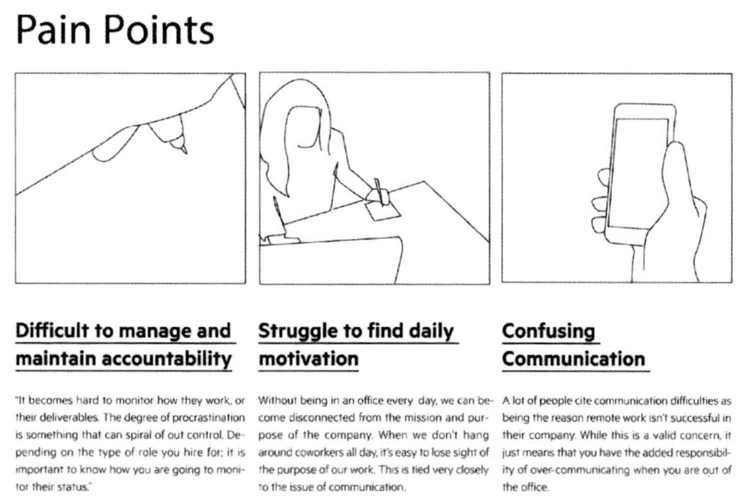

Figure 3.4
Pain points of remote workers (from Cosmos. by Team Laundry. Used by kind permission of Asli Akdemir, Lynn Lei, Nathan Lu, and Yozei Wu).

3.7 GETTING TO THE TRUTH

Armed with this understanding of what we want to know from our user research, how do we acquire that information from our interviewees? When we "interview" we tend to think of asking people questions, yet prepared questions channel the subject into answering what was asked. This is good in the sense that we can directly verify certain expectations, but bad in that it "leads the witness" to provide us answers that we may want to hear. Put more bluntly, our interviewees lie (Lupton, 2011, p. 27).

I apologize. I'm being rather disingenuous. They don't purposefully lie; they just may not completely reveal the truth due to what is called the expectation effect: where our subject may start to provide us answers they know we want to hear (Lidwell, Holden, & Butler, 2010, p. 84). For example, when I chat with someone where I'm from, especially someone I do not know well, they rarely air their dirty laundry. This has a lot to do with the culture of where I grew up. In contrast, where my wife is from, people are fairly blunt. But my compatriots come from a mindset where remaining positive and upbeat is often to their advantage because they do not want to be thought of as annoying. In their mind, being blunt will cause people to avoid them and reduce their social contacts. They are not really lying to me, and their positive outlook comes from a noble spirit, but they are not being completely forthright with me either. One of my favorite examples of this came from a design team tasked with redesigning the walker. They visited the leading rehabilitation center in our area and met with an expert in the field. He went out of his way to tell them that they are wasting their time redesigning the walker because the device is already perfected. Then he proceeded to tell them all the problems that the current walker had. Don't always listen to what they say, tap into to what they honestly feel.

3.8 APPROACHING THE VISIT

There are ways that we can approach a user interview that can improve our acquisition of what we want to know and how our subjects honestly feel about it. When our visit starts, we should strive to make our interviewee comfortable. We should introduce ourselves, our project, and why we are visiting them, but don't reveal too much detail in the beginning so that we can avoid the expectation effect. Progressively reveal details as necessary as the visit proceeds so that we elicit honest feedback. Although through magic moments, scenarios, and user stories we may have considered several possible design solutions, it's often appropriate at this early stage to avoid being specific about solutions altogether to preserve our interviewee's objectivity. This will allow us to come back to them later in the design process without them having been tainted by prior design solutions. We start with observations and efforts that break the ice, then we lead to a more directed means of gathering information.

3.8.1 General Observation

To promote honest feedback, we should initially find ways of building trust. We can do this by finding out about them, engaging in activities, and having them show us things they cherish. Instead of asking direct questions, observe and try to understand who they are as individuals. What they like and dislike. This breaks the ice and allows them to be more honest with us.

General observations and questions that get to know our subject as a person can allow us to establish trust with our interviewee. If they claim they appreciate good design, what does the interior of their house look like? What "well designed" objects have they surrounded themselves with? What is their aesthetic? If they claim they like to read balanced opinions, what books are on their bookshelves? What news sources do they read? What shows do they watch? Our interviewees may not be entirely truthful, but their environments rarely lie.

This is why it's best to conduct the visit at their place if you can (Saffer, 2010, p. 82). This presents a challenge, though, because people often don't feel comfortable inviting strangers into their homes. They may have to get to know us better first. Do they have an office? Is there a community area in their apartment if they have one? If not, have them suggest a venue; that decision alone can be something of interest to us and our research. Why did they choose this particular place? What do they like about it? What do they dislike? What do they think of the people there?

If the system we intend to design is for a certain locale, try to visit your subjects in that locale. For example, if we are designing a new fitness system for gyms, it's instructive to meet with subjects at the gym itself. This way we can get their feedback about their routine, what things they like and dislike about the equipment, what they think could make things better. Have them try to achieve the goals you intend for your future system, but with the tools of today.

The best way to document observations is through photos of our subjects going through a process, with key points highlighted that provide insight (Figure 3.5). Make sure your subject is fine with being photographed, or possibly photograph them from an angle that obscures them (see Figure 3.1, for example). If you feel they aren't comfortable with photos, quickly sketch their process in your journal or take notes.

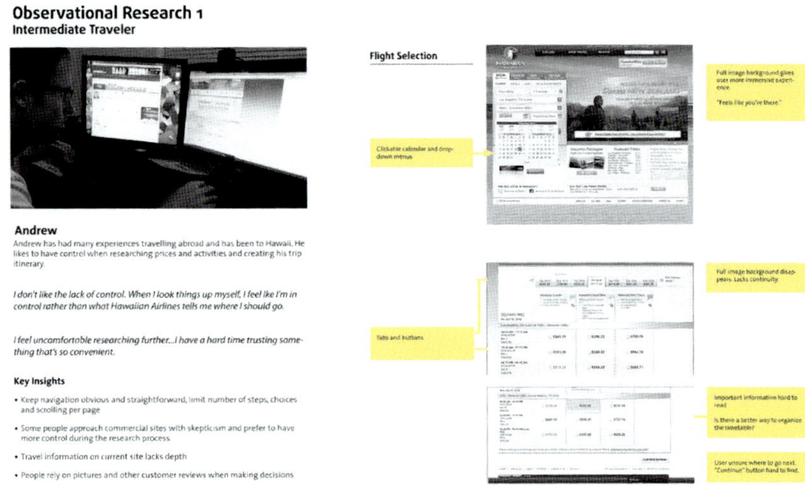

Figure 3.5
Directed task observations of using a travel site with the goal of signing up for a trip (from Hawaiian Airlines, by Oliver Lo, used by kind permission of Oliver Lo).

3.8.2 Activities

Beyond general observations, activities are also revealing (Saffer, 2010, p. 89). What activities do they like to engage in? Have them show you if they can and document the process. What they do and how they do it can provide a great deal of insight into what they value. Even nuances such as how they arrange the pieces of a puzzle that they're putting together can provide insight. Are they organized? Haphazard? Do they put together one section at a time or try to build the whole thing at once? What does this mean in terms of how much they appreciate organization or structure?

A highly directed activity is to see how they use technology. Since often we are designing technological artifacts, this is particularly useful. Are they comfortable with technology or awkward? Do they gravitate to specific things? How do they use those things? How do they behave with things outside of their normal use? Do they get frustrated?

3.8.3 Directed Task Observations

Having the interviewee demonstrate activities they like to engage in reveals much about them and things they like to do, but it may not reveal a great deal of information about achieving the goals we wish our system to provide. To better clarify this, gracefully transition from having the interviewee showing you things they like, to showing you how they now achieve the goals of the system we're trying to design. How do they achieve those goals now? Are those goals even possible? What is their current scenario? By having them perform this directed task, we can observe where there may be hiccups in the process—points of friction that reveal opportunities for our solution.

Prompt them with tasks to perform, such as planning a trip or searching for a book on a certain subject, and then see how they do it. The task they are given should be similar to those we would expect our design to satisfy. Is there a feature that could help them that they are not provided with? What are they confused about? What are points of friction or pain points that they experience? Are there things that work particularly well? After the session, list the findings or highlight them using call-outs on the documentation photos.

Observations, although much more time consuming than the standard user interview, often yield more honest information. Users may not be skilled at determining whether they're struggling or not with an interface, so asking them directly is not very dependable. They may say that they like the interface or it works well for them, but the real truth comes out when we observe them.

3.8.4 Transitioning to Questions

After our observations and activities are complete, we can move into a set of interview questions that are open-ended: In other words, they are not satisfactorily answered by a simple yes or no. This allows the subject to explain things which may lead to more information than was intended by the initial question. For example, don't ask, "Do you drive to work?" Ask, "How do you get to work?" They may simply say, "I drive", but that has the potential of leading to other things more than just the answer "yes." The more open-ended the question, the more information you will receive. Asking something like "What was your favorite trip?" should open the floodgates.

3.8.5 Framing Questions

The most direct user research method is the interview. It may be limited in its scope, and may not be completely trustworthy, but it's efficient. And sometimes, if the user is distant or otherwise inaccessible, a set of questions may be our only recourse. What we get out of a question and answer session greatly depends on how we ask the questions themselves. Let's explore what makes a good question better by sharing a few examples.

Say you're building an app which analyzes the parking restrictions on a street. It tells you if you can park there and for how long. We may use a question and answer process to ask a potential user if that would be useful to them. They'll most likely say yes. This kind of question is very direct and gets right to the point, but it may not be reliable. Most people will say yes to something because it sounds great, they may want to please you, or because they're not fully aware of the friction involved in such a system.

A more accurate way to ask the question would be to provide your subject with a little context. Maybe we're considering a possible solution where a parking app can read signs. This would require our user to stop, get out of the car, and take a picture of the sign. My hunch would be that if we were clear about this type of situation, the user would have all kinds of problems with it. That energetic "yes" would be long gone. Revealing more context allows us to get better information about a possible solution.

The original question of would they like something that informs about parking restrictions is still completely valid. It indicates that, in general, there is a market for the idea, but start with that and then lead to specific possibilities to understand what they would want and what they wouldn't. We need to progressively disclose the details of what we want to know so that we limit leading the interviewee to the answers they think we want to hear.

Another way of cloaking our expectations is to ask our subject about a group of solutions. Some may be ones we are considering; others may not. All should be fairly valid, though. See if you can get your subject to rank the possibilities. Open questions or ranked choices allow the interviewee to inject their own personal experiences into our investigation. This allows us to discover possibilities we may not have considered previously.

3.8.6 Consistent and Unique

One of the drawbacks of basing what we learn about each user on our interviewee's personal experiences is that we may come away from our visits without being able to compare our subjects. They may seem unique and distinct from each other because their answers are so different. Less open-ended questions can serve to unify our interviewees so that we can draw possible conclusions through comparison. If we ask the same question to each individual, we can see a baseline or pattern start to emerge. We can also begin to interpret their differences from each other through this baseline.

By asking each subject the same question, such as what place they would like to visit more than anywhere else, and why, can provide us with insight into how they compare with each other. This is where breaking from the norm of the open-ended questions may prove beneficial to some degree. If we ask a question and all our subjects say "yes" or they all say "no" or they split 50–50, we can draw various conclusions about them. Open-ended questions often don't fit well for this type of comparative analysis.

We can also provide subjects with multiple choice or other question formulations that have a finite number of responses, such as prioritizing a list of items based on the same criteria. Demographic information such as gender, age, income, weight, political party affiliation, or anything that we can draw statistical data from is just such a type of question. And the beauty of demographics is that we not only can use this information to compare our subjects to each other, we can also use it to consider how each subject relates to segments of a larger population, such as that of an entire country.

The thrust of all this is that it's important to balance our questions. Many are shared, some are tailored to each individual, some are spontaneous. Many are open-ended, some are less so, and a few have a very tight set of results to be used for comparison. Open-ended questions are usually more helpful earlier in the design process, when we are trying to discover ideas and possible solutions. Tighter, more directed, and less open-ended questions are generally better later in the process, when we would like specific answers to specific issues. Open-ended questions become more challenging to analyze against a larger sample size, while questions with finite answers or statistical information become less error prone as the population grows.

3.8.7 Observational Verification

After we've interviewed our subject, return to observations. Study their environment if you are in their home or office. Does it support what they've said? Ask them about things you see, and, if they let you, photograph those things as well. On this note, be careful with photographs and recordings, since people may be apprehensive about them. Handwritten notes and drawings are almost always accepted—so bring your journal—but always ask before taking a photograph or turning on a recorder.

3.9 USER RESEARCH FINDINGS

When we've completed our visits, we should put together our findings in a way that is presentable. A wall of text of the questions and answers may be accurate and should certainly be kept on record, but it's not presentable to a larger audience. The presentation format we found to be most effective is based on one often used to present personas, where each subject is devoted a single page (Figure 3.6) (Saffer, 2010, p. 82). We will see how this format is used for personas later in this chapter.

Interviews

I like to contact people in the destination or friends that live there and have them show me around. I want access to real people so that I get a true feel for what the local culture is like.

Yee

Age 41

Occupation
Graphic Designer

Hobbies
Working out, fixing and restoring cars, martial arts, swimming, biking, yoga, hiking, fishing, going to museums, movies, dancing and yoga

Describe your ideal vacation.
No cellphones. Ideally going with a date. I'm not one of those types that like to go alone. I like nature and would not take a vacation to New York to party. I go on a vacation to get away from the usual things and from the big city like LA. I am looking for leisure and relaxation and something I'm not used to in my daily routine.

What are you looking for in a vacation?
I want to experience the culture of the place. I like to learn about how other people live, how people value things differently, how the cuisine differs in each culture and what aspects are special and exciting.

Does Hawaii fit your idea of an ideal vacation?
For the most part. It has nice, romantic places to bring a girlfriend. It has beaches, nature and friendly people. But the aspect that's not appealing to me is the "touristy" thing. I want to experience more unique cultural thing other than the typical image of Hawaii. If I went there I would try to find out what daily life is like there, what issues the people face, what island fever is and if it's some place i would retire to.

Describe how you plan a vacation.
Check weather and see when is a good season to go Find out the attractions, what hotels are highly rated, what is different to see there, what natural things to see and what food.

Ask friends, conduct online searches and look at the touristy stuff first and then read blogs or website that is not run by the department of tourism, something more grassroots. Look at travel books.

Pick a place based on word of mouth. Like more unconventional places, the process of discovery and experiencing something haven't seen before.

Like to have certain things planned but leave room to explore

Search for ppl online in the destination or friends that live there and have them show me around

I shop around for flights using sites like Travelocity but I don't always get deals. But not usually picky. Will choose a seat within 20% price increase if it has better amenities.

What is the most challenging part of trip planning?
I don't like to worry. I'm not the type of person that has a list. I plan things last minute and enjoy being spontaneous.

Insights

- **people go on vacation to experience something new and unconventional, enjoy the sense of discovery**
- **demographic generally turned off by "touristy" and fabricated cultural experiences**
- **having a local guide or expert is valuable and provides a more authentic, off the beaten path experience**
- **limited time makes trip planning challenging**

Figure 3.6
Presenting user research discoveries: the vacation traveller (from Hawaiian Airlines, by Oliver Lo, used by kind permission of Oliver Lo).

The page has a photo of the subject or drawing, or some image identifying them (maybe they chose one for us?). It contains demographic information about them and a paragraph about who they are. We present the answers that made the most impact on us and a quote that identifies some unique and useful perspective they may have had. We also have a section that indicates insights we may have gotten from them, including aspirational adjectives, possibly some images of their environment, inspirational imagery, and how they use things in context.

This formulation should be fairly glanceable because there may have been several interviewees and our reviewers may only have a short amount of time to devote to our presentation. But they should also carry enough information to provide detail if there are questions. These profiles form the core of the user research in our presentation.

3.10 INTERVIEW SYNOPSES

Whether we have five user interviews or 50, an important part of the process is to summarize our findings (Saffer, 2010, p. 101). This focuses us on the wealth of information we just acquired and puts it into a useful fashion. When we return from our visits, we should get into the habit of writing up our findings immediately while the experience is still fresh. We can come back to it later to add additional insights we may have realized while we gave it a rest, but we shouldn't avoid documenting the experience as soon as we can.

When doing synopses, look for the big notions that keep coming up repeatedly. Look for the most problematic pain points and especially those that could be best solved with the product we're considering. Tease out these ideas and narrow them down to the most important, then consider the features we could integrate into our product that may be able to alleviate these issues or provide more capabilities for your audience (Figure 3.7). Eventually, this will stream into the feature set for our product.

Figure 3.7
Synopsizing user feedback and drawing design conclusions (from Mio, by Audrey Liu, used by kind permission of Audrey Liu).

WHAT THEY SAID	WHAT IT MEANS
• the interface should be simple	• limit physical buttons to the most important functions.
• the form should be compact, lightweight	• the overall size should not be compromised by extra buttons or a large menu screen size.
• varying screen sizes for varying tasks and scenarios	• the projection should be adjustable as well as the screen itself. perhaps a folding mechanism
• screen stability might be an issue	• the screen should be attached to the device to increase stability
• screen should not be cumbersome	• integrate the screen with the overall design so that it is not a separate element
• the community aspect of the device is a good bonus feature	• concentrate on the personal aspect first being able to link up is an added perk
• I hate useless features like the contacts and calendar menus on the iPod	• keep it simple and specific to portable media Do not try to make it do too much It's more important for it to be small than for it to bundle too many functions

After we've interviewed our subjects, determine what we learned from them as a group, what insight they may have provided us individually, and what each of those things mean in terms of how we are to approach our design (Figure 3.8). How can these be translated into design criteria? (See Figure 2.20.) Additionally, consider any aspirational adjectives that may have consistently arisen during the interviews. What feelings would inspire them within the context of the design you're pursuing?

Figure 3.8
Synopsizing research into criteria (from Kairos by Team Kairos, used by kind permission of Tanya Chang and Jon Hsiung).

	PERSONAL DOWNTIME	PROFESSIONAL APPEARANCE	HEALTH
INSIGHT	The allowance of personal downtime brings happiness.	Efficient time management allows people to appear more professional.	People prioritize health in time management.
OPPORTUNITIES	· Promote scheduling downtime. · Allow users to understand the benefit of downtime.	Promote usage of time management tools.	Promote benefits and importance of health, increase awareness.
CRITERIA	· Provide visualization of physical and mental benefits of downtime. · Allow the system to provide downtime options.	· Make the time management system more seamless and accessible. · Integrate with things they already use. · Make device/tool less noticeable.	· Visualization of user biometric data. · Show negative effects on health as a result of bad time management.

3.11 RE-ASSESS THE STRATEGIC VISION

Prior to our user research, we assessed the opportunity presented by our concept and formulated its strategic vision through competitive landscapes, SWOT analyses, positioning matrices, provisional persona, positioning statements, design criteria, and text scenarios. It's more than likely that our interviews have impacted these significantly. Since these form the foundation of our approach, they need to reflect our updated understanding of the challenge at hand. They need to be re-addressed and refined based on our user research.

3.12 STRATEGIC REFINEMENT

As mentioned previously, designers do research but are not researchers. Analysis is not our end goal. In fact, it's just the beginning. Our research should flow into design and provide the credibility that our design needs to convince stakeholders to move forward with it. This means not only ideating with every research effort we are involved in, but also actively turning our research into principles that are valuable for our design. To do this, it's critical to take a good hard look at our user's goals. Before we visited actual users, we had a notion as to what was important for them, but it probably was a little off. How have those goals changed? What have we learned from our interviews that led to that change? How have those alterations changed our design criteria and why? Again, see Figure 2.20 and revise your criteria as exemplified by Figure 2.21.

The strategic vision we had before our user interviews was based on conjecture. We could be fairly correct with that insight, but chances are we missed on a few, if not several, things. Whenever a designer tells me that their interviews completely substantiated their hypotheses and that very little needs to be changed, I don't believe them. If you are of this opinion, don't believe yourself either. Either you're not being honest with yourself, or you're not being sensitive enough with your research. Your goal should not be to verify that your insight was correct, but to find those moments where you and the agreed upon cliché of your user base was incorrect. These formulate the opportunities for your design. If you just go on whatever everyone else assumes is correct, you have found zero advantage.

Treat interviews as an investigation. You are a detective trying to find those opportunities where you and the assumed understanding of your market is wrong, then revise your strategic vison to address this new understanding. Those nuggets are there, you just need to find them.

3.13 THE PERSONA

One of the frameworks that is usually most impacted by our user research is our persona. In fact, prior to our interviews we called this a provisional persona in that its primary role was to aid us in selecting a group of users to interview. With those interviews now in hand, we should inject that knowledge back into this framework and upgrade it from a provisional to an actual persona.

Our interviews provided us a great deal more insight into who our concept is for and who it's not (Karjaluoto, 2014, p. 106). The more user research, the better we know the scope of our audience. To continue to refer to that research, to pore over interview text and notes, is often time consuming and can take the designer out of the flow of creating solutions. This why the target persona framework exists. It's much easier and more direct for a designer to consider a potential user than to read pages of user research.

The persona is the archetype of the user for whom we are designing. It's debatable whether this person should be real or fictitious, with those who support a fictitious persona claiming that no single individual contains all the aspects that are important to the design, while those who support using a real person claim that at least their design is for a real someone as opposed to a fictional nobody (Portigal, 2008).

Regardless of this debate, our persona should be very narrow. Don't say we're designing this for everyone. That's doomed. To design for everyone means we're designing for no one. It gives us a design that, at best, is bland, and, at worst, is confusing. Target one persona per user role in our system. If our system is for a customer and an employee, be specific about each. Know who they are, what they do, their likes and dislikes. By doing so, our job as a designer will be a lot easier.

The important thing is that you get this persona right. Instead of getting mired in the debate of whether our persona should be entirely fictitious or entirely real, we prefer to approach them as a mix of both. For details and verisimilitude, we identify someone in the interview set who is as close as possible to our target. Then we add and subtract characteristics from them to arrive at a composite persona that frames the aspects we feel are important. Once that's done, we detail out the persona by trying to provide them with an identity. In this way, our persona seems real because they are grafted onto a real person.

What does your persona like? What are they attracted to and why? Conversely, what annoys them and what do they try to avoid? We should have asked these questions of our interview subjects, so we should ask them of our persona as well and weave the answers into the fabric of their personality.

More than any socio-economic data, what someone likes and dislikes provides us with insight into the choices they will make and how interactions need to be designed. Do they get into reading text in detail or do walls of text become a tedious blur? Do they want to be more careful about reading the text in detail, but not have the time? Answering these correctly may be the difference between our design being a success or a failure.

Advertising creatives often take the persona one step further and create what's called a "Mantra". This is a manifesto of sorts that states who the persona is in more inspirational and less clinical terms. It is exclusively aspirational: less about gaining empathy with a pseudo-real person, and more about gaining inspiration from the persona archetype. Consider whether including a mantra is helpful for you.

The persona may be fictional but should contain enough realism so that they aid us in making design decisions. Would our persona be frustrated by this behavior? Would a particular visual approach be acceptable? Would it be inspirational? Answering these questions is one of the greatest values of the persona construct.

Also valuable, the persona gets a team on the same page. If the depiction seems real, and the team becomes intimate with that persona or set of personas, design discussions transition from being about whether *a team member* likes or dislikes a design. They become about whether *the persona* would or would not like the design. This abstraction becomes useful in making these debates less about personal taste and more about whether the system is satisfying its design goals. Design discussions become more objective.

We present our persona similar to the way we presented our provisional persona: with an image, demographic information, expressions of some wants and needs, a pull quote that frames who they are, and imagery depicting things that they like or spend time with (Figure 3.9).

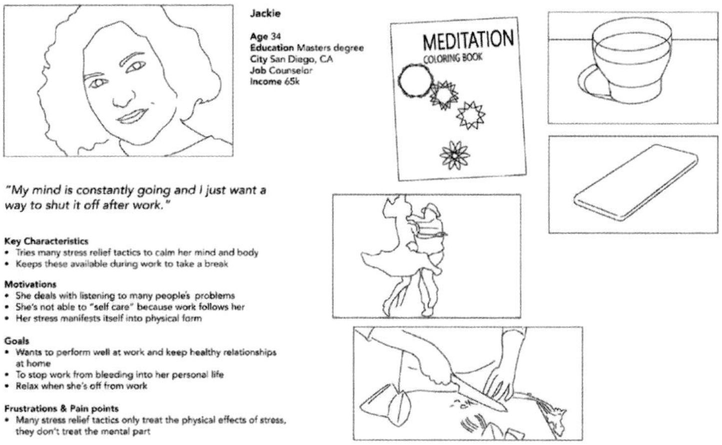

Figure 3.9
Persona presentation format, from Tranquillo, by Team My Favorite, used by kind permission of Busarin Chumnong, Elly Nam, Mariko Sanchez, and Xiaoyi Xie).

3.14 REVISITING THE TEXT SCENARIO

In the previous chapter, we pointed out how we use scenario based design to create our solutions. Our user research has invariably altered the text scenario we established previously. What did you learn about the pain points your users endure in the current scenario? How would your users ultimately like to achieve the goals your concept provides? It's possible that we may only need to revise a few critical details against our competition in order to help our user significantly, or we may see that a fundamental change in approach is called for. Whether our modifications are evolutionary or revolutionary, it's critical that our scenario needs careful reconsideration.

3.15 ASPIRATIONAL ADJECTIVES

The entirety of a design incorporates both style and substance. As our process evolves, you will notice activities we propose that explore not only what our system does or what it contains, but how it feels: Its emotional impact. Our effort to refine how we want it to feel will eventually affect the style and aesthetics of our system.

What we mean by feel here is, of course, not whether its surface is rough or smooth (although that can sometimes get us what we want), but how it feels emotionally. In a physical interface feel and style are often closely related. For example, a pickup may have a hexagon as a recurring theme throughout its design because it refers to bolts that convey the feeling of being rugged. For this reason, features that in other cars may be just plain circles may be expressed as hexagons on a truck. With a rugged looking hexagonal bolt-like knob, a plain old radio dial delivers on that feeling. When we talk about how a design feels, we are getting into the realm of branding: The aesthetic personality of a product that distinguishes it from its rivals.

Too often we design things for our own aesthetics and forget that we are not the target. That being said, we also need to recognize that we bring our sense of aesthetics into the equation as well. Even if we're designing for seniors, maybe they want to be a little edgy, too? When our competition designs things for seniors that look as if they belong in a hospital, we may stand out because ours has a little youthful vitality to it. As long as we are well aware of our audience's turn-offs, it's perfectly fine to explore how far we can push things. By doing so, we may discover approaches that allow our system to stand out.

Use the persona construct as inspiration to come up with a list of words that convey how our system should feel to the user. You can use a mind map to aid you in this process (Figure 3.10). Nike uses dark imagery and world-class athletes in its campaigns to convey performance and aggressiveness. Not because the guy buying shoes in its outlet store is a world-class athlete, but he aspires to perform at a high level with the product. He wants that feeling. We call these words aspirational adjectives because that's what they are: The feelings we would like our audience to aspire to when using our system.

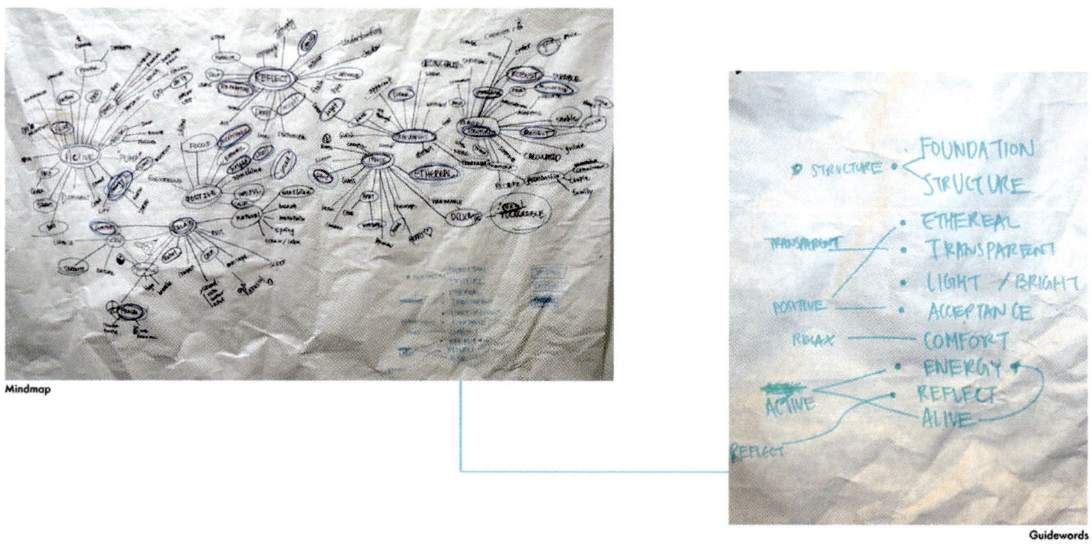

Figure 3.10
Ideating descriptors for guidewords, from Addmit, by Team CTX, used by kind permission of Emily Harrington, Tammy Hsieh, and Lars Fiva).

3.16 GENERAL MOODBOARD

We may be clear about the meaning of our aspirational adjectives, but they may not be entirely clear to the people we're trying to present them to. The term "sophisticated" may have a different meaning to us than to our client. This is where moodboards come in. These are visual expressions of the mood our project is striving to convey. As Dan Saffer points out, "They are a means for the designer to explore the emotional landscape of a product" (Saffer, 2010, p. 149).

During your interviews, did you find some imagery that was both inspirational to your audience and to you? Consider your aspirational adjectives. What do you mean aesthetically when you consider these terms? For example, if one of your terms is "sophisticated" what does that look like? Were there objects or imagery that both you and your interviewee felt conveyed the feeling of "sophistication"?

The moodboard is a distillation of these images. What images do you think best typifies feelings you wish to convey? We will be developing a number of these boards throughout our process with varying levels of specificity, but for now it's instructive to simply choose any image that seems to appropriately convey the feeling we wish to achieve. This is our general feel moodboard, or simply general moodboard, and they can contain any form of image, from art, design, photography, performance, architecture, sculpture, illustration, nature, even abstract imagery.

3.17 YOUR MISSION

It's appropriate at this stage to use your further understanding of the design problem you face to create one more statement of the vision of your project: Your mission.

At its core, the mission statement answers the question, "What are you and your design team trying to solve?" Our design hypothesis may be: "Drivers don't know that a freeway is congested until they're stuck on it, so we believe informing them before they get on will relieve traffic congestion." Our mission would be something more succinct, like: "Our mission is to relieve congestion on freeways." While the hypothesis proposes the problem and a possible solution, the mission states our ultimate end goal. It is quite simply the highest-level directive guiding our design effort.

The mission should stem directly from the research we've performed in consideration of what it is we're designing. It shouldn't go into detail about how our design achieves the goal; it should just state the goal itself. It should not be wordy: It should be clear, concise, easy to memorize, and easy to say to people who are unfamiliar with your project. If we are in an elevator going up only a few floors, and someone asks us what we are doing, the mission should be the first thing out of our mouth. It needs to be quick to say and accurately reflect the research we conducted (Figure 3.11).

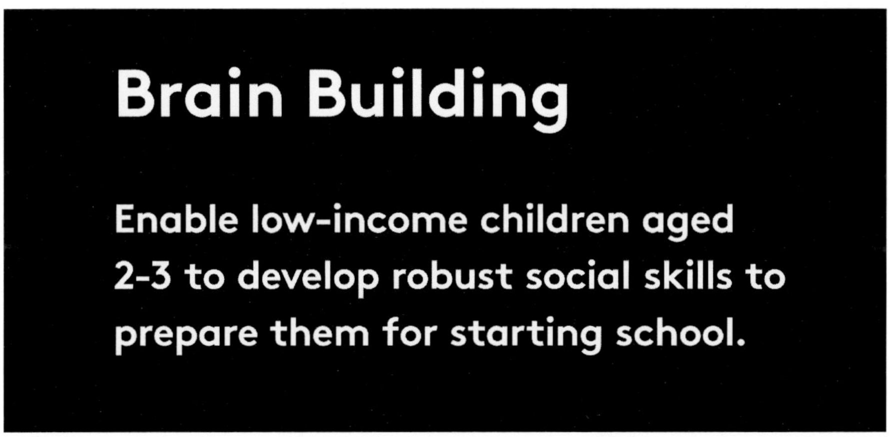

Figure 3.11
A mission statement for brain building (from Canary, by Team Frank, used by kind permission of Justin Babikian, April Cheung, Kelsey Chow, India Hillis, and Joe Tsao).

To construct a mission, we need to consider what is essential. What we want our system to do and what we don't. Often we are distracted by the notion that our system should do everything, but keep in mind those systems more than likely do nothing well. Even the most versatile object in our possession—our computer—is circumscribed: It creates, manipulates, and deletes information, but does so in an almost infinite number of ways. However, it does not (at least at this writing) fold your clothes or wash your dishes.

When we see a well-written mission statement, it looks easy, but creating one is often not. We have a habit of being confused and distracted by things that are unimportant and these things infiltrate and pollute our mission. It's not uncommon to refine a mission statement over and over for weeks until it seems right. To paraphrase Blaise Pascal, It would have been shorter if I had more time (Pascal, 2014)[2]. Mission statements are often hard work. Don't be discouraged if it takes time to develop one. Eventually, you will roll together both your primary research on users and your secondary research on opportunities into a presentation that summarizes the most critical takeaways (Figure 3.12).

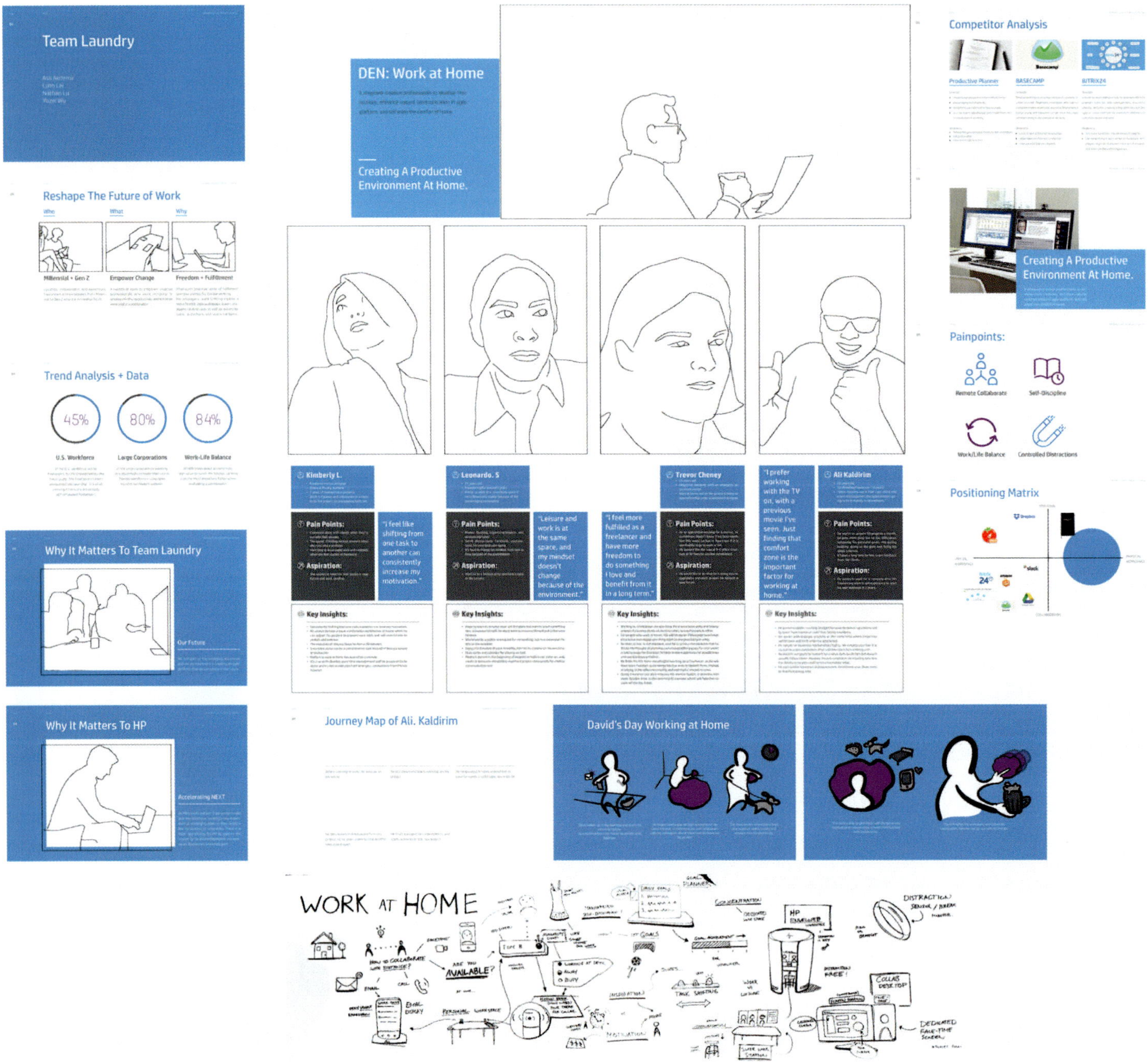

Figure 3.12
Research presentation for work trends (from Cosmos, by Team Laundry, used by kind permission of Asli Akdemir, Lynn Lei, Nathan Lu, and Yozei Wu).

Notes

1 References from Toyota executives, Scion Project, Art Center College of Design, 2007.

2 Letter XVI (December 4th, 1656). Commonly attributed to others, including Winston Churchill.

4 Approach Exploration
Users and Features

Through our opportunity and user research, and the establishment of our strategic vision, we should have a solid platform on which to explore possible solutions. Through the evolution of our text scenarios, we have been engaged in that process, but it was somewhat on the sidelines, as our main focus was on research. But now possible solutions become our central effort.

We use the term "possible" at this point because we are in an exploratory phase. One of the most pervasive problems we see from both novice designers and even experts sometimes is their desire to latch onto a single solution too early. It's very easy at this point to come out of performing research with a singular approach in mind and begin executing a design on that immediately. That approach to our system may be very good, and may even be the foundation for the final approach we land upon, but as our design progresses, considering other possibilities becomes exponentially harder. Now is the time we can explore many different approaches, not just one. To that end, we will spend this chapter discussing ways of creating approaches inspired by characteristics of our user. Central to this discussion is how we can we can gain inspiration to generate a multitude of solutions.

4.1 UNCONSTRAINED IDEATION

It's often useful to begin the approach stage of design by producing simple ideations based on what we think the system should do. These may relate to our magic moments, or they may be entirely new ideas informed by our research. Indeed, we suggested just this at the beginning of our research effort—that as we research we should be ideating possible solutions in our journal as well. Now is a good time to review those ideations and jot down any more that may be bouncing around inside our head. Which possibilities look promising? Can we take them further? (Figure 4.1).

This style of ideation, sometimes called brain dumping (Lupton, 2011, p. 62), coming up with ideas unconstrained by any specific process or methodology, can yield a wide range of solutions. This is distinctly an expansive process, not reductive,

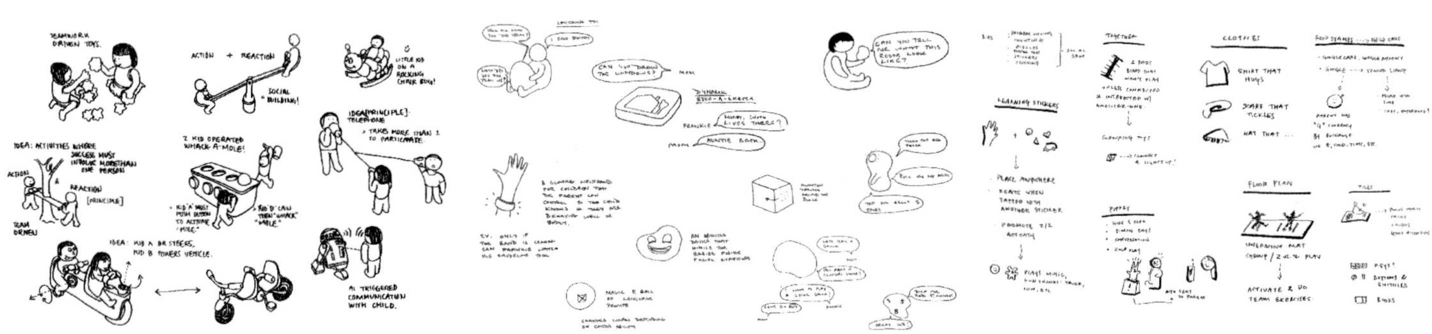

Figure 4.1
Make ideation easy to review later (from Canary, by Team Frank, used by kind permission of Justin Babikian, April Cheung, Kelsey Chow, India Hillis, and Joe Tsao).

so don't let the thought that an idea may be bad inhibit you from putting it down. It may lead to something else that is useful. It may be a singular magic moment, a text scenario, or an isolated interaction. Whatever it is, capture it. The only bad idea is the one that doesn't make it into your journal. But often we need activities to trigger ideas, and that's what most of the following three chapters on approach is about.

4.2 GOALS TO FEATURES

Besides ideation, another, more systematic, method of creating approaches is to gain inspiration by our user goals. The system we are designing will eventually be a set of features intended to deliver on the design goals we define. As discussed previously, goals are things users want to achieve with your system, while features are the attributes of the system that allow them to achieve their goals. Features should be derived from user goals, not the other way around. Since features are what our system contains, understanding our user's goals and the features required to achieve them is both a necessary and vital step in establishing our design.

Features can go one step further as well: We use the term "distinguishing features" to identify those things our system provides that distinguish it with respect to its competition. Sometimes the concept of "features" and "distinguishing features" are muddled. Make sure you're clear about which one is the topic at hand. For our current purposes, we are not discussing distinguishing features, but the collection of features the system needs to allow our audience to achieve their goals.

What are our user's goals? What do these goals tell us about features that are needed? It's useful to brainstorm a mind map by starting with user goals and extending out by asking the question "What do we need to provide to achieve this?" (Figure 4.2.) As an example of deriving features from goals, recall the system we proposed to relieve freeway congestion. The user's goal in this instance is simply to avoid congestion, and can be broken down in the following way:

1. To be informed early enough to be able to choose to enter the freeway or not.
2. To stay safe.
3. To be able to absorb the information quickly.
4. To be able to access the information regardless of what technology they have.
5. To be able to trust the information.

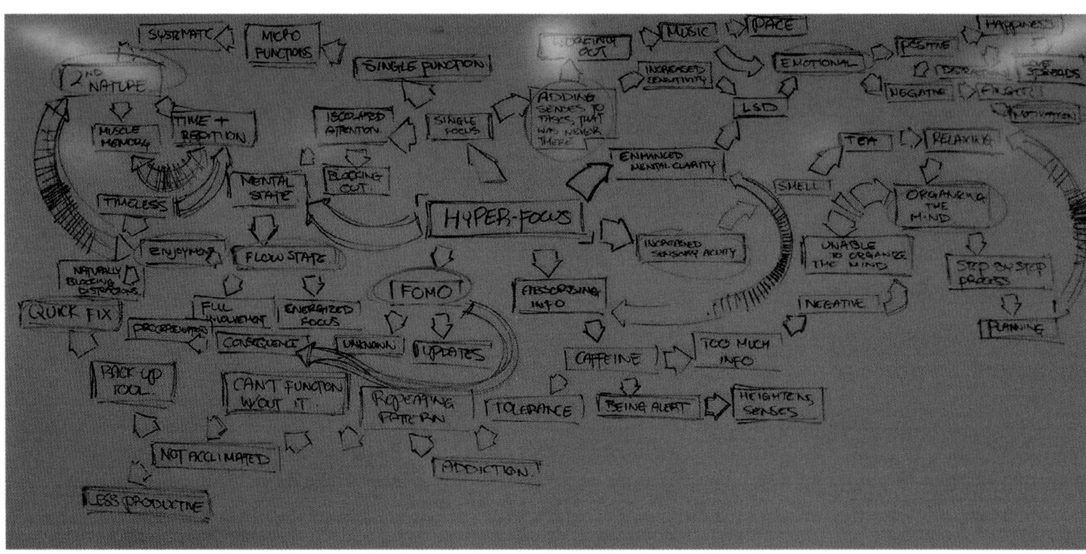

Figure 4.2
An example of mindmapping from project goals to derive features (from Knoq by Team Cheeseburger, used by kind permission of James Chu, Chloe Kim, Juno Park, and Yidan Zhang).

These, in turn, translate into features required by the system. For example, the first and fourth items in the list above imply a signage system placed well before the onramp. This defines a particular feature of the system: well placed signage. In items 2 and 3, safety and clarity work hand in hand to imply that the signs have features that make them simple and clear. With these, we can see that the most critical feature of the system would be to present to a driver trustworthy congestion information in a safe, clear, and approachable manner. And it should be done in a way to allow them to safely take an alternate route.

Our freeway congestion system may be functionally complex, but, from a user's perspective, it should be very simple and straightforward or the clear and approachable attributes would not be met. For the user, there would appear to be very few features: It really only does one thing, and should do that thing exceptionally well. Other systems, such as financial management systems, may have tens or hundreds of features. The main user goal may be to be able to optimize the management of their money, but to achieve that goal they would at the very least have to be able to see their financial positions, have access to their accounts, be able to move money in and out of those accounts, and possibly even be able to purchase or sell financial instruments, get tax documentation, and plan their financial future.

We need to explore the features of our proposed system whether they are simple or complex. We can do this by brainstorming a mind map or sticky note wall by starting with the user's goal or goals at the center, and continuing outward to define features in increasing detail by asking the question "how do we do this" until we cover all the features we think are relevant to the system.

4.3 THE MUSCOW CHART

Some features of our system are critical, others less so. Some may be possible because they rely on things necessary by required features, and some may be just plain nice to have. If you're using a sticky note wall to capture and organize your information, things may be fairly cluttered at first (Figure 4.3). We need to rigorously consider all of these and use our vision statements to guide us in determining what is necessary, what is nice to have, and what the system should not have (Figure 4.4). Reflect on this organization for a bit. There may be features that are duplicated. Strive to consolidate them. To a large degree, this will form the basis of the structure of your system, so this is not some trivial exercise.

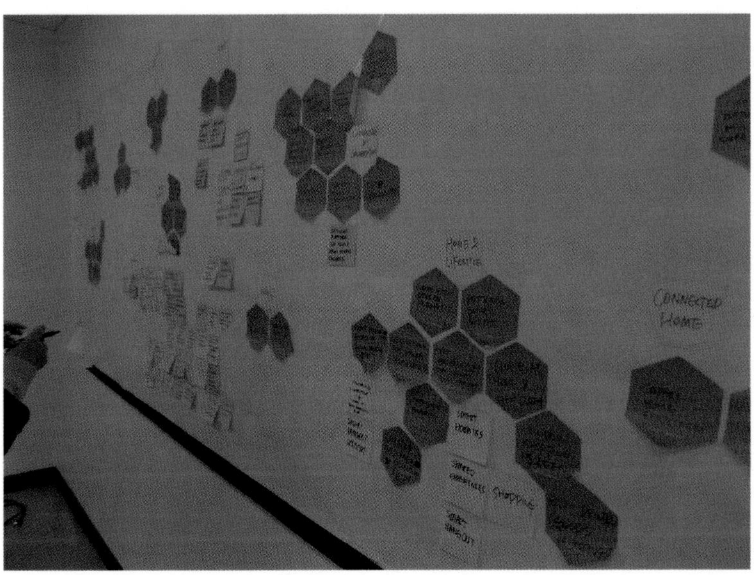

Figure 4.3
Sticky note wall (from Kin, by Team Ha, used by kind permission of David Huang, Kristy Lee, Vincent Zhang, and Yuni Choi).

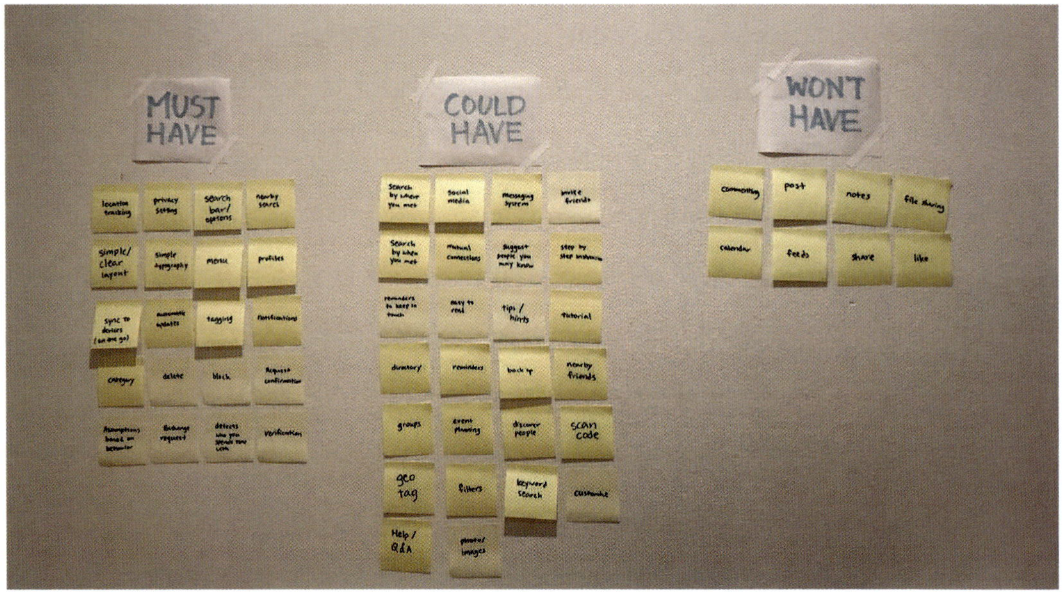

Figure 4.4
Prioritizing features (from Keepintouch, by Amber Wang, used by kind permission of Amber Wang).

Considering what it won't have may, in fact, be more important to the success of our project than what it will have: Tightly focused products are not only easier to create, they're less error-prone and easier to adopt, providing a greater likelihood of success. Doing one thing well is far better than doing several things poorly. This is the concept central to creating a minimum viable product, or MVP. What is the most minimal feature set that makes our idea viable? If our MVP works in the marketplace, then we will be better positioned to attract the resources to extend it later.

Often, it's difficult for reviewers to see the final features that result from a brainstormed think map, so, for the sake of clarity, it's a good idea to list these features separately. This is where a documentation framework called the MUSCOW (or MOSCOW) chart comes in. What the chart does is list the features to be considered in the system. It breaks them down into those that MUSt be done, those that COuld be done, and those that Won't be done. The capital letters spell MUSCOW (Figure 4.5).[1]

Figure 4.5
MUSCOW chart of a vacation travel system (from Tiny Traces, by Aska Cheung, used by kind permission of Aska Cheung).

Must include

- A way to dodge the crowds
- A map to show the distance between travel spots
- A suggested schedule based on the user's duration of stay
- Freedom to edit one's schedule
- Filter costly places
- Price Labels
- Suggested spots by locals
- Feedback by locals
- Strong Imagery
- Suggested mode of transporation

Could include

- Day by day weather
- Notifications about when to leave for another destination
- A guide on the country's transporation
- Rating System
- Feedback from fellow travelers
- Have fun themes for travel schedules
- Offline Access
- Interactive media to give you a sense of what the place is like
- Useful digital coupons
- Emergency button

Won't include

- Turn by turn navigation
- Money management
- Translator/Language Guide
- Generic tourist spots
- Hotel booking
- Mobile payment
- Heavy text

Those features that "must" be in the project are those that are critical to its success. Those that "could" be done are those that are easy to implement because much of the work would be done for the must-have features, or those that are easy to implement and would be nice to have, but are not necessary. Finally, those that won't be done could be infinite, so we only list those that are likely to be considered, but we want to expressly avoid. These may be features that competitors may have, or things that may be easy to implement but would distract from our goals. The items in the MUSCOW chart not only indicate the features we are considering, but also prioritizes them. We can assign our effort to them according to that prioritization.

4.4 USER STORIES

The essence of user based design is to keep the user the central focus to the design process. But features are attributes of the system and may take our eye off the user's wants and needs. The agile design process has made effective use of a means of expressing features that keeps the user front and center: the user story.

User stories reframe features from a user's point of view. These have many formulations in the industry, but they should contain a clarification of the user, the context, what they want, and why. Since we've spent time on developing a persona, we suggest leveraging that persona in our user stories. Say, for example, the name of our persona in our freeway example is Steve. We may formulate Steve's experience with our system as this: "Prior to Steve driving onto the freeway, he wants to be able to determine if there is congestion in order to decide to enter the freeway or not."

Our user story approach provides a number of useful details. First off, we're considering Steve, who should come with a great deal of profile information that can help guide the approach of both the aesthetic and structural design of our system. Second, his context is that he is driving and on the verge of entering the freeway. The display and presentation of the information needs to be able to handle this challenge. Next, we have the central thing he wants to do: Determine if there is congestion. The final detail is the why: whether he wants to get on the freeway or not. This may not provide any guidance at all with things we need to make, but it does one very important thing: It provides us insight into why we are building these things for Steve. It continues to further our empathy with him during our information breakdown process, which is often a cold and analytical activity.

If you notice, a framework that we have previously explored is coming back again: the strategic pyramid. The "What is it, who is it for, why do they want to use it, where and when is it used" set of questions is exactly what we would want to know from our user stories. Identify features in the MUSt have and possibly the COuld have column in our MUSCOW chart, and create user stories of them.

Note that we remained at a fairly high level when we created our user story for the freeway system. We should remain at this level as we consider the general approach to our system. Once we're clear on its high-level features, we will drill down into detail.

4.5 A DAY IN THE LIFE

Considering our user goals and breaking them down into features is a fruitful way to generate the content of our system, yet, as previously mentioned, it is rather analytical. This is certainly not a bad thing, and it ensures that whatever features we have can be intrinsically tied back to our user's goals. Yet, when we are dealing with features, we run the risk of becoming distant from the experience of our users. User stories help keep us connected to them, but on a piecemeal basis. Because of this, it's also useful to consider inspiration targeted at a more personal approach: That of looking at how our users experience their lives and the impact that may have on what we want to provide for them.

If anything we design does not make perfect sense to our users, it should not be in the system. So, let's leverage what we've done already to understand our users and get to know them a little better. Let's first consider their lives in general. Every day our users embark on a journey through their world. We could look at the specific journey we'd like them to have with our product or service (Cooper, 2015, p 136). But, at this stage, we suggest going more broadly and exploring their life journey.

Our typical user probably engages in a ritual of activities that are fairly consistent from day to day. There could be work days and play days, and each may have their unique characteristics. Considering how these days play out provides us with insight not only into who they are, but possibly reveals unmet opportunities to interact with our system that fits more seamlessly into their lives than their current scenario. It changes our perception of the scope of the problem, thereby increasing our ability to see more unique solutions.

During the user research process, we should have gathered insight into our user's typical day. However, we are not talking about specific users here. We are talking about the archetypal user: our persona. It's instructive at this point to formulate those discoveries into a picture of a day in our persona's life. Let's clear off some wall space or roll out some paper and begin laying out what we think they do throughout their day (Figure 4.6).

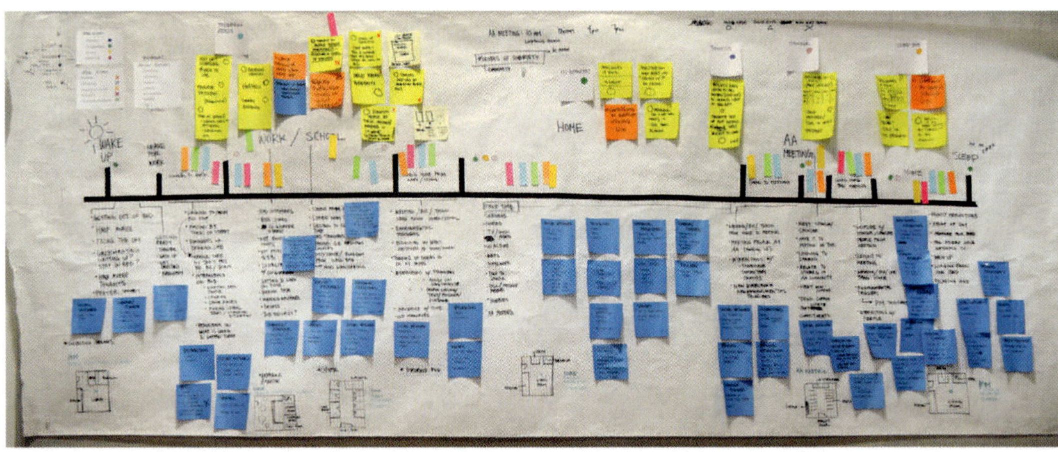

Figure 4.6
Day in the life brainstorming (from Addmit, by Team CTX, used by kind permission of Lars Fiva, Emily Harrington, Tammy Hsieh, and Michele Lee).

This work should be distilled down to the key points in our user's day that could be opportunities for touchpoints with our system. This can be executed in many ways, from text to storyboard, to something more diagrammatic (Figures 4.7, 4.8, and 4.9)).

If we are to be presenting this to our team or stakeholders, we need to be sensitive to their time constraints and possible lack of familiarity with the details of our effort. Text may be the easiest and most detailed way to present the

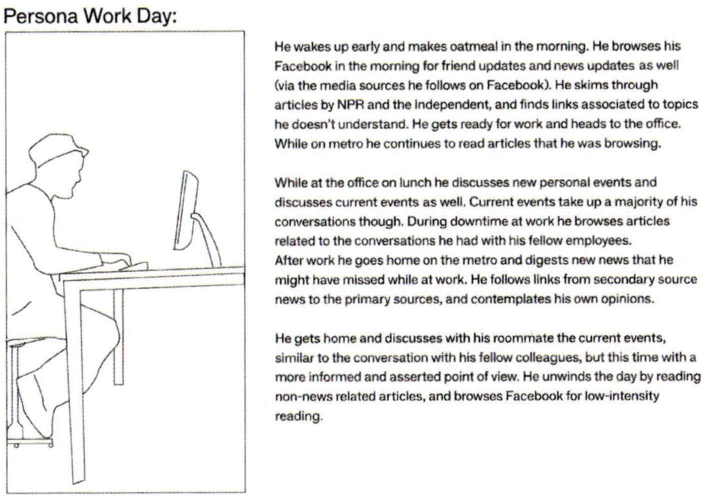

Figure 4.7
Text version of a day in the life for a news aggregator (from Sourced, by Jonathan Nishida, used by kind permission of Jonathan Nishida).

Figure 4.8
Scenario version of a day in the life for a remote worker (from Cosmos, by Team Laundry, used by kind permission of Asli Akdemir, Lynn Lei, Nathan Lu, and Yozei Wu).

Figure 4.9
Diagrammatic version of a day in the life for a fitness tracker (from Tier X, by Schei Wang, used by kind permission of Schei Wang).

information we are working on, but it is also somewhat intimidating. It is certainly time-consuming to absorb. Although more work for you, something more image-based, such as storyboards or diagrams, will be much easier for them to swallow. We need to keep these things in mind when we're working on material meant for general consumption.

4.6 JOURNEY MAP

The work we've done on our user's day in the life sets us up to express a journey map. Journey maps look at not only a time frame in our user's life, such as a typical day, but additional information about certain aspects we wish to track throughout that time frame. This new information can be presented graphically or diagrammatically and indicates things such as our user's emotional highs and low, or their engagement throughout the time frame. Again, it's a tool to broaden our perspective (Figure 4.10).

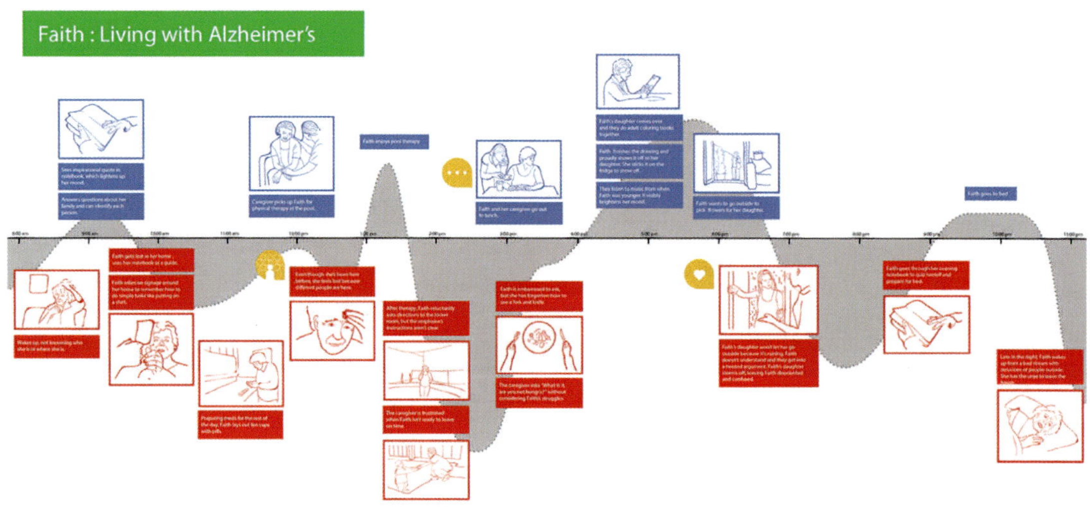

Figure 4.10
Journey map for an Alzheimer's patient: Storyboard version (from Emma, by Team Delta, used by kind permission of Devin Montes, Naomi Tirronen, Joshua Woo, Angela Dong, and Jenny Kim).

These diagrams focus our attention on opportunities we may be able to leverage in our design. How can we make things work better throughout our user's daily activities? Can we envision a suite of contexts or devices that work more seamlessly throughout their day than what is currently being offered? How can we provide them a better, and possibly more fulfilling, experience?

The specific formulation of a journey map is not all that rigid. We can rely on storyboard-like imagery, such as in Figure 4.10, or be more schematic such as is shown in Figure 4.11. The essence, though, is to depict someone's experience through time and indicate how their journey affects them. As such, it serves several purposes: It allows the designer to become more empathetic with the target user by allowing them a window into the target's day. It becomes a valuable tool to stimulate ideation, and it provides us with a presentation framework whereby we can discuss how to make our target's life better.

The most common time frame of a journey map depicts a day in the target's life, but it may not be the only one. Timelines don't have to span hours, but could also span days or years. Whatever is most pertinent to the question at hand. For example, we may be considering not how our audience uses our system day to day,

Journey Map

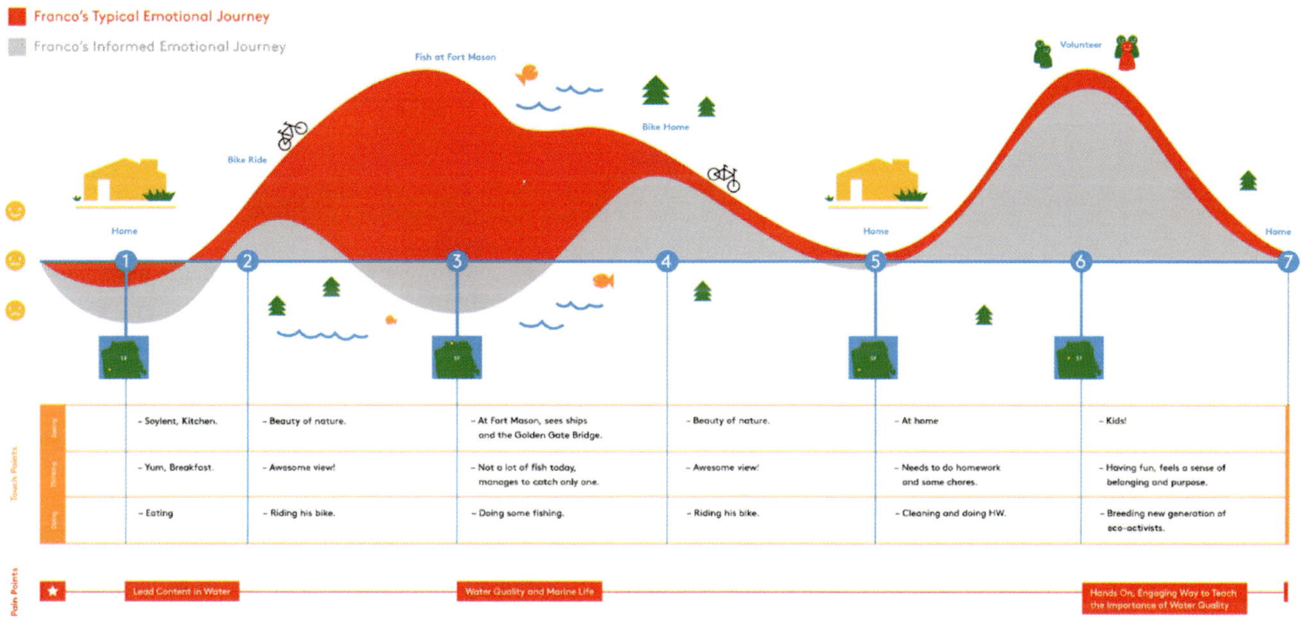

Figure 4.11
Journey map for citizen scientist system: Diagram version (from Canary, by Team Frank, used by kind permission of Justin Babikian, April Cheung, Kelsey Chow, India Hillis, and Joe Tsao).

but what stage in their life it is for (Figure 4.12). If you're designing something to be used by Alzheimer's patients, you may have to position it at a point where the patient is beginning to suffer problems, but is not yet at a stage where they can't interact with the system. A journey map of the progress of the disease may be helpful to illustrate where your system fits in.

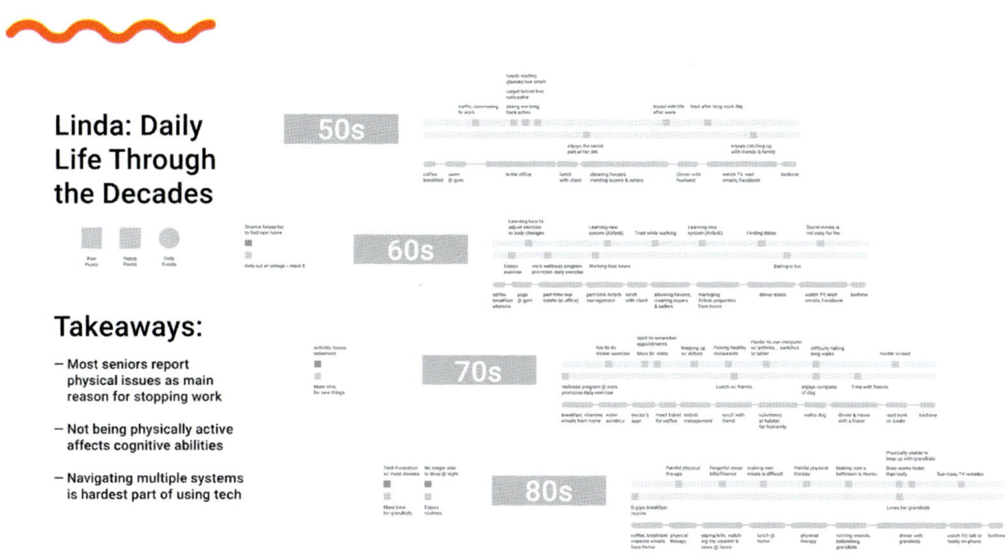

Figure 4.12
Broad time frames in the stages of Alzheimer's (from Playground, by Team WeeFee, used by kind permission of Trevor Cheney, Caitlin Conlen, Cindy Hu, Michelle Lee, and Chase Morrison).

Whatever the time frame, method, or data depicted, the journey map allows us to consider the target's experiences temporally, and indicates aspects that are critical to the overall design of our system.

4.7 INSPIRATION BY JOURNEY

Journey maps and days in the life change our scope of the problem. They allow us to consider and present for discussion larger aspects of the user's experience than just the current scenario. By adopting this perspective, we are now looking at issues across their daily routine, their life, and their emotional journey. These frameworks and the discussion that results should trigger a new round of possible ways of achieving the user goals we want our system to provide. Let's explore these by engaging in another round of brainstorming.

At this level of concept development, we can revisit the same techniques we used in breaking down our user goals into features (mind maps, sticky note walls, and then text scenarios), but our perspective now has the benefit of context. What goals would they want to achieve and when should they do it in the journey of their day? How should our features be distributed along the path of that experience? Instead of using words for our brainstorming, let's begin to use a combination of words and imagery to create an ideation mind map (Figure 4.13).

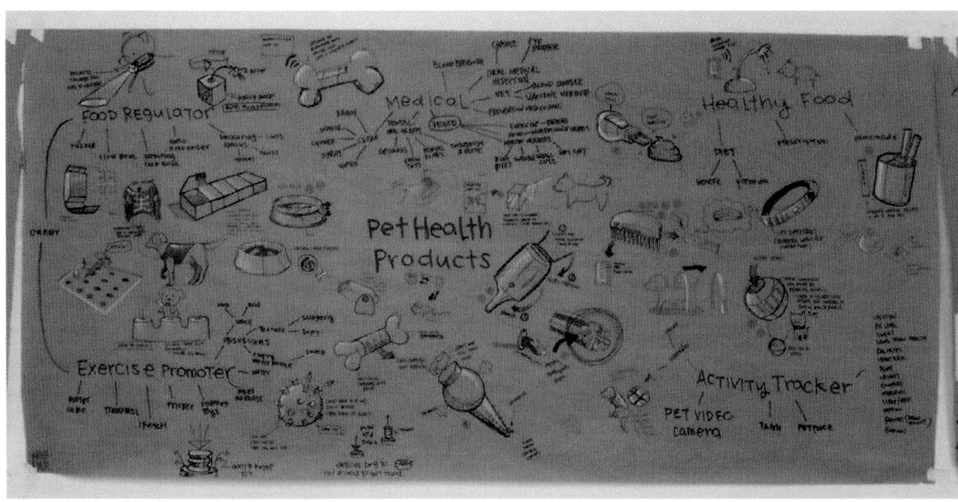

Figure 4.13
Ideation mind map for pet care (from Munio, by Team Wolf Pack, used by kind permission of Judy Chu, Tina Ou, Jane Park, and Jade Tsao).

Our perspective has broadened due to our increased understanding of our user's day and life, and we are better positioned to brainstorm approaches for them. While doing this, make sure to keep in mind the foundational layer of our strategic pyramid: what it is, who it's for, and why they would want to use it. Strive to get beyond just evolving their current scenario. Forget about how things work today, brainstorm, ideate, create magic moments and text scenarios around user needs and how things should work. This is the time to be revolutionary, not simply evolutionary. Where does this lead you?

This effort may become a little uncomfortable to the more conservative members of the team or organization. They may feel that proposing revolutionary ideas carries substantial risk, and they're right. But, at this stage, we are only talking about ideas. It's good to know what the extremes are even if we don't end up going down those paths because one of our competitors just might. Knowing this may make even a slightly evolutionary solution better.

4.8 INSPIRATION BY EMPATHY

Recall that the current scenario is the experience that the user currently endures to achieve the goals of the system you wish to design. Revisiting this is a good place to start to develop ideas about how to approach your design, but instead of having a user research interviewee communicate it to us, let's explore some heuristic analysis: Let's become the user ourselves. This approach is one of the most effective methods of becoming more empathetic with the user, and, as John Kolko states, empathy is the underpinning of Interaction Design (Kolko, 2011, p. 160).

To begin, create rough props to stage the experience. Tape, foam core, paper cut-outs will do. A large space is also useful in that it can be imagined into anything from a kitchen to an office to a street or a section of a stadium; whatever the context or set of contexts should be for our target's situation. You can engage in this process solo, or, better yet, recruit team members or friends to become actors. Don't forget to feed them!

Go through the current scenario. We should subject ourselves to the challenges and difficulties our target faces. Make sure that the experience is documented by photographing it, and have someone who is assigned to take thorough and clear notes. As we progress through the experience indicate to the note taker trials, tribulations, thoughts, and possible solutions. When we're finished, we edit the photos, print them out, and use sticky notes to comment on them (Figure 4.14).

What were the pain points? What could be improved? What worked in the current scenario and should not be lost? What do you as a team feel is the most critical problem to be solved? These pain points and ideas become a directed source of inspiration for further ideation and user experiences. Break out that journal and consider more magic moments, interactions, and text scenarios. The results from this process are usually well grounded in practical reality.

Figure 4.14
Finding inspiration by identifying pain points within the current scenario (from Reset, by Team Lechee, used by kind permission of Sara Ferris, Wenzhou Liang, Karim Merchant, and Jenny Chen).

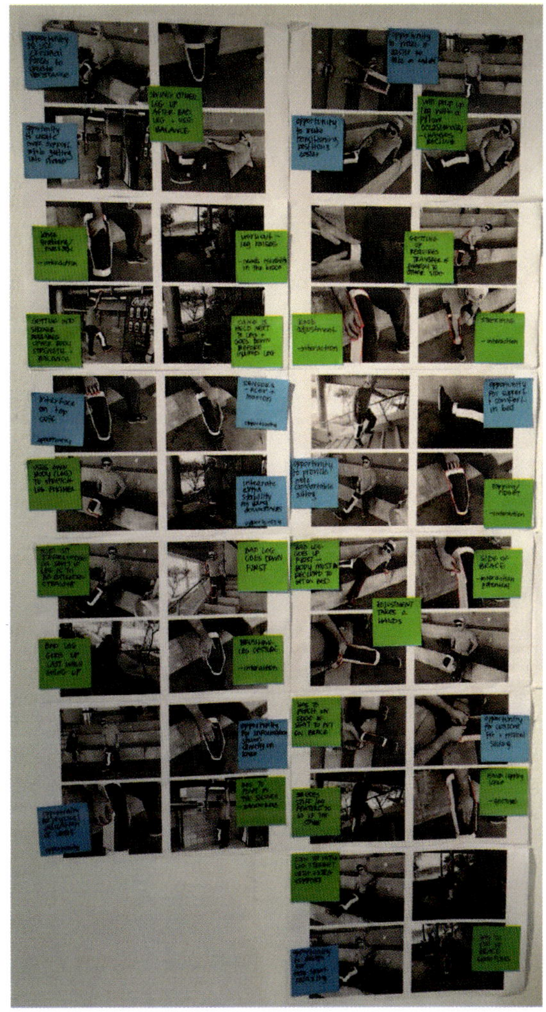

4.9 THE PRIMARY USE CASE

Up to this point, we've relied mainly upon magic moments and text scenarios to express our user's experience. We've assessed how our user flows into and out of experiences with our system as their life carries them along. We could consider all kinds of experiences with our system, but if we did we may tend to fall into an activity we call "boiling the ocean": Doing a lot of work with diminishing returns. Instead, let's be focused on the most important experience: the primary use case.

The primary use case is the flow through the system when it is working as intended. The interactions the user encounters along this path illuminate the most critical features of the system. Some of my colleagues call this the "happy path", which I think is more fun and descriptive of what it is: It's the story of the best use of the system that we hope empowers users and provides them with delight. Hence, the happy path.

It's important to note that the primary use case is not the process someone goes through when they first encounter the system. That is called "onboarding" and we'll go into detail about that a little later. Suffice it to say here, though, that onboarding usually requires that the user engages in activities that are outside of the normal operation of the system, so they're not true indications of what we intend to happen day in and day out when everything in our system is functioning smoothly.

The primary use case, on the other hand, is when the user has engaged with the system often enough so that all of its critical features have become apparent. When we look at the primary use case, we are not looking at beginning users, or even advanced users, but intermediates who have performed all the efforts necessary to make the system run as intended.

The primary use case simplifies the design process. We will flesh out other cases later, but if our primary use case doesn't work, those other cases will most likely fail as well.

4.10 EXTERNAL CONTEXT

Our user's experience is intrinsically linked to the real world, the "where" and "when" of the second layer of our strategic pyramid. It's not enough just to think of what's happening on a particular interface without thinking of what the user may be physically doing.

For example, if I'm considering map interaction on a mobile app and I've integrated pinching as a way of zooming, that seems to be a very optimal and delightful solution because pinch to zoom is fun. But now consider that my user is late, walking to a luncheon with a coffee in one hand, and they need to use my system to find where to go. Pinch requires a two-handed interaction—one hand to hold the device and the other to pinch. Now my user must perform either one of two activities: They either need to stop walking and put their coffee down to use two hands, or they must hold and pinch with one hand. Both are frustrating and not the least bit delightful.

If an external context is critical to the success of the system, the appropriate design approach would be to develop solutions around that context. For the example above, our system should be able to be used by a single hand. This is why contextualization is important in the understanding of the flow of your user. Scenarios focus our attention on these situations, which all too often are overlooked.

4.11 EXPLORING APPROACHES THROUGH TEXT SCENARIOS

Up to now, we've been fairly casual with the elements required by our design solutions. They could be magic moments, text scenarios, or brief interactions. But now it's time to evaluate which of our several approaches is best. To do this, focus on the primary use case and consider multiple approaches for it.

To illustrate, let's say that we're tasked with the responsibility of making doctors' visits more efficient. First off, when we say efficient here, we must consider whether we are making it more efficient for the patient or the doctor. In considering the current system (as of this writing—I have a hunch that this will change dramatically in the coming years), the visit is pretty efficient for the doctor: The patient is scheduled for the convenience of the doctor; they must come to the doctor's office, not the other way around; they must wait until the doctor is available to be seen; and all information must be supplied in a form that is convenient for the doctor, not one that may be convenient for the patient. So, when we say "more efficient," we probably mean more efficient for the patient. But we must realize that any solution must be reasonably efficient for the doctor, too, or the approach will not be adopted.

There are many approaches to making the visit more efficient. First, we could consider leaving the current approach intact and developing solutions that fit within it in a fairly unobtrusive way. For example, using the web or an app to allow the patient to fill in their information before arriving at the doctor's office.

This improves efficiency because the patient can now fill out the form more on their time than at the time of arrival at the office. This may not only make things marginally better for the patient, but also better for the doctor as well, in that their office may not need to input the data into the computer. They can rely on the patient to do that.

But this does not remove the most jarring pain points from the patient's point of view: The need to visit the doctor's office not on the patient's time, but on the doctor's time. An approach to solving this would be to reinstitute a doctor's house call visit and have them do so on the patient's schedule. This approach would be great for the patient, but bad for the doctor, whose resources of time and services are restricted.

Doctors may be an extremely limited resource, but nurses are less so. And, in fact, much of a patient's visit to a doctor's office entails interaction with the nurse, not the doctor. So, what if the nurse visits the patient's house and communicates with the doctor? This approach could be viable if the nurse's time is not too costly and the communication with the doctor is effective.

Finally, if the approach of the nurse's home visit isn't effective, possibly a satellite office staffed by nurses would be. This could be closer to the patient's home than, say, the doctor's office itself, it could house a rudimentary set of devices that aid the patient's assessment, and it may be able to run on evenings and weekends, allowing it to connect better to the patient's schedule.

These illustrate four different "approaches" to the problem: An information app, a central station primarily staffed by nurses, a nurse home visit, and a doctor home visit. There may be many more, but, as we can see, we have not yet considered the details of each. We are keeping things at the level of a collection of possible approaches; hence, we classify these as approach scenarios.

Through multiple approach scenarios, we gain insight into the experience of the stakeholders, the patient, nurses, and doctors in this case, and extend the comparison of our ideas accordingly. But, if we dive too deeply into the details of one scenario or another, we may not only be wasting time on something that will get tossed, but we may tend to lock into a particular solution too early in the process. This may blind us to other possibilities that present themselves (Carroll 2000, pg. 54).

Approach scenarios need to focus on general aspects of how the system is configured, not the details. We've found that text scenarios with their inherent strategic ambiguity and focus on the user's experience are effective in doing this. Consolidate your approaches into a small set of text scenarios and provide each with a name. For our health care example above, possible names could be "information app", "central station", "nurse home visit", and "doctor home visit". With our approaches clarified, arrange them in a way they can be easily compared.

Consider the resources necessary for each approach. This will prepare us to weigh our solutions against each other. Which are simple to implement, which are more difficult? Which match well with the resources at our disposal, and which do not? Which align with the development timeframe of our concept, which take more advantage of the opportunities we uncovered in our research, or which do we think are better matched to our target user? Some approaches will make more sense than others.

One way to compare approaches is to line them up along a couple axes: For example, one axis could be feasibility and the other is how radical they are. Feasibility is the amount of effort we or our team feel will be needed to create and sell the idea. How radical it is, or radicality, is a measure of whether the idea is revolutionary or evolutionary. Often, we will see a strong correlation between these axes: The more conservatively evolutionary an idea is, the more feasible it is. The more radically revolutionary it is, the less feasible. But this isn't always the case, and if you've found a radical idea that's feasible, that's definitely something to look into further.

Another axis that can come to bear is near term and far term. What ideas can be built tomorrow and what are more like ten years out? Often clients or project leadership want to see a range of ideas. Understanding our ideas along these axes allows us to select those along a range. We can also mix and match axes, as well as providing ones that may be aligned with our design criteria.

4.12 TOUCHPOINT IDEATION

To further clarify our approaches, it's useful to analyze our most successful scenarios and reflect on the points where they refer to "the system". Recall the text scenario depicted in Figure 2.22. When we use the term "the system," we are expressing a touchpoint; the moments at which our user metaphorically and sometimes physically touches our system (Saffer, 2010, p. 99) (Figure 4.15).

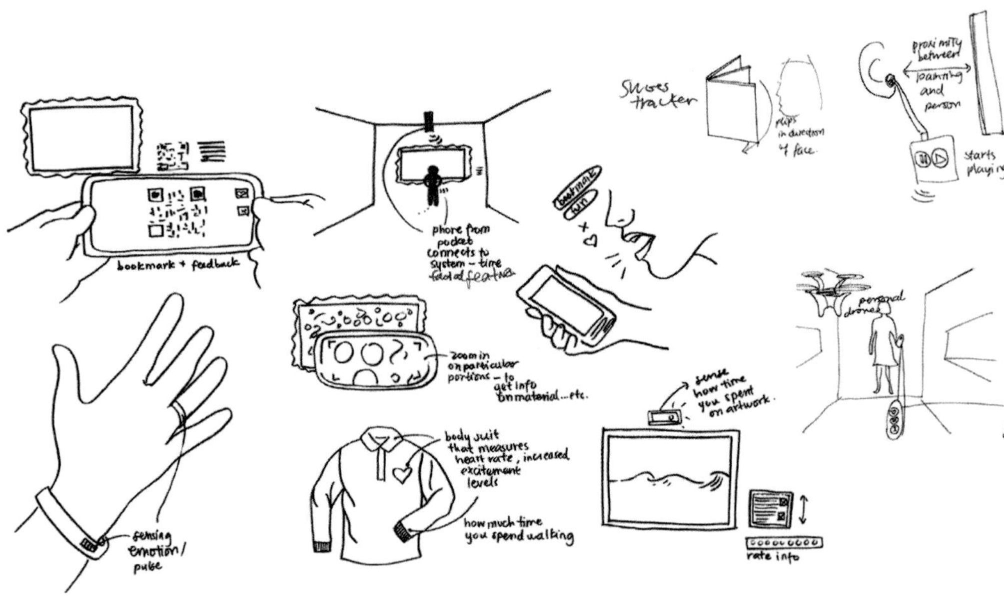

Figure 4.15
Touchpoint ideation for a digital museum guide (from Artbug, by Radhika Kashyap, used by kind permission of Radhika Kashyap).

Touchpoints themselves provide us with a great service in that they indicate our points of interaction, and each can be used as a source of inspiration for ideation. We call out each touchpoint in our text scenario and fill a page or two of ideation using the touchpoints as inspiration. This effort allows us to explore possible specific solutions for our intentionally vague and ambiguous text scenarios.

Identify a few approaches, three to five say, that are the most fruitful. We next should look to ideation that can make these approaches less vague and more specific. Identify the critical points of interaction—the magic moments if you will—of all these approaches and turn them into scenarios. Since they are meant to be specific, text scenarios will no longer do. You may wish to make mock-ups of the devices and interfaces, and photograph these scenarios. We will be doing a substantial amount of this later, but there's no reason to avoid doing it now if you're so inclined.

Keep in mind that these are still in the realm of approach scenarios, so details are not all that important. As long as the scenario provides the gist of the touchpoint, the user's interactions in the broadest sense, and indicates the relevant technology that may be used, they've done their job. Approach scenarios are somewhat of a balancing act. Our goal is to consider different approaches to solving the design problem without providing the level of detail that may be distracting (Figure 4.16).

4.13 POSTURE STUDIES

As we've seen, when we begin to address approach scenarios in more detail, we are beginning to address issues of context: we're climbing to the second tier of our strategic pyramid. What is our audience doing when they are most naturally interacting with our system? What are those touchpoints? Where are they? When is this happening?

In this phase, we consider different approaches to the design of our system, and often the features that most clearly distinguish them revolve around these differences of context. Therefore, a better understanding our user's situation will allow us a better understanding of which approach is best. Posture studies prompt us to consider this by focusing on the contextual issues themselves, independent of the experience story or the system interaction. As you will see here and in chapters to come, the concept of postures is central to the design process used throughout this book.

We use the term "posture" because of its physical nature. Discussions in the process of Interaction Design use the term to describe to the presentation of the system itself (Cooper, 2015, p. 206), but we have found it effective to expand the concept to indicate the posture of the audience while they're performing interactions with the system. Postures need to include not only the presentation of the system, but the way the system is used.

The framework we use when considering postures is the posture study. These studies are derived from the touchpoints of our system and our user research. When we researched our users, one of our tasks was to notice how they behaved throughout a typical day. Do they spend leisure time in the morning at the table while they're having breakfast? When they work, are they mostly at a desk, or are they running around? Do they like to be productive while they're commuting, and if so, what are they doing? Are they driving, walking, or taking mass transport? How do they spend their time when they're doing those things? This gives us insight into a set of user inspired situations where we can position our product's interaction—its touchpoints.

In addition, our text scenarios and magic moments have provided us another set of touchpoints inspired by the intended user experience with our system. Sometimes touchpoints inspired by user behavior and those inspired by our user's posture agree, sometimes they don't. For those that don't, how can we adjust the system's posture so it can better agree with the natural behaviors of our user? This consideration may inspire a new set of approaches. Ideate them. If some seem promising, turn them into text scenarios.

Certainly, the most user-friendly approaches will be those that match our user's natural behavior most seamlessly. This formulates one of the underlying principles of postures: *The posture of the system should agree with the posture of the user.* To determine if they indeed agree, let's consider in more detail what those situations are by asking a few questions:

1. What is the context where our touchpoints most naturally reside?
2. Do the physical, cognitive, and sensory demands of our user match what our system intends for them to do?
3. Does the posture agree with contexts we are considering for a particular approach?
4. Are we asking our user to do too much?
5. Are we offering too little?
6. Are there situations in which it would be convenient for our audience to use the system when they aren't being bombarded by other distractions?
7. Can a touchpoint be slipped into a context in their journey throughout their day that is not currently being taken advantage of?

Figure 4.16
Approach scenarios for a workplace assistant (from Kairos, by Team Kairos, used by kind permission of Tanya Chang and Jon Hsiung).

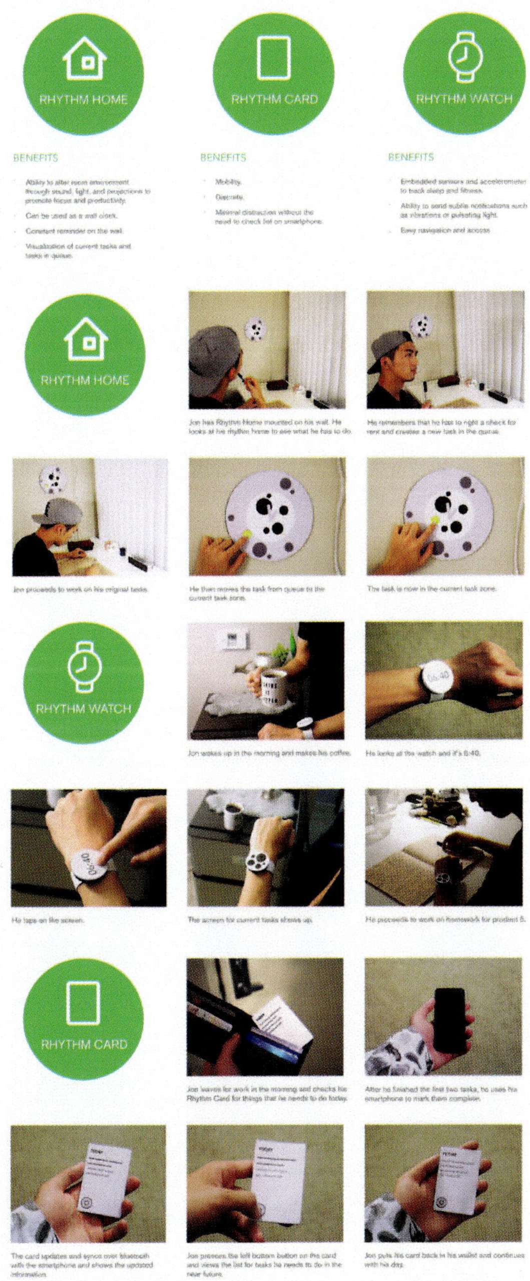

Posture studies allow us to look at our user's postures in the abstract and consider how our system can be designed to work with them.

Refer to our primary research and the day in the life of our target, and identify the moments throughout the day that are ripe for interacting with our system. Detail the physical aspects and limitations of our target within those situations. Are they standing, walking, seated, or lounging? What is their level of dexterity in those situations? Do they have both hands available, just one, or none at all? If they can use a hand, can they use all their fingers or only a few? What is their cognitive focus? Can they apply their full attention to our system or are they distracted by other things? If they're distracted, what's the level of attention they can give our system? What's the level of attention they must give to something else? Are they able to use the full force of the recognition capabilities of their eyes, or should the visual aspect of our system just be glanceable? How about hearing and audio? Is the environment loud or quiet? Is audio appropriate? Do they need to keep their hearing available to better sense dangers in their immediate surroundings? These questions of our user's physicality, or posture, greatly impact our system's design.

Posture studies are not just for considering various approaches. In fact, because they keep us in touch with our user's situation, we should be referring to them throughout the entire design process. If they are wordy and bogged down in detail they will be ignored and, hence, be useless. So, it's important that they are presented in a manner that doesn't overwhelm us with minutiae when we look at them. They should be quick and easy to understand. We've found that a formulation relying on images and iconography works best (Figure 4.17). This presentation form may not be rich in detail, but it's glanceable and indicates the essentials: those aspects that are available from the user to interact with our system. If we need a deeper description, that can certainly be offered by text material associated with the visual presentation.

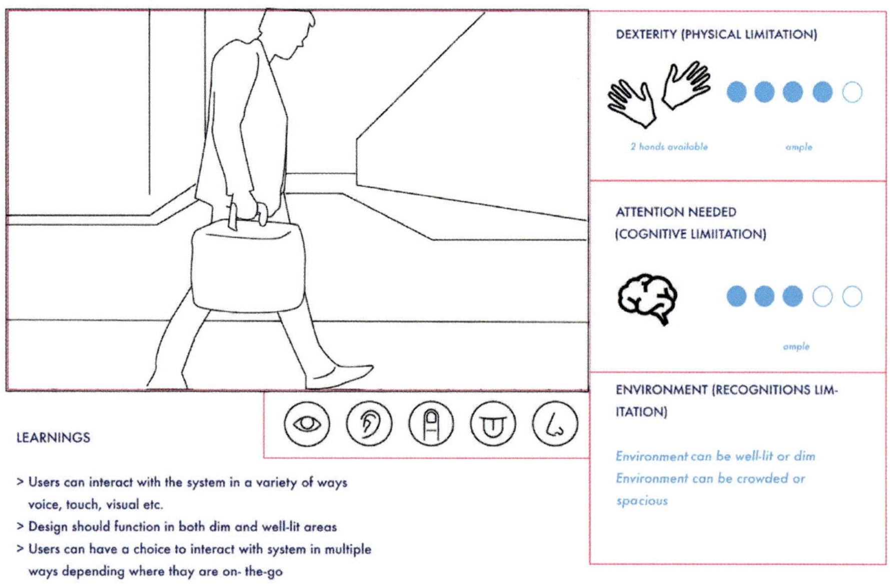

Figure 4.17
Posture studies using image and iconography (from Artbug, by Radhika Kashyap, used by kind permission of Radhika Kashyap).

We indicate an image of the posture itself, the level and aspect of the dexterity of the user, the amount of cognitive focus they can supply to the interaction, and can also include how much visual or aural recognition the user can provide. All of these will impact the system's design. For example, a high degree of cognitive focus will translate into the ability to pack more information onto the screen. The level and aspect of the dexterity will provide us with insight into whether we can use two-handed gestures or single-handed ones. We are not making these decisions yet, but our posture studies will help us make them when the time comes. For now, we can use these studies to determine how effective various situations will be in their ability to handle our system's interactions, what goals we should offer our users when, and what are the critical aspects of these contexts that can inform an exploration of possible device ecosystems (Figures 4.18 and 4.19).

Figure 4.18
A posture study of a personal projector (from Mio, by Audrey Liu, used by kind permission of Audrey Liu).

Figure 4.19
The design interpretations of the posture (from Mio, by Audrey Liu, used by kind permission of Audrey Liu).

THE POSTURE	WHAT IT MEANS
• one hand will be needed to navigate the menu, and the other to situate the screen	• the process of setting up needs to be quick and seemless
• the environment's lighting may vary	• it should be easy for the user to adjust the brightness of the projection with one hand
• the environment may be crowded	• the device must be able to be held with one hand and be small
• the user will be getting on and off the train or bus quickly	• the device should be able to be packed away quickly. it should have an auto sleep/shut off function when the screen closes
• the user may be standing while operating the device	• the device must be one handed • the functions for scrolling, zooming, etc. must be accessible with the one hand that is holding the device. The projection itself could be inter active, recognizing simple gestures

4.14 INSPIRATION THROUGH PHYSICALITY

If our approach proposes new products or devices, with a set of posture studies we can begin to explore what these may look like. These can start as ideations in our journal, but then extend out into the real world with quick mock-ups (Figure 4.20). With these mock-ups, don't worry too much about details—all we're doing is considering the user's relationship with the system in broad strokes. Shape, size, and a vague notion of how the interaction may work are all we need, things that may be depicted by tape balls and quickly cut foam core.

Figure 4.20
Physical sketch prototypes for a pet care system (from Munio, by Team Wolf Pack, used by kind permission of Judy Chu, Tina Ou, Jane Park, and Jade Tsao).

It's best to use a little contextual inquiry by placing ourselves in the situation of our postures as closely as possible and considering how well certain mock-ups work. Get on a commuter train or sit behind the wheel of a car (don't put yourself in danger by driving though, just sit there), put on garden gloves to simulate arthritis, put petroleum jelly on glasses to simulate poor eyesight, then interact with your mock-ups as if you were using them. What works? What doesn't? If you can't experience the situation, mock it up as closely as you can with the resources available to you, and then role play (Figure 4.21). Modify and iterate your mock-ups to see if something works better.

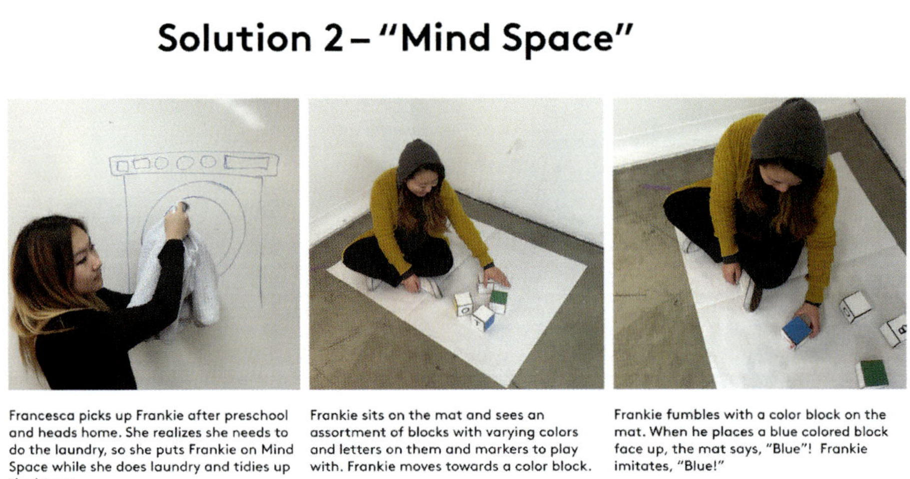

Figure 4.21
Exploring child play through role playing (from Canary, by Team Frank, used by kind permission of Justin Babikian, April Cheung, Kelsey Chow, India Hillis, and Joe Tsao).

Even if we're not designing new devices, it's still a good idea to role play our postures to see what the critical aspects are. We shouldn't just sit in our chairs and imagine the posture. There are things that become clear during the act of physically engaging the posture that we may not have realized before. Get out of the chair, engage in the real world, and act.

4.15 INSPIRATION THROUGH TECHNOLOGY

Our posture studies and physical explorations most likely have triggered questions of whether something is technologically possible. We may have uncovered some of these technologies earlier in our research phase, but, with this contextual approach, we may be facing a whole new set of possibilities because we are exploring solutions more broadly and deeply than we have before. Just because we are no longer in the research phase *per se*, does not mean we should abandon research. Continue to learn, continue to explore, and continue to engage in what is happening throughout the entire process of design. Use these questions and concerns to research possible solutions (Figure 4.22).

HAPTIC TECHNOLOGY

- Provides digital tactile feedback
- Restores the sense of touch to otherwise flat, cold surfaces
- Adds tactility to simulations that often rely only on visual and audio feeback
- It does "for the sense of touch what computer graphics does for vision"
- Can deliver pressure sensitivity interfaces, vibrations, and localized reactions

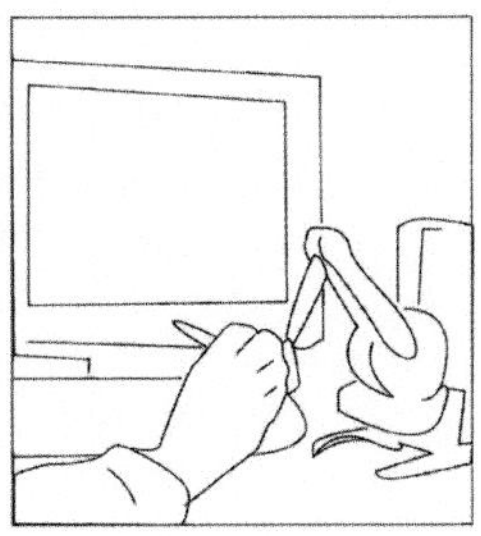

NEAR FIELD COMMUNICATION

- Set of standards for smartphones and similar devices to establish radio communication with each other
- Based on existing radio-frequency identification (RFID)
- Personal area network
- Passes information by proximity

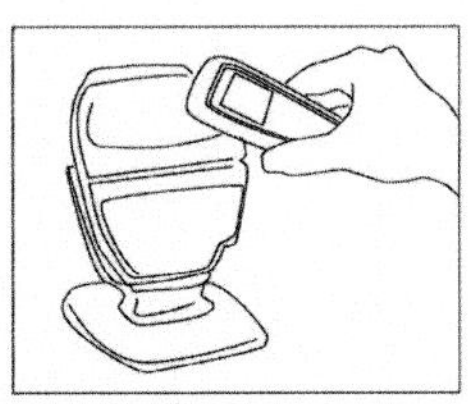

Figure 4.22
Continue to research applicable technologies (from Culina Metra, by Team Culina Metra, used by kind permission of Katrina Hercules and Neal Smith).

How do these discoveries affect your ideation? Can you use them to inspire more detailed solutions for your approach scenarios? What are some other issues besides technology that have come to light through text scenarios, posture studies, and physical explorations? How about solutions that rely less on technology and more on social innovations? How could these be manifested into an approach?

4.16 INSPIRATION THROUGH ACCESSIBILITY

Systems should be made accessible to the widest range of people so long as the approach does not dramatically affect the usability of the product for the target. In fact, products that are made more accessible are often products that are easier

Maron

Issue that she came to me with:
- she was stuck on a pinwheel on her laptop, didn't know a program had crashed
- her email had signed her out and she didn't know phone specific:
- she had no idea what the little pictures were and what they meant
-going back from an imessage stuck on the new gesture drawing feature

Main problem:
-getting in and out of things.
- the back arrow had been replaced with an 'x' for this screen and she didn't recognize how to get back

Most used apps:
- email, messaging,

My questions?
- do you like the icons?
I like them, I just don't know what they are
- which icons do you remember?
i just read the bottom of what it says under (she was talking about app thumbnail)
i know all the basic ones that are on every one I just do not know the ones are new on each one
- what gestures are you familiar with?
scroll, click.
same issue with the others, sometimes they clicked too hard and sometimes they clicked on the wrong part of the clickable area (clicked the email senders name and the another screen came out)

Needed:

Icons that she already knows
One back/ exit button
Limited icons
Limited gestures
Clear clickable area

Features for gestures:

No subcategories when you click hard vs. clicking light
All clicks and taps and presses are registered at the same level
Scrolls recognize that it's a scroll and momentarily stops clicking

How does this design make you feel:
I feel dumb sometimes (didn't get the question), liked the simple contact and IM messaging layout

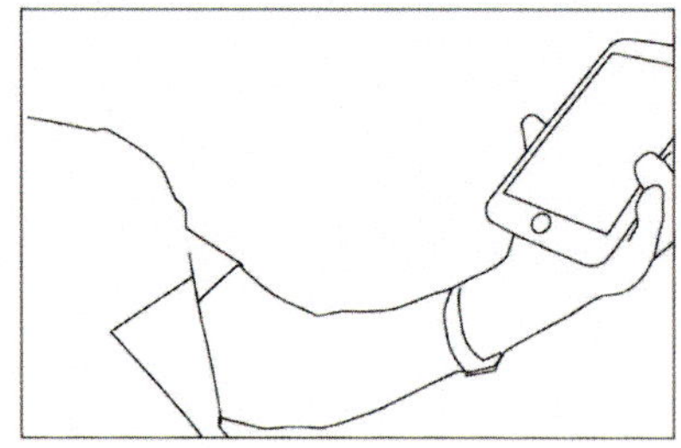

CUTTING SCENARIO

COMMERCIAL BREAK • LOW VISION SIMULATION

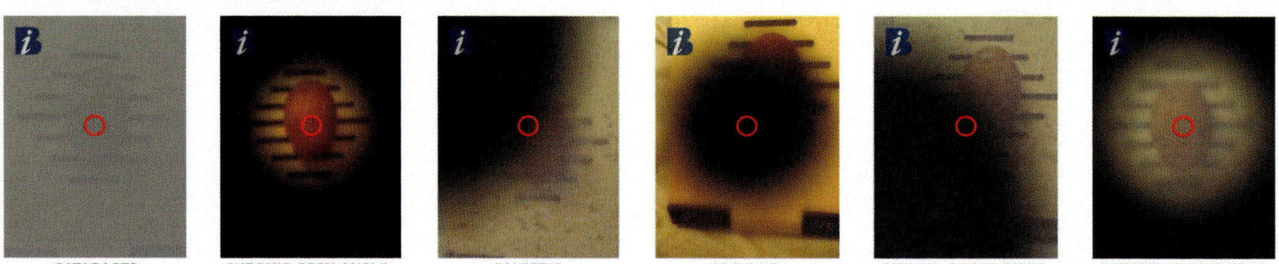

Figure 4.23
Accessibility issues for the elderly and the vision impaired. Top: Golden, by Diana Choung; bottom: Culina Metra, by Team Culina Metra, used by kind permission of Diana Choung, Katrina Hercules, and Neal Smith).

for everyone to use. A case in point is the Good Grips line of products from OXO. They were designed by Sam Farber after he noticed his arthritic wife Betsy having trouble with their peeler (OXO, 2017). We may not be designing kitchen utensils (or maybe we are), but the same could hold true of our system. If our target tends to be from a population with a certain set of disabilities or are at a certain developmental stage of life, we need to make things easier for that population. We need to consider accessibility issues and formulate design requirements for that population (Figure 4.23).

What are the perceptual limitations of this audience? What are the requirements to which we need adhere to design for them? Is there a range of perceptual abilities for this audience, such as there is in color blindness, or children just learning to read? If so, what are those categories and how many of the affected population are in each? Is there a range of capabilities such as levels of sightedness? How do those play out over the population? Research and become knowledgeable with the accessibility aspects of the disability.

Even if our population is not predisposed to certain limitations, we should consider the essence of who they are for other reasons. What trends is our audience obsessed with? For example, young users are obsessed with social media. If we are designing a system for them and social connections are not considered, it may have a high risk of failure. On the other hand, intense social throttling may not be as important for the elderly—that's not to say they don't do it, just not every thirty seconds, as millennials and those belonging to Generation Z might—so social media connectivity may not be as important. Know your audience and what considerations need to be made to best target them.

What contexts are appropriate for your audience? Are there accessibility issues that need to be considered? Are there trends that need to be considered? How do these considerations affect the design of your ecosystem?

4.17 THE BLOB SCENARIO

Text scenarios were useful because they were relatively quick and injected a clear strategic ambiguity into our depictions. Speed was necessary because we were developing many of them. Ambiguity was necessary because we didn't know the contexts within which our solutions would be manifest. But now, after performing posture studies, we have a much clearer notion of what these contexts need to do. Text scenarios and the ambiguous "the system" are no longer effective in capturing these new considerations. We're moving on with our scenario design process. We need to transition our scenarios from vague text to a slightly more accurate representation of the user's experience in the physical world.

Yet, we are still considering approaches, not interface details, so strategic ambiguity is still important. We need to take things further certainly in detail and possibly scope, but we still need to keep the focus of our design effort at the right level. How do we maintain this strategic ambiguity, yet shift to more accurately depicting things? This is where a "blob" scenario comes in.

A "blob" scenario portrays a user's physical relationship with the system, but the thing that is being interacted with is turned into a "blob". In other words, it is intentionally left physically vague. The reason for this ambiguity is the same as that with the text scenario: At this stage the designer's focus should be on the general approach to the system and how it works within the day-to-day activities of our user, not specifically how the solutions should be physically formed.

The trick with a blob scenario is determining how much detail to reveal, and how much to keep vague. To achieve this balance, our blob scenario needs to answer the question of how our audience uses our system in general and how it fits into their lives. We are not communicating buttons, screens, and interactive components at this stage. We are describing our system's overall role in our user's lives.

If you heeded the advice earlier in this chapter and went through the process of physical exploration, essentially, you created a blob scenario. Those mock-ups were the blobs: fairly formless artifacts devoid of detail, yet instructive in elucidating how our system fits into our user's lives.

Select your top ideas. Using your text scenarios for guidance, refine a set of props in shape and scale. Heuristically evaluate the experiences by testing these prototypes on yourself. Make sure you take care to be honest when conducting these evaluations. As Dan Saffer instructs: "Walk through the prototype as though you hadn't designed it and didn't already know everything about it and why features are the way they are" (Saffer, 2010, p. 184). In other words, play-act a role where you know nothing about what you've done, and assume the role of your user fully and completely. Be critical of nuances and small points of friction as well as confusing structures and flows. Are you making assumptions that your user knows things they don't? Or are you being too careful to protect them when you don't need to? Become one with who your user is and what they would want.

Photo-document the process of creating your blob scenario, and refine the experiences further until you've developed an approach or set of approaches that seem to be working. Then photograph them in final form and *voila*! You've created a blob scenario.

4.18 GUIDEWORDS

We've spent a great deal of time considering what our system should contain, but what about how it feels? What should be its personality? Answering this question will form the basis of our aesthetic design.

Much like our design criteria, this effort begins with the establishment of a set of words that keep our design focused. While from a branding perspective these words are called brand values, from a design perspective they are called design guidewords, or simply "guidewords". Although the term "brand values" is used when we are considering heavily branded experiences, and "guidewords" is used for the rest, we tend to use these terms interchangeably. Regardless of the terms we use, these words describe how the system should feel to its audience. If a brand is supposed to convey the feeling of sophistication, for example, that should be delivered by the design of everything the brand's audience experiences, from its advertising to the design of its stores, the packaging used on its products, down to the contents of the product itself. Where do these words come from?

Recall the aspirational adjectives we derived during our user research. Our guidewords are derived from these. Determine those aspirational adjectives that are the most relevant. What is the handful that we think best reflects the feeling we want? Take care to keep the number of your selection small. If we select too many, we may lose sight of what the feeling should be, too few, however, and we run the risk of it being derivative. We usually go with only three to five words to give us guidance. Let's consider a few principles to refine these words further.

4.18.1 Avoid Things You Should Do Anyway

What should the best words be? As designers, we strive for certain things automatically. We'd like our interface to be well organized and easy to use. Terms like "organized" and "simple" are almost a given. You have only five precious words to express how your system stands out from the rest; don't waste them on things that you should be doing as a designer in the first place. If you ask the opposite of the word and it sounds ridiculous, it's probably something you should be doing as a designer anyway. For example, the opposite of "organized" and "clear" is something like "cluttered" and "confusing". As a designer we would never say "I want to design a system that is cluttered and confusing." That's ridiculous. Therefore "organized" and "clear" are things we should be doing as designers automatically.

4.18.2 Be Distinctive

If our brand values aren't unique, how our product feels won't be unique either. Words like "professional" or "playful" are inherently vague. What kind of "professional" do we mean? What is "playful" in your mind? How could we clarify these better? We should strive to push our guidewords away from being clichés and into the realm of descriptors that are unique (Figure 4.24). Surprising or unexpected words work well. They stand out and make us think about what they really mean. They push us and motivate us to strive for something beyond the norm.

Scrumptious
Wondrous
Pure
Delightful
Rugged

Figure 4.24
When creating criteria, strive for distinction, range, and tension (from Canary, by Team Frank, used by kind permission of Justin Babikian, April Cheung, Kelsey Chow, India Hillis, and Joe Tsao).

4.18.3 Strive for Range and Tension

Avoid words that have essentially the same meaning. For example, if we are using the word "lighthearted," why would you also use the word "playful"? Those things that convey playfulness could also provide our system with a lightheartedness as well, so why use both? Choose one. In the example shown in Figure 4.24, above,"Wondrous" and "Delightful" convey much the same feeling. One can be eliminated or transformed into another word. Again, we have only a few words, so choose them wisely to communicate a breadth of feelings.

These words should be harmonious in some respects, but it's a misnomer to think that they all need to have a similar sensibility. Words that are complementary, or even conflicting, tend to provide that spark of originality that may make our approach unique. This tension provides spice. What does it mean to be "aggressively casual" or "seriously whimsical"? I have no idea, but whatever aesthetic approach these would lead to, I'd be curious to see. This tension within our guidewords can supply a level of uniqueness and specificity to terms that tend to be vague. As noted above, the term playful is vague, but when we say "elegantly playful" we begin to get a unique picture of what we mean.

4.18.4 Avoid Media Terms

As a final note, it's good to avoid terms that have direct referents within the context and media forms you are designing. What we mean here is that if we're designing a visual interface, try to avoid using visual terms such as "bright", "gridded", or "image rich". If we're designing an auditory interface, avoid things like "loud" or "noisy". These are less about feel and more about the approach a design would have to achieve a feeling. When we find ourselves using words like this, we should take a step back and inject a little more strategic ambiguity into them. Why do we want things to be "bright"? Is it because we want them to be energetic? Technologically aggressive? Whimsical? Fall back on those terms instead. This will allow us to have more latitude in our detailed design phase.

Using these principles—uniqueness, breadth, tension, and strategic ambiguity—select a handful of words, only three to five, that best describe the feeling you feel your system should convey.

4.18.5 Guidewords are not Design Criteria

Because both guidewords and design criteria are sets of words that aid us in design, designers tend to confuse them. They are similar in form because each is a small collection of words that provide us with guidance, but they are not the same and are used very differently. Design criteria guide us in the conceptualization of things our system should contain, while guidewords or brand values guide us in how it should feel. Guidewords lead to form, criteria lead to content and functionality. Guidewords lead to style, criteria lead to substance. This is precisely the same distinction we have been making between our aspirational and actual target: The aspirational aspects of our design are driven by our guidewords or brand values. Those features that provide functionality and content that our users need are inspired by design criteria.

If, after our system is built, we would ask one of our users how our system felt, our goal would be that they would answer with one of the adjectives in our set of guidewords. If we were to describe the brand communication of Nike, for example, we might use the terms "active" and "aggressive". Or, for Apple, we may use the terms "simplified" and "sophisticated". These words not only help us with ideation but when used well—and tightly adhered to—they are the bedrock of the brand communication of our product.

We could also say that the features of Apple products are simplified and sophisticated, so guidewords and criteria can certainly share words. But if we were describing a Lego set, for example, we may use the words "modular" and playful. "Playful" is definitely a "feel" word and probably related to the color and form of the product. Hence, it is a guideword. "Modular" is a description of how it works or its function and, hence, is a design criteria. In the end, these words are for you, the designer, to keep you on track. If the images that come to your head when you say "modular" impact your perception, such as color and form, touch and texture, well, then, so be it. For you, it may be a guideword.

Criteria results in things the system contains, guidewords result in how the system feels.

4.18.6 Guideword Moodboards

Since we're working on refining our aspirational adjectives into guidewords as a form of inspiration, we should also revisit our moodboards. But, instead of making one poster for the general feel of our system, let's explore the visual impact of each word separately: Make a guideword poster for each guideword. As in our previous moodboard effort, the images that appear on these posters can be anything that conveys the feeling we wish to express, as long as they honestly convey the feeling expressed in that particular guideword (Figure 4.25).

Figure 4.25
Guideword moodboards: A poster for each guideword (from Tranquillo, by Team My Favorite, used by kind permission of Busarin Chumnong, Elly Nam, Mariko Sanchez, and Xiaoyi Xie).

4.19 USER FEEDBACK

Although our approaches may still be rather conceptual, this is a good time not only to consider them within our design team but gather together a group of potential users and get their feedback. This effort provides us with a wealth of information that we may not be aware of within our hermetically sealed design bubble. But take care with this feedback. Because our ideas are not fully refined, or even remotely close to that level, the feedback may lack some accuracy: Users may say things that may not be true of the final implementation. Take care, but also we should not be so concerned about it that we avoid a little user testing. In the end, it's just information. We are the designers and the design is our decision, whether a user's anecdotes affect it or not.

Revisit some of the users you interviewed. Show them your blob scenarios. Visit others who are your target whom you may not have interviewed yet. See what they think. Make sure to give them a sense of what their goals are and the contexts in which they will be using each approach. Make sure to photographically document the process, and, finally, make sure you review and reflect on the things they told you. Are there any issues that seemed to come up often? Was there one single thing that someone said that struck you? What do these things mean for your approaches and how would you change them? Are one or two approaches beginning to stand out more than the others?

4.20 FEEDBACK ON AESTHETICS

When presenting your scenarios and ecosystems to others, don't forget also to get feedback on your aesthetic vision, such as the selection of guidewords or the emotional impact of our moodboards. What images do reviewers associate with our words? Do their answers agree with ours? What are the differences?

Start with your general feel boards and ask reviewers what feelings they think the images convey. Are those words similar to the ones you've been using to select the images? Find out why, whether or not they've iterated your words. This exploration usually gives us insight into either our guidewords or our image selections, or both. Strive to have a conversation with them about the images to gain a deeper understanding of feelings that are motivational to them.

Does this provide any insight into how to adapt our guidewords to reach them better? In the end, keep in mind that our guidewords are essentially for us and our design team. As long as our team is on board with what they mean, and those results have the impact on our audience in the way we desire, then it doesn't matter if our users come up with the same words or not. It's just that we may learn a thing or two that we didn't know that could be used to guide our designs.

4.21 A/B TESTING

With multiple approaches, one of the most useful results we can derive from our users is which approach they feel is best. A/B testing is a method whereby we present two or more ideas to a subject and collect their feedback as to which they think is better, and why (Saffer, 2010, p. 183). Often, the results are not as definitive as that one is better in all aspects, but more likely that "A" is better in one area, while "B" is better in another. Gather their feedback about what they feel about each.

A/B testing is not only useful for the approaches we've been developing, it's also valuable for eliciting their response about the selections on our guideword moodboards and inspiration posters. This is less about what is "better" and more about what the images on the posters make them feel. Remove the adjectives from your boards and present them to your test subject. What words do they think your images represent? Their feedback can be surprising.

Note

1 Some formulations postulate must, should, could, and won't (International Institute of Business Analysis 2009), but there is ambiguity about what constitutes "must" and "should", so we narrow the framework down to must, could, won't.

5 Approach Exploration
Context and Structure

The effort of defining the elements of our system can be fairly straightforward, or incredibly complex. This depends on the amount of content our system holds. At one end of the spectrum are large-scale information systems, such as a website for a financial institution or control systems such as that on an airliner. We classify these as complex information or control systems, or simply complex systems. At the other end of the spectrum are displays like simple warning signs or devices with simple controls, like a light switch or a mechanical toaster. These we classify these as information or control sparse, or simply sparse systems. Most consumer targeted interactive systems fall somewhere in between. They are rich enough in information and control to satisfy the required tasks, but not so complex that the consumer faces a steep learning curve to engage with them in a meaningful way.

I do not know if your system is sparse or complex. If it's sparse, the diagrams and activities you perform in these next few chapters will be relatively simple. If it's complex, you may spend a great deal of time and effort detailing its structure. You must assess the scope of your structuring effort based on your system's level of complexity.

5.1 SYSTEM HIERARCHY

Before we begin the discussion about your system's content, it's useful to clarify a bit of terminology. An interactive system comprises several different levels. Often, these levels do not fall into neat categories, but are more like a continuum. That being said, we can think of a system roughly in this hierarchy: The highest level is that of the system and the device ecosystem. Below that is the expression of the system on each device: its context. Each context has an interface that allows the system to communicate with the user. The interface comprises an organized collection of content and control that we call quiescent states—the screens on a mobile device or pages on a website. Quiescent states are often organized into sections to help group information for better comprehension. Sections further break down into the lowest level of our hierarchy: the elements of each bit of content and the system's interactive components —the specific controls the user interacts with. Let's look at these levels in a little more detail.

5.1.1 System Level

The system level is the macro level: that which comprises the highest level of organization of the product. This is sometimes referred to as the "platform", but we use the term "system" or "product" here because often the term "platform" can be confused with "device", especially in industrial design. For entities with multiple product offerings, such as Google, Apple, or Facebook, the term platform serves to collect and identify all those products together, but that level is beyond the scope of this book. We are looking at a specific product, such as Google Docs, and how that product manifests itself across an ecosystem of devices.

We may experience the expression of this system or product across a range of devices. For example, we experience Google Docs on a desktop computer, a mobile device, or a tablet. The system is experienced through each of these devices via a software application, or "application", or just simply an "app".

As mentioned above, commonly products have just one expression per device, but that may not always be true. For example, Strava, when it first came out, had both a running and a cycling app on mobile devices, but they formed different parts of the same system. Eventually, the company merged them.

5.1.2 Context Level

The next level down from system is the "context". This includes both the physical device and the expression of the system on that device, the context. We say things such as "a web-based context" or "a mobile context", meaning that it is a particular expression of the system as a website or on an app on a mobile device. In this way, the term "context" means a particular combination of app and device.

There is commonly a one-to-one relationship between device and app, so the terms "context" and "device" are often used interchangeably. But this is not always the case: Facebook has both an app and a fairly sophisticated web app that runs in a mobile browser. So, on mobile, there is an app context and a web app context. To be precise, "device" refers to the physical object, while "context" refers to an expression of the system on that object.

5.1.3 Quiescent State Level

The "quiescent state" level is a bit more complicated. On a website, this is the web page. On a mobile device, this may be called a "view" or a "screen". But these terms are inherently visual and don't apply well to auditory or tactile systems. Hence, we use the term "quiescent state" so that we remain sensitive to contexts beyond the screen. Later in this book, we may use context-specific terms such as "page" or "view" or "screen", because of the ubiquity of these terms and the clarity of what we are referring to, but whenever we do, they should be regarded as context-specific synonyms for a quiescent state.

How do we define a quiescent state, though? A quiescent state is a presentation of the system in which it is largely at rest, waiting for user input or action. The system is quiet or idle, waiting for input, hence the term "quiescent". This doesn't mean that things aren't going on: There could be animations happening on the screen, or the system is going through some cycle such as a voice menu, but the system is waiting for the user to act to take it to another quiescent state. Where this possibly becomes confusing is in situations where we may click on something that expands or contracts information. Is this a new quiescent state or not? Our approach is that it isn't, because most of the information has been delivered to the display, just some has been revealed or hidden.

In terms of a system's structure, the quiescent state is arguably the most important construct: It is how we break down and organize our system into smaller, more easily manageable parts. A web page, the web version of a quiescent state, usually presents content reflecting a particular topic. This can be about a single topic, such as a description of a destination you may wish to visit, or it can present a collection of several places that may be of interest. Whatever the topic and scope are of the page, the system displays the page and waits for you to select what you want to do next.

A screen on a mobile device or tablet is in a quiescent state that works in much the same way as a web page. We enter the screen through some means such as clicking a menu or link, and we are presented with a screen of content. As in a web page, this content can be some collection of text, image, video, sound, and/or controls. The user can navigate the content in some way, such as scrolling, and scan it for things that may be of interest. The system stays in that quiescent state until the user selects something that transitions it to a new one.

Auditory systems, such as the ubiquitous (and often frustrating) phone menu are also organized in this way. We enter a quiescent state and are presented with a menu of options. We select one and are brought to another menu of options until we have (successfully, one hopes, but often not) fallen into a quiescent state where we hear the information we want. Apologies for being derisive of phone menus, but they often force us to spend time listening to a host of options that we do not want, and lead us down paths where we don't want to go. On the other hand, a quick question to a trained operator or intelligent natural language system often provides more accurate information much more quickly.

Physical products present quiescent states as well, but these are relatively sparse, so that we may often overlook them as such. But when my device is off, it's definitely at rest. If I flip its "on" switch, the state of the system has definitely changed and we've entered a new quiescent state, that in which the system is on. A further level of complexity is something like a stove. When all the elements are off, we understand the stove to be off. When we turn an element on, we understand the stove as being on. But what happens when I dial the flame up or down? Do I transition to a new quiescent state with each turn of the dial? Not really. The stove is still in the "on" quiescent state, but the flame is a little higher.

A quiescent state is when the interface is at rest, but the system itself may be performing some fairly complex work. Take, for example, a commercial airliner or a nuclear reactor. If the plane is on autopilot or the reactor is operating at normal levels, the pilot or operator may not be doing much. But the system is performing a wealth of complex machinations behind the scenes to keep the plane flying and moving toward its intended destination, or keep the reactor balanced at normal levels. So "quiescent" may mean "quiet", but it may be quiet only from a user perspective. It may be extremely active behind the scenes.

As with our stove example, quiescent states are not devoid of interaction. If the plane is in a state where the pilot is guiding it, every action by the pilot is not really changing its state. It's only in a manual mode that allows the user (the pilot in this case) the ability to use flight controls to guide the system. Similarly, if I'm on a web page, I still can scroll up and down the page. The same is true with a mobile device. I may even be provided with a set of controls that allow me to manipulate the interface, yet not change its quiescent state. Pinching a map, for example, is not transitioning me from the map's quiescent state, it's just allowing me to zoom in or out of the map in that state.

In the end, if we get too confused about whether a system's mode is a quiescent state or not, it's important to realize that quiescent states are constructs for us to clarify a certain presentation or system state to design. With this construct, we can say "design the landing page," or "design the navigation map screen," or "consider what can and cannot be done in autopilot mode." We really shouldn't be spending a great deal of time getting knotted up about whether or not something is a quiescent state, just use them to provide definition to our design.

5.1.4 Section, Content, and Control

Travelling on down the structural hierarchy, a "section" is simply a section of a quiescent state useful for information organization purposes. Sections and quiescent states themselves comprise two types of elements: content and control. Content is the media we read or see or play; control elements are those we interact with, such as a button, a link, a slider, or a steering wheel. We may synonymously call control elements "components" or "widgets".

Most systems are a combination of content and control, and, in the structure phase, we are tasked with the responsibility of discovering associations between them that indicate how best they should be grouped, content with content, content with control, and control with control. For complex systems, we would most likely devote a great deal of effort to organizing the structure of the content, while sparse systems do not usually present this kind of challenge and the information organization is simple and straightforward to the point of being almost a non-issue.

5.1.5 Elements

Elements are individual items of content or control that are usually not divided any further. An image is an element, a headline is an element, a menu item is an element. Body text is an element, too, but we may see that it can be divided into paragraphs, sentences, and individual characters. But for the most part—unless we are designing a writing system—we lump characters, sentences, and paragraphs together as the body text because the user is not dealing with anything of smaller granularity than that.

With these terms in hand—system, device, context, quiescent states, sections, elements, content, and control—let's begin to discuss the process of defining the general structure of our interactive system itself.

5.2 DEVICE ECOSYSTEMS

When we were considering our approach in the previous chapter, we looked at the general structure of our system and attempted to answer the question of how an approach achieved the user's goals through the appropriate arrangement of features. We were looking at the aspects of the system level of our concept's hierarchy. Let's consider the next level down: the contexts that allow our users to achieve their goals. To effectively compare contexts, each approach we are considering should propose a suite of device possibilities: They should specify a device ecosystem. These ecosystems are provisional at first because we are in the approach phase of our design, exploring possibilities. Through exploration and consideration, the collection of contexts that comprise our ecosystem become more resolved and less provisional.

In biology, an ecosystem is a collection of organisms in an environment that work together to sustain one another. Likewise, a digital ecosystem is a collection of devices and contexts that work together to support one another. Apple products are a good example of this: The Mac, iPhone, iPad, Apple Watch, Apple TV, and iCloud are products that strive to work together, sharing information such as email, photos, videos, locations, contacts, passwords, notes, and reminders. And they do this through multiple applications. Google, Microsoft, and Amazon do this as well.

When we use the term "ecosystem" in this book, we are not necessarily referring to systems as expansive and complex as Apple's suite of devices and applications, but we are more often considering it in the more limited sense of an integrated application that is experienced through a set of contexts. The term ecosystem emphasizes that these contexts should work together as seamlessly as possible. So, when we talk of our device ecosystem, we are talking of the set of devices or contexts in our system, and the role each of them plays (Figure 5.1).

For example, although a mobile device may be one—if not the main—context in our ecosystem, it may not be able to perform all the actions the website can. The Strava app on mobile is its primary context, intended to record and post an athlete's endurance activities as well as commenting on your friend's efforts. It's also good for finding possible routes on which to ride or run. But the mobile app does not present a deep data analysis of one's athletic performance; for that we must use its website.

This orchestration makes sense with Strava's product. The things we can do with the mobile device are things that are essential when we're on the go. Things that we do on the website are intended to take advantage of moments when we have

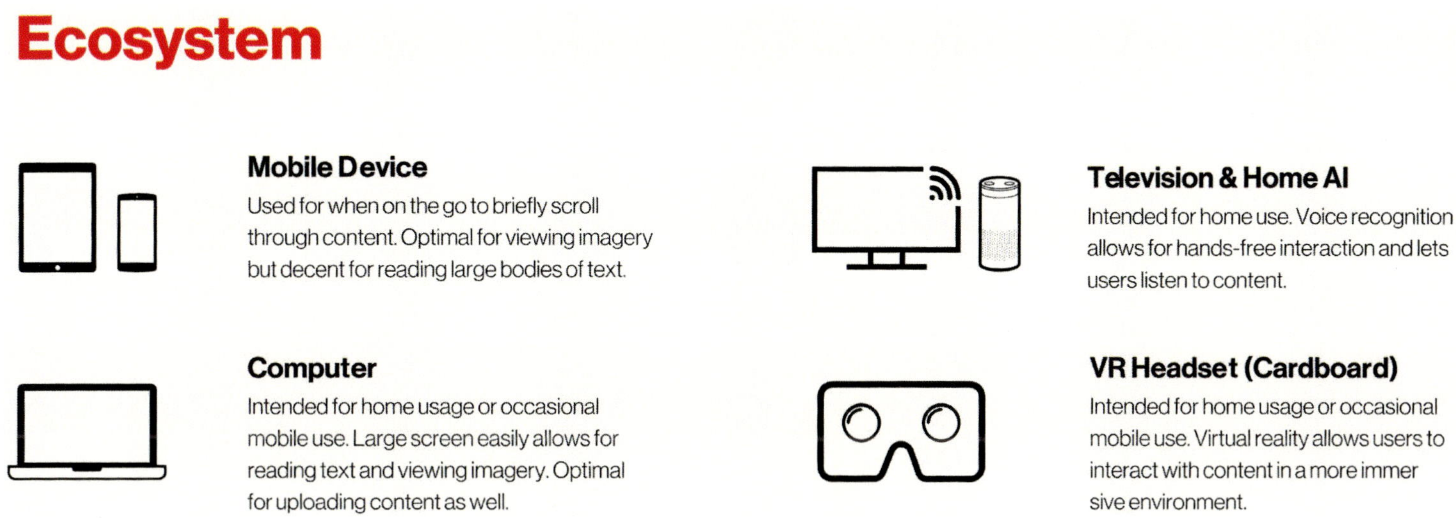

Figure 5.1
An ecosystem and the role each device plays (from Sourced, by Jonathan Nishida, used by kind permission of Jonathan Nishida).

some downtime at home and want to analyze our effort more deeply. Although the mobile app is the main context in the system, it doesn't have everything. It has just what it needs to be effective in the situation it's used.

Our goal in this phase is to consider various ecosystem approaches and determine which is the best fit for our design challenge. For each approach, we need to determine what contexts are required to allow the system to achieve the user's goals. Some contexts in our considered ecosystem may be critical, some less so. For Strava, the mobile app is essential. The website is extremely useful, but without the app, the system would more than likely fail. If they had a natural language app, such as something that would run on Amazon's Echo, it could be nice, but certainly not essential. What are the devices and contexts we are proposing for a particular approach? Which are essential, which are extremely useful yet not essential, which would just simply be nice to have, and which would be a waste of time and effort to build?

5.3 ECOSYSTEM ORCHESTRATION

A system could be considered as a set of features distributed among a collection of contexts that allow the user to achieve their goals. If its features are not distributed correctly across these contexts, the user may get lost, confused, frustrated, and not be able to achieve their goals. This distribution of features is what is called "orchestration," in reference to the arrangement of a symphonic score distributed across instruments that serve the greater purpose of creating a well-orchestrated sonic flow. If the features are orchestrated well, our audience should achieve their goals with little effort; if not, they will not want to have our system in their lives. Without good orchestration, our system will fail.

To structure things correctly, we need to explore a number of possibilities and consider myriad questions: Is a particular ecosystem configuration the most efficient and effective way to lead our audience to this point? Is this the most appropriate device for them to use, given what we expect them to be doing? Are we considering the correct context on that device if there are, indeed, more than one? Do users have all the information they need to make an informed decision for the selection they make? Is its information grouped in such a way as to make sense to the user? These are questions that need to be addressed when we lay out its structure.

As an example of an ecosystem structure, Garmin has a suite of athletic performance devices that allow endurance athletes to track their progress. When I run or swim, I use a watch that records my workout and provides me splits on time and pace. The ecosystem provides a heart rate monitor and a footpod so that I can track my heart rate and get accurate recordings of my pace. When I cycle, there's a bike computer within the ecosystem that I place on my handlebars that records performance data and gives me metrics such as speed, cadence, and distance traveled. It even connects to my bike's back hub to provide me power information as I ride. All of my athletic efforts are recorded and posted on a suite of apps called Garmin Connect. I can view and analyze my performance on these apps on mobile and web. The ecosystem provides connections to third party extensions as well, such as Strava and Training Peaks, which extend the features and functionality of the system.

The Garmin performance tracking system is a complex suite of devices and contexts that are orchestrated extremely well. For example, the bike computer does not have the data analysis features that the Garmin Connect app has, which would be dangerous to review while we're riding at 20 miles an hour in traffic. Although the bike and the watch are fairly similar in what they do, one provides information pertinent to running and the other provides information pertinent to being on a bike. Although the watch can be used to track bike information as well, it's much easier and safer to glance at a screen on the handlebars right in front of my face than to take my hand off the bars to look at my watch. Additionally, the size of the bike computer's screen is larger and displays information better when my head is bobbing due to bumpy asphalt. The heart rate monitor, footpod, and bike hub have no interface at all and act as "dumb" devices that simply supply the watch or bike computer with information. The components of the ecosystem are well orchestrated in the sense that the features for each context are exactly appropriate for the posture of the user, no more, no less. And the entire system provides its audience with the larger goal of being able to track, analyze, and reconsider the proper training methodology to reach peak performance exactly when needed during the race season.

This system is well orchestrated because the designers were well aware of the different roles each context plays within the ecosystem. The role of the "dumb" devices, such as the heart rate monitor, is simply to supply accurate performance information to the tracking device in the system. They have no user interface at all. The tracking devices, such as the watch or the bike computer, record the data and have a limited interface that presents the user with information they may need during the activity itself. They tell the user what's happening right now. Historical data is there, but not that easy to reach. The Garmin Connect apps are where the historical performance analysis comes into play. I can see where I rode or ran, my power distribution or pace along that path, and compare it to other performances I did on that route previously. I can get further analysis through connected apps such as Training Peaks, or a better social experience and data analysis through Strava.

Although the devices and contexts are very well orchestrated, it's interesting to note that I often do not use the Garmin Connect app to review my stats. I use Strava instead. The reason is that Strava seems to have orchestrated the differences between the mobile context and the web context much better than Garmin Connect. Connect allows for detailed data analysis on mobile, which one would think is great, but what it does is clutter the interface with several layers of navigation and information that I often don't want while I'm walking down the hall. I just want to easily see an overview of what I did and what my followers are doing. Yes, it's powerful, but it's not appropriate for what I need to know when I'm using that device. For Strava, the mobile app is for quick information about fairly recent history, while the web app is for detailed analysis. This makes better sense because I want to perform deep analysis at my desk or in my comfy chair, not on the go.

For an ecosystem to be effective, each device and context needs a role. They are like actors in a play who all serve the purpose of the greater message. For the Garmin/Strava ecosystem, the "dumb" devices just capture data, the watch or computer record and present information just about the immediate performance, the mobile prioritizes recent history information interesting for those on the go, and the web context is where the analytical heavy lifting occurs.

Given your ecosystem, what roles do your contexts and devices assume? What should they do, and, often more importantly, what should they not do? Since we should be user focused in our approach, as opposed to device focused, we can reframe these questions from a user perspective: as user stories. What should the user be able to do with a particular device? What should they not do? For example, with the Garmin watch, we should be able to see information pertinent to my current run, so that I know that my immediate performance is on track with what I'm supposed to be doing during that workout. I should be able to easily see my pace, my heart rate, how far I've run, and how much time I've run. And all this needs to be easily viewable while I'm running, yet not be clouded or obscured by other less pertinent information.

5.4 USE CASTING

Each context will have a role to play in our system, so it's useful to cast them as such. To group features, consider the role of a device or context. For example, even though we know we may need some form of mobile device in our ecosystem, we may not as yet know whether it should be a watch, or a phone, or something that is custom designed. Referring to a context not as the device itself, but, rather, casting it as the role it plays abstracts it to allow us to consider a multitude of possibilities before making a final determination of what it should be. The term "moment of active update" in Figure 5.2 casts the posture in a role, as opposed to a device. These roles should be reflected in the ideation of possible devices within our system (Figure 5.3). Additionally, use casting makes the design prompt more user-centric because it focuses us on its role for the user, as opposed to the device itself. Users care more about what it does and how it works with them than what it is.

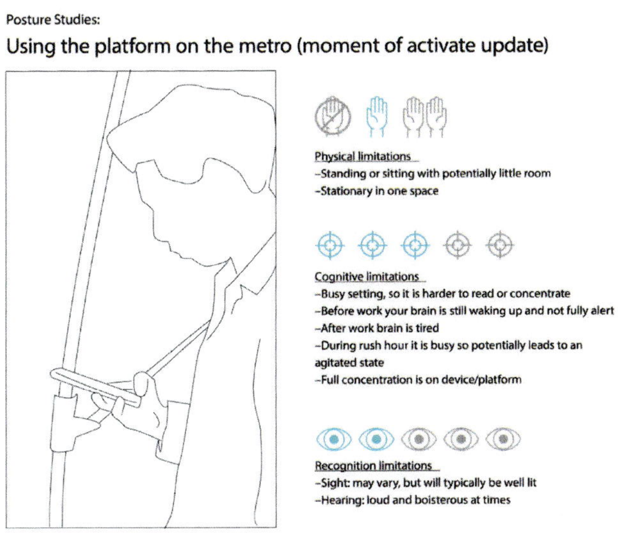

Figure 5.2
Use casting a news aggregator (from Sourced, by Jonathan Nishida, used by kind permission of Jonathan Nishida).

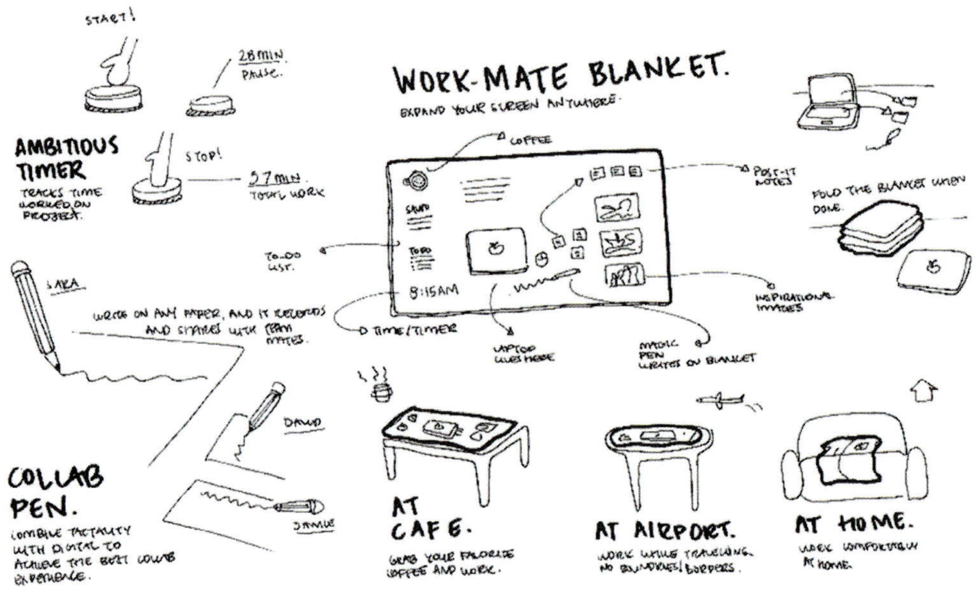

Figures 5.3
Approach ideation using use casting (from Cosmos, by Team Laundry, used by kind permission of Asli Akdemir, Lynn Lei, Nathan Lu, and Yozei Wu).

5.5 POSTURES AND CONTEXT

As we weigh the value of different approaches to our system, we need to consider how the contexts we are considering play out against the natural postures we've studied for our user's experience (Figure 5.4). When our audience uses the system, they are subject to a particular external context, and the system manifests itself in a context or set of contexts as well, so essentially our agreement principle that *The posture of the system should agree with the posture of the user* can boil down to *the context of the system should agree with the posture of the user*.

For example, a device to be used on a bike will offer a much different set of goals and features than one intended for our user's office desk. The goals and features for each touchpoint within an approach must make sense for each context it

Figure 5.4
Critiquing contextual needs with respect to postures and device requirements (from Aroma, by Bessy Liang, used by kind permission of Bessy Liang).

suggests. We created our blob scenario, we built scratch mock-ups to provide us a sense of the kinds of devices that might be useful in our ecosystem, given our user's experience. Now that we are looking precisely at the context level of our system, it's instructive to go through this process again, but with a slightly finer level of detail. Instead of cardboard or paper tape, we may begin to consider materials that can better hold form, such as clay.

We should also be asking more questions about the general characteristics of our devices. Are they large or small and why? How are they held or how do I interact with them? Do I act on them with two-dimensional gestures, three-dimensional gestures, voice, tactile controls, or through an interactive device such as a mouse, keypad, or touchpad? Do I need to do so on the surface of the device itself, or from a distance? What are the ways it can respond to me? Via a screen, lights, movement, or sound? What combination of these?

What do our postures studies imply from their analysis of the user's level of dexterity, cognition, and recognition about the general characteristics of the devices and contexts in our system? Can they focus full attention on a screen for a long period of time, or do they need to pay attention to other things? How does this affect the context of the system and how they interact with it? When does it make sense for the user to transition from one device to another in the ecosystem? Be

Figure 5.5
Inject strategic ambiguity even if particular devices are being considered (from Artbug, by Radhika Kashyap, used by kind permission of Radhika Kashyap).

creative and consider other possibilities than those that currently exist. For any posture, what would be the ultimate arrangement of devices that can capture what users want to communicate to the system, and how it presents back to them what they need to know?

Even though we may be considering a particular context, such as a mobile device or laptop, it's instructive at this stage to inject strategic ambiguity into the consideration by simulating these objects with blank forms (Figure 5.5). This allows us to avoid being influenced by current realities, and consider what could be as opposed to what currently is. Create a form out of foam or foam core, for example, that fits in the hand like a mobile device and consider how to act on it and how it can communicate back. Or, keep your phone turned off, yet hold it in your hand as you're walking down a hallway and imagine interacting with your system.

5.6 USER STORIES, REVISITED

Given your ecosystem, what roles do your contexts and devices assume? What should they do, and, often more importantly, what do they not do? As responsible user-centered designers, let's reframe these questions from a user perspective. For example, with the Garmin watch, we should be able to see information pertinent to my current run so I know my immediate performance is on track with my workout. I should be able to easily see my pace, my heart rate, how far I've run, and how much time I've run. And all this needs to be easily viewable while I'm running.

Let's recall the expression of features as a user story. Our persona from the previous chapter, Steve, is no longer a driver considering whether to get on the freeway, but an endurance athlete who has adopted the Garmin ecosystem and is using a Garmin watch. We can formulate our user story for this context with: "As Steve runs, he wants to be able to review his running stats in order to make sure he's on track with his workout."

Let's again break down the details of Steve's user story. Steve is the persona along with all that entails. His posture is running, while the role of the system at that touchpoint is such that it can present stats to him while he runs and he can interact with it in a limited way. His central goal is to review his running stats. Why? In order "to make sure he's on track."

Garmin's watch is only one possible solution, but it's a pretty good one. His external context requires that he pay attention to cars, curbs, and sticks on the sidewalk. He needs to be able to glance at his interface to receive information—not study it. As such, the presentation of information on the interface should be "glancable": meaning it needs to be legible in quick glances while he runs. A large watch face with large type achieves this because Steve can glance at his watch quickly, and perform brief tactile interactions with it. But it could also be achieved by other means, such as a head-up display projected on his glasses, assisted by an interactive "thimble" on his finger. There could be numerous possibilities. This is the stage where we explore them.

We have once again applied the framework of our strategic pyramid questions to arrive at our user story, and we can also use the organizational structure of the MUSCOW chart to determine which features are important, and which aren't. We're still expressing things at a fairly high level, but now we're making assumptions based on context rather than the feature set of the system in general.

5.7 THE PROCESS OF EXPLORING CONTEXT

When we're dealing with context, we need to consider how the features indicated by our user stories are grouped. This is the essence of our system's orchestration. We will need to express that structure by mapping it out in some way and the flexibility of the tools we employ is critical for this: We don't want to avoid exploring a different structural approach just because it's too much effort to change things. You can use a sticky note wall, mind mapping software, or cards on a table. We hope that affordable, wall-sized high-resolution gesture screens will be available in the very near future just for this purpose, but as of this writing they are not. For now, though, what we often use is the sticky note wall. See the sticky note wall in Figure 4.3 for an example.

We cover an entire wall with these notes, arranging and rearranging them and photo documenting each iteration (Figure 5.6). The notes themselves express features with simple single or few word descriptions. If you include a simple user story on the back of the note that expresses that feature, you can have the added benefit of creating a user story list as well. In agile development, this is called a backlog (Gothelf & Seiden, 2016, p. 118). If we want to rearrange the notes on our wall to explore other possibilities, we photo document them before we proceed to the next arrangement.

Figure 5.6
Consider multiple organizational approaches by rearranging sticky notes (from So Cal Modernist, by Alex Kasper, used by kind permission of Alex Kasper).

5.8 ECOSYSTEM DIAGRAM

To effectively communicate our solutions to our stakeholders, we will need to express the attributes of our system's ecosystem. A useful framework for this is an ecosystem diagram: a schematic that presents a high level view of the system's components—including its contexts, devices, user types, their most pertinent postures, environments, and the flow of information throughout the system. An audience should be able to look at an ecosystem diagram and understand the general structure of the system (Figure 5.7).

Done well, the ecosystem diagram can serve as a central communication tool for our system. It is not uncommon to use refined versions of this diagram as a unifying element in the final design pitch. At this stage, however, it's useful to provide us, our design team, and other project stakeholders a broad understanding of the elements that comprise our system. This, in combination with the structure map that we will discuss in later chapters, provides a general overview of our system's

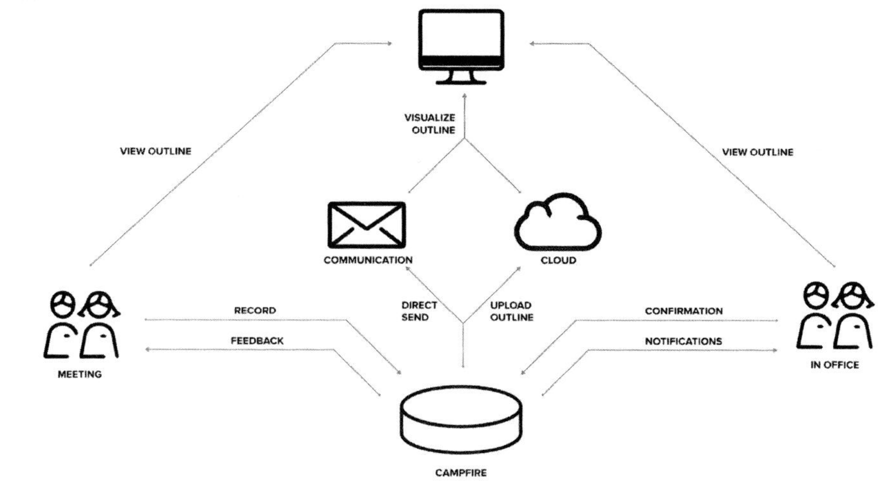

Figure 5.7
Ecosystem diagram for a note taking device (from Campfire, by Team Seamrippers, used by kind permission of Matthew Benkert, Derling Chen, Ian Liao, and Mike Rito).

structure. In the approach phase, however, an ecosystem diagram allows us a quick way of determining the contextual differences each approach entails.

5.9 FLOW-CENTRIC ORGANIZATION

There are a few standard ways of challenging ourselves to explore different feature arrangements for our ecosystem. The most straightforward is to organize them by user flow. This relates strongly to the scenario approach we've been using to define and describe our user experience so far. We've used this in developing our approach and our primary use case scenario, so it seems natural to see what happens to our information when we look at it from this point of view. Let's return to this to see how we can arrange our features to better aid our user's experience.

How do users flow through these tasks to achieve their goals? This can stem from the primary use case, as clarified by the approach scenario, and include critical alternate paths as well (Figure 5.8). As Dan Saffer points out, user flows "show where . . . users will have to perform certain actions" (Saffer, 2010, p. 148). What tasks need to appear in what physical context during our user's experience with the system? Consider the MUSCOW charts you built for the devices and contexts in your ecosystem. With these, we can see what features need to appear where, and begin to have an idea of what content and control needs to appear on each interface. Look at Figure 5.8 and take it one step further by establishing commands the user should execute (Figure 5.9).

Note also that this flow diagram not only indicates what the user is doing, it also indicates what the system is doing in response. This is useful for itemizing the processes that need to be built for the system to achieve its goals. Based on the importance of the use case, production priority can be given to these processes.

What do tasks look like when they're organized by the user's flow? How can you make those tasks easier for them? Consider your user's flow as a guide to organize the features on your sticky note wall. Does your user's experience seem to make sense from their point of view? Do the tasks make sense with the role at that touchpoint? Are critical user goals achieved? Is there anything redundant that can be removed?

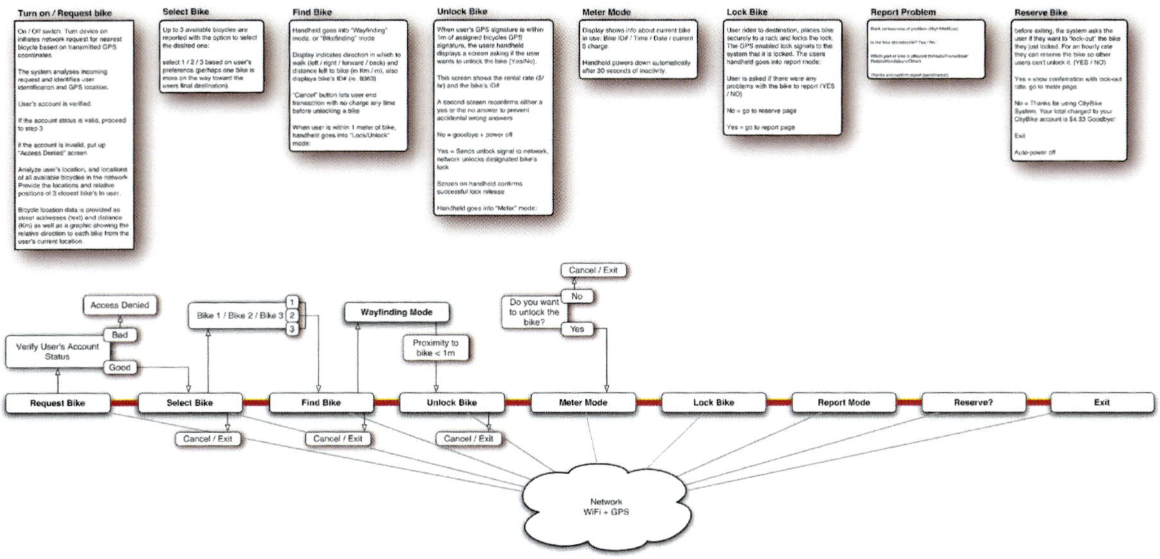

Figure 5.8
A task flow for a bike-sharing system (from Citybike, by Johnathan Abarbanel, used by kind permission of Johnathan Abarbanel).

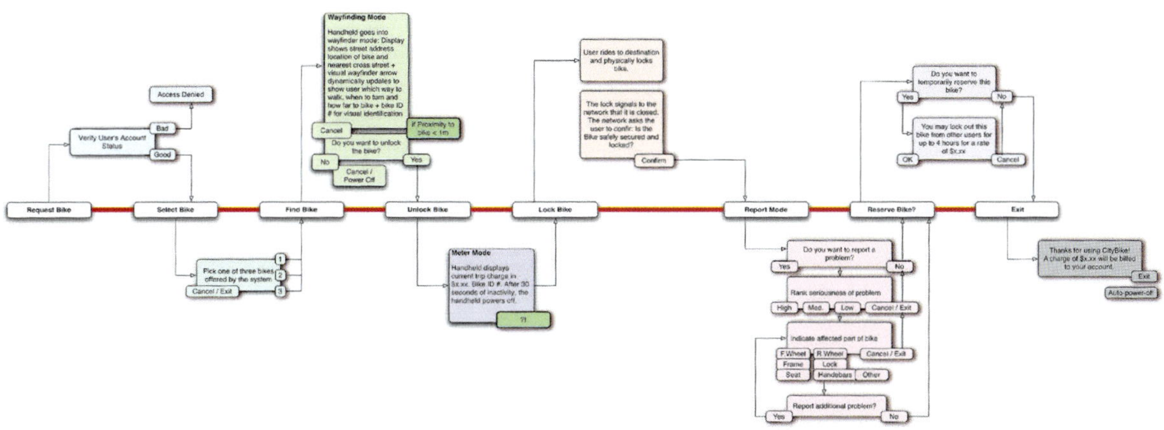

Figure 5.9
A flow-centric structure for a bike-sharing system (from Citybike, by Johnathan Abarbanel, used by kind permission of Johnathan Abarbanel).

5.10 DATA-CENTRIC ORGANIZATION

What if we did away with contexts altogether and looked at the organization of our features as simply a system of data? What could that organization look like? Start with your user goals and ask: "What things do we need to achieve these goals?" Break those items down even further, level by level, until you get to the most basic elements of the system (Figure 5.10).

The approach I'm putting forth here is one that is often used by data analysts and back-end developers (Morville & Rosenfeld, 2007, p. 73), yet is also used in the hierarchical layout approaches common in websites where we have a main menu, sub menu, and detail pages. Think of your system in its most abstract terms as a collection of data objects. To use a familiar example, let's think of the general data structure of Facebook.

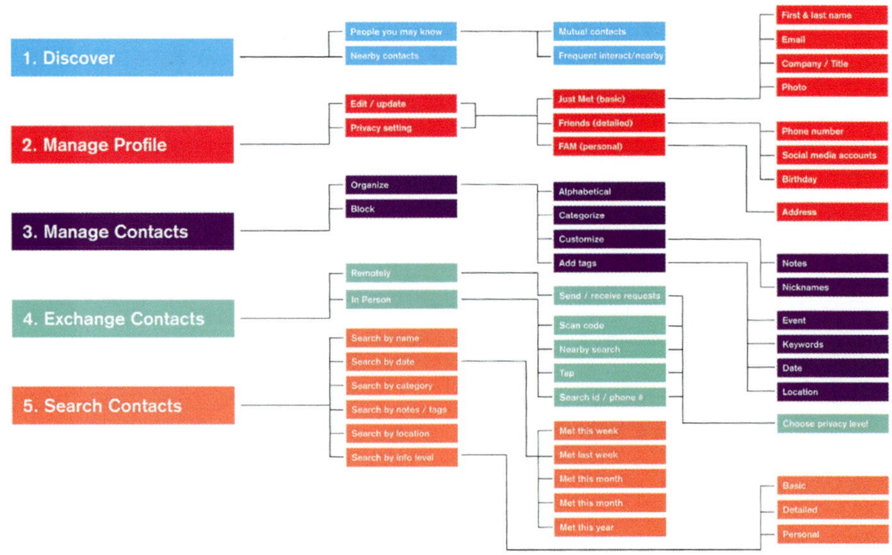

Figure 5.10
Information breakdown: Breaking tasks down into information (from Keepintouch, by Amber Wang, used by kind permission of Amber Wang).

Facebook comprises a collection of users. Each user has a profile and a collection of friends they follow. This is the data object of the user. It also contains a collection of posts, and each post can have words, images, and videos. The most critical information in a post, besides the content of the post itself, is its author. And it is through the author that a post is associated with a user, the user's friends, and, ultimately, the user's feed. The author is the "key" that links it to these other structures.

There are many more data collections in Facebook, but people and posts are the most important and will serve our descriptive purposes here just fine. For each of these data objects, we will need a way to create an item, update an item, and remove or delete the item. This is referred to by the pleasant acronym CRUD (CReate, Update, Delete). We create a user profile for ourselves by signing in for the first time. We can update that information on our profile page. And we can destroy that profile if we wish—although reportedly it isn't easy. Likewise, we can create a post by updating our status and we can delete posts as well. Updating or editing a post was something desired by early Facebook users, but wasn't allowed for quite some time.

Facebook users certainly care about their posts in order to read comments and satisfy their narcissistic behavior of counting the number of likes they have, but they also care about what's happening to their friends. This is where the feed comes in. It is constructed of our friends and their posts organized by time. We can also comment on their posts adding to the information of the post data object.

In this way, we have the system, Facebook, comprising two primary data objects—users and posts—that combine to create two more objects—friends and our feed—and besides navigation, the interface is all about providing users the ability to CRUD—create, display, update, and delete—items in these four data objects. "CRUD"ing those data objects needs to be provided for users to have a worthwhile Facebook experience, and "CRUD"ing our data objects had better be on our sticky note wall when we're considering what features go where.

As you may see, a data-centric method isn't very good at revealing what is essential to our users and their flow, but it's an excellent way to trigger questions that may have eluded us in other information organization scenarios, such as considering how we update or delete a post. By considering a data-centric architecture and how to "CRUD" our data objects, the inclusion (or absence) of these operations is no longer happenstance, it becomes a conscious design decision.

5.11 THE PRIMARY USE CASE TEST

When you have something like a sticky note wall representing an arrangement of features and contexts that seems to make sense, consider how it works with respect to your primary use case. Are the user's most important goals being achieved? Is it easy or awkward to flow through the proposed contexts? Would it make sense to them? Are there points of friction that can be removed? What is the minimum viable product or MVP? Are there redundant contexts that can be removed or could take a secondary priority?

5.12 PRIMARY CONTEXTS

Just as we are focusing on the primary use case, we can explore approaches by focusing solely on our primary context. If, for example, we are considering a GPS navigation system, is its primary context held in the hand or installed in the dashboard of the car? Or is it a hand-held device used in the car? Are certain features available when we are driving and others available when we're parked or out of the car? Determine the primary context of your system and ask the question: "Can the features that make up the MVP of my system be supported on just the primary context?" If so, what would that look like? Arrange your feature set to reflect this approach. What would be the user's experience in that case? Aspects may not be as approachable as a well-considered multi-context ecosystem, but the reduction in production and distribution costs may be so extreme as to prohibit any other approach for the system's launch. In other words, the business goals would make more sense.

Many design efforts use a "mobile first" design approach where we design for a mobile device before we design anything else. Owing to the screen limitations of mobile devices, this approach forces designers to pare down the expression of their system to the information and features that are most necessary—the MVP. If mobile is the primary context in our system, mobile first works well, but if not, this approach may not leverage the system's features appropriately. Recall that we need to consider devices that match well with our user's experience. So yes, mobile first if that's the best device for our user's experience, but no if their experience points to other interaction methodologies for the system's primary context.

5.13 OTHER ORGANIZATIONAL APPROACHES

Our flow-centric structuring approach is essentially how our user progressively engages with the contexts of our system in executing the tasks necessary to achieve their goals. It's a mix of different organizational approaches: contexts, tasks, and user goals. In the end, it may be just this kind of combination that is the most effective, but, like our data-centric approach, if we consider other ways of organizing things we may uncover questions and concerns that we hadn't arrived at before. The same is true for the approach of considering our primary context.

We can also be futuristic, in the sense that we could consider approaches where we strip away any assumption that we are limited by contexts, especially contexts that are currently available. In this case, the only driving concern would be exactly what the user would want and when. This is an extreme user-centric approach that is unconstrained by any contextual limitations. How would features best be arranged in this approach? What would happen if anything could have an interface and everything can be interactive? It is interesting to see how this approach could structure our features. What are the similarities between this and either a user flow or data-centric approach? What are the differences? Think about this and rearrange your sticky note wall of features accordingly.

On the other hand, say we worked for a company that was good at a particular suite of technologies. How would a technology-centric organization of the features on your sticky notes look? What are the differences and similarities between this and a flow-centric approach? Or, consider the relative familiarity of your user base: How would things be organized for the novice? The intermediate? The expert? What if you have different user roles, such as a student, faculty, and administrator? How would the flow be best arranged from the perspective of each of these individuals?

There are numerous ways of addressing structural organization, and now is the right time to explore them. But bear in mind there will always be trade-offs. One approach may be excellent for one issue, but inadequate for another. We need to organize our features, consider things we learn from that organization, analyze its relative strengths and weaknesses to other organizations, and reorganize again. Finally, what approach or combination of approaches seems optimal for your target? How can we take advantage of the benefits of that optimal organization and what can we do to alleviate its challenges? It's quite possible that the most optimal configuration of our system reflects a little of each of these approaches.

5.14 FRICTION

Since we're considering the relative value of one structural approach versus another, it's appropriate at this point to discuss further the topic of friction. Friction results from activities an interface imposes upon a user that makes it more difficult for the user to achieve their goals. These points of friction can be something dramatic or something that is almost unnoticeable, but even the most subtle form of friction could be the difference between the success or failure of a system.

A dramatic example of the removal of a point of friction was Apple's abandonment of the stylus as a means of interacting with a mobile interface in favor of just the finger. The elimination of this led to an entirely different approach to the interface: touch. It required an entirely new kind of interface to make feasible. It was the elimination of points of friction like this that led to the iPhone's dominance in the mobile phone market.

An example of resolving a more subtle point of friction is Amazon's placement of its add to cart and one-click buttons at the top right of its item page. These could have been placed below the description of the product, but they are exposed right at the top so it's less "fricative" for the user to select them: They don't have to scroll down to easily purchase a product. At first blush, this may seem minor, but, I guarantee you, if Amazon moved them down—to below the fold—sales would drop significantly.

At the stage we've reached, we're primarily considering the macroscopic structure of our system. Why should these details of friction be important to us right now? Because, as we can see by the lack of the stylus for the iPhone, sometimes the removal of an element of friction shoots right to the core of how our system is designed. When we are considering different approaches for organizing our system, we need to look at them in terms of removing as much friction for our primary user as possible, while still making it usable for alternate targets. If our system is primarily targeted at students, but intended for faculty as well, it had better be as smooth as possible for the student, but it can't be impossible to use for faculty.

The threat that confronts us when we consider the creation of a system from scratch is that our competition already has a user base. We have a huge hill to climb to compete with them. Yet, the advantage we have is that our competition has organizational approaches that are deeply baked into their system if not their entire corporate structure. If those assumptions are no longer correct, or were not correct in the first place, they often lead to points of friction that are not easy to remove. For example, the restaurant-centric approach to Yelp makes it extremely difficult, if not impossible, for them to adapt to a user and image sharing approach to meal ideas that is so successful with Instagram. A new, or newly revamped, system is nimble. It has the opportunity to turn founding assumptions on their head and provide a better experience. So yes, the elimination of friction is entirely relevant now and may be the most significant opportunity we have to gain a foothold in the marketplace.

5.15 THE IMPACT OF STRUCTURE

In addition to eliminating points of friction, how we structure our system has other impacts as well. Consider a system designed to provide a user with information about restaurants near them. For example, if the restaurants can be organized by popularity, it implies that there needs to be a way of judging popularity in the first place. How exactly do we propose to do that? Is our organization going to curate this information by having a reviewer visit each restaurant and judge its popularity? Or is this content going to be user-generated? The former is the way Zagat's guide works; the latter is Yelp.

The choice we make about how content is supplied not only defines other aspects of our system, that is, screens needed to input that content, but it impacts our organization's personnel structure as well. With the Zagat approach, we will be paying for an army of reviewers to visit restaurants. How do we generate the revenue to pay them? The point here is twofold: We must consider each decision we make about our system's features very carefully, and reflect on how we are obtaining the information each feature requires and what that means for our organization; further, if we're going to motivate our users to acquire that information, what features does *that* require? How are we going to arrange that in our interface?

Eventually, when we've considered all these factors and our sticky note wall reflects the best arrangement of contexts and features we can muster, it's time to document a breakdown of our system's features in terms of the requirements of each object in our ecosystem. We do that with a structure map.

5.16 STRUCTURE MAP

Wherever our analysis leads, eventually we'll want to build a structure map of the features of each context. This is sometimes called a blueprint, or, in web design, it's called a sitemap and indicates the major information groupings of a particular context of our system (Karjaluoto, 2014, p. 111) (Figure 5.11). The structure map of a website shows the pages of the site and indicates their structural hierarchy (Van Dijck, 2003, p. 108). But we can use this presentation of structure for more than just our web context: The manifestation of our system in each context has a structure, and we will need to build a map of that structure for them as well.

Again, we should consider if the arrangement we've arrived at is the most efficient for our user. We should test the structure by considering our user stories and observing how our users flow through the system for those cases. It's very common that we will have to adjust things somewhat and may face some tough decisions along the way (Van Dijck, 2003, p. 108). An arrangement that may make one task more efficient may make another less so. To resolve these concerns, it's useful to prioritize our use cases and allow the more critical cases, such as our primary use case, to win out over those that are less so.

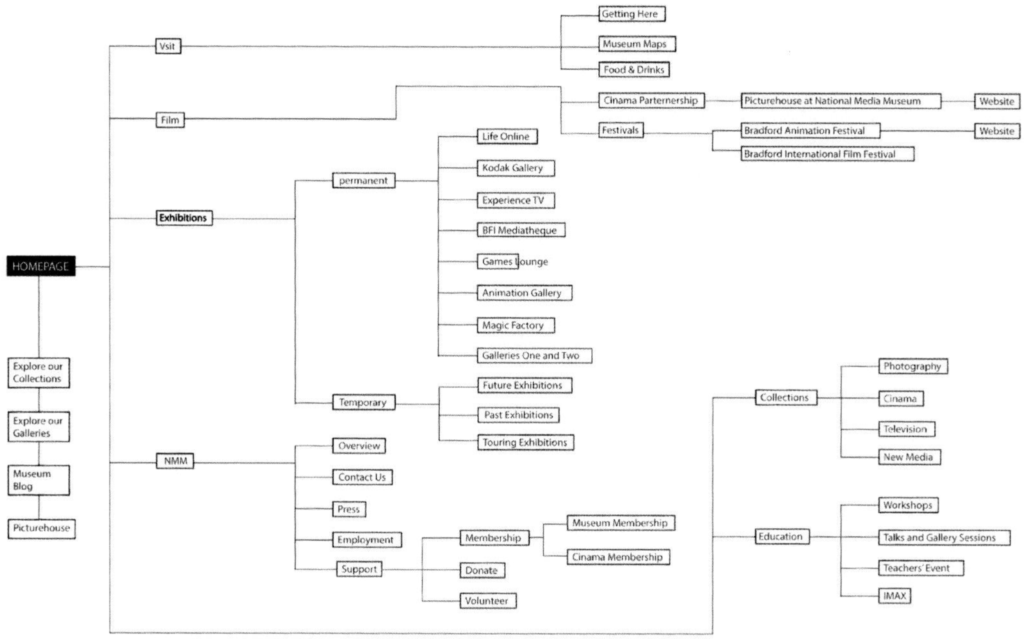

Figure 5.11
The structure map of a museum website (from National Media Museum, by Tanya Chang, used by kind permission of Tanya Chang).

5.17 REFINING THE BLOB SCENARIO

Earlier in this chapter we used the postures of our audience as inspiration to explore mock-ups investigating scope, scale, form, and general aspects of use. Through the use of blobs, we strove to keep our mock-ups resolved enough to consider our user's relationship to our system, yet strategically ambiguous so that we didn't fall into the weeds.

We should retain a level of ambiguity, but it's completely natural at this stage for contexts to become even more resolved. Maybe we're beginning to consider how our users act on the system to best align with the role a context needs to play. Does it make sense for them to use a trackpad, touch, three-dimensional gestures, or spoken word? We may also be starting to consider how our system talks back to our users. Is it appropriate for the system to communicate using a screen, a voice, physical movement, or just a simple light? This level of specificity is entirely appropriate and leads us into the interface discussions of the next chapter. Yet, we're still considering approaches—at this point, approaches to the configuration of our ecosystem—so don't lock in, explore.

Our explorations should have produced a few approaches to a context ecosystem that we should be inspired to take further. Take these ecosystem explorations through the entire path of the primary use case and see if they hold up. If they do, turn them into a scenario. Since we are considering the physicality of our contexts, the appropriate form of scenario is no longer a text scenario, but what we call a blob scenario. To create a blob scenario, your mock-ups as props, and use your team or a group of friends to play-act the scenario. Photograph their performance creating a visual storyboard. If you've addressed some detail of a device or an interface, make sure to shoot it in close-up so your audience can see what's going on.

You most likely have several scenarios representing several different approaches. Put these scenarios together as a set of storyboards: a storyboard for each approach, name each of your scenarios in such a way as to identify their central characteristics, and present them to your team to further discuss their relative strengths and weaknesses. The next stage in our design process takes us down to the interface level, increasing exponentially the complexity and amount of information we need to handle, so strive now to narrow the choice of possible approaches down to only a few.

6 Approach Exploration
Tasks and Interactions

In the previous chapter, we looked at the approach to our system in terms of context. These contexts could be traditional or more speculative depending on our project's goals. Our focus on context allowed us to consider the role each device would play in our ecosystem and how we could best distribute its features to into those roles to improve our user's experience, but roles are not the whole story when we consider context.

Interactive systems are just that: interactive. The system provides our users with the ability to act on the system, and the system responds to those actions in some way that communicates back to the user. The actions that we can perform on a bike and the appropriate responses we can receive there are completely different than what can happen in a comfy chair. What our system should provide in each of these situations not only depends on what we want at those moments, but how we are able to act on the system and perceive its response. In other words, to determine context, it's not enough to consider features, we need to consider interactions as well. To determine those interactions, we need to define what our audience does with our system; the tasks we are asking them engage in. Then, we look at how to configure our system's contexts to best achieve those tasks in a way that supports our user's posture.

6.1 FEATURES TO TASKS

We've engaged in several considerations to inspire solutions to our system. We've focused on user goals, features, and contexts. And although things are still somewhat vague, through those solutions our system has become more valid and refined. However, with an understanding of goals, features, and contexts, we can delve more deeply into exactly what our users should be trying to do with our system; when, where, and with what contexts they will be doing those activities. These activities are commonly referred to as tasks, or user tasks, and they stem from the features our system offers to help our users achieve their goals.

Recall that when we brainstormed the features of our system we started with our user's goals—those things they wish to achieve with our system, and mindmapped those into a set of features. Features are things the system provides in order to deliver upon its user's goals. Now, with features and contexts further refined, we can reconsider our user again and ask the question "Given what our user needs in each context, what activities are we asking our users to perform to achieve their goals?" The result is a task breakdown, which is a "raw list of activities our system will need to support" (Saffer, 2010, p. 100).

Goals are derived from our user's wants and needs, features provide users with the means to achieve those goals, and tasks clarify how our audience uses the system's features to achieve those goals. These tasks will eventually lead to the elements—the content and control—our users need to complete their tasks, and how those elements are organized and arranged across contexts will, in turn, clarify what is needed for our interface. Goals to features to tasks to elements to interface—those are the layers of the onion we are peeling away. The point where we are right now is further refining the tasks.

We've defined many of these tasks already: Our approach scenarios, either through text or blobs, indicate touchpoints that our audience uses to execute specific tasks that deliver on their goals. Now we need to specify in more detail what those tasks are. We do this by revisiting our scenarios and performing a task breakdown.

In our text scenarios, we used the term "the system" because we were avoiding the specificity of the context. Similarly, the "blob" in the blob scenario avoided specificity as well. At this stage, we have a better idea of what those contexts could be, and the features necessary in each context to deliver on our user's goals, but we don't know specifically the activities our users need to perform to achieve those goals. We will get there, and very soon, but let's avoid the context details right now and break down the features of our system into tasks in such a way as to remain somewhat context independent.

To illustrate this effort, consider the example of a system our audience would use to find a restaurant. For this challenge, our text scenario may have stated: "John accesses the system and searches for a Chinese restaurant near him." How is this done? Breaking this down we realize that the system will need to know several things:

1. Where is John?
2. What kind of restaurant is he interested in?
3. What restaurants are around him?
4. Which of those match his interests?

These are the minimum to be able to solve this question. But it would also be useful to know another thing:

5. What restaurant or restaurants would John most likely prefer?

With these, the system could not only figure out what Chinese restaurants are near him but also be able to present them in such a way as to leverage what he likes. What is the minimum that John has to do to have these items supplied to the system? Let's consider each question one at a time. The question of "Where is John" could be provided by a mobile device with a GPS, or a kiosk where the system knows its location. The set of restaurants that are around him could already be in a database in the system, as well as information indicating the type of cuisine. It will most likely be John who supplies what he is interested in.

Item 5 is much trickier, but also fascinating, and can be supplied in several ways. With an understanding of John's previous history, for example, the system could match John's historical preferences with other users in the system (the classic "those who like also like" feature). It could be supplied by more quantitative information such as distance from him or price. It could be some combination of these. Regardless of the approach to item 5, the minimum that John would have to do to achieve his goal would be to indicate the kind of cuisine in which he's interested. His task at this point in the system would be simply: "Input cuisine."

How, specifically, is this done? We may not know yet because we may not have decided on a final device ecosystem. We may know the roles our context should play based on our user's day in the life, but we may not have completely determined whether it is a mobile device, a car-based system, or a kiosk on the street. Eventually, we will have to determine this, but as long as we use appropriately abstracted language—"input cuisine", as opposed to "type cuisine into a search bar in your mobile device"—we can specify the user tasks of the system while still allowing enough room to explore context possibilities. This can be broken down as a structure map—see Figure 5.11 in the previous chapter—or, alternatively, an outline that starts with the goal and breaks things down into tasks and subtasks (Figure 6.1). Either are effective.

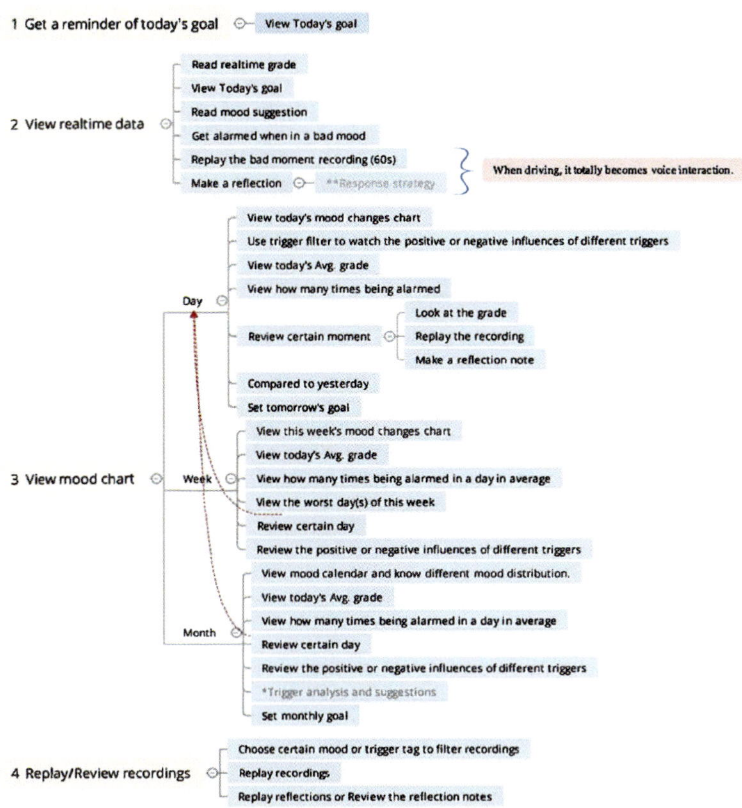

Figure 6.1
A feature to task breakdown for a mood changer (from Odmo, by Hui Ye, used by kind permission of Hui Ye).

While features indicate what the system provides, tasks indicate what the user has to do (Saffer, 2010, p. 100). Notice also that tasks begin to use the language of our interface: "Input" cuisine, "edit" destination. We don't know how the inputting or editing happens, just that it should. It's also important to note that tasks often come with a hierarchy of expression. We could say "get address," or we could say "search in map for location, zoom into map, select location in map for address." Although the latter implies some sort of visual context, both are relatively context independent. These activities could be done on mobile, or at a kiosk, or in a car. But, at this stage, we don't need the detail of the latter expression, we just want some level of indication of the tasks, and the choice of "get address" provides that just fine. In other words, at this stage, a broader description is sufficient and a lot simpler to generate.

The other thing we can avoid at this step is an exhaustive consideration of all aspects of the system. Instead, we focus on the primary use case and any important alternative cases that may serve to deliver on our critical user goals. We don't need to dive down the rabbit hole of taking into consideration every single fringe case or error handling. At least, not yet.

6.2 INTERACTION AS A LANGUAGE

By defining our user's tasks, we are clarifying how they interact with the system. But what are interactions really? They are a means by which users communicate with a system and how the system responds: In essence, interactions can be considered to be a language: A language an audience uses to communicate with a system. User goals and use cases are the stories we want our audience to be engaged in, tasks may be considered the paragraphs used to reveal those goal "stories", and the interactions themselves could be thought of as the sentences used to resolve those task "paragraphs".

But these stories are not movies or novels; they are conversations. Saffer points out that for us to communicate with a digital device, we need some intermediary with which to communicate. And that intermediary is the interface (Saffer, 2010, p. 170). In its most basic form, the system presents an interface to the user, and the user acts on that interface. The system talks to the user by presenting information as well as a set of choices or things to interact with. The user responds by selecting an option or performing an action with those interactive components. The system then responds in turn and presents a new or modified interface for the user to act on again. This simple process is the feedback loop and is like a chat we may be having with a friend where they say something, we respond, and they say something more. One hopes they say something that continues the flow of the conversation, and if they don't, we may get disinterested, walk away, and think twice about conversing with them again.

It's is the same with interactions. If, within the feedback loop, the system responds in a way that is confusing or inappropriate, the user will lose their sense of flow. At best, they may get tripped up and have to think a bit before responding. Systems that do this break what usability expert Steve Krug calls the first rule of usability: "Don't make me think" (Krug, 2014, p. 11). At worst, users get frustrated, leave, and think twice about engaging with the system again. As a designer, we need to know our audience—their context, needs, and wants—in order to understand the interactions with which to provide them to maintain their sense of flow. Keep this in mind as we break down our user tasks and assign them to contexts and postures.

Just as sentences have a grammar, interactions have a grammar as well. Underscoring this, we can effectively describe interactions in an imperative verb/object/result combination such as "input cuisine to get restaurant suggestions" or "search map to get address" (Cooper, 2015, p. 590). Framed in this way, we can consider Interaction Design as the discipline of designing a structured conversation between a digital system and a person or set of people.

But, at this stage, we may not know what the system presents, or we may wish to reserve some ambiguity for creative reasons. "Input cuisine to get restaurant suggestions" may not lock us in too much—there is no definition on how the restaurant suggestions are presented to us—but "search map to get address" may. What if we want to consider a natural language system? We won't be presented with a map, but we still may want to "get address."

For these reasons, we often leave off what the system does and frame tasks as what the user does. For example, to plan a trip, we may want to "review places to visit", "select a place", "compare options in visiting there", "determine travel plans", and "purchase tickets". What the system presents is implied in these imperative directives. Clearly, the system needs to provide the means by which users can select places, compare options, determine plans, and purchase tickets. The imperative language of user tasks is contextually vague, allowing us a framework within which we can explore myriad possibilities. It also makes the effort of performing feature breakdowns into tasks a little easier in that we don't have to worry about the system side. At least, not yet.

Consider your user's goals and the features you think are critical for your system, then break down your system from goals, to features, to tasks. These should resemble the breakdown shown in Figure 6.1 or that in Figure 5.10. Frame tasks in an imperative form, and strive to make them contextually ambiguous.

6.3 POSTURES AND TASKS

With our tasks, we are not only beginning to have an indication of what should happen, but, through being associated with context roles and features, we are considering when they should happen and where. Alternatively, we also have in hand a set of posture studies that indicate the physical reality of our user and the limitations imposed by that reality. What happens when we merge tasks with

Posture Studies

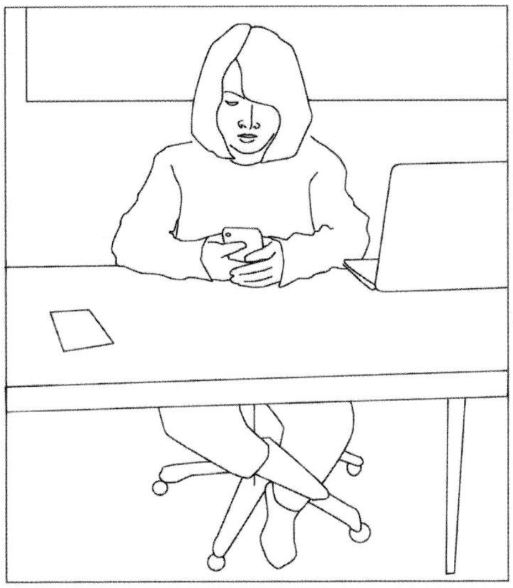

Posture 1

Physical

Cognitive

Recognition

The user is sitting down at a desk in an office space. There are some physical limitation, she is able to reach area within arm length and move slightly left and right with the rolling chair. Space is well lit, everything can be see clearly. It is quiet and there are not much distraction so the user can focus on her tasks.

Posture & Tasks

The user is sitting down to through her contacts to verify, edit, updating her information, and search for contacts. First time user may be setting up her information in this posture.

_ Setting up
_ Updating information
_ Organizing / grouping
_ Adding tags
_ Search by location
_ Search by name
_ Search by event
_ Search by time
_ Search by tags/ keywords
Find recent add
Customize
_ Search nearby / approaching contacts
_ Confirm suggestions
_ Verify information
Block

Posture Studies

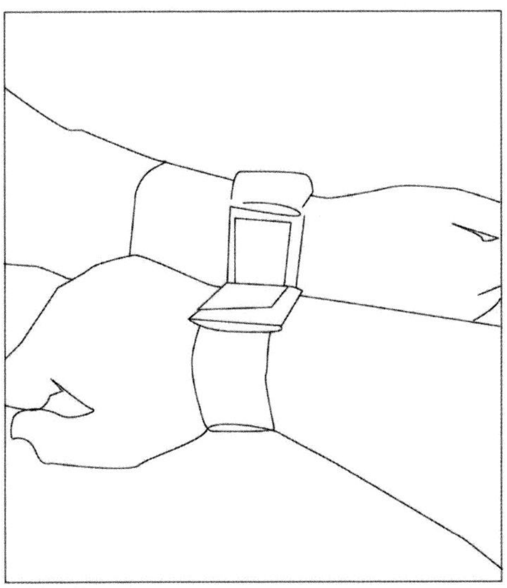

Posture 4

Physical

Cognitive

Recognition

The users exchange contacts by tapping one device with another. The exchange is seamless and can be easily done without interrupting the users' interaction and conversation.

Posture & Tasks

The two users exchange their information by tapping one device with the other.

_ Exchange Contacts

Figure 6.2
Assigning tasks to postures for a work assistant (from Keepintouch. by Amber Wang, used by kind permission of Amber Wang).

posture studies? What kind of contexts or contextual roles do these situations imply? While associating these, recall the agreement principle: The context of the system should agree with the posture of the user. Do the "what", "when," and "where" of the tasks make sense within the dexterity, cognition, or recognition limitations we indicated in our posture studies? Do these agree with the approach we've selected?

To focus our attention on these questions, we add the tasks to our posture studies, and supply a short scenario or magic moment depicting our system's use in that context (Figure 6.2). When we combine both tasks and postures it should become clear whether the task is appropriate and whether we are asking the impossible of them.

Also, be sensitive to overloading a particular context with tasks that may not be necessary. If we're on the go with our mobile device, do we want to analyze reams of statistical data? We may want to save that for a context (such as the web) where the audience can absorb a high resolution presentation of the data and has a quiet moment to reflect on its complexity. Just because we *can* assign a task to a context does not necessarily mean we *should*.

6.4 APPROACH IDEATION

Associating critical tasks with postures provides us with a launch pad for further ideation, developing interface possibilities for these postures. We may find it useful at first to sit in our studio, refer to our tasks and posture studies, and ideate away. This is certainly reasonable for a first stab at things, but our inspiration may quickly dry up. When is does, remember that becoming more empathetic with our user often yields better results. Leave the desk and engage in a little contextual inquiry by transporting yourself into the role of the user.

If the posture we're considering is in the car, take a drive. If it's while the user is working out, go to the gym. If it's not possible to immediately experience their context, then use your imagination, yet be as realistic as you can. Animators, when they are coming up with the action of a scene, often physically act out the scene. This allows their body to feel the movement so that they can draw it better. As designers, we should do the same. Act out the situation. Ask ourselves where and how would be the best solution for interaction. Feel it and sketch it or mock it up (Figure 6.3).

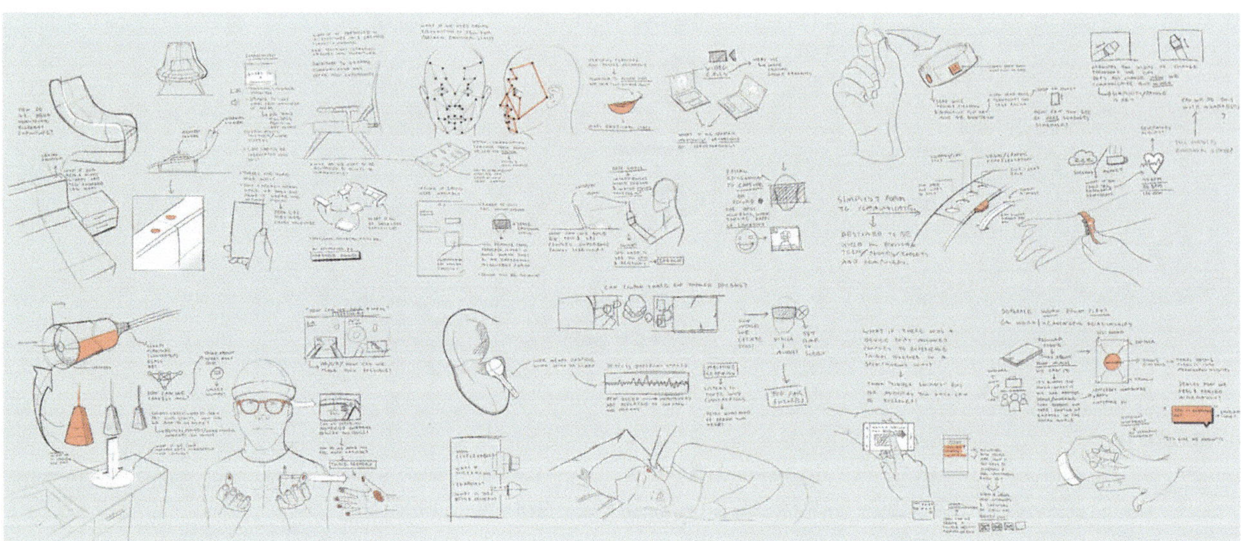

Figure 6.3 Approach ideation for a system helping those in distant relationships (from Sync and Harmony, by Team ABC, used by kind permission of Ofir Atia, Calvin Lien, Serena Jorif, and Alice Yu).

Put together simple physical mock-ups. See if performing the interactions of the tasks intended for a context are effective or annoying, given the posture of the user. We should not only mock up objects, but document our explorations by taking photos as well. These low-fidelity mock-ups, or "prototypes," are "meant to be assembled (and thrown away) quickly: in just enough time to test a concept" (Saffer, 2010, p. 177).

6.5 FINDING INSPIRATION

When we start hitting a wall based on our knowledge or experience, we should further our research. Are there any analogous experiences that can help us better see into our user's situation? If we're trying to develop devices for airline commuters, it's probably beyond our budget to book a flight just for a simple ideation exercise, so think of an analogous situation. Wouldn't it be great if that seat in the plane were similar to our comfy chair? What makes our chair that way? What things do we surround ourselves with that would allow us to sit there for hours? What is similar about our chair and the seat on the plane? What is different? Try to come up with ideas that could improve our flying experience based on these similarities and differences.

Emerging technologies can be another fruitful source of inspiration. What new or novel things do we see appearing on the market that could be useful in the contexts we're considering? We did this before in our research phase, but there's no reason why we can't do this again now that we're looking at things in finer detail.

For example, at the time I'm writing this, there are several excellent websites and apps devoted to cooking, but cooking is inherently a messy task. It's difficult inserting a touch screen or a keyboard into a kitchen context. Natural language systems are more useful, but they suffer from the fact that kitchens are noisy and our user wants to see examples, not hear them. In terms of sheer interaction with the recipe, it would be great to have a butler following us around, telling us what the next step is and showing us what our current stage in the process should look like. This butler is our analog. To mimic this with interactive technology, we could consider having a visual and voice-based hybrid where screens are displayed in easy to view places in our kitchens such as on cabinets or refrigerator doors. How could current developments in digital ubiquity, device sensing, projection, holography, AI, robotics, and possibly screens deployed on micro-drones help us? You can see how the near term and far term game can help you with your ideation here: What would be the ultimate long-term solution? What would be a solution using technology on the market today?

This process is almost the same as when we were initially coming up with our concepts, but, at this point, we're no longer interested in answering the general question "what is it," but "what are some of the best ways of doing it?" It's instructive to revisit not only user empathy, analogs, and technology trends as sources of inspiration, but other idea generating methodologies as well, such as group mind maps drawn on a large sheet of roll paper, or tightly scoped creativity cards. Your observational research should offer many possibilities as well. What things or objects did your subjects enjoy using in the contexts you're considering? Social trends and cultural limitations may reveal approaches that emerging technology cannot, especially in situations where technology is limited.

Become acutely aware of the physical or cognitive aspects of your target and don't shy away from limitations: They're often a rich source of inspiration. If you're designing education solutions based on connected mobile devices and your subjects are having trouble just merely getting water to their home, you probably have to rethink your solutions. If you're designing a smart wayfinding system for an airport, how would you design one for the blind? How would you design one for the deaf? Could it help the lost child who can't even read?

Speaking of children, one of the things I love to consider at this stage, when relevant, is what I call the toddler test. How would your device fare in the hands of toddlers who have no experience of even the most basic ways we engage with objects, who are always trying to put things in their mouths, and who come up with the most ingenious ways of destroying things or harming themselves? If a toddler can use it correctly, anyone can. Also, if your target has a toddler in the house, how could you protect both the child and the device?

Finally, have you been ideating all alone? Start ideating in a group. It's not only fun, but also the improvisational play off others often leads us to results we've never considered. We may even find our creative endurance improved because when one person is fresh out of ideas, another can take over, giving the first a rest and providing them a little critical distance (Figure 6.4).

Figure 6.4
Group Ideation for an activity tracker (from Knoq, by Team Cheeseburger, used by kind permission of James Chu, Chloe Kim, Juno Park, and Yidan Zhang).

6.6 RECONNECT WITH THE BIG PICTURE

Ideating based on postures and tasks is excellent for developing features and functionality. But the process may lead us to lose sight of the big picture: the magic of our idea. Once we've pushed ourselves down the task and posture path for a while, it's instructive to stop and shift gears. Review the magic moments that initially inspired you. Reconsider them and recreate them if they've been modified based on the work we've done up to this point. Reflect on your guidewords. Have you lost your way? Has your design become clinical and devoid of passion? Leave the left brain behind and spend some time ideating from the right: What does your heart say? Eventually, you may be able to discover a synthesis that brings both the analytical task and posture approach and the emotional "magic moment" solutions together.

6.7 GOOD CLIMBING HABITS

A well designed system should make sense at the system level, the context level, quiescent state level, all the way down to how our user engages with elements themselves. When we look at the system or ecosystem level, we are looking at the macro view. The more we consider the details, the more micro. Our system needs to support both these macro and micro views. In case you haven't noticed, over the past few chapters we have been considering the macro aspects of our system first, descending down our system's organizational hierarchy to the micro view. This doesn't mean that starting with the micro and rolling up to the macro view is wrong. In fact, there are certain advantages to that approach: We are then focused on what the user does as the primary driving force and our system is organized around that. Our macro to micro approach is so we don't get lost in the weeds (i.e., details) and work on things that have a likelyhood of being thrown out later.

But is there a way that we can take advantage of both approaches? In essence, that's what we're doing with our scenarios. We may be considering the macro arrangement of our system first, but we are using the detail of cause and effect actions in our scenarios to provide us with a form of checks and balances. If we explore a possibility at the system level that makes no sense when we depict our audience flowing through the use of our interface, we must change it. We characterize this as having good climbing habits: The ability to consider high-level changes and see how they manifest themselves at the level of interactions. We should be able to climb up as well: The ability to see how adjustments made at the micro level changes things at the macro level.

Also critical to good climbing habits is strategic ambiguity: We strive to keep things open and flexible so we can explore modifications at any level of the design. Our features at the system level may be clarified, but we are using context roles and use casting to make sure we've maintained strategic ambiguity at the context level. We've kept the language we've used for our interactions somewhat context independent to maintain strategic ambiguity at the task level as well.

But if we are dealing with a system of even moderate complexity, as we progress from here forward we could be facing a great deal of effort managing large amounts of data that needs to be supported by our system. To keep our effort manageable, our exploratory effort needs to come to a close. We should begin making decisions about the configuration of our system. This is even true for sparse systems. There's a point where we need to put a stake in the ground and commit to an approach so that it can be tested and survive or fail on its merits. Prototyping begins to inject those specifics into our process.

6.8 PROTOTYPING

To aid us in refining the approach to our system, let's look at the concept of mock-ups, or prototypes, more deeply. By definition, a prototype is a model. It simulates something without being that thing (Karjaluoto, 2014, p. 152). Prototypes are used to simulate systems because building them is an expensive endeavor in both treasure and time, and it's a good idea to get aspects of the system correct before it's built in final form.

In Interaction Design, we use prototypes throughout the design process to explore whether our design decisions are correct. Saffer points out that "Aside from the finished product, prototypes are the ultimate expression of the interaction designer's vision" (Saffer, 2010, p. 174). As we start with rough ideas and head into things that are more resolved, our prototypes begin rough and become more resolved as well. This level of refinement is often referred to as the "fidelity" of the prototype. Low fidelity is rough, and high fidelity is much closer to the real thing.

Rough prototypes are sketches in the same way an illustrator or painter may use sketches to explore how to render certain aspects of their image. These should be fast and disposable explorations of the system, intended to be carried out repeatedly, that allow us to consider different possibilities. They should contain more detail in terms of size, shape, and interface than the props we used in our blob scenarios because we are now better informed of our user's external context, but they should still be highly disposable.

We've been creating physical mock-ups, now we need to add interfaces (Figure 6.5). These can be represented by 3 x 5 cards, sticky notes, thick pen drawings on paper, or even stickers to stand in for buttons. At this stage, we should never commit so much energy and effort to a prototype that we become irrationally wedded to it. Everything must be built with the intention that it will be thrown away.

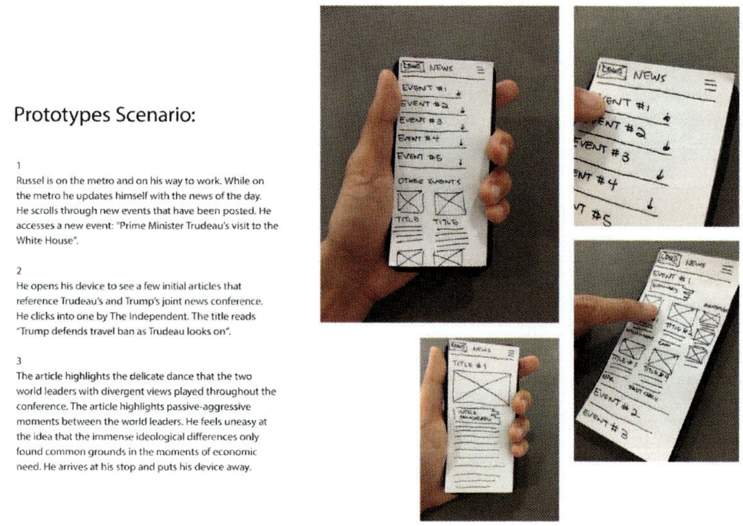

Figure 6.5
Adding a quick interface to a mock-up with 3 x 5 cards and a thick pen (from Sourced, by Jonathan Nishida, used by kind permission of Jonathan Nishida).

Some designers have so much fun building prototypes that they forget the most important reason for their existence: to explore and refine ideas. Build a prototype, simulate its use, determine where the issues are, and build it again. First, we will probably use just ourselves as the subject because things are so sketchy that they may be tough to explain to others. After resolving the prototype to a point where we've eliminated the most glaring problems, we may like to invite a group of designers to give us feedback. This will invariably launch a whole new iteration of sketchy discoveries.

As we march down this process, our prototypes should start becoming more resolved. Our mock-ups should begin to give way to higher fidelity approaches, possibly constructed of foam and more tightly resolved interfaces that are still on paper, yet contain real text and imagery. At this point, our prototypes may still be sketches, but with enough detail to be ready to show to people who are not familiar with the design process and are more typical of our target user. As when we showed our prototypes to our fellow designers, this process will expose another set of glaring issues that neither we nor our design team imagined, thus sparking yet another round of ideation.

6.9 CONNECTING IDEAS INTO SCENARIOS

After we've explored a wealth of possibilities through our sketch prototypes, it's time to consider what's effective and what's not. What are the most critical situations where we think our target will most likely use our system? What type of tasks make sense for each of those situations? What type of interactions work well with the user's postures in those situations to allow them to perform those tasks? What contexts of the system would most appropriately deliver those interactions? And finally, what kind of arrangement of the interface presented by those contexts agrees with the interactions the user is able to perform in those postures?

Begin considering the central challenge of Interaction Design: to design a system so that the interactions we provide our users are the most appropriate for fulfilling their goals in the situation they're in. Which approach is best for solving this question? Which approach is best given our resources?

Some of our ideation will survive this challenge; others will fail. For those that survive, return to your MUSCOW chart and positioning statement. Can our approach address all critical features? Does it agree with the position we claimed would achieve success in the marketplace? If these bases are covered, let's push further to see if we can stitch things together into a well-formulated scenario.

6.10 THE SKETCH SCENARIO

In the previous chapter we role played our user's experience and used that to revise mock-up props and interfaces to refine our blob scenario. Much of that process is still useful in refining our scenario even further. Since we have a better understanding of our ecosystem and the tasks our users need to engage in, our props should be evolving into sketchy objects with a semblance of form containing rudimentary interfaces quickly drafted on paper or sticky notes. These props form the basis of a "sketch" scenario.

Our prototypes, although paper-based and very rudimentary, may begin to present interface components. We will dive much more deeply into this in subsequent chapters, but here we can start addressing general actions and begin considering how well they agree with our postures in scenario form (Figure 6.6). One of the main

Figure 6.6
Sketch prototype scenario, performed and photographed (from Pingo, by Team Hakuna Matata, used by kind permission of Suguru Ogata, Tina Tsung, and Rosalia Hosseinzadeh).

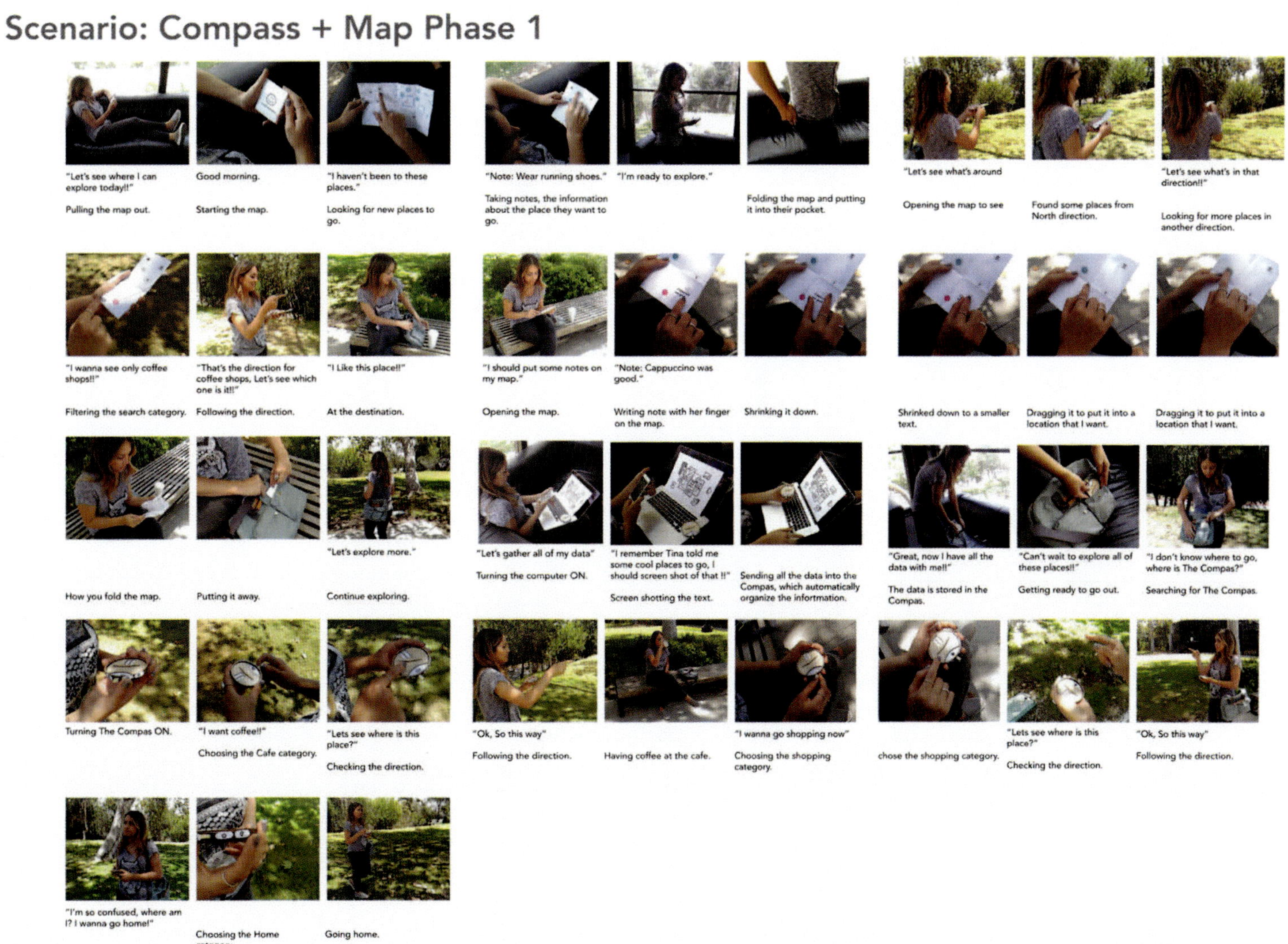

benefits of sketch prototypes and our sketch scenario is that it is much easier to take on the road than the text or blob scenario: We can present it to an uninitiated audience without much additional clarification. This was most likely not true of our blob scenarios.

We can also express the detail of this scenario more rigorously because we are armed with a better understanding of the details of our user's postures and how their wants and needs are manifested into tasks. The "approach" nature of our blob scenarios now give way to more precision. As such, we no longer classify these as approach scenarios steeped in strategic ambiguity, but as sketch scenarios that are beginning to explore the details of interaction and interface.

Either photograph or draw your imagery in storyboard form to effectively deliver the story you wish to tell (Figure 6.7). Regardless of your approach, no longer should we simply photo document our performance, now we should control the communication by using good cinematic language.

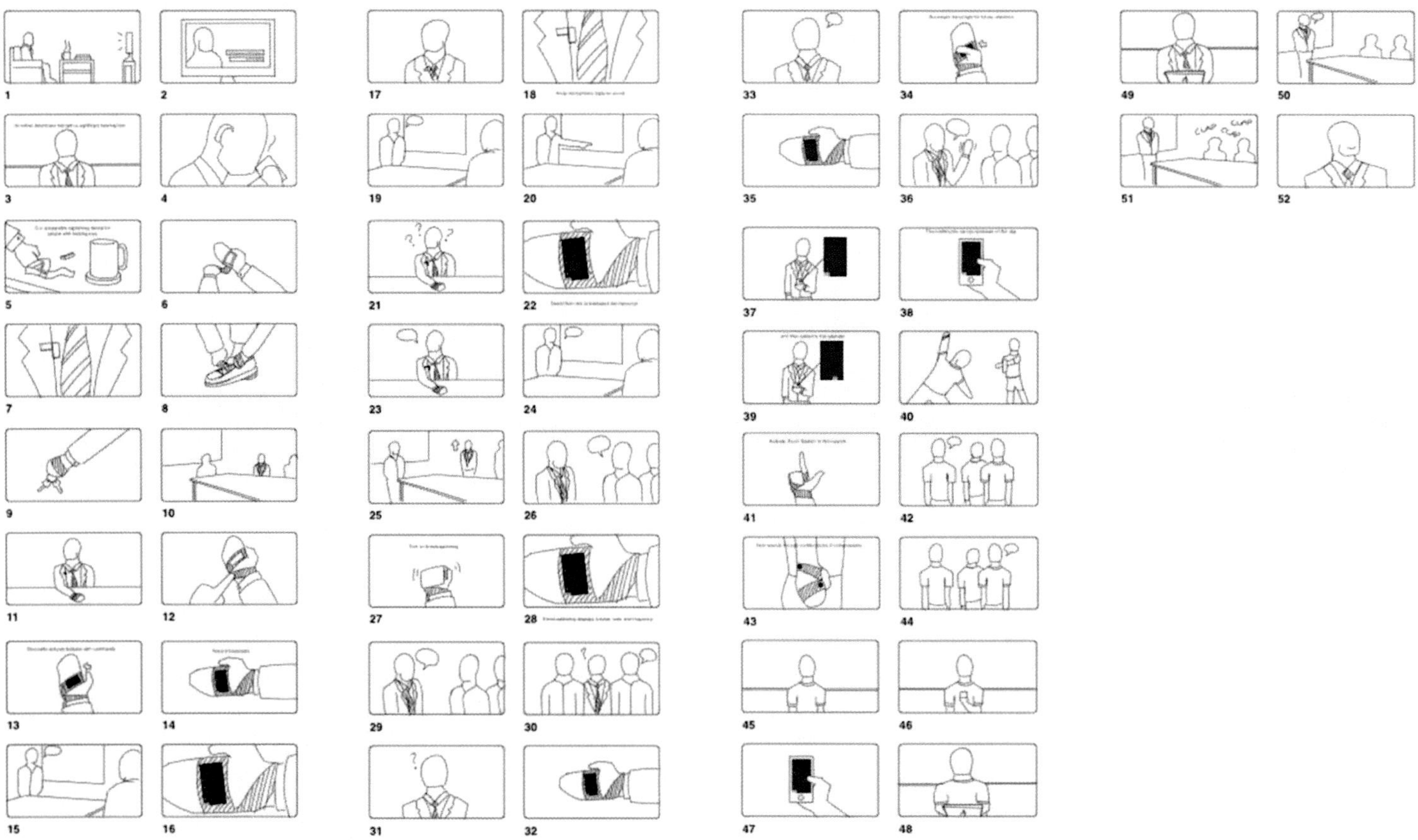

Figure 6.7
Scenario storyboards: Control the communication using cinematics to deliver both external context and details (from Q, by Team Inyerface, used by kind permission of Daniela Cardona, Leah Demeter, Emin Demirci, and Jeff Smith).

To be effective, visual storytelling needs a great deal of nuance. It's important to understand, at least at a very basic level, the language of cinema, such as communicating cause and effect, shot structure, and adherence to the concept of one image, one idea. You don't have to go to film school to be able to do this, but there are a few rules to bear in mind. We've provided a brief outline of the principles of cinematic language for your benefit in the web resources for this book (go to InteractionForDesigners.com, navigate to the Additional Content section, and select on the "Cinematics for Scenarios" link).

If our ability to produce sketch scenarios is limited, the next best thing to do is to play-act the scenario ourselves, and either sketch draw solutions, or use a tripod as the cameraman and photo document ourselves going through the primary use case. This is often much slower than working with a team, but has the added benefit that we can do it at any time: We don't have to arrange the schedules of a bunch of people. Drawing a scenario is not as forgiving as photographing it, since we put a substantial more work into each image, but at least we are limited only by our imagination. Photographic scenarios need a little more willingness to suspend disbelief on the part of our audience.

If we decide to draw, we shouldn't just sit at our table. Mimic the photographic process by acting out the scenario as animators do when they draw a scene. We should use our body to lead to discoveries that we may not have been aware of if we stayed at our desk. It's not uncommon for designers to explore interactions in a personal setting with a tripod before doing it with a larger group. We can even shoot some point of view shots along the way to help guide our illustrations as well.

Regardless of how we execute this, our goal again is to create not just one viable sketch scenario, but a few. Possibly one that is near term, and one that is far. Or one that is economical and another where cost is no object. Or one that is for communities with a great deal of infrastructure, and others that are largely off the grid. By considering extremes, we'll be able to consider a range of possibilities.

Remember, don't boil the ocean: Focus on the primary use case—which means not only focusing on the most engaging features of the approach, but refraining from depicting the onboarding or other alternate cases. By the end of this stage, we should not only have a set of well-documented sketch scenarios, but should have explored many design possibilities along the way.

6.11 INSPIRATION BOARDS

We may have refined our guidewords down to a select few—three to five for example—that accurately reflect the aspirational feelings we want our product to convey. They should avoid clichés and provide a good balance of synergy and tension among themselves. Through our guideword moodboards, we should also have imagery assigned to each guideword that accurately reflects what each word means.

Guideword moodboards may illustrate the feeling we wish to convey but, as a precise design reference, they are not all that useful. For example, we may have chosen the word "sensuous" and selected as one of our images on our moodboard a photo of the undulating curves of a slot canyon. This may certainly visually convey the feeling of sensuality we are striving for, but how does an exquisite photograph of a slot canyon tell us anything about type or layout? Not much. To provide us with better guidance in our design effort, it's often useful to create a second set of boards for each word that uses references more connected to the attributes of the thing we are designing. If we expect to use type, our examples should have type. If we expect to have controls on the surface of our devices, our examples should have these as well.

These boards present images of designs that can serve to inspire us in approaching our project (Figure 6.8). As such, we refer to them as guideword inspiration boards. Certainly, when we are in the trenches of detailed design, these boards may be more useful to us than our moodboards, but both have their roles. In fact, designers who are more experienced often need less explicit references. They can translate feelings into comps quite effectively from not only their guideword moodboards, but also their general moodboard, and even directly from guidewords themselves. However, the explicit examples of our inspiration boards are often critical for those designers who have a little less water under the bridge of experience, but all can benefit from their use.

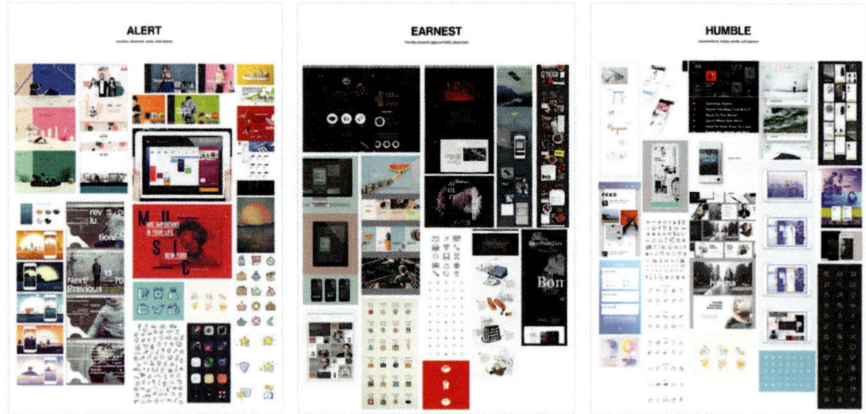

Figure 6.8
Guideword inspiration boards (from The Making, by Hanna Yi, used by kind permission of Hanna Yi).

The process of using guidewords not only can inspire, but can provide a means to test our approaches as well. What approaches in your journal makes the most sense for your persona and their aspirations? What makes sense for our guidewords? Is there one approach that seems to exhibit the greatest association to all our guidewords simultaneously?

6.12 FEEDBACK

This chapter guided us in the refinement and creation of a number of materials that can be used to elicit feedback, from both our design team and potential users alike. Take advantage of this opportunity and take these materials into the field to garner the reaction of different individuals (Figure 6.9). In fact, each stage we take you through in this book is often an opportunity to elicit feedback. We are designing systems that others will use, so it's best to gain insight into what others think. Often, that experience is humbling, and results in substantial changes, but it's better to learn those things earlier rather than later.

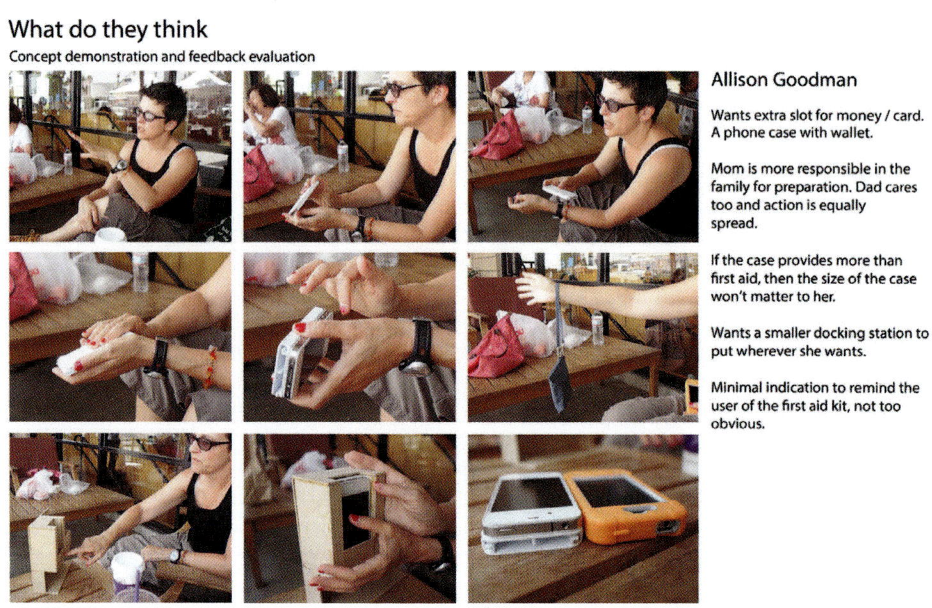

Figure 6.9
User feedback for a digitally enhanced medical kit (from Provision, by Team Provision, used by kind permission of Joey Cheng).

7 Structure

When we observe a building being constructed, we first see the land prepared, then the foundation is laid, the internal structure lofted, the walls go up, and, finally, the interior is arranged. Preparing the land is equivalent to establishing the design strategy for our project: Making sure the conditions are right for our project to be built. Laying the foundation is the approach: creating that substrate on which everything will be built. We are now at the phase where the structure is going up.

The structure of the system is the skeleton on which all the moving parts are supported. It is what is also known as its information architecture. Traditionally, an information architect organizes a system's information so users can find what they are looking for (Morville & Rosenfeld, 2007, p. 8). We've done a great deal of this already by breaking down our goals into features and features into tasks. In this chapter, we will break things down even further, from tasks to the information necessary to complete those tasks, and contemplate ways of organizing that information to deliver on the best user experience possible.

At this point, we should have arrived at a set of tasks that allows our users to achieve their goals and explored interactions in an effort to identify what we need for our interface. In this chapter we continue that process, but look at the information in detail, consider ways of organizing it, and introduce the framework of wireframes and flowboards to aid us in the structuring process.

If you are designing an informationally complex system, the information organization efforts outlined in this chapter will take a great deal of consideration. If, on the other hand, your system is fairly sparse, information organization will be rather straightforward and simple. It may even verge on the non-existent. You need to consider how the content in this chapter applies to your particular challenge. But regardless of the level of complexity of your system, wireframes, flowboards, and paper prototypes are important for all.

Given the tasks we are asking of our audience, what type of content and control do we need to provide so that they can achieve their goal? To answer this, it's useful to begin by ideating ways our information should be structured in terms of an interface (Figure 7.1). We've considered our design at the system and context level through

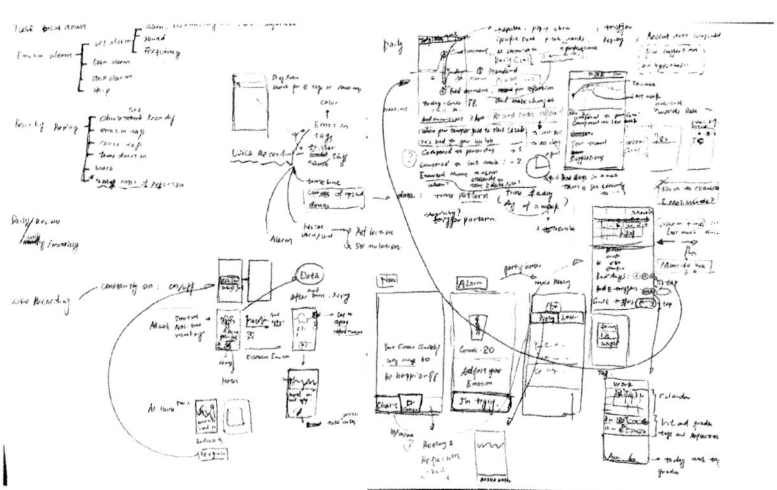

Figure 7.1
Exploring information and interface structure (from Odmo, by Hui Ye, used by kind permission of Hui Ye).

feature and task breakdowns, now we shall prepare ourselves to be able to consider approaches to the interface at the quiescent state level by conducting an information breakdown.

7.1 TASKS TO INFORMATION

As an example of an information breakdown, let's return to our restaurant app that we introduced in the beginning of the last chapter. For John to achieve the goal of finding a restaurant where he'd like to eat, our system could provide a list of restaurants near him. In turn, he would need to engage in the task of identifying the restaurant of his choice. But we may not have provided enough information for him to make that decision. What information does he need?

The type of cuisine our user wants may be useful as well as a menu with prices and pictures of the food. What else? Think of when you're wandering a street and looking for a restaurant. What is useful? For myself, a good indicator is if there are people there. This can be translated into something that indicates its popularity, such as a rating if people like it or that it is "hot", whatever that means.

Where the restaurant is and how close it is to me are also important factors. Its name and possibly what it looks like from the street so John can find it; a route to it may also be useful when he's finally chosen to go there. It could be assumed he may want to explore and compare several restaurants before making a final selection. There should be an easy way to select those he likes from a list and be able to compare them side by side.

The above analysis provides us with a collection of information that John needs in order to fulfill his goal of selecting a restaurant. How we derived that information is that we started with the user's goal: Find a restaurant near John where he'd like to eat. We identified features our system needs to provide, such as a list of restaurants near him. Given that feature, we reflected on the tasks we expect John to perform to select a desired restaurant, and indicated the information needed to complete that task: Cuisine, the restaurant's popularity, its proximity, et cetera.

Through a series of breakdowns—user goals, system features, user tasks, and the system's information—we arrive at the things we need to design: The feature breakdown derives features from user goals. The task breakdown derives tasks from those features given what the user wants to do. And now, the information breakdown derives the specific bits of content and control needed to achieve those goals. From this, we can begin to design our interfaces. We should perform an information breakdown for each context in our system.

Given a particualr context, how should its content and control best be organized? This will be laid out in this chapter in detail, but you may have some ideas already. Use your journal to sketch them out in an interface as in Figure 7.1. Play around with the organization: For example, do we show all that information for the possible restaurants all at once, or do we have a brief selection list with just essential information first, and allow the user to drill down into more detail by selecting on an item in that list? By performing these activities, we are now considering how our information is to be structured.

7.2 INFORMATION TAXONOMIES

In the previous chapter we found that considering tasks generates an interaction language for our system. In the development of this language, we may begin to see a few common patterns or structures appear. For example, above we had the task directive "Input cuisine to get restaurant suggestions". In this case, we begin to see that the concept of "cuisine" and list of "restaurant suggestions" are emerging as structures that will need to be addressed in the design. What are the relationships between these? Certainly, we will need to collect restaurants which will have several things associated with them, such as their name, their location, and *their cuisine*. Hence, the data object "restaurants" will most likely contain the information "type of cuisine".

Notice we are creating a hierarchical relationship of items: Restaurants are the category and cuisine is the subcategory. Our breakdown process, going from high-level user goals down to low-level content and control, usually leads to such a hierarchical structuring. This effort builds an information "taxonomy" of our system: A well-defined set of categories with a clear and often hierarchical relationship to each other. The naming of these categories such as the term "restaurant" and "cuisine" and their hierarchical relationship, is a taxonomy in the same way that science has divided all living things into kingdoms, classes, and species (Morville & Rosenfeld, 2007, p. 69). Mammals are a category, and humans are a subcategory of mammal (although they have several layers of classifications between them).

As we define and clarify the structure of the information needed in our system, we should be teasing out these organizing objects, naming them, and considering the structural relationship between them. Are they related or are they independent of each other? If they're related, how so? Is there a form of parent–child relationship between them, or are they more like siblings? This is precisely the same activity we engaged in when we assessed the data-centric approach to our system. That process resulted in hierarchies of features, and this results in hierarchies of information. Hierarchies are extremely common and useful, but there are other structures as well. We will discuss these structures shortly, but, for now, create a preliminary taxonomy of the required objects in your system and express them in a form such as that shown in Figure 7.2. Notice the similarity of structure between this and Figure 6.1. They're the same thing, just Figure 7.2 has taken the structure down to the level of the informational elements, the content and control, while 6.1 just left us at the level of tasks.

- Play
  - Playlists (Library of media files)
    - Select song
      - Edit media
        - Delete
        - Cut
        - Copy
        - Paste
        - Splice
        - Undo
        - Smooth out a glitch
      - Review sounds
        - Review button
        - Review files on one screen and replay
      - Save media
        - Name media
    - Create media
      - Display notes
        - Display keyboard
      - Select notes
        - Visual feedback of selected media
      - Edit media
        - Delete
        - Cut
        - Copy
        - Paste
        - Splice
        - Undo
        - Smooth out a glitch
        - Organize sounds
          - Sequence sounds/Layer sounds
          - Display a window that allows for the user to make individual folders to display separate files
          - Layer window will allow for grouping sounds together
      - Review sounds
        - Review button
        - Review files on one screen and replay
      - Save media
        - Name media
- Capture media
  - Record
    - Display record button
    - Start recorder
    - Display button recessed
    - Button changes color to red
    - Stop recorder
    - Display button popped out
    - Red color turns off
  - Edit media
    - Delete
    - Cut
    - Copy
    - Paste
    - Splice
    - Undo
    - Smooth out a glitch
    - Organize sounds
      - Sequence sounds/Layer sounds
      - Display a window that allows for the user to make individual folders to display separate files
      - Layer window will allow for grouping sounds together
    - Review sounds
      - Review button
      - Review files on one screen and replay
    - Save media
      - Name media
  - Adjust Volume
    - Adjust speakers
      - Volume up and down
        - Volume button
        - Mute
      - Sound balance
        - Visual indicate of left and right speakers
        - Adjust with scroll window
        - Mute
      - Mute
        - Mute button
  - Review media
    - Fast forward
      - Fast forward button
    - Rewind
      - Rewind button
    - Pause
      - Pause button
    - Repeat
      - Repeat button
      - Repeat one
      - Repeat all

Figure 7.2
Outlining the structure of information (from Puppymate, by Nairi Khachikian, used by kind permission of Nairi Khachikian).

7.3 LABELING

When we break down a system into its component parts and begin organizing, we need to develop labels for the groupings within our taxonomy. This is not some mundane effort that has little meaning in our final product. Quite the contrary: The concise, clear, and accurate naming of taxonomic groupings directly affects the usability of our system. Many of the labels we place on the organization of our information will stay with that information throughout the design process and have a high probability of becoming menu titles or page names.

Consider, for example, we determine that there needs to be information such as a business phone number, address, and email. In our structure design process, we could label these items "Business Information." Then, with that title, we start adding other stuff such as when the business was founded, who founded it, what type of work it does, etc. This all seems to make sense when we organize it, but we did so based on the label we chose: "business information".

But what if we originally choose that initial information because we wanted people to be able to contact our business? It's been grouped with, and most likely buried with, a bunch of stuff we didn't want—our business story—and didn't associate with the goal of that information in the first place, just because of a poorly considered label. Now, if we called it "Contact Us", it would gather the information that served the goal for the user. The point is, take care with labels. Make them clear, concise, and accurate in terms of what they mean for your user. Have them relate to your user's goals.

7.4 CARD SORTING

Are we using the right organization? Are we using the correct labels for our groupings in that organization and would our users group these features under these labels? These are questions that can cause us a great deal of concern for an information architect, especially if the design's effectiveness is measured by click-throughs.

Fortunately, we often don't have to guess. We can test our labels with our audience. A powerful means of doing this is with a technique called card sorting. Place the information of your system on a series of cards and ask a user to arrange them in the way they think makes the most sense. Have them indicate what's important and what's less so. Then ask them how they would label those groupings.

To do this correctly, we need a decent sample size of people so that we know those things that are shared, and those that are anecdotal. Select about five to ten people and see how they sort your cards, arrange them, and label them. If a common organization emerges, and especially if a common labeling system emerges, we can have a great deal of confidence that's the way a large portion of our users will see things. Card sorting can do a great deal of organizational work for us.

7.5 BEYOND HIERARCHIES

Going from high-level goals to low-level content and control may lead to a hierarchy, but that may not be the best way to structure our system. Consider this: You have a problem with your phone bill and you want to discuss it with the phone company. You call them and the voice menu system gives you five options to choose from. You select one, and it gives you another five to narrow your selections. You continue to do this to about seven levels, only to find that their way of hierarchically organizing their information is not your way, and the final selections you're presented with have nothing to do with what you want. You've wasted about five minutes of your life on navigating a hierarchical system with no result, and you're frustrated. Welcome to hierarchical phone menus.

What would you really want? You'd want to dial the phone number and have them magically determine that you had a problem with your phone bill and be able to discuss it with you right then and there. That's essentially a knowledgeable service representative: The system we had up to the mid 1990s. This exemplifies issues that we will address in the next chapter when we discuss some of the principles we need to consider in Interaction Design, but suffice it to say here that although a hierarchy may be the most natural result of a top-down breakdown process, it may not be the best arrangement of our system.

Challenge yourself to look beyond a hierarchical organization and towards the raw information itself. Look at how the audience uses the system and provide them with exactly what they need when they need it. What happens when we organize things by task instead of a hierarchy? How about by user or audience? Can we think of a metaphor that can lend itself as a guiding principle for organizing our system? Most likely the best result is a hybrid of many of these, and we need to explore them all to see what aspects of our system fit which organizational principles most naturally (Cooper, 2015, pp. 63–68). By "natural," we mean how should our information be organized such that it can be easily found and absorbed by our users. Saffer uses the term "functional cartography" to refer to the concept of determining where functions should live (Saffer, 2010, p. 141). And this is not only true of functions, but of all elements of a system's content as well. What is our system's cartography? To determine this, it's useful to have an understanding of some common concepts of structuring information.

7.6 OVERVIEW OF INFORMATION STRUCTURES

Information has some basic structural concepts that help us in its organization. The most basic item in a structured information system is the element. Elements can be anything—animals, paint chips, stars in the night sky—but the elements we are interested in are those of our system: elements of content and control. A collection of elements is a set. A linearly ordered set where one and only one element follows another is a list. There are a few classic ways of organizing lists: by number, alphabet, time, and category. Category is kind of a catch-all for other ways of ordering things, such as by color or classification. These are sometimes called the "five hat racks" (Lidwell, Holden, & Butler, 2010, p. 100) and if you notice, we have only four. The other classic way of ordering elements of information is by location. Location is clearly not a list in that it maps to a two-dimensional surface on the earth, or a point in a three-dimensional volume of space.

There are other structures that have elements following one after the other, though, and those are sequences, cycles, and spirals. Sequences are things like slideshows with a beginning and an end, cycles are lists where the end connects to the beginning, such as a carousel, and spirals seem odd, but in fact are very common. Our calendar that flows linearly from day to day, but every seven days cycles around to the start of the week again, is an example of this.

Moving on from the list type object are those where elements are connected to other elements not one after the other, but one can be connected to many. A hierarchy is one such schema. In a classic hierarchy, each child element has only one parent, yet each parent can have multiple children. Hierarchies are powerful in the way they allow us to organize vast amounts of information. For example, your file system has hundreds of thousands of files. It would be next to impossible to find a file in that set if it were a linearly organized list. However, our file system is organized as a hierarchy, and, as such, we can usually find any file within seconds.

Polyhierarchies are similar to hierarchies, yet there is the possibility of getting to an element through more than one path. These are like having aliases in your file system.

Hierarchies are powerful, yet problematic. They hide information. If you don't know the categories, you're pretty much out of luck in being able to find things. Most organizational schemas have positives and negatives about them that make them appropriate or inappropriate for a particular task. Hierarchies are no different.

The most general schema is the web. In fact, lists and hierarchies are simplified versions of webs. Webs are elements that have more than one other element connected to them. They don't have the parent–child relationship with them, as do hierarchies, but are considered "flat" in the sense that every element is neither more nor less important than another. The most ubiquitous example of a web structure is simply the World Wide Web. Websites connected to other websites through links.

The final form of organization that is useful to consider are faceted structures. They are essentially a flat set of information where all the connections between elements are gone, and in their place are facets, or what we better know as tags or metadata. This is where searches or search results come in handy. If elements have tags, they may have no structure, but we can build a structure in any way we want through searches that organize the elements through tags.

This was a very brief overview of some very basic organizational structures in information theory. For a more in-depth description of these structures, please visit the web resource (go to InteractionForDesigners.com, navigate to the Additional Content section, and select the "Information Structures" link).

7.7 EXPLORING STRUCTURE

I usually ask my designers to go through various organizational structures and consider what a particular set of information would look like if it were organized, say, in a hierarchy, or ordered as an alphabetized or numerical list. Is it best presented spatially or temporally? Should it be cyclical? Does location have any relevance to the data? If so, how would that look? What categories are natural for our data? Would our audience be able to understand those categories implicitly? What would a polyhierarchy look like in the interface and is that useful? How about a faceted structure of tags? This is the time to ask these questions so that we can develop the correct set of structures for our system.

As mentioned earlier, describing the complete architecture of a complex information system is a daunting task. There could be hundreds, if not thousands, of elements that need to be considered. Any tool we use for this task needs to be able to organize items into hierarchies, nodes, sets, and lists, and sometimes be able to draw associations to other elements that may be outside any hierarchical structure. Information structuring tools are good for this, such as that which we used in Figure 6.1, or as just our run of the mill sticky note wall (Figure 7.3).

Figure 7.3
Working with a sticky note wall (from Knoq, by Team Cheeseburger, used by kind permission of James Chu, Chloe Kim, Juno Park, and Yidan Zhang).

To manage the information explosion, we may not have to go all the way down to the element level, but stay at the level of sets of information. For example, the components of a news article may contain the elements of a header, a sub-head, an image or two, body text, and possibly a list of associated comments. But if this structure is valid consistently, and each of these individual items has no relationship with other items in our system, we can effectively encapsulate this structure with an item called merely "article". This may not give us the complete picture, but may make our daunting task more manageable.

As we explore how our information can be grouped, we should keep in mind a few general types of organizational structures and approaches: sets, lists, organizational schemas (the five hat racks), sequences, cycles, spirals, hierarchies, polyhierarchies, nodes, webs, and faceted structures. Consider these structures and ideate information organization approaches in your journal.

7.8 NAVIGATION DESIGN

The more complex the system, the harder it is for users to navigate to elements within it. The perfect system would be one that had no navigation: It would know what the user wanted and provide it to them immediately. This is what I call the "genie in the bottle" solution: We rub the bottle, the genie appears and gives us exactly what we want. We don't even have to ask for it.

You want a book? No problem. The Amazon genie knows precisely the book you want, what you want to pay for it, and how you want it delivered. Bang! There it is on your doorstep. You want to fix something? Shizam! The YouTube genie knows precisely what you want to fix and it shows you a video on how to fix it. You want a date? Your eHarmony genie knows who you want, and poof! they appear at your door, with flowers. With a genie in a bottle we don't need navigation any more because the genie is there, and the genie reads our mind.

This is, of course, ridiculous to an extreme, but it highlights the necessity of having to muck around an interface to find things: the act of navigating the system. In the perfect interface, navigation doesn't exist, but in the real world it must, because reality has limitations: screen sizes, devices, and an imperfect knowledge of you and your wants. We have navigation because of these limitations. We could say the same thing about design—that it exists because of limitations—but that's another book.

Consider this: In complex information systems, most of what we design is navigation. This not only includes the menu bar on a website or a pull down on our desktop screen, but it also includes our file systems, home screens, how we scroll through lists and other content, the Google search field, even how we arrange content into sections and subsections on an interface. All these allow us to navigate that content better.

Browsing and searching are mostly navigation behaviors, while manipulation and consumption are not. We browse or search so that we can get to the things we want to manipulate or consume. Since search is commonly just an input field or a question we pose to a natural language system, it's those patterns we use for browsing that are the ones we associate most directly with navigation, such as the top menu, pulldown menu, and links. It is the act of browsing content and control that we should strive to make as simple, direct, and usable as possible.

Navigation is necessary, but interacting with navigation is most likely not the thing our users came to our system to do. When we design navigation, we should keep this in the forefront of our minds: It is quite literally the means to the end, not the end itself. Because of this, navigation should usually be as direct and straightforward as possible while still being effective. The caveat to this is if our users came to our system to browse; to window shop. If that's the case, then certainly consider flowing through possibilities as the end itself. But, even in this situation, the navigation flow should be made easy and simple.

Although most of the time we should strive for navigation that is easy and simple, unique signature interactions do have their place even in navigation—as we will come to understand later—yet, for the most part, those who design navigation shouldn't be in the business of making a statement with their design as much as striving to design themselves out of a job. We want to have navigation be as usable as possible, so our users don't have to struggle with it very much. This is why design patterns are so pervasive in navigation design.

7.9 DESIGN PATTERNS AND NAVIGATION

Design patterns are arrangements of designed artifacts that are commonly shared. Because they are shared, they allow users to apply what they already know so they don't have to relearn the interaction. But the pattern needs to fit the information being interacted with—in this case navigated—and there's always the case of a paradigm shift where the shared means of navigating may not be as efficient as one we may come up with. So, by all means ideate and explore navigation possibilities, but if you don't arrive at something just as good or better than what currently exists, be careful about implementing it just because it's different. If you make things harder, your audience will hate you.

Although the effective use of design patterns is an essential element in good navigation design, we have made a conscious decision in this book to avoid discussing design patterns. We would need another hundred or more pages or an entirely new book to have addressed patterns with any level of respectability, so we've decided to encourage the reader to reference other sources. Several authors have made valiant attempts at the topic in print (Cooper, 2015, chapters 18–21; Neil, 2014; Tidwell, 2006), yet we are of the opinion that since patterns are continually being introduced, revised, and updated, it's a better topic for media that is more dynamic. However, these books provide a solid basic understanding of fundamental patterns, and, together with the wealth of internet resources that present design patterns (UI Patterns, 2017; van Welie, 2017), we feel the topic is well covered in other literature.

Consider your structure map and how you envision your users navigating it. It's a good approach to ideate a few possibilities on your own before exploring traditional patterns. Then, familiarize yourself with patterns that you feel may be useful and ideate possibilities anew. These ideations will become useful when we consider wireframes, next.

7.10 WIREFRAMES

Let's return to the structure map that we created when considering features, and may have updated when we broke down those features into tasks (see Figure 5.8). Make sure it's updated with your current organizational approach, and then let's climb down the information hierarchy to the bottom, to the micro view. At this level are the elements our user sees on an interface. Roughly how should this look? How much information can the display limitations of our interface handle? How much information can our users absorb before they reach cognitive overload (Johnson, 2010, p. 83)? What should be the general structure of that information so that it is as comprehensible as possible? These questions are handled by the wireframe.

Wireframes are the skeletal manifestation of the information we think should be displayed in a given quiescent state. They are schematics that show the structure, information hierarchy, controls, and content of an interface, and are arguably "the most important document that interaction designers produce" (Saffer, 2010, p. 151). At our current level of fidelity, these are rendered as interface sketches intended to be created quickly to explore different organizational possibilities. They are not designed in an aesthetic sense, but reflect how the elements should be organized in an information design sense (Van Dijck, 2003, p. 144).

In fact, wireframes that are more aesthetically pleasing may pose problems: When a pretty wireframe is presented to a client, their critique may veer away from questions of information organization toward issues that we have no intention of addressing at this stage, such as whether our client likes a particular typeface or hates the color green. Because of this we often impose limitations on wireframes so they remain sketchy. For example, we may restrict them so that they use only black or white; they use only a certain standard well-structured typeface, like Helvetica or Univers; we can only use a Sharpie on a 3 x 5 card to make them; or images should only be represented as a box with an "x" through it. Whatever the collection of limiting features we impose, the role of the wireframe is to present the information we intend to include on a screen or quiescent state, and, through position and scale, indicate things such as how important something is and what other elements it should be associated with (Morville & Rosenfeld, 2007, p. 307). That's it.

Wireframes are a construct born from screen design. Designers that have projects where no screen is involved often feel left out when wireframes are discussed. This should not be the case. If you are focusing on the interactive aspects of a system that are mainly or entirely physical, when we use the term "wireframe" in this book, interpret it to mean "mock-up".

Wireframes come in an assortment of levels of fidelity. Low-fidelity wireframes, or lo-fi wireframes, are very rough. Often these are drawn on paper such as 3 x 5 cards, with lines representing text and boxes representing images. At the other end of the spectrum, high-fidelity—or hi-fi—wireframes contain all the information we'd expect our quiescent state to present (Figure 7.4). We create these on the computer using real pictures that contain images we'd expect to see there, real headings, sub-heads, and dates. We greek the paragraphs using *lorem ipsum*.

Figure 7.4
High-fidelity wireframes (from Odmo, by Hui Ye, used by kind permission of Hui Ye).

When we say "high-fidelity wireframes" or "low-fidelity wireframes", the physical product designer should interpret this to be "high-fidelity mock-ups" or "low-fidelity mock-ups". When we instruct the screen interface designer to use 3 x 5 cards or lines to represent text, the physical product designer should interpret these to be rough mock-ups that consider scale, functionality, and use, but where the detail form is absent.

Wireframes exist because it's not only inefficient to visually design every screen in detail during the structuring process, but it's also psychologically problematic: It's harder to let go of a design if a great deal of effort has been placed into it. We shouldn't be pouring our screens in visual concrete until the structural work is done. Allow wireframes to have the detail they need to bring important issues to light, but don't be so detailed as to bog down the exploratory process. Consider a wealth of possibilities through iteration, keep the good stuff, throw out the bad, until the information of the system comes into focus.

Let's return to breaking down our information, but now let's consider our interfaces: The displays or presentations our user experiences directly. What information should appear where? What content and control does our user need to achieve their goals? When do they need it? In other words what does our user need to execute their tasks, and when is it needed? We've found that organizing and reorganizing a sticky note wall is particularly effective for exploring and developing solutions to these questions, then resolve them into a structure map and a set of low-fi wireframes.

7.11 CONSIDER THE PRIMARY USE CASE

To aid us in considering the structure of our system's interfaces, let's return to our primary use case scenario and revisit how our user flows through the structure of the system. What tasks are they required to provide at each step? What content and control do we need for those tasks? What does this say about the elements that appear on each of our quiescent states?

Recall that the primary use case is that which demonstrates the most salient features of our system. It is that use case that is being employed when the system has all the information it needs, and the user is reasonably comfortable with it: the happy path. We consider the intermediate user here, not the novice or the expert. The primary use case should handle the lion's share of our user base when everything is up and running as expected.

What contexts does your user flow through in order to achieve their goals? We may have entered this project with the mindset that we were designing a mobile app. But is a mobile app really appropriate for all the postures our user goes through? Rather than focusing on one single context exclusively, we promote the approach of looking at all critical contexts from the beginning so we can consider how they are orchestrated together right at the outset. Our primary use case should flow into and out of all these contexts within the ecosystem. As such, we call this the "systemic" primary use case.

Yet, all systems have a primary context. What is yours? If you think your audience will be primarily mobile based, you should make your mobile flow the hero of your systemic primary use case. If it's the web, or a voice-based system, that should be the hero. Don't avoid the other contexts, but prioritize the consideration for the hero.

We suggest designing and testing the primary use case before considering alternate or less critical cases. Remember, the primary case should directly reflect the success goals of the system that we spent a great deal of time and effort formulating in the research phase. If our system doesn't achieve these, our design will probably be unsuccessful. It's critical that our primary case works.

7.12 WIREFRAME INTERFACE EXPLORATION

How should we group the information on our screens? We may have explored some of these possibilities in our journal ideation, but now, with our architecture in hand, we have a much better idea of the kinds of quiescent states a particular context may need, and the structure of the information within each quiescent state contained in that context. Let's ideate these possibilities further (Figure 7.5).

Figure 7.5
Wireframe ideation (from Artbug, by Radhika Kashyap, used by kind permission of Radhika Kashyap).

As we have a much better understanding of the role each context plays, we also can begin to make more accurate choices about whether an interactive component should be presented virtually or physically (Figure 7.6). And we can start to explore the ways components and data can be shown to ensure better comprehension (Figure 7.7). As we ideate in our journal, we begin to gravitate to certain structures that seem to make sense. When this starts happening, it's time to transition to formal wireframing methods.

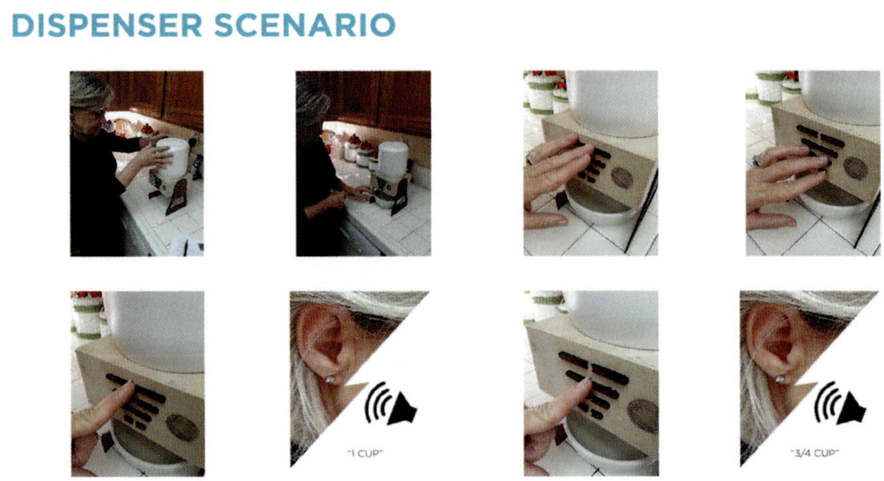

Figure 7.6
Considering physical interactions (from Culina Metra, by Team Culina Metra, used by kind permission of Katrina Hercules and Neal Smith).

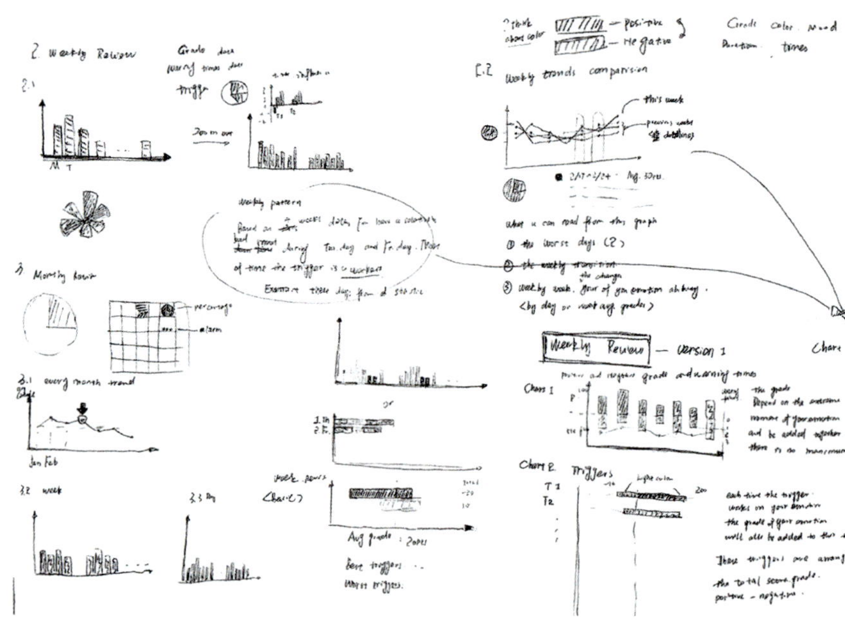

Figure 7.7
Ideating data visualization (from Odmo, by Hui Ye, used by kind permission of Hui Ye).

7.13 LO-FI WIREFRAMES

At this point we may have a strong desire to jump over to our computer and begin detailing our interface. Slow down. We are going to be doing this a lot, so there is no rush. Your favorite computer drawing tool has tons of capabilities to control the precise visual design of your interface, and we often see our designers get seduced into "noodling" their wireframes—obsessing about insignificant details—their first time out of the gate. Stay off the computer. Draw them instead (Figure 7.8).

Figure 7.8
Roughing out a lo-fi wireframe flowboard (from Keepintouch, by Amber Wang, used by kind permission of Amber Wang).

It's useful to use pieces of paper or index cards to build our interface at this point: They can be moved around, removed, or added to with relative ease. In this way, we can begin translating our information design into a sketch version of our interface to get a feel for how it will work. Use your structure map as a guide to begin laying out your wireframes in a manner that reflects how users would flow through the system. Think about how they go through each screen, given the primary use case. Does it work? Especially, does the structure map make sense? Can it be improved? Can it be made more efficient, clearer?

7.14 TEST THE WIREFRAME FLOW

With lo-fi wireframes, we begin to experience a sketch version of our interface. If we have arrived at an organization of our information on a sticky note wall or a table, before we move on, we need to photograph or otherwise document our arrangement. Integrate the information into lo-fi wireframe sketches, and use the wireframes to experience the interface.

We strive for as much verisimilitude as possible by placing our wireframes on the devices where they will be used. We stick them on cell phones, computer screens, or tablets. If the device is not available to us, or we have yet to design its physical structure, we can refer to our posture studies, build sketchy physical mock-ups of

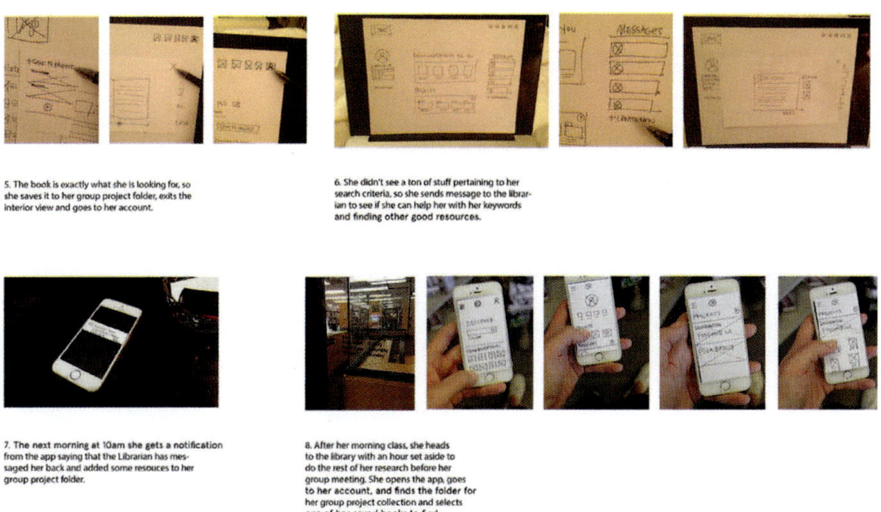

Figure 7.9
Experiencing the primary use case using paper prototypes (from Stacks, by Mary Louise McGraw, used by kind permission of Mary Louise McGraw).

them and place our interface on them (Saffer, 2010, p. 146). We can also place our sketch interfaces on devices themselves (Figure 7.9).

To test if our interface is working, become the user. This is where our target persona comes in handy. Absorb the essence of that person with all their attributes and concerns. What are their goals? What are they doing physically? Where are they? What are their distractions? We need to place ourselves in their situation. If they're a kid, become a kid again. If they have problems seeing, we need to squint our eyes. If they're in their kitchen, go to the kitchen. Don't just do these things in your mind, actually do them. The physical experience allows us to discover things we would not necessarily uncover if we just did this mentally. And, in addition, it's fun.

Experience the interface using your primary use case as the guide. Focus on the hero context, yet also strive to experience every context in the ecosystem. The goal of this process is to leverage empathy and focus on making the system as efficient, engaging, understandable, and usable as possible.

7.15 REVISE

After a round of testing, how did the design hold up? Chances are it didn't do very well. In fact, I'd say that if you think everything worked great, you're probably deluding yourself. Become very self-critical and sensitive to every bump and seam you run into. Worry about friction. Can we get rid of a click or a swipe? No inefficiency is too small to contemplate smoothing out. Removing a single superfluous step in a task is often the difference between users choosing one system over another.

Get accustomed to throwing away wireframes and re-doing them. That's why we're using lo-fi wireframes in the first place. Also get accustomed to photo documenting: we may arrive at a solution early in our process that we may want to come back to. Photos will help us remember those, as well as providing a more objective means of considering the effectiveness of various iterations of our interface later.

7.16 MAGIC MOMENTS REVISITED

As we dig deep into the structure of the interface details, we should also employ good climbing habits: As part of the interface exploration process, it's useful to re-address our magic moments to ensure that we haven't lost sight of that "magic" that we originally wanted to deliver. Our magic moments allowed us to clarify our user goals that differentiate our product in the marketplace. When we're digging in the details with our wireframes, it's good to keep our magic moments in mind. Are we doing what we set out to do?

7.17 THE WIREFRAME FLOWBOARD

We've been using our structure map to illustrate the structure of our system and wireframes to express the information on our interfaces. But there is a presentation framework that integrates both: The wireframe flowboard, which is essentially a structure map with the nodes replaced by wireframes.

A flowboard is so named because it is a combination of two things: A *flow* diagram which indicates the main ways users can flow through the quiescent states of the system, and a presentation *board* of the quiescent states themselves. We connect quiescent states to those we can navigate to from that state with lines. Keep in mind that the flowboard presents the main structure of the context, so not every state to state link is depicted, simply the major ones that are often reflected in menus, sub-menus, and content detail links. The board is usually expressed as a hierarchy and we usually have one flowboard per context. If there is only one context in the system (for example, there is only an app), there is usually only one flowboard. If we have multiple contexts, we have multiple flowboards.

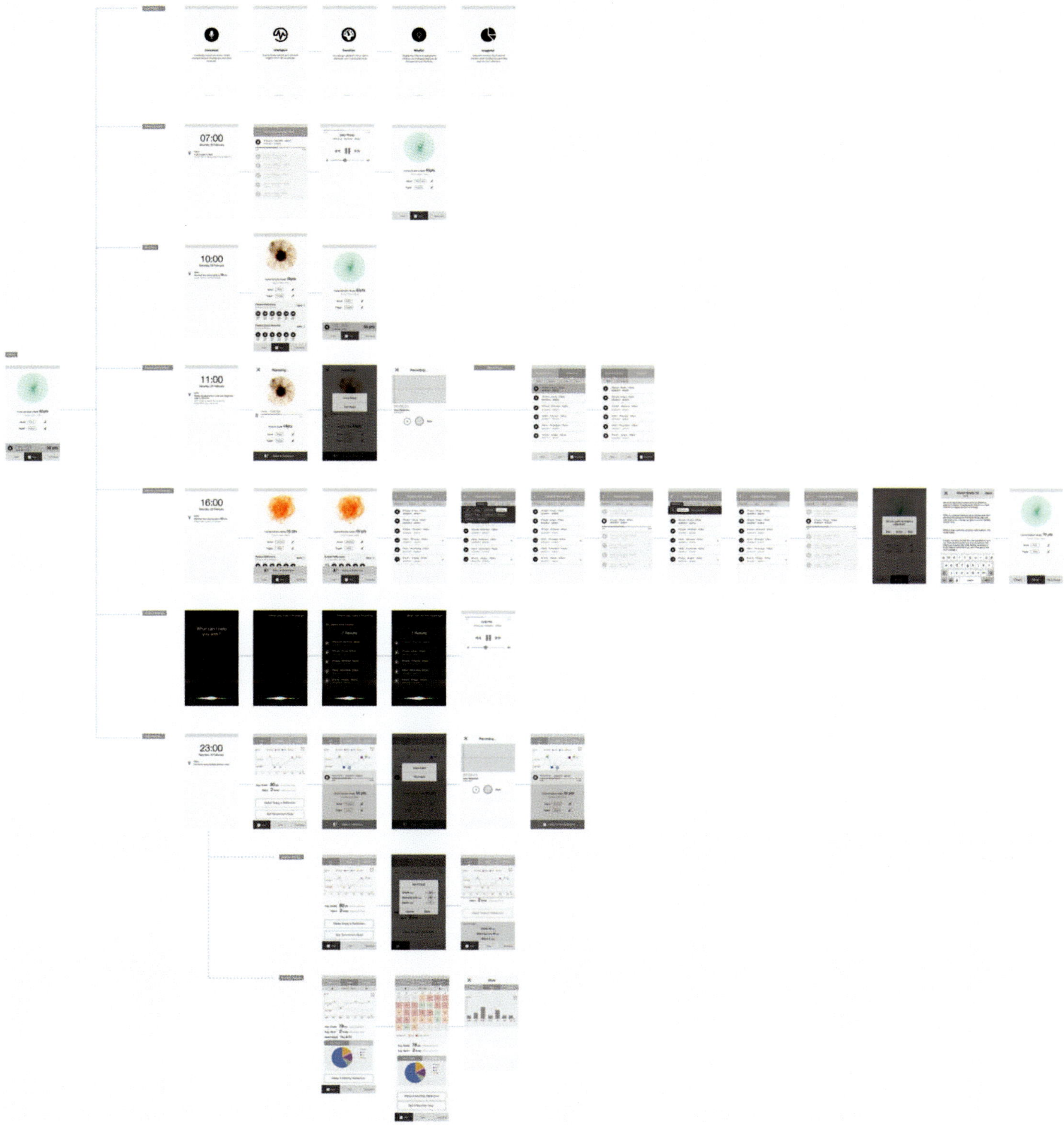

Figure 7.10
High-fidelity wireframe flowboard (from Odmo, by Hui Ye, used by kind permission of Hui Ye).

Flowboards can be done at any level of fidelity. We will start to use them now for our low-fi wireframes, such as we showed in Figure 7.8, through mid- and high-fidelity wireframes (Figure 7.10), and will continue to use them up to and including our final interface designs, at which point they are no longer *wireframe* flowboards, but *final* flowboards. But most of our structure is determined in the wireframing phase, so wireframe flowboards—those that use wireframes to depict the quiescent states—are the ones we deal with the most. Wireframe flowboards allow us to consider both the macro and micro aspects of the arrangement of elements within our system in a fidelity that we can easily iterate.

There are a few conventions in this type of diagram that are important to consider: Flowboards are read left to right, top to bottom and should have a clear start point. In this way, either a top-down or left to right to down version of the flowboard is the clearest. Look again at Figure 7.10 for clarification.

The structure map is the precursor to the wireframe flowboard. We can use it as a guide to lay out our board (Figures 7.11 and 7.12). Often our system exhibits a hierarchical formulation, which is natural, given that we're asking our audience at each level to make a selection that refines what they want to see and do. But sometimes the form of the flowboard is relatively linear with very few branch points. This happens in specific instances, such as payment processes, where users must perform actions in a stepwise fashion. So don't get confused about whether your system is hierarchical or not. Just insure that it expresses the most common flow patterns we envision our users to take.

The wireframe flowboard allows us to see both the structure map and the wireframe of a particular context: the macro and microstructure of our system. Flowboards are often large, but because of their scope, breadth, and detail, their usefulness lies in that they allow us to perceive the organization of our system in a way that few other diagrams can.

The most common error we see is that designers don't use the flowboard properly. They create one board, make a couple of adjustments here or there, and think they're done with their system's design. We are formulating our interface in wireframes for a

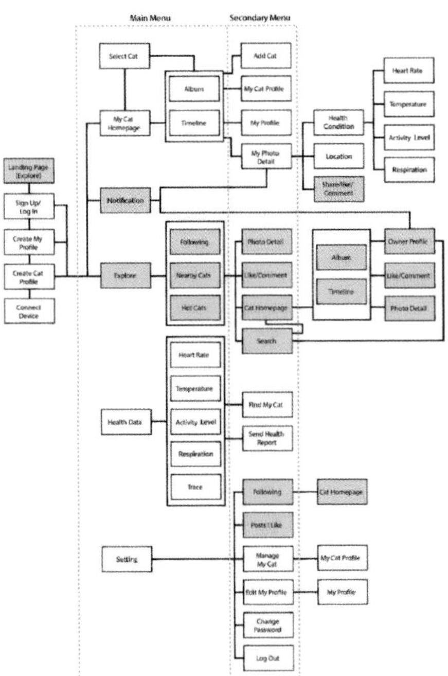

Figure 7.11
Using the structure map as a guide for a wireframe flowboard (from Snapcat, by Zhihan Ying, used by kind permission of Zhihan Ying).

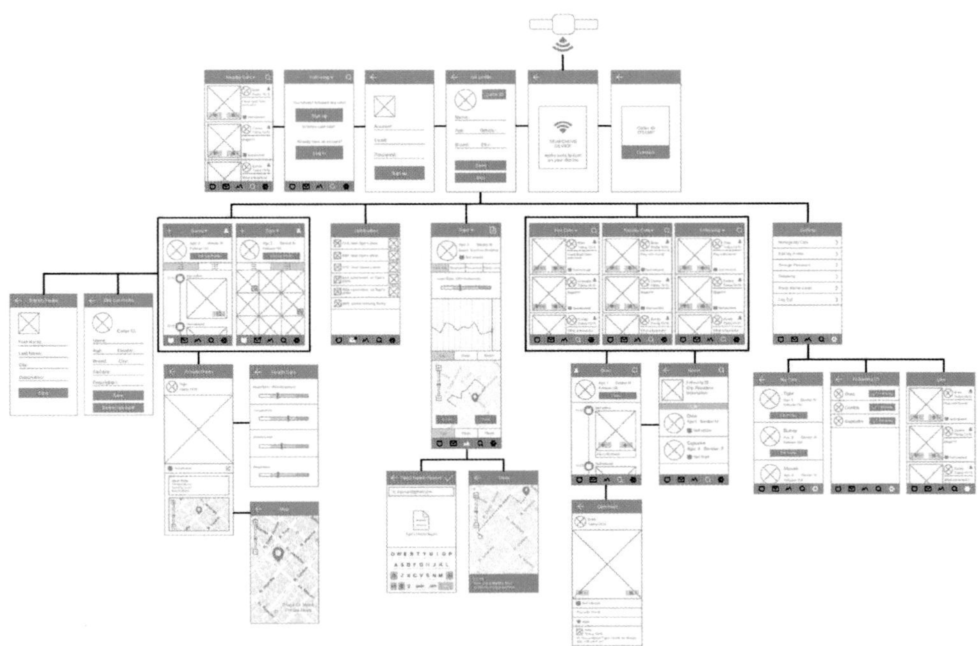

Figure 7.12
A wireframe flowboard built from a structure map (from Snapcat, by Zhihan Ying, used by kind permission of Zhihan Ying).

reason: They are easy to change. We lay things out as a map for that reason as well: It's a lot easier to move things around than it would be if we coded them. Use the wireframe flowboard in the way it's intended: Iterate with it to determine the most salient structure of your system. It is, essentially, our system's roadmap.

Update your structure map if that's not already been done. Create your wireframe flowboard by replacing its nodes with the wireframes of your system. Identify nodes that are not yet wireframed and wireframe them using appropriate information organization principles.

7.18 THE LO-FI (PAPER) PROTOTYPE

Consider the experience we're building. As we've mentioned previously, iteration of this experience allows us to refine our design quickly, discovering glaring errors and improving subtle features. Often, we do this by ourselves or with our close team members, but we need to keep in mind we are designing for a particular group of people who are very likely not us. Even if they are like us, everybody is unique with their own set of issues and concerns. Once we think we've removed most of the glaring problems with our system's structure by ourselves, it's time to take it on the road and see how others feel about it. To do so, we need a prototype.

Prototyping is a means of experiencing a design. It simulates multiple states of a design without having to build the system (Zaki Warfel, 2009, p. v) and its value is that it's generative: It allows us to see issues and spark ideas iteratively, so we do not have to expend a great deal of time and effort building a fully working system (Zaki Warfel, 2009, p. 3).

In the design process, we usually proceed from low fidelity prototypes where our priority is on speed and exploring the broad strokes of the experience, to high fidelity prototypes where our priority is on precision and exploring subtlety. But it's important to note that the appropriate fidelity of the prototype should not necessarily depend on the phase of the process, but rather what needs to be tested (Zaki Warfel, 2009, p. 44). Regardless of the level of execution, bear in mind that all prototypes are models of the real thing, not the thing itself. And, as such, our audience's expectations need to be appropriately managed for the prototype to be useful (Zaki Warfel, 2009, p. 46).

At this stage in the design, we really don't have anything functional, but we can use our paper wireframes and our device mock-ups to prototype our system (Figure 7.13). Remember that what we care about at this point is testing whether the system's structure is sound. And it is most likely not, if this is our first round of prototype testing.

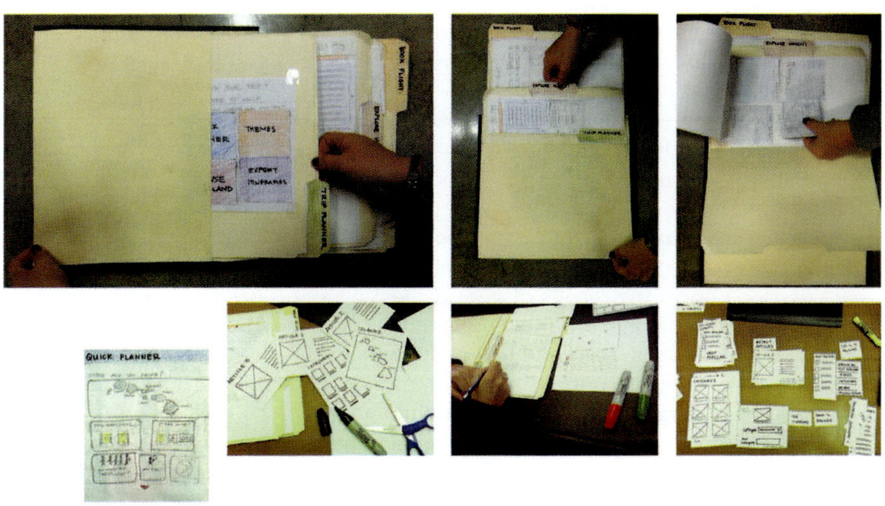

Figure 7.13
Making a paper prototype functional (from Hawaiian Airlines, by Oliver Lo, used by kind permission of Oliver Lo).

As in low-fi wireframing, paper allows us to do two things: It enables a quick and dirty way of exploring if something works (Saffer, 2010, p. 178), but, like lo-fi wireframes, it also forces us to stay away from noodling our interactions as we may be prone to do when we use digital prototyping tools. It's often this latter reason why we use paper first: My designers have pointed out that they could probably create digital prototypes faster than paper ones, but the urge to "make it really work" becomes so strong that they end up spending a great deal more time on them than they would with paper. Paper provides a restriction that forces the designer to look more at the broad strokes rather than the subtle details.

When we say "paper" we should also make it clear that we may not necessarily mean paper in reality. We may mean masking tape or cardboard, anything that gets our ideas down quickly, and provides little concern if we have to throw it away. What we mean by "paper" is that the objects that are created are easily disposable sketches. The main focus should be on quickly iterable depictions of our interface where we are able to get informative user feedback (Figure 7.14).

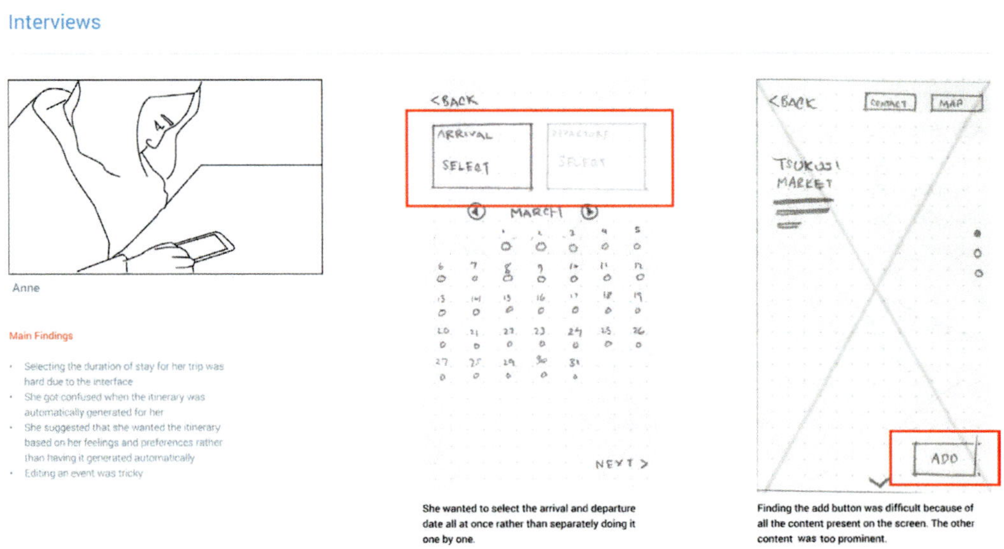

Figure 7.14
Highlighting feedback for a paper prototype (from Tiny Traces, by Aska Cheung, used by kind permission of Aska Cheung).

7.19 FEEDBACK SHOULD TRIGGER IDEATION

We need to take the test discoveries back to our system and use them as inspiration to iterate the design both physically and virtually (Figure 7.15). If our testing revealed a new set of requirements to guide our design, how could they be applied to our system?

How can we modify our designs to solve the problems we encountered? Do we need to reorganize things to have them make more sense? Do we need to add some features that they feel are missing? Should we remove, revise, or de-emphasize features that may be confusing?

As we work through this step, remember to bear in mind that we are the designer. Although user testing provides excellent feedback into issues we may not have been aware of, don't apply the results of our user test blindly. It has been widely claimed that users would have rejected the iPhone had it been user tested before its release. We may take this story as an illustration of the genius of Apple, but also keep in mind that Apple was not without their fair share of failures: They probably wouldn't have destroyed their market share in video editing systems with their failed revamp of Final Cut Pro if they had adequately user tested it (Elmer-DeWitt, 2011).

The point is that there is a balance. The user is neither the word of the almighty nor completely clueless. Their insight is merely useful information that we can use to guide our design. In the end, we are the designer, and design decisions are our

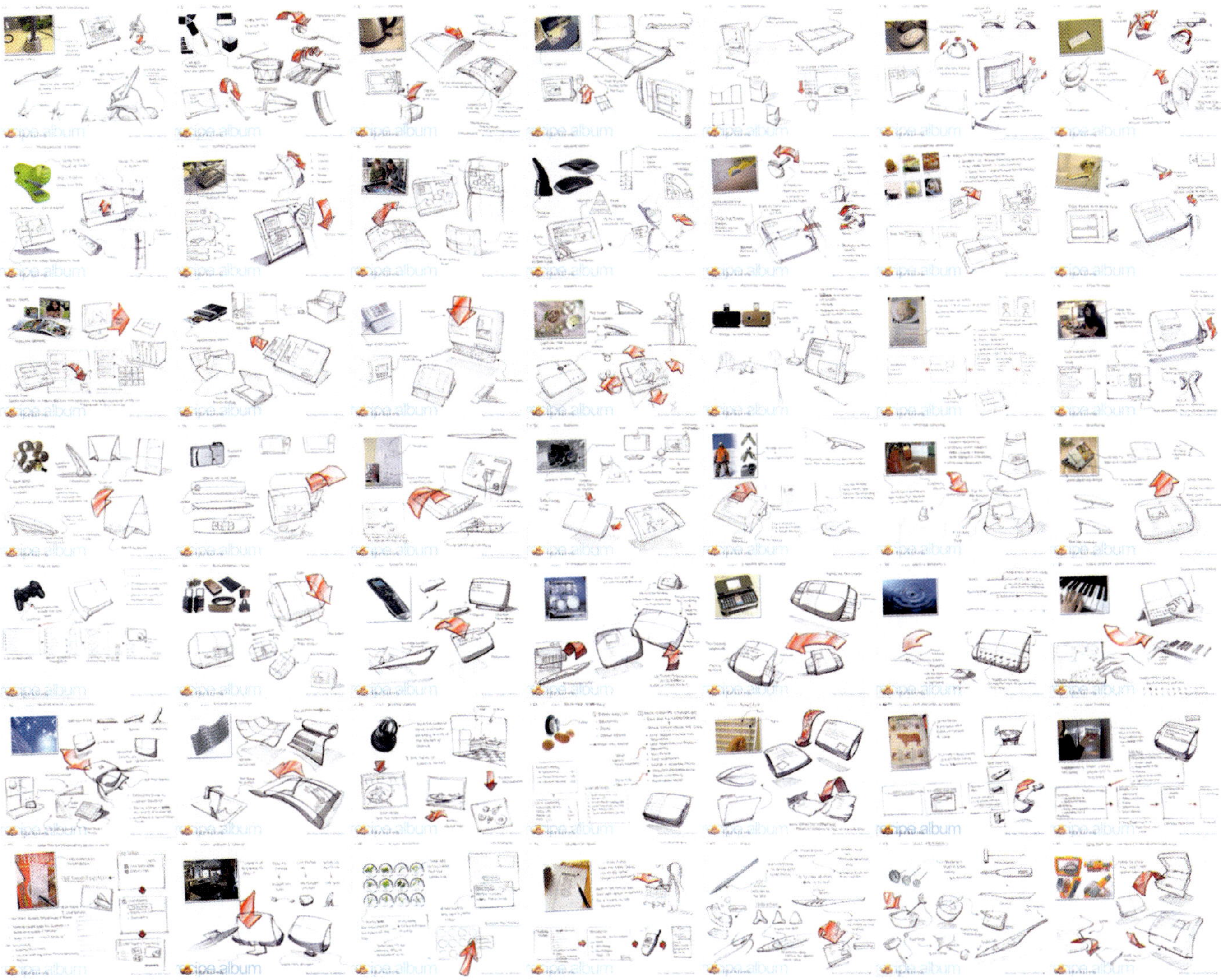

responsibility, not theirs. So, we need to prioritize their responses based on our design goals and reflect on what makes sense with the design we are making.

Figure 7.15
Device ideation inspired by user feedback (from Aroma, by Bessy Liang, used by kind permission of Bessy Liang).

7.20 THE PAPER PROTOTYPE SCENARIO

In the end, all this information architecture, lo-fi wireframing, mockup iteration, paper testing, and design modification is rolled into a scenario. Revise your paper prototype based on your user tests, and leverage that effort in the creation of your scenario. A small snippet of your scenario may look something like Figure 7.16, use proper cinematics to communicate both context and detail. Make sure your interfaces are presented clearly within the frame so the audience can see them. Finally, make sure that the scenario is both detailed and comprehensive. Only six images will not cut it. You get zero style points for short and sweet when it comes to scenarios at this stage. Put the effort into clarity and completeness. Recall the scenario in Figure 6.6 for guidance.

Continue to focus on the primary use case. Just make that experience as clear and complete as possible. Resist the temptation to subject your audience to endless screens of settings and other tedious experiences. This is about clarifying what makes your system great. I sincerely doubt that includes your settings screen.

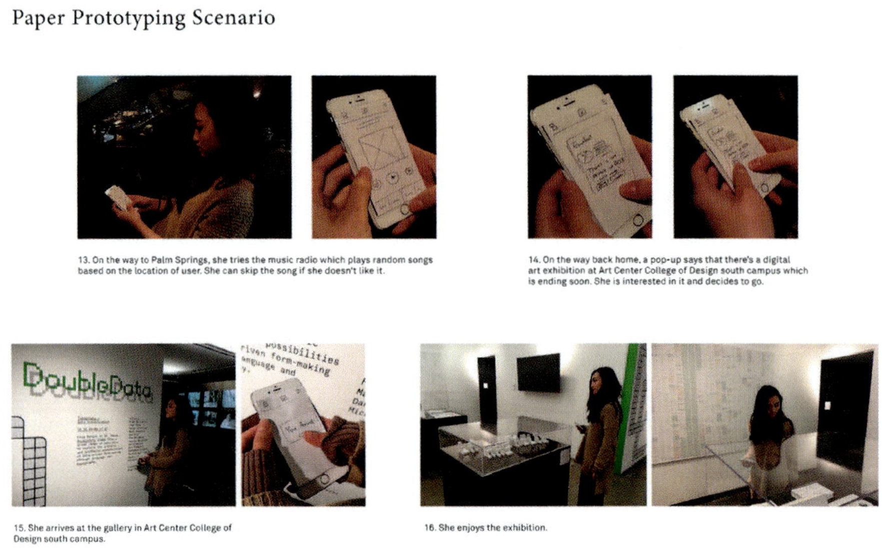

Figure 7.16
Using a paper prototype in a lo-fi scenario (from Lastmin, by Chufan Huang, used by kind permission of Chufan Huang).

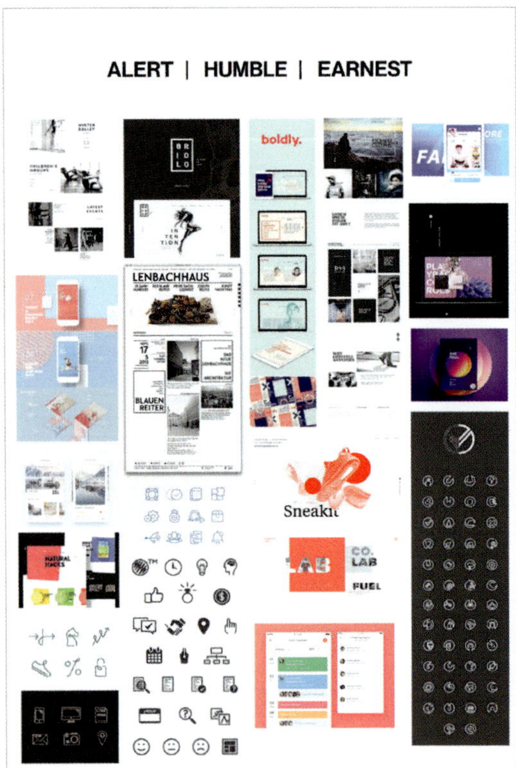

Figure 7.17
A comprehensive inspiration board (from The Making, by Hanna Yi, used by kind permission of Hanna Yi).

7.21 COMPREHENSIVE MOODBOARDS AND INSPIRATION BOARDS

In addition to revisiting our scenarios, revisiting our guidewords also injects an emotional component into our ideation. The moodboards we've developed for our guidewords have established what each word aesthetically means in terms of general feel and inspiration. But any one of these images is not the full picture. An image on a guideword poster for the word "spicy" are just images for that specific word. If we claim that our design is to promote the feeling of those guidewords all at once, each impression or touchpoint needs to communicate all our guidewords *simultaneously*.

To take our guideword inspiration to this level, let's create another set of moodboards and inspiration boards for our guidewords. These are similar in form to those associated with each word individually, but this time *every* image that appears needs to reflect all our guidewords at the same time: If our words are spicy, scrumptious, and sleek, every image should feel spicy, scrumptious, and sleek. We call these comprehensive moodboards and comprehensive inspiration boards (Figure 7.17).

Developing comprehensive boards is tough, and it should be: If they were easy the look and feel of our system would not be distinctive. We need to spend time with this to get it right. During this effort, don't be discouraged that we may not be being productive in the sense that we are building our system, because we are being productive in the sense that we're gaining a great deal of insight into how to design our solution aesthetically.

8 Interface

The presentation frameworks of our previous structural explorations—low-fidelity wireframes, prototypes, and scenarios—began to clarify how our users should interact with the elements of our system. But what issues should guide us in the design of our interfaces? Answering this is the thrust of this chapter.

For a moment, let's forget about the overall structure of our system and simply focus on the interface level: those things our user acts on and how the system responds to those actions. At this point, we should have a series of sketched screens or quiescent states that follow our primary use case across the critical contexts of our system with particular emphasis on our primary, or hero, context. For what we need to explore in this chapter, let's limit our focus only to these primary use case screens, and enter the realm of interface exploration. But before we get to the nitty-gritty of our interface exploration effort, let's discuss how to approach this exploration in the first place, because it's a little different than what we've been doing so far.

8.1 CONSIDERATIONS, NOT PROCESS

Design is an open-ended discipline. It is not like hard science, where there is usually one solution best fit for a particular problem. Correct solutions for design problems may be infinite. Additionally, every design problem we face presents a new and possibly unique challenge. Because of this, the way we go about solving each design problem is very likely different for different projects. They are non-deterministic hard problems.

The central issue of a book about design process is just this: I am attempting to outline a process for problems that may have radically different solutions and radically different ways of developing those solutions. There are phases to this process that I've seen have very similar steps—although they may require a little adjustment of emphasis and arrangement on a project-by-project basis. But there are other phases that do not lend themselves as neatly to a clear process. These usually appear when we're addressing the precise results of our design considerations. We are beginning to enter such a phase right now: the design of our interface.

Developing good solutions in such a phase is often less about the steps we take and more about the things we consider. As such, this chapter dispenses with the largely step-by-step process in which we've been engaged, and presents a set of considerations instead: things to think about when you design. My hope is that these considerations provide you with useful guidance in solving your own unique design problem in much the same way that process has provided you with guidance up to this point.

Okay, so much for the meta-discussion. Now, let's re-engage in the effort of designing. Below, I describe several considerations to guide your design. I realize it may be next to impossible to keep them all in your head at once, so I don't expect you to do so. If you're at a loss as to how to work through this, we'd suggest taking each consideration individually and ideating interface possibilities inspired by each consideration.

The hope is that these considerations trigger a flood of explorations. We've been working with hand-drawn interfaces up to this point to avoid excessive detail and noodling, but if you are more comfortable exploring things on your favorite digital drawing tool, then so be it. If you're comfortable exploring by continuing drawing on cards, then do that. If you'd just like to ideate in your journal, go right ahead. You may even want to mix and match these approaches for different reasons. In our experience, we've found journal ideation to be the most fruitful and comfortable way to capture ideas. See Figure 7.5 for example. But that may not be your style. Whatever method allows you to generate a wealth of useful possibilities quickly should be the ideation method you choose.

8.2 THE CONTENT TRIANGLE

To provide relevance to the considerations below, we need to understand that not all content in our system is the same. When we enter a library, we will find that it is organized by fiction and non-fiction. Some genres are a little of both, such as historical fiction or infotainment, but, for the most part, we can place the contents of a book along a continuum from those that are primarily to educate and inform to those that are primarily to experience and entertain.

Digital media can be divided up in pretty much the same way. There are media outlets that provide us with news and information, and those that provide movies or games that are intended to provide enjoyment. But what about software that allows us to perform specific tasks, such as editing a movie or processing a photo? Those certainly aren't entertainment, and although they may be more in the realm of information, they really aren't that either. They are tools.

Because some digital media can do things, the medium is not like print. It presents a third type of content: utility. Elements that provide utility are like tools in a toolbox in that they help us make or modify things. While, in general, print has two classifications—fiction and non-fiction or entertainment and information—digital media has three: entertainment, information, and utility. I like to consider these content types as sitting on a triangular axis with the three corners referring to the extremes of the three types of content (Figure 8.1).

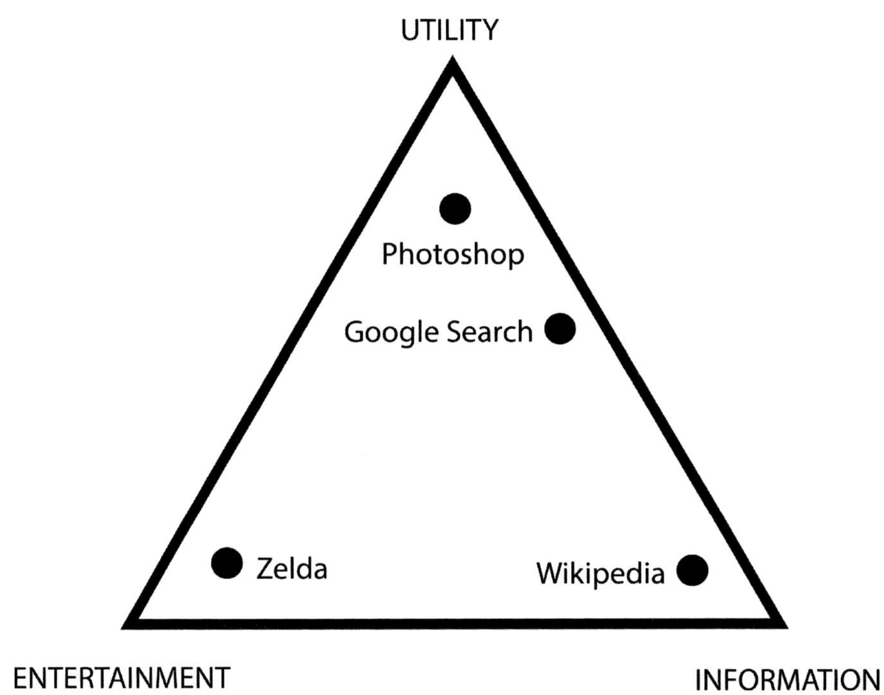

Figure 8.1
The content triangle.

Your digital system resides somewhere on this triangle. Photoshop or the device that controls my sprinkler system sits at the utility corner; Halo or Zelda sits at entertainment; Wikipedia sits at information. Google search, because it's a tool we use to find things, lies near utility, but because we get information from it, it may be a little towards information as well. It's definitely not about entertainment (unless Google searches are how you like to spend your free time), so it sits on the edge between information and utility, probably closer to the utility side. Facebook resides along the information–entertainment edge, and Mindstorms mixes entertainment, utility, and education with more emphasis on entertainment than the others.

Where a system resides on this triangle provides us with insight into how we should approach the principles that guide our interface design. For a system at the utility extreme, control is desirable, and proficiency is a common trait among its users. For systems that target news and education, the user is often more casual, so the complexity of control may give way to simplicity.

Systems whose purpose is to entertain are often different altogether from the other two. In fact, challenges and conflicts are an integral part of the gaming experience, so many of the principles below may have limited relevance to gaming systems. But before you game designers throw them out, consider that the interface elements used to *control* a game are different from the challenges and achievements of the game itself. The principles below very much apply to the control interface of a game. This is where efficiency, usability, branding, and clarity are critical, and the gamer is as demanding as the professional animator who needs their controls precise and robust to do their job.

Where does your system lie on this content triangle? How does its genre tell you what may be important and what may not? Are you considering your user's goals correctly and, if so, what impact does that have on the interface? Know your user well. Even though utility is more for the professional and information is more for the casual user, there are numerous exceptions to these assertions.

As we address those things we should consider while doing interface design, be clear about who your user is and why they are using your system.

8.3 INTERFACE CONSIDERATIONS

The relative importance, or unimportance, of a particular consideration relates to the realities of the system you are designing. For example, if you are designing a complex information system, the considerations below that relate to the organization of information, navigation, and content are of high importance. Yet, if you are designing a sparse system that relies more on tactile interactions, the importance of organizing information will give way to considerations that are more physical in nature, such as posture agreement and ergonomics.

Weigh all the considerations below, but be more acutely aware of those that are important to the challenges posed by your design problem.

8.4 CONSIDER THE USER'S SITUATION

Many of our previous exploratory activities were centered around the physicality of our user. For example, our posture studies capture the realities of our user in their external context and should have been central to the derivation of the solutions to our ecosystem (Figure 8.2). We use posture studies precisely because a user's external context is one of the most important things to consider when we design our system.

Given the environment and posture of our user and the context of our interface, do our wireframes make sense? For example, if our user is driving a car, are we asking them to do things that will cause them to crash? When we're driving, we have

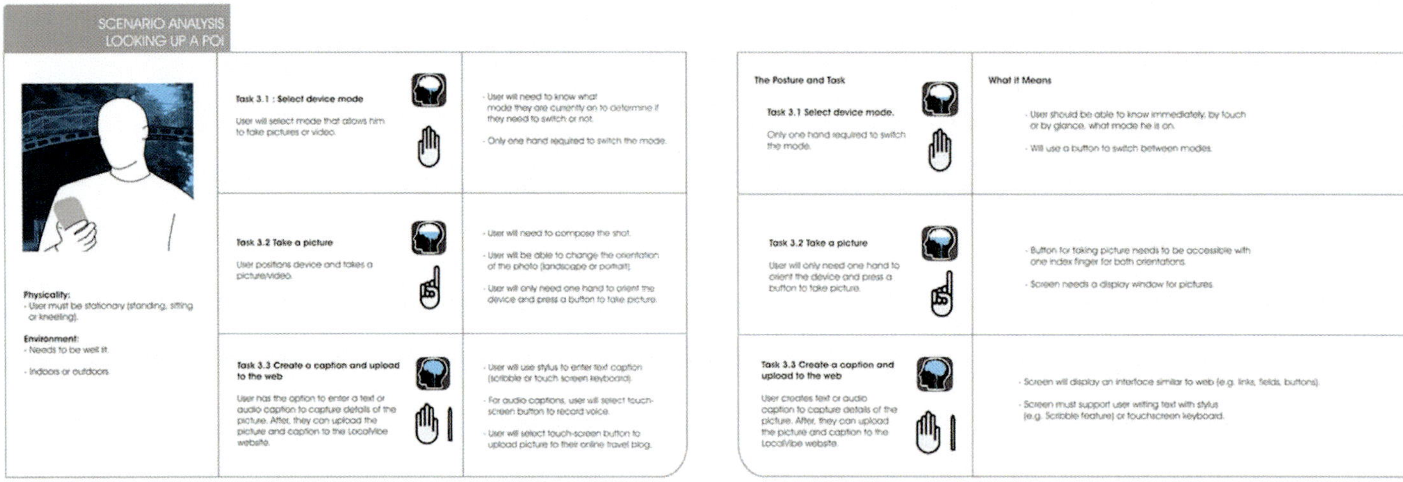

Figure 8.2
Postures and context for a digital travel guide (from Local Vibe, by Gabe la O', used by kind permission of Gabe la O').

about a single second to glance at something before we get into danger; therefore, automotive screens must be of minimal distraction (Cooper, 2015, p. 232). They must be clear, simple, and uncluttered. We use the word "must" because we mean it. We do not mean "should". These aren't suggestions but are tightly regulated standards to which our automotive system must conform. In general, type needs to be large, simple, and glanceable. Interactions should be able to be done with one touch and hotspots should be few and large. These requirements create severe restrictions on what is presented on the screen. We need to keep these in mind when we are considering how much information can appear and how it is used.

The example of a driver of a car is a rather extreme posture, but even how we intend our audience to use the ubiquitous mobile device has substantial ramifications for our interface. For example, do we expect our user to be carrying things while they're interacting with our app, or do they have both hands free? How do we expect them to zoom in or out on a map if they don't have the use of both hands? If this is a substantial issue, we need to design a workaround for the problem.

Important aspects of our user's situation not only revolve around their relationship with the interface, but also concern the user's environment. Are we asking our user to listen to something in a noisy room? Are we asking them to look at a dim screen when they're outside and it is extremely bright? What are the circumstances of the environment they are most likely in? How could these affect our interface?

A recent trip I made to Yellowstone National Park provided a good example of a failure in environmental context. As you may know, Yellowstone is famous for its geothermal activity and a fact you may not know is that it is home to almost two-thirds of the geysers on earth. Led by Old Faithful, its geysers are the park's main draw. Rangers can predict the eruption of Old Faithful and several others of its significant geysers within minutes. Naturally, visitors want to know when these will erupt.

Rangers calculate these timings each day, and their primary way of distributing the schedule to the public is through an app. This all sounds great until you realize that pretty much the entire park is an internet blackout zone. Cell or wifi service is practically non-existent. The park service does have a solution, though: Just call a number and the times will be read off to you. But as of this writing, not only does the park lack internet and cell service, all the pay phones have been removed. How do we find out? Ask a ranger. The solution they've had for the past hundred years.

The Yellowstone app is clearly a bad idea for those within the confines of the park—exactly those people who want up-to-the-minute geyser schedules. The information phone line is less egregious because it's cheap to build and operate, and there are a few cell hotspots in the park. (Although they are in the same places where you'll easily find rangers.) The money poured into the app would have been much better spent on a kiosk or display system at various connected sites, such as visitors' centers, hotel lobbies, and campground entrances. These all have internet for the employees, so connectivity would no longer present a problem. And I would wager the cost of a collection of monitors and a displayed website would be well below that of an app.

This example serves to illustrate the impact of the environment on our system. It seems like a pretty obvious failure, but these disconnects happen all the time. Whenever we feel stupid or frustrated interacting with something, more likely than not it's not we who are stupid, it's the designer (Garrett, 2003, p. 17).

Review your user's postures along with their tasks for those postures, and consider their likely external context. Explore interface possibilities for those tasks in full consideration of your user's situation.

The context should agree with the user's situation.

8.5 CONSIDER DEVICE

It's fruitful at this stage not only to consider our user's posture, but also the physical aspects of the device our system is on. Just like the consideration of external contexts, above, devices and contexts should have been a central source of inspiration for our designs, but it's useful to check that our approach conforms with context.

A page on a website has the screen real estate to contain a great deal more information than the screen on our mobile device. Also, the spatial precision of a mouse or trackpad on a desktop computer is much higher than our sausagey fingers on a mobile device. We can almost select single pixels with a cursor, while our finger on a touch screen easily covers about 50 pixels in both width and height. The result is that we can both display and interact with a great deal more precision on a desktop than we ever can on our mobile device. When we ideate our wireframes, they should reflect that precision or lack thereof (Figure 8.3).

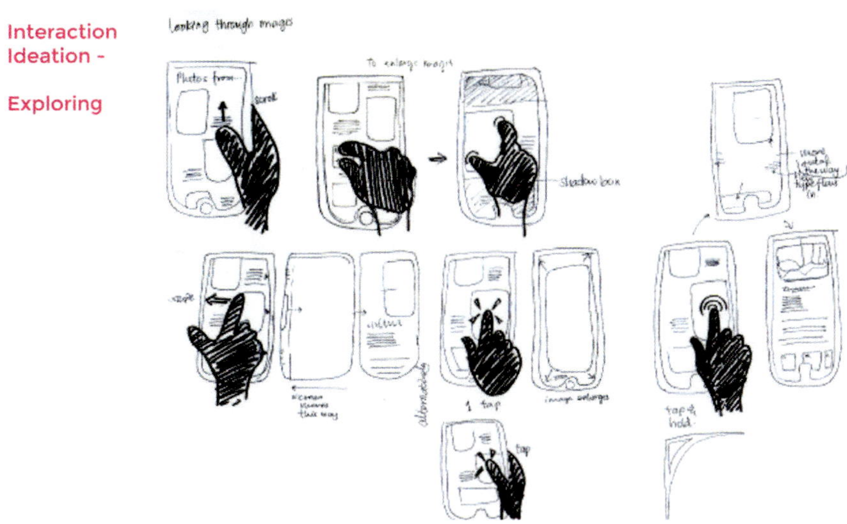

Figure 8.3
Ideation considering device limitations (from Artbug, by Radhika Kashyap, used by kind permission of Radhika Kashyap).

We should also be aware not only of input limitations, but output or response limitations as well. This includes screen sizes for visual displays, speaker limitations for auditory contexts, and physical feedback limitations for haptics. Our consideration of these doesn't have to be precise at this stage: We don't have to create two sets of wireframes for two different mobile devices with screen sizes that may differ by ten pixels. We just need to know that the general dimensions and resolution of the mobile devices are around a certain size, and that those sizes and resolutions are entirely different from the laptop context for which we do produce a different set of wireframes.

The device should agree with the user's situation.

8.6 VIRTUAL VS. PHYSICAL

Physical interaction components are those things that we manipulate physically to communicate with a system. These are as simple as an on/off switch or as complicated as a gyroscopic hand controller for telesurgery. The advantage of physical interaction components is that they offer direct manipulation and tactile sensation, and this produces a more "flow inducing interface" (Cooper, 2015, p. 315). We get the sensation when we turn the steering wheel of our car that we are directly turning the wheels, but that is not the case in the modern car. We are communicating with a set of actuators that control hydraulic pumps that in turn steer the wheels. But because the steering wheel not only turns the wheels but also gives us just the right balance and resistance, we feel that we are actually turning them.

This haptic feedback—this "feel"—is no accident. It is carefully designed by the automakers to provide the impression that we are turning something reasonably heavy, but not too heavy. They could easily make a steering wheel turn with no resistance at all. But this effortlessness would probably result in us wildly turning the car back and forth. Too stiff and it would be both tiring and challenging to turn the car at all. The steering wheel's action and haptic feedback combine to allow us to safely control a ton of hurtling metal at quite literally breakneck speeds.

Although many touch-based interactions can give us the sense that we are directly manipulating an object—such as swiping the screen provides us with the impression that we are moving the screen contents left or right—touch systems have none of the physical feedback that comes with well designed physical components. Try flying a drone with a smartphone vs. a well-designed controller: It's much more difficult. Even a simple game controller provides more control than virtual buttons and sliders on a mobile device.

Another benefit of physical components is that we can use our sense of touch to feel where a knob or button is. This is extremely important in automobile interfaces where we don't want to have our audience take their eyes off the road. Virtual components don't provide us with that sensation, so we must use our eyes to see where the manipulator is. Because of this, a great deal of care should be taken when integrating a touch-based system into a car. Taking our eyes off the road places the passengers at risk.

But there are several drawbacks of physical components with respect to those that are virtual. First, we can easily overload a device with physical components to the point of being utterly overwhelming to our audience. Consider the control panels for commercial airliners just to get a sense of how daunting this component clutter would be if we had a physical controller for almost everything. It even takes a little while to get a feel for the controls of a new car. Indeed, we can instantly grasp how to steer it, accelerate it, and stop it, but the audio system, HVAC, lights, and wipers may take a little longer to understand—and it's probably a better idea to figure out those things before we hit the road rather than doing so while driving.

Another drawback of physical components is that, for the most part, they have fixed roles. Just because we use a wheel to steer a car and a wheel-like circular knob to tune a radio station doesn't mean it's a good idea to reduce the component clutter to have the steering wheel double as the radio tuner. Steering wheels are assigned to steering, tuner dials are assigned to tuning. This one-to-one relationship between control and result makes for the explosion of components that causes overload (recall the cockpit of an airliner).

However, this one-to-one mapping between component and result is not always true—consider how we can manipulate video games ranging from flight simulators to hand-to-hand combat with a simple game controller. Now also think of the instruction we must absorb to learn those controls. Many to one mapping of physical components usually means a steeper learning curve. However, the vast majority of physical components typically have one result: a singular component to a singular action specificity.

Virtual components have little of this baggage. On one screen we can be using a left to right movement of our thumb to manipulate a slider, while on another screen we may use the same gesture to swipe to the next screen. We are very comfortable using the same interaction for entirely different things. This lack of action specificity allows us to design a wealth of different interactions with only a few physical actions. The actions we use to steer a drone are precisely the same actions we use to turn up the volume of our music. Virtual interactions traditionally have a great deal more flexibility than physical components.

This can provide us insight into determining whether a feature should be controlled by a physical or virtual interaction component. If we are designing for a pre-existing platform, such as a laptop, we have little choice but to conform it to the interaction components and languages associated with that platform. But if we are developing our own system with a custom set of devices, we may very well face this physical vs. virtual decision.

If our goal is feature flexibility or our system requires a great deal of customization from the user, then it's most likely that our feature should be controlled virtually. On the other hand, if the feature is critical to the operation of the system, the user needs fast access to it, and tactile feedback is essential, then a physical interaction component may be the correct solution. But keep in mind, as was mentioned before, too many physical components cause the system to become overwhelming.

Consider whether a particular interface element should be virtual or physical. Physical controls are more direct, faster to use, but are rigid. Virtual controls take longer to get at, are more prone to interface friction, yet are infinitely malleable. A physical surface can only handle a finite amount of controls, yet a virtual interface, because of scrolling lists and hierarchies, can handle thousands. If a control does not change and is one of a very small number that is critical, it likely resides on the surface of the device. If it's less critical and relies on situation or context, it would most likely be virtual within the interface.

Determine if an element should be virtual or physical.

8.7 PHYSICAL CONTROLS

If the answer is physical, we need to address how those controls should be designed on the surface of our device. What are the things we need to keep in mind when we design them? To illustrate this, I like to use a negative example. Something that frustrates me every time I use it: my alarm clock.

The clock beside my bed is an almost perfect example of a poorly designed set of physical interaction components. Yes, I really should get a new alarm clock, but my cell phone has pretty much taken over that role. Getting a new clock is a fairly low priority in my life, and I've come to like having it next to me: Its bad design reminds me of the importance of good design.

The clock has only buttons for its interface: for setting the time, the alarm, switching the alarm mode, tuning in a radio station, and switching from AM to FM. Using buttons to switch from AM to FM makes sense, but to travel up and down the radio dial, it's fairly ridiculous. I have to click several times to get a station or press and hold to make it travel faster. Of course, the result when I press and hold is that I always overshoot the radio station. This interaction is frustrating. A dial would have been much more usable.

All the buttons are the same size and shape and have little to distinguish them than a raised icon in the center. However, the icons identifying them are small and of the same black plastic as the rest of the clock. They are not visible enough to see clearly nor are they large enough to feel. The buttons are aligned in columns and rows, so their arrangement provides no indication as to their use either. Also, the black color of the buttons is challenging to see in the dark.

The buttons are on the top of the clock, which may not seem like a bad idea if you assume the clock will be controlled by someone looking down on it. But my clock is placed on a nightstand at the head of my bed. This is probably a fairly common arrangement. When I'm lying in the bed, the controls face the ceiling and are difficult, if not impossible, to see. Fortunately, at least the clock face is on the side and viewable from the bed.

The clock looks slick, but its interaction design fails miserably. We can use this example to build a set of design considerations:

8.7.1 Information Coherence

Buttons are fitting for on/off switches or selecting our favorite radio station, but are poor when intended to control a continuum of values, such as frequencies along a radio spectrum. Dials or sliders are much more appropriate for this task.

Physical controls should agree with the information and data they control.

8.7.2 Fit In, but Stand Out

If controls are the same, it leads to confusion. If size and shape are not used to distinguish a control, then the product graphics must be clear enough to take that role. Graphics should be large enough and distinguishable enough to be seen.

Physical controls should fit with the overall design of the device, but be distinctive enough to be distinguishable from each other.

8.7.3 Sensory Agreement

If a physical control has a high probability of being felt rather than seen, the distinction should be in its feel to the touch: It should be shaped differently or have physical features that separate it from the rest.

8.7.4 Chunking

Chunking is the act of putting elements together to aid comprehension. If we have a set of buttons that allow us to select different stations, it's helpful if they're grouped in a specific place on the interface and are shaped similarly.

Physical controls with similar functionality should be grouped together either spatially or formally or both.

8.7.5 Posture Coherence

If a device is intended to be used by a person in bed, both the face and controls should be designed for that posture. This also means that it should be ergonomically correct for that posture as well. The controls for my clock example should not only be understandable by someone in bed, but also usable by someone in bed.

Just as context should agree with posture, physical controls should agree with posture as well.

8.8 VIRTUAL COMPONENTS AND POSTURES

Both virtual components and physical components need to exhibit good design principles, but virtual components differ from their physical counterparts in many important ways: They are not tactile, their visual presentation is incredibly dynamic, and they rely more heavily on the aesthetic principles associated with graphics and communication design.

The lack of tactility means that they require the use of the other senses, such as sight and hearing. This means not only the uninterrupted attention of these senses, but these are senses that are more demanding of our concentration than the feel of an object. They can quickly subject the user to cognitive overload if they force users to multitask, such as demanding attention while the user is driving, or is listening to the flow of conversation in a meeting.

Whatever an interactive component is asking of our users, make sure it agrees with their critical postures in a way that neither distracts nor overloads them.

8.9 ORGANIZING VIRTUAL CONTROLS

The principles of organization—good modularity, hierarchy, and layout –are just as important in virtual visual interfaces as they are in those that are physical. They may be even more so because of the preponderance for virtual interfaces to be more visually complex than their physical counterparts. A major point of differentiation, though, between physical and visual interfaces is their use of type. (The same can be said of the spoken word in auditory systems.) The virtual interface is the main delivery pathway of the system's content, so, in a visual context, the principles of well-organized typography and grid are critical.

With respect to your wireframes, be sensitive as to how well your interactive components work with elements used for graphic organization.

8.10 VIRTUAL CONTROL CONSIDERATIONS

The considerations we developed based on my failed clock are not just for physical components; they can be applied to virtual components as well. Let's go through them with an eye toward our virtual interface and see how each applies:

8.10.1 Information Coherence

What data are we asking our audience to control? We don't want our users to be clicking on a button when a slider is more appropriate, regardless of whether the control is physical or virtual. We need to map controls to functions properly (Cooper, 2015, p. 290).

As with physical controls, the virtual widget we control should agree with the input. If the input is a small selection, such as on/off or red/green/blue buttons, this may suffice. If the input is a continuum, such as scrolling up and down a document, then things like sliders are appropriate.

Virtual controls should agree with the information and data they control.

8.10.2 Fit In, but Stand Out

Virtual controls should also fit in with the overall design, but stand out in ways that distinguish them from other types of controls on the interface. For example, links within a paragraph should look different than the surrounding text. If you're using bolds or underlines for emphasis within your text, the same type of bold or underline should not be used for a link. A slight color change may do the trick, but be careful that it's also accompanied by a change in value—color blindness is an inability to distinguish hue, not value.

Other controls, such as buttons and sliders, should also be treated consistently and separate themselves from non-interactive information. Google's Material Design advises designers to use drop shadows to communicate that items are indeed interactive. In this way, the user doesn't have to think much about whether an item is interactive. The visual cues tell them that it is.

Virtual controls should fit with the overall design of the interface, but be distinctive enough to communicate to the user that it is interactive.

8.10.3 Chunking

Our information design groupings—contexts, quiescent states, sections, and elements—could be considered an exercise in chunking on a massive scale. At the interface level, chunking is arranging the layout of the interface in such a way that associated information is grouped together. If we're in the stage of making a purchase, we want all the information relevant for that purchase right in front of us. This is not the time for an interface to distract us with other information that is not essential for that purchase, unless, of course, they are trying to surreptitiously seduce us to buy more stuff.

Virtual elements of content or control that are associated should be grouped together, either spatially or formally or both.

8.10.4 Posture Coherence

If we intend our audience to be manipulating our app with just one hand, we had better design it to be thumbable. If they are likely to be using it in a blackout zone, they had better be able to use it offline. If they are most likely using it on a laptop, this is where we can be comprehensive with our information and precise with our controls.

Just as context should agree with posture, virtual controls should agree with posture as well.

8.10.5 Sensory Agreement

Screens or audible interfaces are not tactile, so, clearly, shape on the screen has little relevance to our sense of touch. But beyond the aspect of physical feeling, sensory coherence is highly relevant to virtual interfaces. If we need our eyes to drive, we had better not be using them to navigate a complicated screen. If we're using our ears to hear oncoming cars while riding our bike, an auditory interface needs to be sensitive to that.

Regardless of whether our interface is primarily physical or virtual, be aware of sensory constraints and consider interface approaches that agree.

8.11 CONSIDER ERGONOMICS AND HUMAN FACTORS

When we delve into physical actions, we also need to consider what is physically doable for a human. And not only any human, but *our* human, our target. Ergonomics applies scientific principles to the design process to be compatible with the needs of a given population (McCauley-Bush, 2012, p. 2). It provides us with a wealth of scientific studies that explore the natural actions and limitations of the body. If we're designing systems where lives are at stake such as in the driver's seat, cockpit, or operating room, it's required that we have a solidly scientific rationale for both our physical and virtual interfaces. Although consumer-based systems that have no threat to life or limb may not need this level of rigor, they should still fit our audience naturally.

Since ergonomics deals with aspects of the human body, the literature of ergonomics is heavily weighted on the side of medical language. Human factors as a discipline is similar to ergonomics but is more typically used in design contexts. Texts on human factors are usually more approachable for the designer but still are necessarily rife with scientific detail (Tilley, 2002). These considerations are of vital importance for physical systems in the workplace, for example, but are likely overkill if we want to build a social app. However, there's no reason why we can't conduct a little ergonomic research on our own to make sure we aren't coming up with interactions that are difficult or uncomfortable for our audience.

For example, I am often surprised how a simple understanding of single-handed vs. two-handed interactions in mobile apps escapes scrutiny. A "thumbable" interface—one where we can do everything with just our thumb, allowing for single-handed interactions—is one that we can truly use on the go, while pinch gestures require us to stop and put down whatever we may have in our hands in order to use both. Anyone who has dragged a suitcase down the streets of Manhattan

Figure 8.4
Heuristic evaluations of the ergonomics of thumb sweeps for interface controls, Chris Wu, used by kind permission of Chris Wu).

while simultaneously trying to find their hotel on a mobile map has endured this frustration.

Contexts should not only agree with posture, but do so *ergonomically*.

What are the ergonomic issues surrounding our system and its contexts? We don't have to dive into a ton of scientific studies to get a handle on this. Doing some heuristic evaluations on ourselves or a group of target users can provide ample information about what we are asking our audience to do (Figure 8.4). Have users hold things the way you think they should, look at things that they need to see, and manipulate things you think they should be manipulating. What are they physically doing? Are you asking them to do things that are difficult, tedious, or painful? Look for the points of friction. What would be more convenient, comfortable, and engaging for them? How does this impact your design both physically and virtually? Use this to explore possibilities.

8.12 CONSIDER USABILITY

When we say something is usable, we mean that it's easy to learn and use. This often boils down to usability expert Steve Krug's assertion: "Don't make me think" (Krug, 2014, p. 11). Confronting something that we have to think about slows us down. When we face something that initially is novel or confusing, it forces us to get out of the flow of what we are doing, stop, and think about what we have to do next. It may even cause frustration. This includes confusing interactions, confusing labels, and content and control that doesn't deliver on our expectations. When a user feels stupid, this is a clear indicator that the designer has not taken usability into account.

Clearly, making things usable is good, and making them unusable is bad. Things that promote usability are those that users are familiar with and conform to their expectations. But making your interactions so that they look like everything else also makes them lack distinction. They essentially become vanilla. So, how do we tackle this conundrum? Fortunately, we don't have to yet. We're simply exploring possibilities and striving to make things as usable as possible.

Look to familiar systems on familiar devices. Do they have features like yours? What can be done to make your interface more usable by acting more like them? In the US, usability.gov provides guidelines for usability standards for the web and other media while usability.net collects them for international standards. Explore these standards and see how they can apply to your primary use case interface.

Your interface should strike the correct balance between usability and distinction, but err a great deal more on the side of usability than distinction.

8.13 FORM FOLLOWS FUNCTION

Design is not art. Beauty in design results from a purity of function, form, and how well it satisfies its user's goals (Lidwell et al., 2010, p. 106). If form is the primary objective and function follows it, we may end up designing beautiful things that are unusable, such as my annoying alarm clock.

My clock is frustratingly difficult to use during the day, and impossible to use at night, but it sure looks great! It has smooth lines uninterrupted by any informative product graphics that could disturb its form; its dark surface disappears gracefully into the night; and its buttons create a symmetrical pattern due to being all the same size and shape. Its lack of graphics, dark color, and its buttons' lack of any semblance of modularity or hierarchy may make it aesthetically pleasing, but it's just those things that make it impossible to use. It's an excellent example of breaking the principle of form follows function. For my clock, function is secondary to form. I guess it worked: I was seduced enough by how it looked that I bought it. It wasn't until I started using it that I learned how problematic it was.

Don't fall into the same trap as the designers of my clock. Function should not be subservient to form. This doesn't mean it should be all about function and form should be ignored. Quite the contrary. As a designer, you should strive to make form and function work so well together that its functional aspects are a source of its beauty (Figure 8.5).

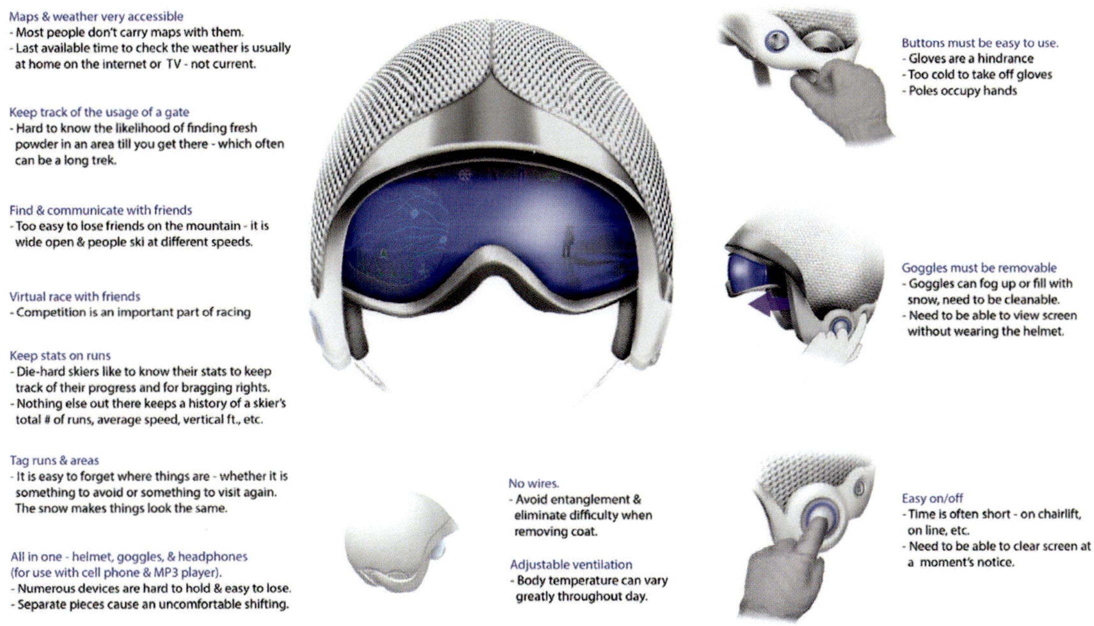

Figure 8.5
Integrating form and function in an HUD wayfinding helmet for skiing (from Traverse GPS, by Katy Dill, used by kind permission of Katy Dill).

Directing our focus to each of our interface components in particular, as opposed to the system at large, what are the details that strike the right balance between functionality and form? Can we develop things so that functionality becomes form? Recall your brand values. Do each of your components exhibit these values well (Figure 8.6)?

The form should follow from function and the ability to be used, not the other way around.

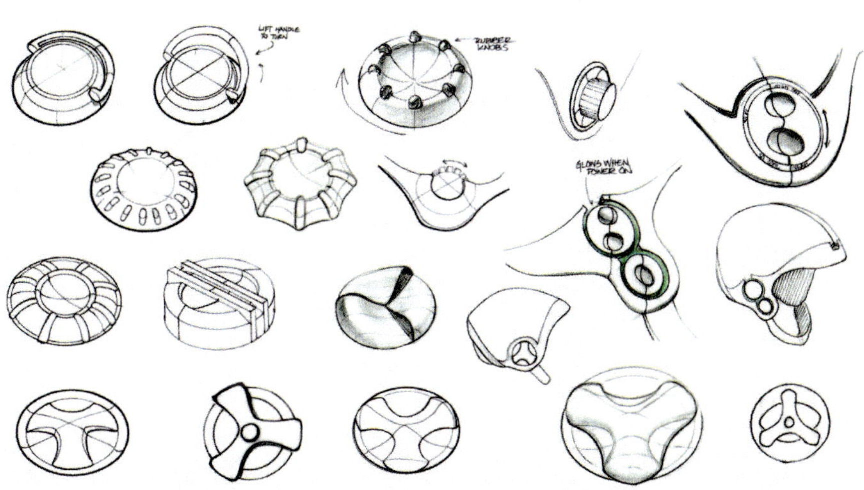

Figure 8.6
Button ideation balancing function and form of the previous HUD ski helmet (from Traverse GPS, by Katy Dill, used by kind permission of Katy Dill).

8.14 CONSIDER ACCESSIBILITY AND INCLUSIVITY

Accessibility is usability, but for those who may be impaired in some way, such as not having full use of their limbs, or sensory impairments such as blindness or significant hearing loss (Cooper, 2015, p. 399). Inclusivity is a little broader consideration where we not only design for those with physical impairments, but also simply poor sight, joint stiffness, or rusty cognitive capabilities, as is typical with old age.

It's always a good idea to tailor our design to be as usable by as many people as possible, and considering accessibility and inclusivity often results in better usability for everyone. If we are designing for an audience with a high percentage of a specific disability, it's not only critical that we become familiar with accessibility guidelines, such as those for the web (WC3, 2017) but familiar with the challenges of that disability as well.

For example, a high percentage of people with diabetes have challenges with their eyesight to the point where many are considered legally blind. At first blush, you may think that designing for a screen-based context such as a mobile phone may not make much sense for this group, but even a cursory study of those that are less than fully sighted will reveal they love their phones. Taking care to use large type, contrasting colors, and clear iconography provides this audience with a rewarding experience.

It's also important to not design down to a non fully abled audience, but to consider usability standards to make your device more sophisticated and more usable for all. When designing for a disability group, we suggest having a target group of people with that disability at our disposal so that we can explore whether design decisions we make are valid (Figure 8.7).

Figure 8.7
Accessibility guidelines derived for a low vision cooking system (from Culina Metra, by Team Culina Metra, used by kind permission of Katrina Hercules and Neal Smith).

LOW VISION DESIGN GUIDELINES

HIGH CONTRAST

People with vision problems naturally have a hard time picking out fine details and detecting subtle changes in color and value. Because of this, it's good to use elements that contrast with each other as much as possible.

BIGGER IS BETTER

Another obvious rule is that bigger type is easier to see than small type. For low vision, a good size is around 15-20 points . Bold type is also useful when designing for low vision.

REDUCE GLARE

Many people with vision problems are sensitive to light and glare and it's important to keep that in mind when designing for low vision. White paper and screens are particularly irritating culprits and it's often wise to output information as white or yellow on black to increase visibility.

This is not just for those with limited senses. In fact, considering how to design for those with limited sight or hearing may make our system easier to use for a much wider audience. We often challenge our designers to ideate around the idea that our audience has some sensory limitation, be it deafness, blindness, or something else. This often results in interesting ideas and adjustments to the system that we would not have considered otherwise.

But, of course, there are downsides for extreme accessibility: First, it's impossible to design for everybody. There will always be a set of people whom our design can't reach. But that doesn't mean we shouldn't consider it. We should design for the largest percentage possible, within reason. Second, usability standards often have an inverse effect on the amount of information one can deliver quickly. For example, large type and icons suck up a great deal of screen real estate and limit the amount of information provided in each screen. Scrolling through screen after screen is a tedious process made more annoying if it isn't necessary for a well-sighted target audience.

Type where our audience has control of its scale can solve this to some degree, but at a certain point, this will break down, too. The overarching goal should be to strive for as large an audience as possible. Take into account those with disabilities and balance this with a clear understanding of your target. This will help you to make informed decisions about accessibility vs. usability conflicts where they may occur. And bear in mind that often there is no negative effect at all.

Good accessibility and inclusivity commonly leads to good usability.

8.15 CONSIDER FLEXIBILITY VS. USABILITY

Flexibility is the ability of the interface to allow the user to be in absolute control of every aspect of the system. Usability is the ability of the system to be easily used. The more flexible an interface, the more complex it will need to be, and, hence, the less usable it is. You will need to balance these against each other by considering how flexible you want your interface to be or how easy it will be to learn and possibly use. Complexity makes things more controllable, but harder to learn and use. Simplicity makes things easier, but less controllable.

Given your audience, strike the correct balance between flexibility and usability.

8.16 CONSIDER HICK'S LAW

When people are presented with several options, it takes longer for them to decide than if they faced fewer. This is what is known as Hick's Law. If we are asking our user to choose an action, it will be less time efficient the more options they face. More options mean more complexity, which then leads to less efficiency. Designers often have to make choices for their audience to reduce the number of options to allow interfaces to be simpler and more efficient.

Strike the right balance between options and efficiency.

8.17 CONSIDER PERFORMANCE LOAD AND COGNITIVE OVERLOAD

Related to Hick's Law is the principle of performance load. The more complex a system, the more error-prone it will be. The simpler, the less error-prone. The goal is to strive for less complexity or fewer steps to achieve the same results. "Designs should minimize performance load to the greatest degree possible" (Lidwell et al., 2010, p. 178). The more complexity, the more it overloads the consciousness of the user and makes things harder.

Our brain also has restrictions that we must consider (Johnson, 2010, p. 82). It's even been asserted that we are not able to handle much more than five to seven items at a time (Saffer, 2010, p. 135). We touched upon this above, in discussing an automobile interface: The cognitive demand of driving is so encompassing and the consequences of failure are so severe, that there are stringent restrictions placed on these interfaces. The brain can easily be overloaded with information to the point where it gets confused or distracted. There are even cases where planes have crashed due to this problem (Traufetter, 2010). Sending an emoji to your friend while you're walking probably doesn't have the same consequences, but, as a designer, we still should ask the question, "Am I supplying them too much information in the posture they're in?" If we're considerate of this—even in mundane circumstances—we'll have a more successful product.

What we mean by considering cognitive overload is that our users have a limit on the amount of information they can hold in their short-term memory. There is a reason why a single quiescent state of the dreaded phone menu never contains hundreds of menu items. It's usually around five to seven, because that's all we can store in our memory. There's even a principle defined for this called seven plus or minus two, that states we can hold in short-term memory only seven items, plus or minus two (Johnson, 2010, p. 82). This limits not only phone menus, but all forms of quiescent states, even the webpage or the mobile screen. We are not saying that we can have only seven items on a web page; what we are saying is that as the amount of content grows on a page or screen, the more short-term memory demand we are placing on our audience, and the less usable the state becomes. It forces us to think harder.

Don't overwhelm your audience.

8.18 CONSIDER REDUCING NAVIGATIONAL DEPTH

When we consider cognitive overload or smaller screen sizes we may need to reduce the number of elements on a screen or quiescent state. But the content we remove has to go somewhere, so we may increase the number of quiescent states to handle it. But by doing so, we begin to confront another problem: navigational depth.

To explain navigational depth, let's consider this thought experiment: We have 1,000 items we want our user to select from. Because we are considering cognitive overload, we know full well our users will have a monumental time keeping all these items in their head in order to choose between them. So, we cleverly divide the items into folders containing about seven items apiece. Now we are left with about 140 folders, and we still are breaking the seven plus or minus two rule. So we add another layer of folders by grouping these into sets of seven as well. Now we have about twenty folders of seven folders apiece. We break this down one more time. In the end, we have a hierarchy of four levels that we need to navigate to get to any one of our items: The top level has about three folders, the second has seven, the third has another seven, and the fourth has yet another seven items.

What if we wanted to make our system even simpler by allowing only five items to be considered? Going through the same process detailed above, we would need to drill down through not four but five layers to get to our items. In other words, although there are fewer items at each level and, by Hick's Law, the more usable the interface is at that level, the deeper we have to navigate to get to any item. This increases the amount of effort we need to expend to get to them. Through this thought experiment we can see that reducing complexity at each state may lead to an increase in navigational depth and make our interface harder to use.

How do we handle this? It's a trade-off between increasing depth and overloading the number of items. We often employ a mixed approach to solving this: We should strive to make items that the audience would most likely use have a much shallower navigational depth, while those things that are used less frequently can have more.

The more something is used, the less deep it should be.

8.19 SURFACING

In the previous section, we mentioned a possible solution to the depth overload conundrum: more popular items are at a shallower depth than those that are less popular. We call this principle "surfacing" because we want our most popular content to come up to the very top, or surface, of our system. In fact, an excellent design approach is to identify the content that our user would want most for a given context and go to the extreme to surface it all the way to the top. In this way, the user isn't looking at a navigational menu right up front, but the content they are interested in.

To surface content, we like to consider the following analogy: It's like taking our structure diagram, identifying the information that is most important, grabbing it and shaking the entire structure so that that content is at the top of the hierarchy. Everything else is below it.

Well-designed systems do this. Facebook, for example, has an information hierarchy with me and my profile at the top, then my friend groups, then my friends, then my friends' posts. But when I launch the system I don't have to drill down this hierarchy to get to the posts. The posts are right at the top, and I drill down to get to the other things, such as my profile or friend groups. They've ignored the information hierarchy and surfaced the content I'm interested in.

Look at your structure map. What is most important? What is most important for each context? How can you restructure the quiescent states of your system to surface that content?

Important elements should rise above less important ones.

8.20 SURFACE THE FUN

What is the "fun" of your interface? Those elements that are most important for each context is what we endearingly call "the fun". For Facebook, it is the feed, for Google search, it is the search results, and, for Yelp, it is a restaurant where I want to eat. These are the things that directly satisfy our user's goals. Everything else is just a means to that end. Every search phrase, every navigation menu, every thumb flick through uninteresting content is stuff we don't want but have to endure to get to the "fun".

When we say "fun" we don't really mean fun in an entertainment sense. We mean fun in the sense that it is what we are using the system for. I don't like doing my taxes, but know that I have to pay them, and need to use a form to do so. The quicker and more efficiently I can get that form done and get presented with what I have to pay, the better. Getting to that final figure and getting that check sent is the "fun," regardless of whether it is fun or not.

Alan Cooper flips this concept around and calls all that other stuff, the non-fun stuff, excise. "Excise tasks . . . don't contribute directly to reaching the [user's] goal, but instead represent extra work that satisfies either the needs of our tools or those of outside agents as we try to achieve our objectives" (Cooper, 2015, p. 272). Excise is friction, and our goal as designers is to eliminate it. When we say "surface the fun," what we mean is that we should have a clear understanding of what the fun is of our system, and what is excise; we should strive as much as possible to get that fun in front of our user as quickly as possible. This may seem straightforward, but it often is not as easy as it looks.

A common case in point is the launch menu. On many apps, when we launch them the first thing we see is a button menu of things that the app can provide us. This may seem natural from an information hierarchy point of view, but is a navigation menu really the fun that the user wants to see? If it's an app where they want to find a restaurant and the first thing they see is a selection menu of cuisine types, that is not the fun. The fun is being presented with restaurants and scrumptious plates of food. But you may say how do we know what the user wants unless we get some information from them? Often, we have that information: If they've been using our system, we have a pretty good idea of what they want. Even if that's wrong, it's better to show them yummy dishes as their launch experience rather than a tedious button menu.

Make some assumptions. Give your user your best guess, and bring up to the surface of your system the thing that they want to see. You can always supply them with a "more" link that allows them to explore a type of content further or a menu bar that takes them to different sections. Eliminate excise, surface the fun, and fill the main content area with the stuff they want.

Surface the fun.

8.21 MENULESSNESS

Users do not open up an app to interact with navigation menus; they want content. Navigation is only a means by which we get to the content we want. It's excise—a necessary evil. Our users would be happy if they had the genie in the bottle: No navigation at all, but the system just inherently knows what they want and presents it to them. It may be far from possible, but it's instructive to consider whether we can eliminate menus altogether.

How do we do this? Let's consider a travel app. If we followed a strict information hierarchy, we might present possible trips to our audience by showing a globe. Then, they could select a country, then a region, then a location to visit, and see trips in that area. This navigation could be contained in a set of hierarchical menus. The system could also have menu items for trips I might want to take based on my history, those for a certain price, and excursions the friends I follow may suggest.

But when I launch the system, do I want to see a menu? No. What I want to see are trips. Instead of showing all these content arrangements as menu items, wouldn't it be better to surface the fun and show them as sections in a list of trips at the launch of the app? It could list trips first by ones I'd most likely want, next, those my friends suggest, third, by region I'd like, and fourth, by the price I'd most likely pay. Each of these sections may present three to five trips themselves, the fun. Not an icon menu leading to a separate screen. If I want more from one of the sections, I can select something that brings me to a new screen, such as one where everything is organized by price.

Not showing navigation first, yet showing content and allowing that content to be navigation, provides users with the things they may want immediately. It may not be exactly what they want, but at least we've made an attempt. Although completely eliminating menus is likely not possible, it's a fruitful exercise to consider what would happen if we eliminated them from the interface.

Surface the fun by considering if the menu can contain content itself.

8.22 MATCH CONTROL WITH PROFICIENCY

The more complex a system is, the harder it is to use, the more time consuming it is, and the more error-prone it may be. But what if we're flying an airplane or managing a nuclear reactor? A simple interface will not cut it. In these cases, systems are complex and their users will need as much control as possible to get out of sticky situations. They may not need this level of control all the time, but it needs to be at the ready, available to be used when necessary.

The more control that is available, the more proficiency the user needs. We could also simply swap out control for complexity, and we'd be correct as well. If your audience has a high level of skill, don't be shy to provide them with the level of control they need. You'll undoubtedly need to be much more careful with error checks and balances, but they will need that complexity, they'll need that control. On the flip side, if you have an audience of casual or infrequent users, you will need to make decisions for them to reduce the complexity of your interface.

The complexity of a system should agree with its user's proficiency.

8.23 CONSIDER PROGRESSIVE DISCLOSURE

The novice wants a simple interface; the power user wants control. One of the most potent aspects of interactive media is that, to some degree, we can allow the user to control the complexity of their interface. They can click on a twirly to reveal elements and click on it again to hide them. We can provide them with a simple search, or they can open up a more advanced set of options. We can supply our users with simplicity first, and allow the interface to increase in complexity as it is used. This is the concept of progressive disclosure, where complexity and control is revealed through use. It allows our interface to simultaneously handle a wide range of users from the novice to the expert.

Increase the usability range of your interface by introducing aspects that can progressively disclose elements through use, allowing for simplicity for the novice and complexity for the power user.

Aid learning through progressive disclosure.

8.24 CONSIDER PROCESS BEHAVIOR

How does your system work? What is the magic that is going on behind the scenes? This is usually the realm of the technology experts on your project team, but there is no reason why designers can't have insight into this area as well. What are your thoughts on how your system might operate? Clarifying these operations and ideating around them can lead to interface elements that we may not have thought about previously.

We certainly don't have to work in a vacuum on this. It's an excellent time to connect with our developers and technologists to gain insight into how they think things may work. Most of our design focus has been user-centric, as it should be, but there is no reason why we should completely avoid exploring more technologically inspired approaches to our interface design.

We've found it useful to list our functional features and then consider what that would mean for the interface, both virtually and physically. We may not know exactly how these elements may be integrated into our system yet; that's not the point at this stage. What is important is that functional features are considered and explored (Figure 8.8).

Understand how your system functionally behaves.

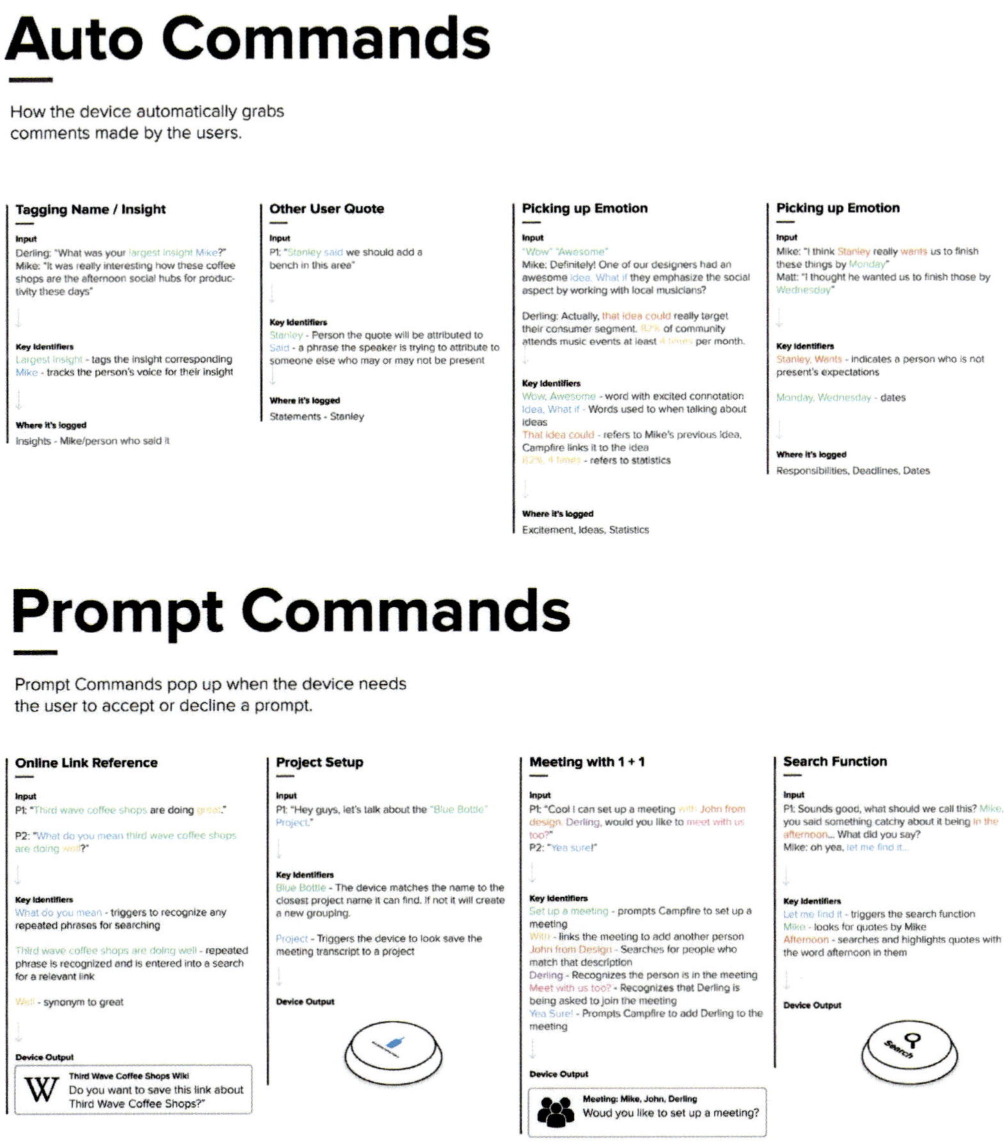

Figure 8.8
Process behavior for a natural language note taking system (from Campfire, by Team Seamrippers, used by kind permission of Matthew Benkert, Derling Chen, Ian Liao, and Mike Rito).

8.25 CONSIDER MENTAL MODELS

We are creatures who have evolved in a physical world. We pick things up, put things down, turn things on, adjust them, open doors, hammer, screw, cut things, and wrap things up. These are the activities that are natural to us. On the other hand, we don't naturally set bytes within CPUs, move things into registers there, and invoke operations on the data in those registers. Yet, that is precisely what is going on behind the scenes within any digital context. Beyond dealing directly with binary data, every single way we work with a computer is a form of fiction. It's a virtual construct that allows our human brain to understand this world of zeros and ones more easily.

These virtual constructs can be language based, as are most programming languages, command line systems, and natural language systems; they can be based on manipulating graphics, as are desktop interfaces and touch devices; or they can be based on selection menus, as are phone systems. Whatever the approach, we manipulate digital devices through these constructs. It is our mental model or conceptual model of how these devices behave that allows us to do the things we want to do (Saffer, 2010, p. 133).

These constructs need to behave, to some degree, as we would expect them to in the real world. If I drag a file from one folder to another, my mental model expects it to be removed from one folder and added to the other. If that doesn't happen, I experience a cognitive dissonance that challenges my understanding of what's happening. I get frustrated and am thrown out of any state of flow I had been in. Now I need to solve the problem of "where's my file?"

When users manipulate aspects of our interface, what mental models do they have of what's going on? Does our interface's presentation and behavior support and reaffirm that mental model?

For the interactive components and constructs on your interface, consider your user's mental models and strive to match them.

8.26 CONSIDER METAPHOR

Metaphors are objects or ideas that are used in place of, and to clarify, another object or idea. We use them in interaction to help users better understand how to use aspects of our interface. We use a folder metaphor on a desktop interface to store files. We use a map metaphor on a mobile device to view location information. We use a clock metaphor on a watch to view time. Bits, bytes, and registers are not how we think. We apply metaphors to make digital data more familiar.

As you can see, metaphor is closely tied to the concept of mental models. The link between them is that if you are using a metaphor to represent some interaction in the virtual world, it should represent the user's mental model of how that thing behaves in the real world. A folder on my computer should behave, to some degree, like a folder in a file cabinet: It should be able to hold documents and be able to be filed, opened, and closed. A swipe should behave like a swipe in the real world: It should be able to push things aside. Your decision about the metaphor to use for an interaction formulates your user's mental model of what's going on.

One of the most revolutionary concepts in digital design was the desktop interface, invented at Xerox and promoted by Apple's Macintosh. This brought computer technology from the arcane world of command line instructions to the visual and menu-driven consumer device we know today. Central to the concept of the desktop interface was the idea of the metaphor. This can be seen in its use of the name "desktop" itself, with items that can be placed on the desktop's surface, its use of a trash can, its use of "menus" that provide the user with clues as to the functions they can perform, and, finally, the browser "window" where we can store files and folders. The desktop, menu, and window all stem from representations of things that we are, to some degree, familiar with in the physical world.

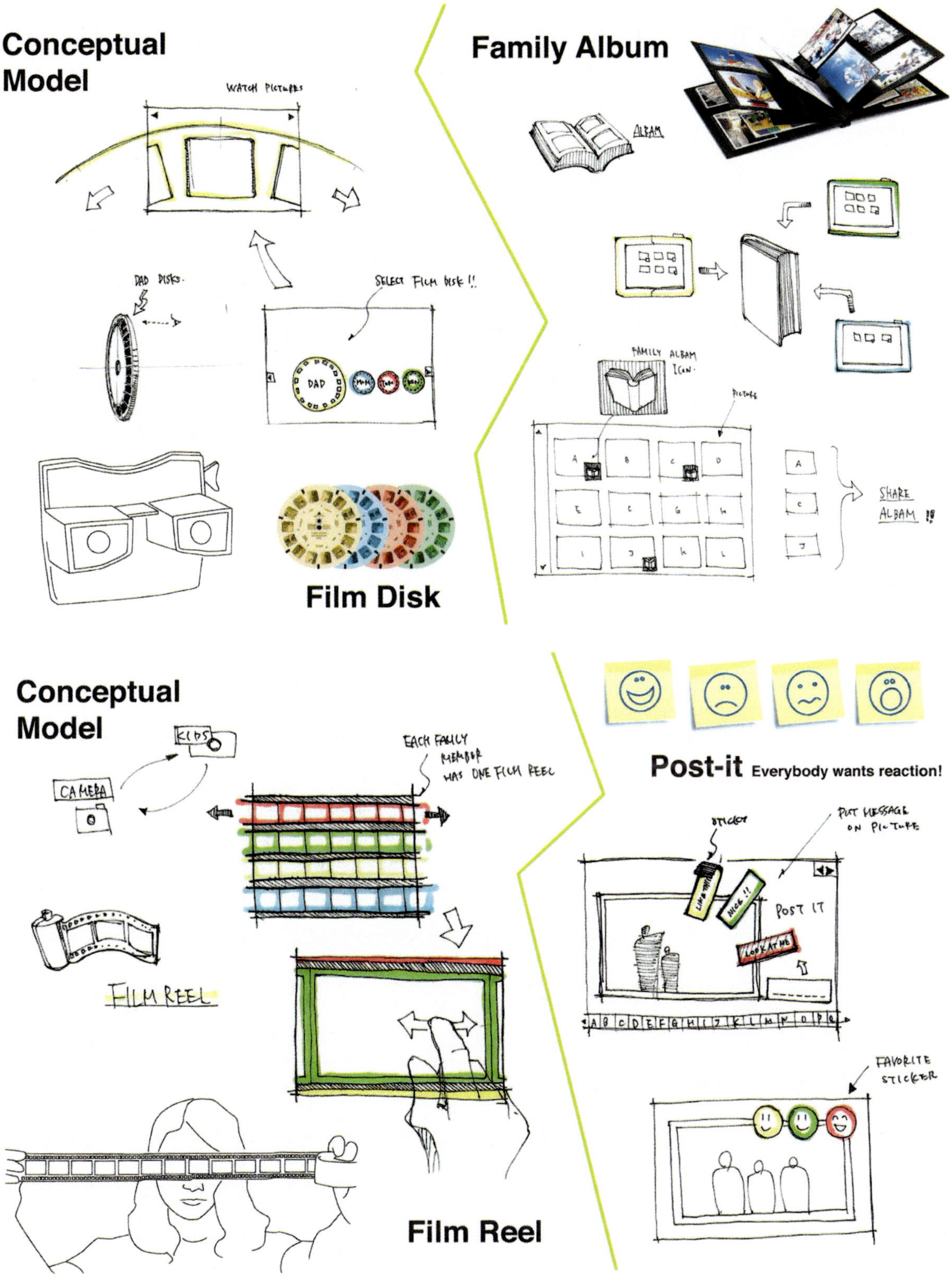

Figure 8.9
Using metaphor to inspire possible solutions (from Kinect, by Tash (Tatsuro) Ushiyama, used by kind permission of Tash (Tatsuro) Ushiyama).

As a designer, it's important to understand that although it's useful to rely on metaphors to help communicate concepts in an interface, there is a danger of going too far. As Cooper points out, excessively realistic metaphors can ". . . cripple the interface with irrelevant limitations and blind the designer to new paradigms more appropriate for a computer-based application" (Cooper, 2015, p. 308). For the desktop to be useful, it doesn't have to work exactly like a desktop. Indeed, I've never seen a desk with pull-down menus and browser windows on it. But we can use the example of a desktop to improve our audience's understanding of how to use things.

This distinction leads some to dispense with the concept of metaphors altogether and identify these items as idioms instead, since they are more like learned idiomatic expressions. When we say "needle in a haystack," we don't really mean needles in haystacks, we mean it's hard to find something. When we say "window," we don't really mean a window looking out at the world, but a scrollable rectangular area that displays the contents of our computer. Regardless of this distinction, we can use metaphors or idioms to allow us to consider other possibilities in the approach to our design (Figure 8.9).

Metaphors should match what you want the system to do as well as matching what the user is thinking. The right choice leverages your user's experience in the real world so that they have a better understanding of how your system behaves, even if they're experiencing it for the first time. A poor choice means that the system will not work as they expect—it does not agree with their mental model—and leads to confusion and frustration.

Metaphors can also be used as analogies to generate interface ideas ranging from the legitimate to the bizarre. Embrace them to push your ideas into areas that you may not have considered. Remember, we are talking about exploration here, so everything is fair game. Consider this an opportunity to explore the wealth of possibilities around the information in your structural design within your scoped what–who–why–where–when.

An important area for ideation and exploration is in the integration of the physical, virtual, and metaphorical aspects of the interface. I will even go out on a limb and say that this is where some of the best interaction design comes from, but sadly seems missing in many interactive devices. What is the mental model that works the best for your system or devices within your system? How can you design both the physical interface and the virtual interface to support this model (Figure 8.10)?

Consider metaphors that help your user understand what's going on with your system's behavior.

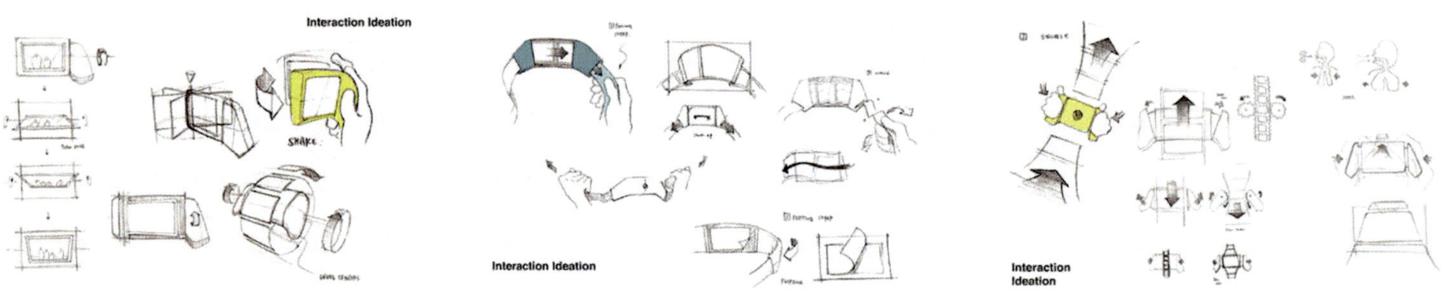

Figure 8.10
Leveraging metaphor to communicate how to use a device (from Kinect, by Tash (Tatsuro) Ushiyama, used by kind permission of Tash (Tatsuro) Ushiyama).

8.27 CONSIDER INTERFACE PATTERNS

Metaphors rely on interaction patterns that we may see in aspects of our lives other than digital contexts. But digital contexts often have idiomatic patterns specific only to themselves. For example, many mobile apps allow us to scroll through lists. Although the lists and their items may be arranged differently from app to app, they are still merely a set of linearly organized items that we navigate through. The list idiom is a pattern, and scrollability is a pattern as well. In fact, scrollability is a common pattern that apps share with many other contexts, including browsers and desktop windows.

Lists are a content pattern because they define an arrangement of content, while scrollability is a behavioral pattern in that it defines a type of action and response mechanism. We introduced the concept of patterns previously in our discussion about navigation, where we pointed out that menus and button menus are patterns. There are also patterns that define controls such as Bezier drawing tools and color pickers. Commonly, patterns combine content, behavior, and control, such as our email or contact list on our mobile device. They are a scrollable list of content items that, when clicked, bring us to a specific email or contact (Figure 8.11).

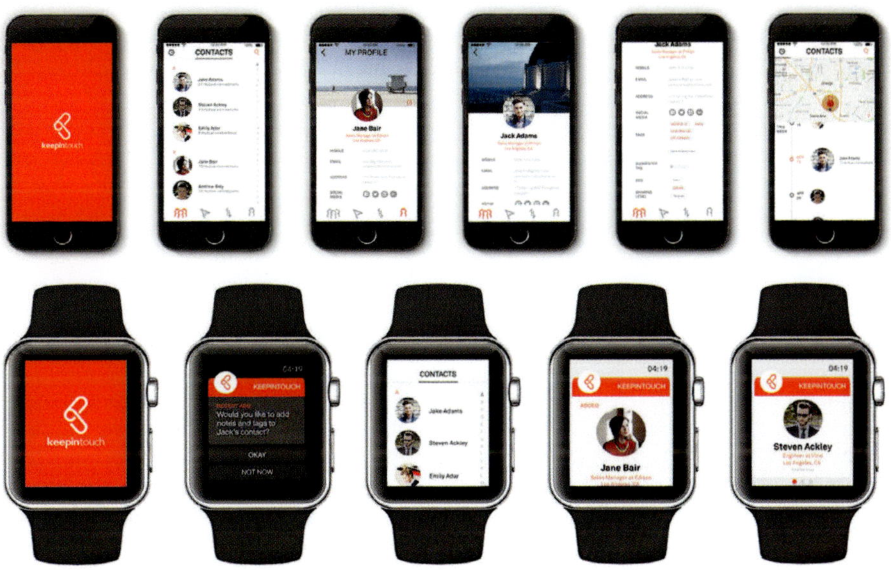

Figure 8.11
A scrollable list pattern across devices (from Keepintouch, by Amber Wang, used by kind permission of Amber Wang).

Although many patterns appear across myriad contexts, such as menus, lists, and scrollability, usually we consider patterns as being associated with particular contexts. Common desktop patterns are windows, menu bars, toolbars, buttons, palettes, and dialogs. Behavioral desktop patterns include selection, drag and drop, and direct manipulators, such as pen tools.

The web has common patterns as well, such as primary and secondary navigation menus, scrollable content, three column layouts, twirlies for hiding or revealing content, search bars, ad panes, parallax, infinite scrolls, headers, and footers. Mobile contexts include patterns such as scrollable lists (also referred to as stacks) (Cooper, 2015, p. 510), menus, search bars, carousels, home screen grids, swimlanes (more prominent on tablets), cards, and drawers. Behavioral patterns on mobile devices include finger click for selection, drag to scroll, pinch to zoom, two-finger rotate, and swiping. Patterns are not just restricted to visual interfaces either: Audio interfaces include selection menus ("please select from the following items . . .), question and answer prompts in natural language systems, and wake up words ("Alexa . . .?").

The list of patterns above gives just some of the most common. As mentioned in our discussion about navigation design, although patterns are a critical component to Interaction Design, a detailed listing and discussion is beyond the scope of this book. However, we should discuss what patterns are in general and the role they play.

Interaction's use of patterns and pattern languages stems from architecture, with its source being the seminal work *A Pattern Language* (Alexander et al., 1977). Within, the authors, spearheaded by Christopher Alexander, present a method whereby a descriptive language is defined and used to create architectural and urban planning programs that are pleasing to their inhabitants. Patterns in Interaction Design can be thought of similarly. We can create a descriptive language to identify patterns that are pleasing to our users.

A pattern's definition should contain a few critical elements: They should have a description and a name; they should have an indication when they should be used, what they are good for, and what they are not good for; and they should have a set of clear examples. If a pattern resource doesn't have these elements, we may end up spending more time than we would want trying to figure them out.

The value of patterns is that they act like metaphors and idioms in the sense that they allow users to understand the interface of a new system without a great deal of prior knowledge. The problem with patterns, though, is that if our interface is entirely constructed of common patterns, it looks like everything else. It has no distinction. Additionally, we may force our interface to conform to a pattern that isn't all that appropriate, thereby losing sight of the unique structure of our information. If applied correctly, patterns make our interface usable, but not distinctive. We usually strive to employ patterns as much as we can, so our system can be as usable as possible, but reserve a few well-considered "hero" interactions that may be uniquely ours through which we can express our own voice.

Improve usability by employing common design patterns.

8.28 CONSIDER INTERFACE GUIDELINES

Many contexts come with a set of design patterns already. These are generally referred to as interface guidelines and include Apple's Human Interface Guidelines (Apple, 2017), Microsoft's Design Guidelines (Microsoft, 2018), and Google's Material Design (Google, 2017). These are suites of design patterns intended to ensure a uniform design approach for applications that run across their devices. The benefit is that if we employ these patterns, our audience will be able to use the knowledge of other applications to understand ours. In other words, they make our app more usable and the learning curve much quicker.

They also give our applications an air of professionalism because they look like other apps. The downside, though, is what was mentioned previously: Our system may lack distinctiveness because it looks and behaves like everyone else's. Regardless of the usability/distinction conundrum, at this stage it's be best to become familiar with the guidelines of the contexts in our ecosystem so that we know the standards. Being aware of them allows us to be in control of when we want to fit in, vs when we want to stand out.

8.29 INTRODUCING AESTHETICS

We've been methodically developing our aesthetic approach over several chapters through the development of our guidewords, moodboards, and identity explorations. Eventually, in a few chapters, aesthetics will not just be playing a bit part, but will take center stage. But before we get to that point, let's address what may be a burning question: What do we mean by aesthetics anyway?

Aesthetics is admittedly a loaded term. It refers to a branch of philosophy as well as a set of principles that define art movements such as Impressionism,

Modernism, or Post-modernism. What we mean by aesthetics in these pages is none of these. Our use of the term refers to the topic of aesthetic judgement, whereby we determine whether the impact an object has on our senses is pleasing or not. For a physical object, this is how it feels in the hand or to the touch, what its surface looks like, what it sounds like when it provides us auditory queues. For a screen, this is what the image looks like and moves like. For an auditory system, it's how it sounds, its voice, the words that are spoken, and its tone. The aesthetics of a system are its surface details. It's what we see, hear, feel, and possibly taste and smell.

In screen-based media, the term "visual design" is often employed in the way we use the term aesthetics in this book. But, clearly, the term "visual design" falls short when our systems cross boundaries into tactility and sound, not to mention getting the nose or tongue involved. We could use terms such as sound design and tactile design, but the impact we may receive from a single design element is often holistic: It may involve a combination of stimuli. A material on a device can have both a look and feel. A good wine is commonly as much smell as it is taste.

We could use the term surface design, but this falls short as well: If we shake an object to hear what it contains, that has nothing to do with the surface of the object. The same is true for the weight and balance of an object. So, we dispense with terms that segment and isolate the senses unless they serve our purpose to be considered in isolation, and we gravitate towards one that celebrates the holistic nature an object has across all the senses: aesthetics. We employ the term to refer to the means by which our system directly impacts our senses.

8.30 ICONOGRAPHY: IMAGE AND MEANING

Icons hold a special place of importance in aesthetics. They can communicate ideas and concepts in a limited amount of space independent of any specific language. For example, the concept of "home" can be communicated with just a box with a triangle on top; search is a magnifying glass; and menu is the hamburger icon (three stacked horizontal lines). Although "home", "search", and "menu" are reasonably small words, these icons can take up even less area. The challenge with icons, though, is understanding their referent—understanding what they mean. For those that are common, this is not too much trouble: Your users have seen the image before and have an idea what the referent is. For those that are not as common, the icon must indicate the idea in such a way that the user gets it without much fuss. It needs to be intelligible.

Simplicity and clarity are critical for intelligibility. Complex forms are not only difficult to reduce to a small size, but they also tend to be more cluttered and more challenging to understand. When considering an idea to iconify, we first explore many possibilities of what it could be. We call this the simulacra phase, because we are investigating the possible images that can serve to represent the idea.

We challenge our designers to explore a range of iconic imagery through ideation between those that are abstract—those that represent a sense or a feeling more than a thing—and those that are representational—those that represent an explicit thing. For example, the concept "to draw" could be expressed abstractly by a flowing line, or more explicitly by an image of an artist drawing at an easel. Neither of these may work. The line may be too abstract to get, while the artist image may be difficult to turn into a simple icon. The artist image has other problems as well: It could mean easel, drawing canvas, inks or paints, or the drawing tool itself. This lack of clarity plagues both images, so why not be simpler so as to make the image easier to scale and possibly easier to remember?

The extremes of impressionistic abstraction and explicit representation are probably not what is desired in the end, but serve to guide us in exploring a range.

It's the stuff between those extremes that is often the most useful. If you're developing an icon for the concept "drawing", forget about expressing the term through the setting of the artist at an easel. Ask what is really "drawing" about this staging: the pencil on the paper. Ask what the feeling is that we wish to convey with the abstract line: possibly a sense of flow? Maybe a happy medium between these two extremes would be a flowing line from the tip of a pencil. Now we have a little bit of representation to ground the idea as well as simplicity and feel.

With the pencil and line as a center point, we can explore a higher degree of representation by including the artist's hand or the artist themselves. We can explore a higher degree of abstraction by de-emphasizing the pencil and emphasizing the line. What are some other ways that we can explore this continuum between abstraction and representation? Challenge yourself to find others and let them guide your ideation. Regardless of whether this method of abstraction/representation is useful, it's essential to engage in the goal of the simulacra phase: to develop many possible approaches to represent your idea (Figure 8.12).

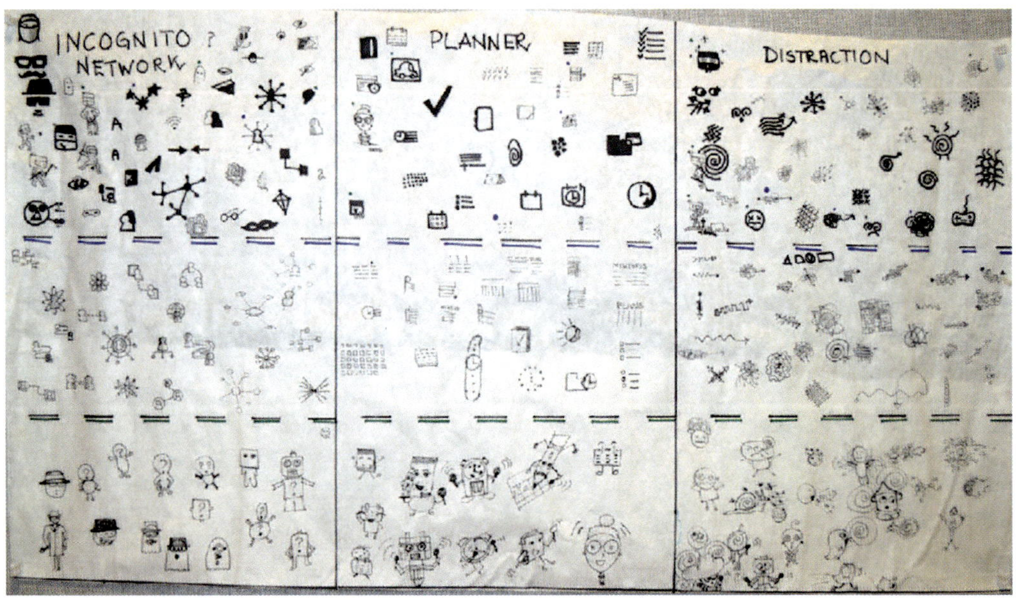

Figure 8.12
The simulacra phase of icon design: Focus on image and meaning (from Addmit, by Team CTX, used by kind permission of Emily Harrington, Tammy Hsieh, and Lars Fiva).

You can test how well your iconic explorations are working by printing them out on cards and showing them to people. Are potential users able to decipher what the image is? Do they have an inkling as to what it is referring to? How well do they remember it? When doing this, it's useful to shuffle a bunch of different ideas together, so the subject has less of a clue as to what images mean what. Remember to reflect on and synopsize this effort for presentation.

8.31 EXPLORATORY COMPS

You may have already been exploring aesthetic possibilities, and, if not, since we have a strong set of guidewords and inspirations in hand, now is the time to begin.

The process of arriving at an aesthetic design with integrity is rarely linear. We may put a great deal of effort into an approach just to realize later that it wasn't right, and needs to be thrown out. We may explore something else, abandon it, and then find that it was what was needed all along. Regardless of this seemingly—and often frustratingly—random through line, there are a few approaches to the effort that we consistently see as providing success early on: Numerous explorations eventually pay off, follow your heart, not your brain, and don't fall in love with any particular approach too early.

To be efficient in exploring numerous approaches, it's a good idea to keep the scope of the explorations small. We ask our designers who are engaging early in the aesthetic process to work on only one or two screens or quiescent states. Forget developing a comprehensive design for the entire system. That's wasted effort. To start the aesthetic process, we select a screen that we want to work on: One that we are chomping at the bit to design. Don't worry about being consistent at this stage: Different design explorations may even have different screens as their subjects, possibly from entirely different contexts. One may be a web interface, and the other may be mobile. Let inspiration be your guide.

When you are designing a quiescent state or screen, don't cheat. Comp them at a level of detail that they look like screen grabs of the real thing. They should have real content and real imagery. Yes, we only have just begun the process of interface design, and we may not yet know exactly what content a particular quiescent state may hold, but these are not finished designs. These are comp explorations. We're less concerned about what the interface contains for this effort, just its style. So, don't be shy, use your sketch wireframes to guide you to what you think will be there information wise, and use them as a basis for your exploratory stylistic approaches. The information will most certainly change, yet so will your aesthetic design.

Keep the effort simple by exploring only one or two interfaces. Keep it inspired by working on interfaces you're compelled to design and keep it exploratory by not becoming too enamored with any particular approach. Your goal at this stage is to generate a wealth of possibilities, not refining the perfect one. Finally, follow your heart, not your head. This should be a welcome break from all the analytical effort you've been working on in your structural design (Figure 8.13).

Figure 8.13
Two different UI approaches of the same interface for a creative brainstorming system (from Cosmos, by Team Laundry, used by kind permission of Asli Akdemir, Lynn Lei, Nathan Lu, and Yozei Wu).

9 Refinement

We should have been using low-fidelity wireframe sketches on paper or in our journal to explore possibilities with the interface considerations listed in the previous chapter. If we were working on physical designs, we should have been using quick three-dimensional mockups or "sketches" of devices. But, at some point, we will arrive at a small set of solutions that we feel need further refinement. For our screens, we need to assess the amount and aspect of the elements of content and control that each quiescent state can hold. For physical mock-ups we need to get a more refined sense of form and function across the object's surface. The level of detail necessary to express these explorations can no longer be handled by low-fi sketches. We need greater fidelity. This chapter takes the work product we've introduced previously, such as wireframes, flowboards, scenarios, and comps, and presents how they should look and what they should contain for the next few phases of design. These are the frameworks to be used to iterate your design to the point where the structure is fairly resolved.

9.1 MID-FIDELITY WIREFRAMES OR MOCK-UPS

Mid-fidelity wireframes are laid out and typeset on the computer (Figures 9.1 and 9.2, also see Figure 7.12). Pictures can still be boxes, but the text should contain the

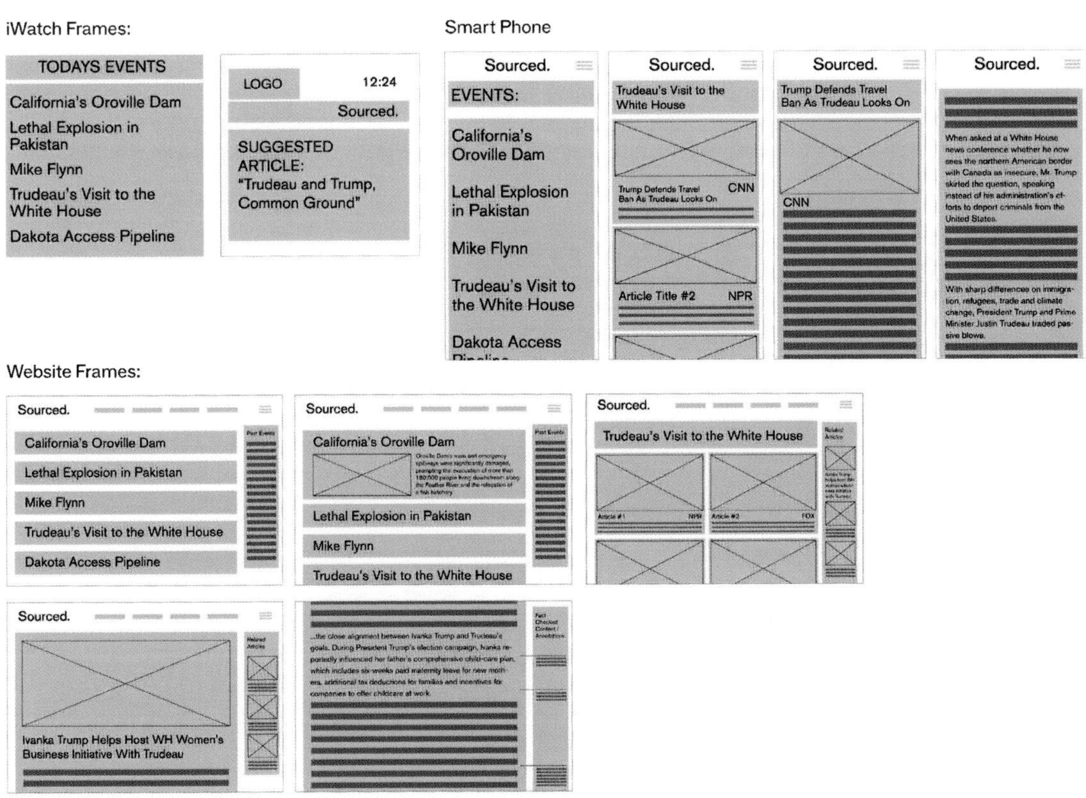

Figure 9.1
Mid-fidelity wireframe example (from Sourced, by Jonathan Nishida, used by kind permission of Jonathan Nishida).

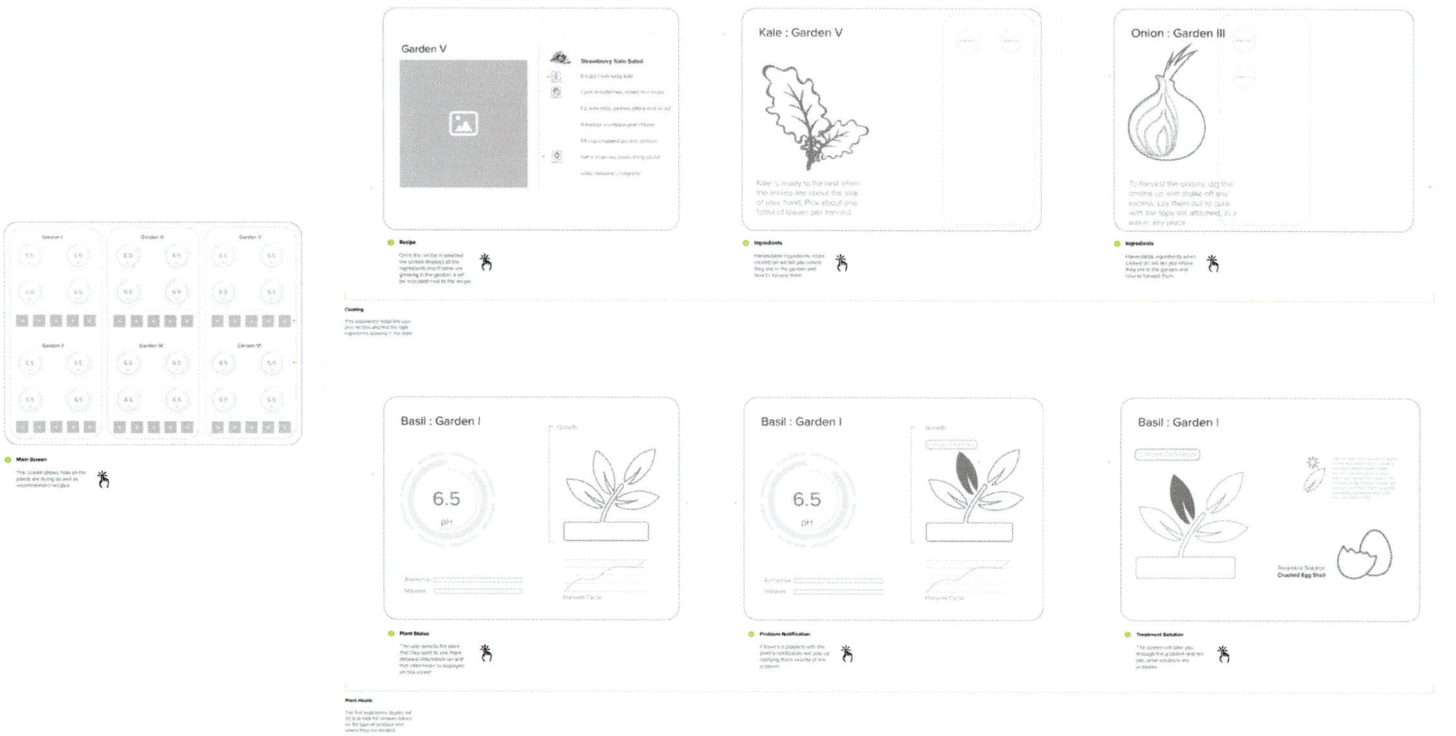

Figure 9.2
Mid-fidelity wireframe example (from Berry, by Team Porkbun, used by kind permission of Justin Nam and Daniel Smitasin).

information they intend to present: Headlines should contain headlines in them, dates should have dates, and menu items should be accurate. Captions and paragraphs can be boxed or greeked out (i.e., *lorem ipsum* can be used), but the number of lines and their line widths should be roughly accurate.

For physical explorations, mid-fidelity mock-ups are done with materials that can carry form and a higher degree of tactile resolution than our quick sketch physical mock-ups. These can be done in foam, clay, or wood. We should begin to assess how their form relates to the physical attributes of our user's posture (Figure 9.3).

Figure 9.3
Mid-fidelity mock-ups should hold form (from Cosmos, by Team Laundry, used by kind permission of Asli Akdemir, Lynn Lei, Nathan Lu, and Yozei Wu).

The danger in moving from lo-fidelity sketches to mid-fidelity is detail seduction: We may tend to start noodling our interface, be it screen based or physical. This is a significant time waster for things that will most likely be revised over and over. To avoid this, rely on restrictions. For screens, we may limit ourselves to using just black and white (not even grayscale), boxes to represent imagery, dingbats for iconography, and use only one typeface that has an ample range of styles, such as Helvetica or Univers. For physical mock-ups, we should limit ourselves in terms of materials that can carry form, but not precise form details. These restrictions make it just about structure, not the style.

Layout and placement considerations begin to emerge at this point, and that is only natural when we must consider the hierarchy and flow of information, but striving for a pixel-perfect placement is not an efficient use of time at this stage. For screen-based content, use simple methods to indicate importance, such as scale or a top to bottom read. Also use simple grids: single columns for narrow (mobile) screens, two or three columns for those that are wider. For physical mock-ups consider general placement in order to agree with ergonomics and posture, but you don't have to be precise at this point. Also, through drawn ideation, we should be exploring the form of any important interactive components that may appear on the surface of devices. See Figure 8.6 for example.

9.2 SECONDARY USE CASES: THE CRITICAL ALTERNATES

Up to now, we've been focusing on our primary use case. What happens when someone uses our system for the first time? What can our system do to take advantage of those who become highly engaged masters? The primary use case has been helpful because it kept our focus on the most essential activities offered by our system, but we may have been blinding ourselves to some critical aspects that make themselves apparent when we consider user flows outside our primary. Let's explore these other cases.

The most important use cases other than our primary are what we call secondary cases, or critical alternates. They feature users who are part of our target but have more detail and specificity. We've been using one of those types already: the intermediate user. The other two most common types are the novice and the power user, or expert. These additional sub-targets do not necessarily flow through our primary use case, but are alternate cases that are still critical to the success of our system. Hence the term "critical alternate".

The intermediate user or "casual veteran" featured in our primary use case forms the most substantial part of our audience but the novice is critical, too. If you have difficulty enticing people into your system, they will never reach the point of being veterans and will never experience the benefits of the primary use case. You'll kill off your audience before they become your audience. On the other side of the skill spectrum, the expert, or power, user is crucial because they have the energy and commitment to drive your system. For example, they may be the ones that upload the lion's share of user-generated content if your system relies on that, or moderate discussions, or create the most pleasing results.

Although the novice and expert are secondary to our primary use case, for our system to be successful, we must expand our scope and design for their success as well. The number of users for these cases may not be even close to the number of intermediate users we have, but their critical nature to the success of the system requires that we need to put as much care and effort into them as we would into our primary.

Let's expand our scope by creating scenarios and structural designs for our novice and expert user, as well as our intermediate. These are the essential users of our system. In fact, if we are approaching this from the point of view of agile development, our primary use case and critical alternates are essentially our MVP. Focus on each of these cases, and consider how the system handles them (Figures 9.4, 9.5, and 9.6).

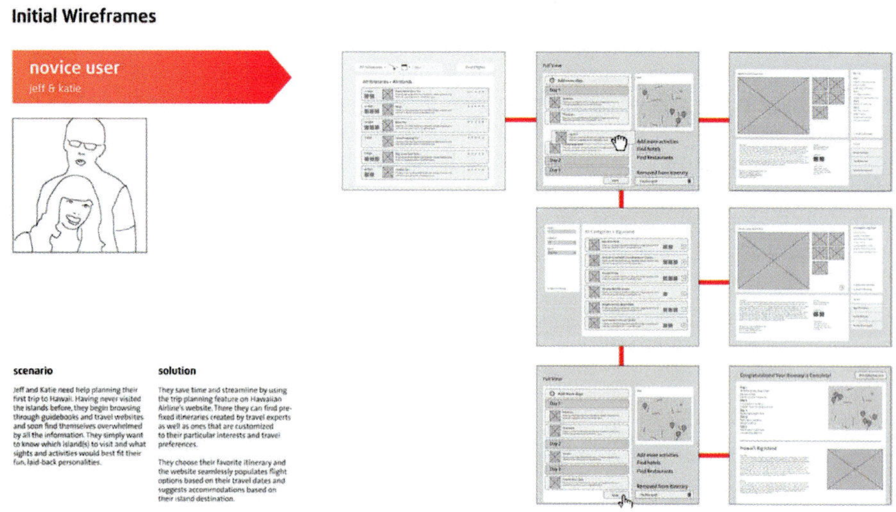

Figure 9.4
Text scenario and user flow of a novice for a vacation travel system (from Hawaiian Airlines, by Oliver Lo, used by kind permission of Oliver Lo).

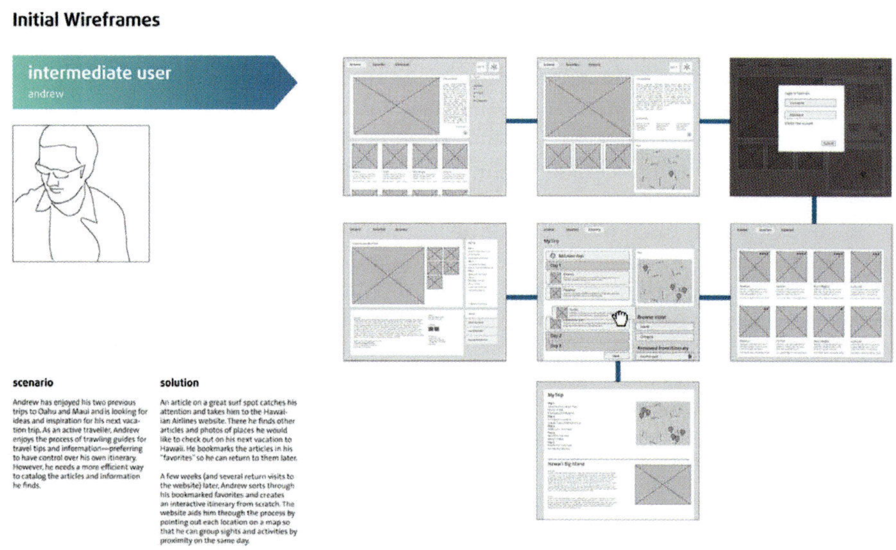

Figure 9.5
The intermediate case (primary use case) (from Hawaiian Airlines, by Oliver Lo, used by kind permission of Oliver Lo).

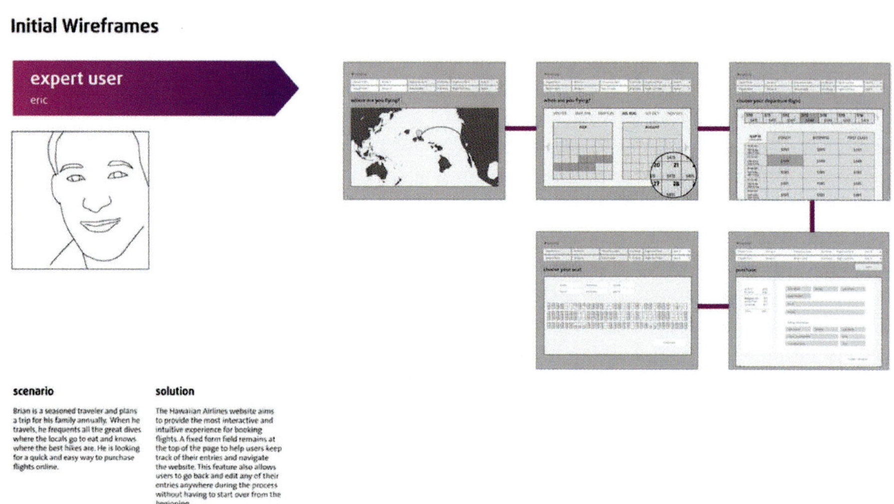

Figure 9.6
The expert case (from Hawaiian Airlines, by Oliver Lo, used by kind permission of Oliver Lo).

Create an inciting moment for each that triggers their need (the "scenario" in the figures), and describe how the system solves that need (the "solution"). Depict how that solution is manifested in the interface. When considering the new use cases generated by these user stories in the example images above, that of novice and expert, bear in mind that the designer didn't start there. They developed these mid-fidelity wireframes flows by using appropriate factorial iteration: They began with user goals, mapped them to features and tasks, and considered them with respect to their posture studies, which were simple in this case, since the context was scoped as a website. They created information breakdowns based on their tasks, and developed lo-fi wireframes from that information. They then user tested and refined these into mid-fidelity wireframes that included micro-interactions. It is this final mid-fidelity result you see here.

What does a user need to do to enter the system for the first time? How quickly can we transition our novice into a casual veteran where they see the full benefits of the system? Look at the information your primary use case requires. What does this tell you about what is necessary to allow your novice to reach the full benefits of the system? How can we make that process easy and seductive? How can we create an experience such that we fill them with delight with the expectation of what our system will do? This is called onboarding: The process by which novices enter the system and become veteran users.

When considering the expert, also look at the information that drives the system. Does that information come from the standard user or power users? Often it comes from the expert. If so, how do we entice the intermediate or casual veteran to transition to an expert? How do we make that transition seductive? When they've arrived at that point, how do we make things powerful and efficient to retain their engagement?

In summary, onboarding should provide our novice user a small collection of well-orchestrated activities so that they are seduced without being overwhelmed. Seduction is key. The intermediate user is provided with tools where they can customize things with little effort and be able to experience the main distinguishing features of the system. Overwhelming them is no longer a problem, and the achievement of the system's main goals is critical. The power user knows what they want and knows how to get it. They desire control, possibly notoriety, and above all, efficiency. The power user wants to get done what they want done, and they want it without any fuss.

Before we end this discussion, it's important to point out another sub-target: the perpetual intermediate (Cooper, 2015, p. 246). The novice certainly wants to transition to the intermediate, but it may not be the case that the intermediate wants to transition to the expert. Most users don't care about engaging with a system to the point of being an expert; they just want to benefit from what the primary use case offers. They have better things to do with their lives. The perpetual intermediate sub-target commonly forms the largest segment of our user base. Allow for intermediates to transition to experts, but not at the expense of making the system more frictive for the perpetual intermediate.

9.3 USER FLOW

The scenario is excellent for expressing the experience of the user: their context and their goals. But sometimes we may want to dispense with context for brevity's sake, and focus squarely on the interfaces themselves. A user flow, also called a use case flow, may be more useful in surfacing these details. They depict a use case—the primary for our purposes right now—just as our scenario does, yet they eliminate the user's external context and present only the interface and how it works. See Figure 9.7. Notice how it removes all contextual imagery. Additionally, the use case presented here is the systemic primary use case—that use case which details the most important features, not only of one context, but all critical contexts of the system's ecosystem: in this case, mobile, TV, web, and watch.

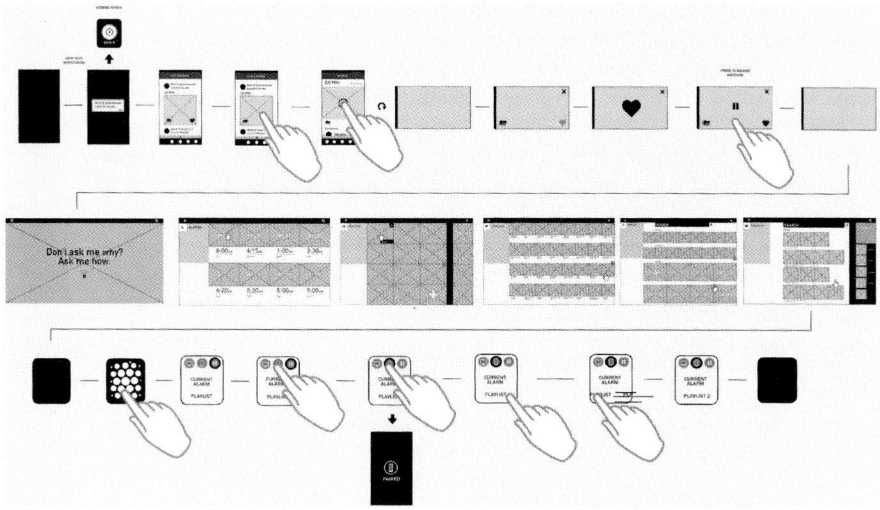

Figure 9.7
User flow of a systemic primary use case (from Inliven, by Elbert Tao, used by kind permission of Elbert Tao).

Due to its lack of external context, the user flow may not be as generally approachable as the scenario, but it has the added benefit that it's easier to create (you don't need settings and actors), and it focuses on what is most important for our design effort: the interactions with the interfaces themselves.

9.4 RED-LINING USER FLOWS

When creating the user flows, it's useful to create a user story for each, establishing who the specific user is and what prompts them to engage with our system (Figure 9.8). Rely on wireframes to identify how they flow through the interfaces to achieve the goals of the user story, such as the systemic primary use case presented in Figure 9.7.

Figure 9.8
Closeup of the user story for the intermediate case (primary use case) (from Hawaiian Airlines, by Oliver Lo, used by kind permission of Oliver Lo).

scenario

Andrew has enjoyed his two previous trips to Oahu and Maui and is looking for ideas and inspiration for his next vacation trip. As an active traveller, Andrew enjoys the process of trawling guides for travel tips and information—preferring to have control over his own itinerary. However, he needs a more e fficient way to catalog the articles and information he finds.

solution

An article on a great surf spot catches his attention and takes him to the Hawaiian Airlines website. There he finds other articles and photos of places he would like to check out on his next vacation to Hawaii. He bookmarks the articles in his "favorites" so he can return to them later.

A few weeks (and several return visits to the website) later, Andrew sorts through his bookmarked favorites and creates an interactive itinerary from scratch. The website aids him through the process by pointing out each location on a map so that he can group sights and activities by proximity on the same day.

Not only is it essential to consider how our audience uses interactions to progress through the interface, but precisely what do they look at, how would they scan the interface, and what would they select? We can indicate this as in Figure 9.9. This

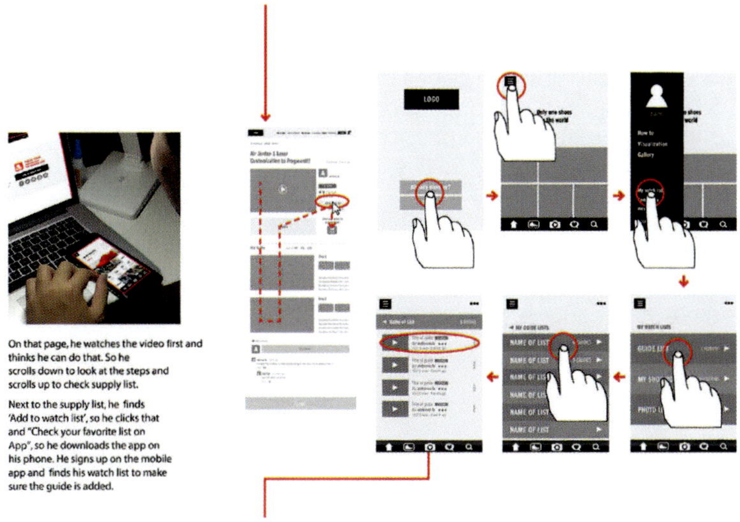

Figure 9.9
Red-lining interactions (from Sneakerzilla, by Jae Hee Jang, used by kind permission of Jae Hee Jang).

is a process called red-lining, because red lines are often used to depict how a user flows through the experience. In this way, we can begin to assess not only what the quiescent state contains, but its organization as well.

9.5 MID-FIDELITY WIREFRAME FLOWBOARD

Updating the fidelity of our interfaces and flows also means updating the fidelity of our wireframe flowboards. We start by using our lo-fi flowboards as a basis, but now the flows may have changed based on the user tests performed with our paper prototypes or considerations we may have addressed in this chapter. Additionally, our consideration of critical alternates should have generated a number of new interface possibilities that we need to integrate into our flowboard.

Our flowboards are the most complete representation of the architectural structure of our system for the contexts within it, so they need to be kept up to date. Neglecting them makes them useless. We need to revise them based on our system's current configuration to keep them accurate and useful. See Figure 7.12.

Yet, we may be facing an explosion of information detail when we transition from lo-fidelity to high-fidelity flowboards. Although this may not be the case with a sparse system, it is certainly the case with informationally complex systems. To handle this explosion, we often reduce the contextual scope of our focus not only to the primary use case, but possibly the primary context as well. It's always good to retain a systemic perspective, but our MVP may only reside on one device, so why consider the rest in detail? If that's true, the answer is that you probably shouldn't. At least not in detail, and not at this stage. What is useful, though, for systems where the MVP is on one device, is to continue to consider the impact of other contexts by keeping them at the level of a structure map. For systems where the MVP is spread throughout the ecosystem, by all means, keep the perspective systemic.

9.6 THE STRUCTURAL PROTOTYPE

To test our designs, it's best to build a prototype that is as close as possible to the system itself, that works on a device as close as possible to the context users will be experiencing. But, as we mentioned before, building a working system on the proposed device is a costly proposition, and, at this stage, we need to iterate extensively to see if an arrangement is working or not. It's not a wise idea to put so much effort into things that are going to get thrown away anyway.

Previously, we used mock-ups and paper prototypes to give us a quick sense of the system. Since we have taken our interfaces one step further in resolution through our mid-fidelity wireframes and physical form explorations, our prototypes need to reflect a more refined level of fidelity as well. This is where structural prototypes come in.

The structural prototype is one that indicates the structure of the system but not its look and feel (Figure 9.10). For screen-based interactions, it refers to a class of prototyping frameworks that rely on pagination and links. A "page" is one of your screens or quiescent states. The links are hot spots that take us to other screens in our system.

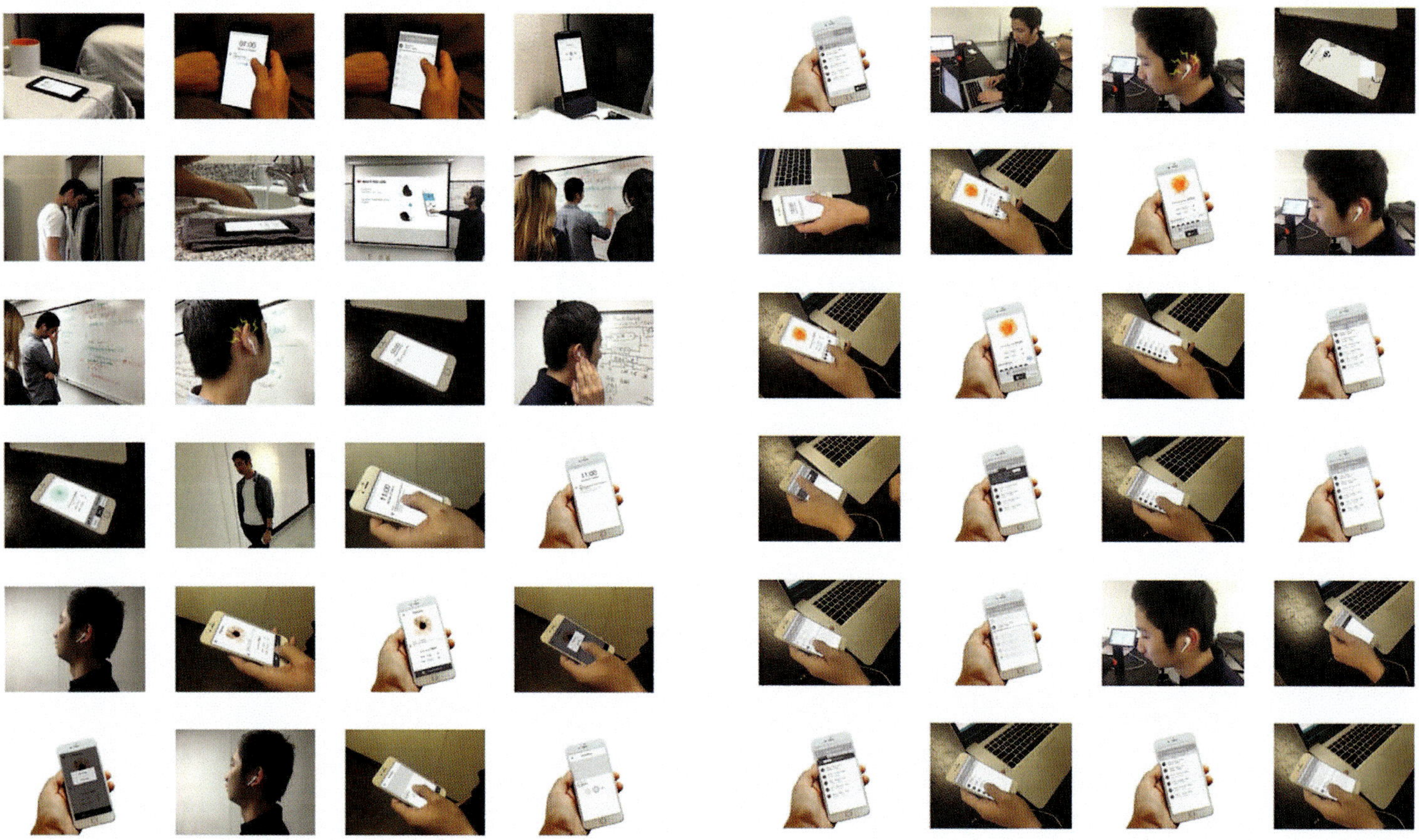

Figure 9.10
A structural prototype used in a primary use case scenario (from Odmo, by Hui Ye, used by kind permission of Hui Ye).

At the time of this writing, Invision is a good example of a page-based prototyping tool for mobile devices. These tools have been with us almost since the beginning of the graphic user interface: A few decades ago a great deal of desktop interface software was prototyped in a tool called Hypercard. I've even seen designers use presentation tools such as Keynote and PowerPoint for this purpose. In fact, Tim Berners-Lee developed the web to be a page-based interactive system to distribute documents (Berners-Lee, 1989). These types of frameworks have been around for decades and will be around for decades to come.

The advantage is that page-based tools are simple to learn, fairly quick to execute, and often can run on a standard suite of devices. The disadvantage is that they are limited in their functionality, often providing only the capability to simply jump from screen to screen based on a click; forget about depicting any unique and complex interactions. This means that if we're using standard devices, such as tablets, desktops, or mobile devices, we're in luck. We probably have a page-based prototyping tool available for us.

If we are proposing a system with custom devices and interfaces, we most likely aren't as lucky. What we do in this case is adapt a standard screen-based device to mimic the interactions on our custom interface. We strive to place the device *in situ*: If our device proposes a screen on a table, we project a computer screen onto a surface. If it proposes a screen on a drone, we mock up a rough drone device, place a small screen on it, and hang it by wires.

As you can see, part of our prototyping effort, from a physical point of view, is focused on creating structures that can represent the devices of the system *in situ*. Even if we cannot quickly construct a form to carry a projection or standard screen, it's useful to create a screen-based structural prototype on a standard device and interact with it. They not only reveal flaws caused by a designer's limited horizon or scope blindness, but they may also reveal hiccups in the way our users absorb information in a context. Through paged prototypes, we can achieve revelations that may not have been evident when we were merely using a flowboard. However, both flowboards and structural prototypes are beneficial in their own way. Flowboards provide a sense of the system structure, while structural prototypes force us to consider the experience of flowing through each quiescent state individually.

This is also the stage where the designers of the physical devices should begin assessing the tactile nature of the system. Exploring materials (Figure 9.11), creating a materials board, and a collection of devices that contain interactive components that we feel may be useful for our system are part of this effort. We may not be integrating look and feel into our prototype yet, but we should indeed be researching it, exploring it, and presenting possibilities to our design team for discussion.

Figure 9.11
A materials board of possible materials to be used for a design.

9.7 THE DESIGN SCENARIO

As a further exploration of how our user flows through the system and how their physicality impacts design, it's instructive to apply our design as it stands into a mid-fidelity scenario. Like our low-fidelity version, the mid-fidelity scenario should

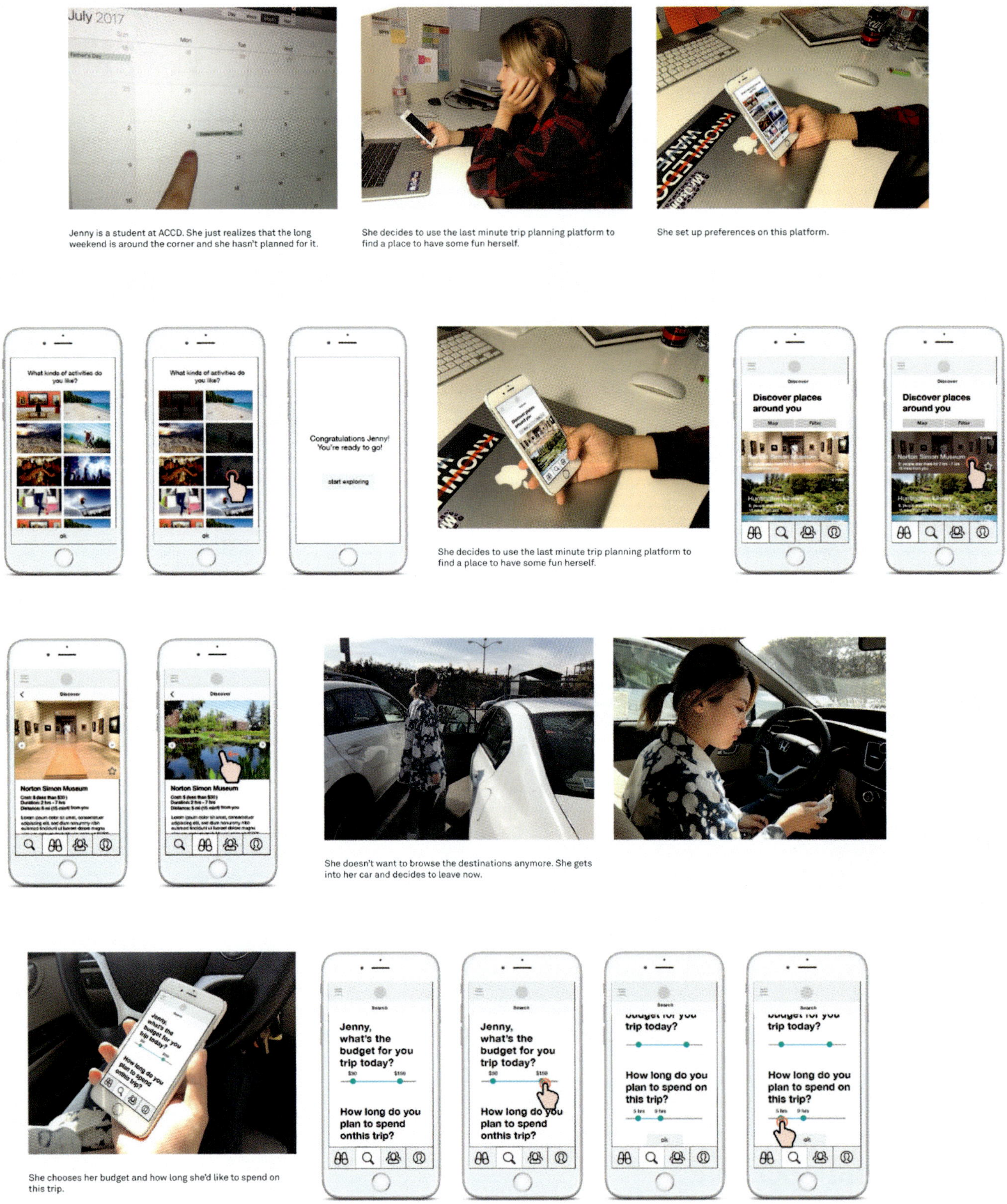

Figure 9.12
In a design scenario, present interfaces face on, so detail can be clearly seen (from Lastmin, by Chufan Huang, used by kind permission of Chufan Huang).

reflect our system's primary use case. The scenario should tell the same story, with the main difference being that it is more refined based on the further refinement of our design.

Because of the level of detail now being expressed, we should add more visual clarity to our scenario using more precise cinematic language and more accurate actors and situations. Also, we should improve the shot style of the interfaces themselves: Instead of relying upon our audience being able to discern the details of the interface within the context shots, it's much better to present the interface face on, using a hand or some sort of indicator to demonstrate how we intend the interaction to work (Figure 9.12). This will allow our stakeholders to assess the details of the interface better because they will see it in its most pristine form.

Our scenario doesn't have to be beautifully shot at this point, but it should be very clear. Employ proper scenario design techniques to appropriately explain what's happening. Your wireframes should be mid-fidelity in that they carry all the information that is expected to be contained in any quiescent state that appears in the scenario. Models don't need to be refined in any sense, but should carry more detail than previous iterations. Physical interaction controls should be included at this point. What we have arrived at with these additions is what we consider to be a complete "design scenario": Still rough, able to be thrown out for the sake of iteration, yet begins to express a clarity of imagery, detail, context, and interface.

The design scenario needs to explicitly present what the user is doing and how the system responds. It needs to communicate cause and effect in detail. Do not get wrapped up in the notion that a design scenario needs to contain a certain fixed number of frames. That's a losing battle. The scenario needs to comprise precisely the number of images that explain the detail cause and effect of the flow along the primary use case. No more, and no less. It is this detail that is important, because we cannot design what we do not know. For the rest of our scenarios throughout the design phase, we should strive for this level detail and completeness.

Because of the increased detail, we can not only reassess whether the flow can be better optimized, but also explore aspects of the interface relative to our projected postures that we may not have been able to consider before. Is the scale of the elements of the interface appropriate for the posture? We can begin considering specific interactions and gestures. Do these interactions seem to work with the postures we've envisioned? Can they be made less awkward?

It's entirely natural to revise and refine the interface while we're creating our mid-fi scenario. If we have several different ideas of how a particular aspect should work or be formed, sketch those possibilities and explore micro scenarios to see which works best. Factor the most successful into the final scenario.

9.8 STYLE ANALYSIS

To continue to keep our aesthetic effort engaged, we are partial to a particularly useful activity that we call a style analysis. It's performed by referring to our guideword boards, in fact, our comprehensive inspiration board in particular. If that board was done correctly, we should have collected a selection of interfaces that we think conveys the precise feel we wish our product to have. How did the designer of that interface achieve this? What are the design elements they are using to deliver on those feelings? Dissecting these elements in a style analysis can provide us with useful insight into these questions.

A style analysis is essentially reverse engineering a style guide based on the aesthetic attributes of a system's interface. As mentioned previously, we use the broad term "aesthetics" because we wish to include not only visual interfaces, but physical, spatial, and auditory as well. However, this process has its genesis and its most significant application in the visual design of screen-based interfaces, so these are the ones we deal with here. Just bear in mind that there's no reason why these cannot be applied to other dimensions as well.

Style guides for heavily branded entities can be books several pages thick. But, in our case here, we build guides of only a few pages. They refer to the visual designs of the interface and express how the brand logo is applied. They indicate the typeface and how it is applied, the color palette, iconography, and how the standard navigation system or systems are treated. They present the look of the iconography, the layout and grid system for each context, and any other design elements that serve the purpose of the visual design.

The goal is that if the style guide were placed in the hands of a competent designer, with that and a particular interface's wireframe, the designer would be able to aesthetically design that interface to fit within the aesthetics of the entire system (Figure 9.13). This deconstruction allows us to see into the design, to analyze the components that make it up, and prompts us to consider attributes that may prove useful for our aesthetics.

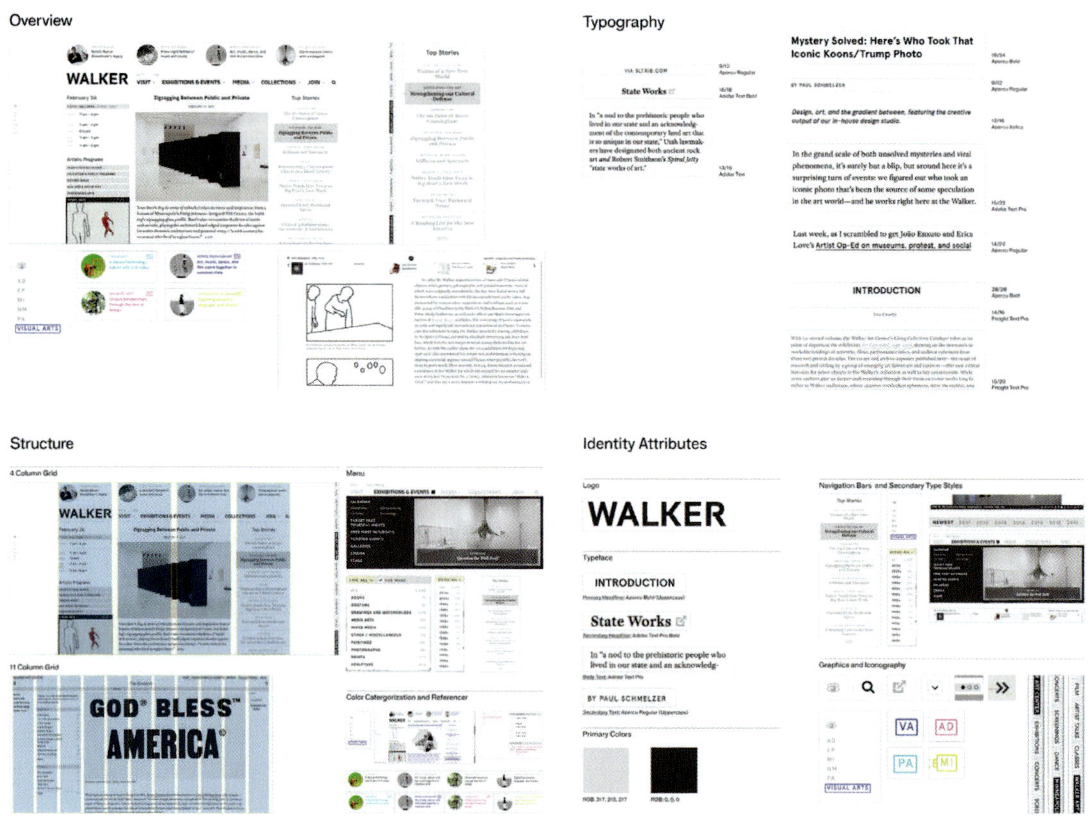

Figure 9.13
A style analysis of a website (from Sourced, by Jonathan Nishida, used by kind permission of Jonathan Nishida).

What colors does the interface use? How does its navigation work? What typefaces are used and what is the typographic strategy is employed? How are photos treated, how is it laid out, what do the icons look like and how are they used? How are separation and hierarchy handled?

There is a conventional narrative that runs throughout the design disciplines that originality is good and derivatives are bad. We are not as dogmatic about this because we see that usability is often enhanced by elements that are shared between systems and we can learn and understand things from other highly successful designs. The problem arises when designers blindly copy others without considering the essence of how things really should work. This may lead to perpetuating a bad set of "best practices" (Karjaluoto, 2014, p. 117).

But we feel perfectly comfortable with looking to successful "others", gaining a deep understanding of how they are done, and then developing our unique designs from both first principles and what we've learned from those "others". We need a little of the familiar if we also are offering the unfamiliar. To have everything be novel will lose our audience, and is just as egregious as being completely derivative. What we are engaging in with a style analysis is not learning to be derivative, but engaging in a form of active visual research (Lupton, 2011, p. 38).

The style analysis prompts us to see what makes the inspiration tick design-wise by having us look at it as a set of design elements. What may seem elusive when it's altogether may not appear as daunting when it's dissected.

9.9 ICON FAMILIES

When we introduced iconography in the previous chapter, we explored their form and meaning individually. The effectiveness of a single icon is one thing; its effectiveness in a group of several presents an entirely different challenge. Clearly, an icon needs to look different from its brethren to express a different idea, but there's a balancing act here: You also want them to have a sense of unity of design that in the end represents your brand values. We want them to look different conceptually, yet not stylistically. To illustrate this, maybe we need an icon to represent "to write" in addition to one that represents "to draw". Both could be expressed by a pencil and a line, and if they both do, our users would have no idea of the difference between them. We could highlight these differences by expressing the drawing icon with a wavy line and the writing icon with a straight line. But is this enough? Will our audience be confused as to which is which? I cannot tell you the answer to this, but it is something that should be explored. It's entirely possible that we will need much more to differentiate the two concepts.

This differentiation is also critical for either one of the icons to be remembered. If our users are confused as to which means which, this confusion may inhibit their ability to remember them. And, since the ability to be remembered is one of the most significant problems of using icons, we run the risk that these icons will inhibit usability, not enhance it.

On the flip side, we want our icons to work together as a team. They need to convey our brand values appropriately, and if they are stylistically unified, they represent one of the most effective means of communicating the overall style of the interface. We like to emphasize this point by referring to them as little idea logos. The effort we would put into making a logo feel right is not unlike the effort we will need to make our icons work.

A smoothed line here, or a framing device there, all placed to make our icons stylistically similar, may have the counter effect of making them conceptually similar as well. These two goals must be balanced so that they are not in conflict. This is where the principle of form follows function comes into play. The function is the concept, and the style is the form. Conceptual separation is paramount; stylistic unity needs to follow from that.

Going back to our process, once we have gone through the simulacra phase with our icons that we initiated in the last chapter, we then need to consider them as a family. Are their respective executions different enough to make them unique? Are there approaches for each that allow them to have similar traits as a family without disturbing these differences? Use these considerations to select the icon for each idea carefully, then start the next phase of their development: the familial phase.

The goal of the familial phase is to establish stylistic nuances that convey your brand values and unify your icons as a family. In this sense, icons are like a well-designed typeface: They need to look as different as the characters in an alphabet, yet have elements that unify them, such as similar heights, curves, aspects, and serifs. In fact, a useful trick is to take the lines and curves of the typeface we may be considering for our interface and create a kit of parts from them: lines, curves, corners, and flourishes. Explore if this kit of parts can be used to form the system's icons. The same can be done with the lines and forms of our identity. If successful, it's a way that we not only can establish a unity of form within our iconography, we can also establish unity with our typeface and identity.

Since the curves and lines in either our typeface or logo should express our brand values, there's a good chance our icons will also. It doesn't work all the time, but for the wealth of benefits that result, it's good to try. Whether this approach works or not, it's important to keep clear sight of the goal of the familial stage: To establish a visual approach for your icons that allow them to stand out from each other, yet fit together as a family.

We don't do this for all icons all at once. We lift a few of the most critical ones—three to five to be precise—and begin working on them together to bring them closer as a family. Use framing devices such as circles or rectangles. Strive to establish a similar level of simplicity and complexity throughout the set. Strive to make their radii, line weights, complexity, and aspect ratios agree. All this effort needs to be done without disrupting the contrast between them that makes them comprehensible (Figure 9.14). Once the formal aspects are established that make them a family, we then enter a refinement phase where we work on applying that style to the rest of the icons, and refine more surface details that tie them even closer to the identity and brand (Figure 9.15).

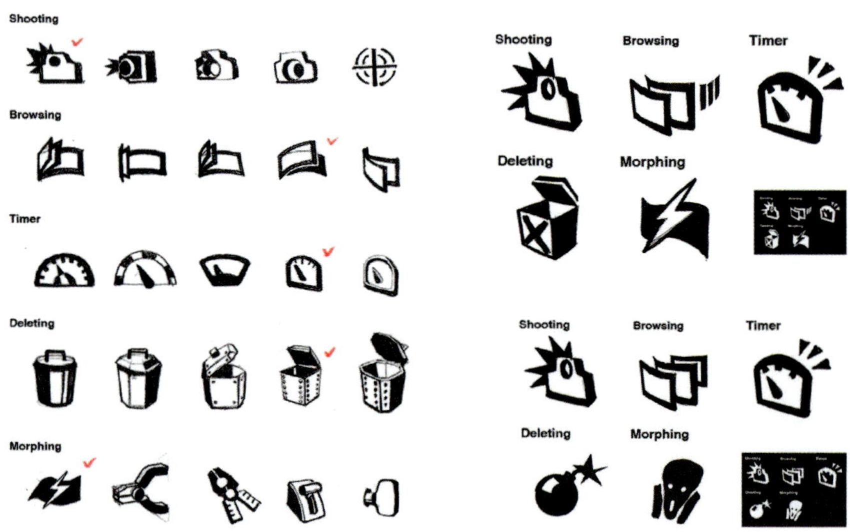

Figure 9.14
Exploring icon forms as a family for a children's camera (from Kinect, by Tash (Tatsuro) Ushiyama, used by kind permission of Tash (Tatsuro) Ushiyama).

Figure 9.15
Iconographic refinement and surface treatment (from National Media Museum, by Tanya Chang, used by kind permission of Tanya Chang).

9.10 CRITICAL INTERFACES

To push our aesthetic design along, we also need to become more strategic with our interface comps. We should move away from choosing any random set of interfaces for our comps, and begin focusing on those that present the most significant challenge to our design effort. Indeed, one of those we choose should be the screen or quiescent state that we consider to be the most central of our system: The one our audience will use most frequently. We call this the "high traffic" screen. Second, we select a screen that challenges our information design the most. It's probably the screen with the most content, the most need for hierarchy, and/or most challenging information requirements. We call this the "information rich" screen.

Finally, we select a screen that may not have a great deal of diverse information on it, and neither is it high traffic, but is one that presents us with the best opportunity to establish our brand values. This may be a landing screen that entices our audience with all the wealth of engaging content we may be providing them, or a detail screen that unabashedly promotes a new product or service to almost the level of an interactive ad. Consider again a travel site promoting a vacation destination. If a detail screen is about a particular tropical beach that we would like our audience to visit, our presentation must make that beach look like the most amazing place on earth. We need to pull out all the stops to make that screen deliver on our brand values. We call this the "brand impact" screen. It's that screen that delivers on our brand values more than any other in our system.

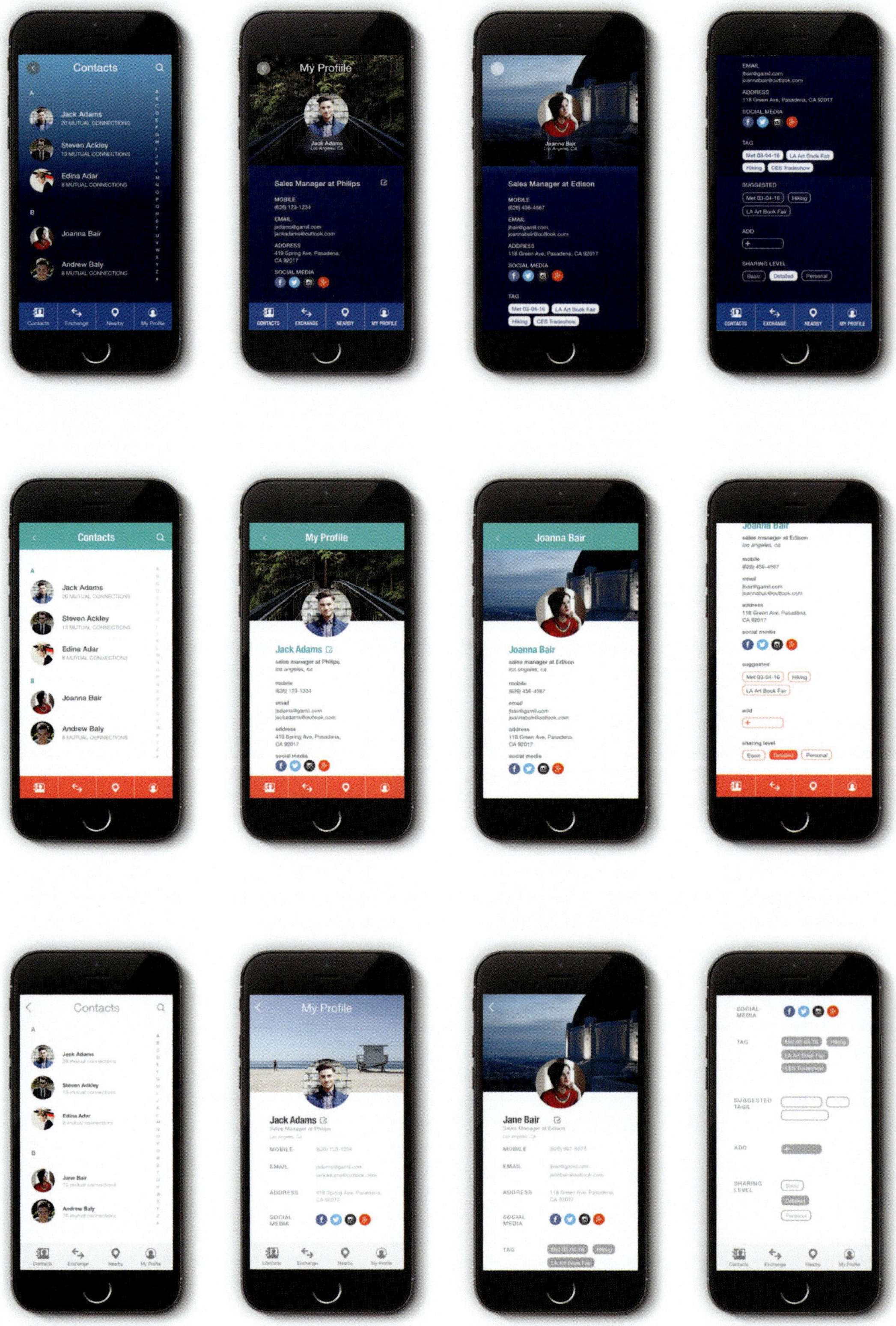

Figure 9.16
Critical interface comps: High traffic, brand impact, and information rich (from Keepintouch, by Amber Wang, used by kind permission of Amber Wang).

We refer to this collection of high traffic, info-rich, and brand impact interfaces as our critical interface set, or, simply, our critical interfaces. This interface set strategically challenges our design approach: The high traffic one needs to be in the mix because of its importance; The info rich interface is the one that most effectively challenges our general layout structure and our typographic hierarchy. It is all about organization; The brand impact interface is the one that presents the greatest opportunity to apply our guidewords or brand values. It is about style. Importance, organization, style: If we get these three interfaces right, we've laid a great deal of the groundwork for almost every other interface in our system (Figure 9.16).

While executing critical interface comps, we must keep firmly in mind the interfaces we chose for our inspiration board. Our inspiration is our ultimate litmus test. Can our comps comfortably sit on that board with our other inspirations? Does our work look awkward, amateurish, or unrefined next to them? If that's the case, ask yourself why, and fix those things. If your critical interfaces are not at the level of feeling, quality, or distinction as the interfaces on your inspiration board, you need to work on them until you get to that point.

10 Microinteractions

We've explored the overall structure of our system through presentation frameworks such as our ecosystem diagram, structure map, and flowboards. We considered context and task through ideations stemming from our posture studies. We've balanced several considerations and used them to stimulate interface explorations resulting in mid-fidelity wireframes. Now, let's drill down to the most basic level of our system, that of the specific interactions our audience has with our interactive components. This is the level of the finest granularity of Interaction Design: that of microinteractions and behavor. In this chapter, we will address microinteractions, and behavior design we will address in the next.

10.1 THE STUFF OF INTERACTION DESIGN

When we are designing interactions, what is it that we are designing anyway? If we were designing a poster, we would be in charge of every square inch of that poster: Type, layout, color, iconography, imagery, content, it's all on the designer's shoulders. We'd create comps and see exactly how the poster looked before we sent it out for the final print run. We could say the same thing about designing a chair, or a package, or even an exterior of a car. Interaction Design is not like that: We never really see it all at once like a poster or a chair. We need a user for the stuff of Interaction Design to come to life. And what is that stuff? Interaction designers are the ones responsible for coming up with how users can act on a system, and how that system behaves in response. The "stuff" of Interaction Design are these interactions and the behaviors associated with them.

10.2 MICROINTERACTIONS AND BEHAVIOR DESIGN

Dan Saffer, who wrote the definitive text on microinteractions, refers to them as contained product moments ". . . that revolve around a single use case—a tiny piece of functionality that only does one thing" (Saffer, 2014, p. 2). These are at the level of elements in our information structure and are the bits of control that make up our interface. We may think of them as almost insignificant in the scheme of things, such as when we compare them to the overall structure of our system or the layout of a screen, but consider this: Everything we interact with in an interface is a microinteraction. The entire system we design is an orchestrated set of microinteractions (Saffer, 2014, p. 20).

The discipline oflnteraction Design is about a lot of things—concept, research, system structure, interfaces, aesthetics—but if there is one thing that we can point to that is the essence of what we create, it is the design of microinteractions. They are to us what letterforms are to the typographer, the most basic element we design with. It could be argued that because of the importance of microinteractions, we should dispense with the somewhat diminutive term "micro" from the word, and just call them interactions. Everything else from interfaces to system structure are in fact "*macro*" interactions. But we'll stick with tradition and call these fundamental interactive moments microinteractions.

But what about behaviors? What is the difference between microinteractions and behavior design? As clarified further in the next chapter, they both encapsulate the same level of an interactive system—that of the most basic level of detail—and are essentially different ways of looking at the same thing. But we address them separately because we use them differently and they accentuate different issues. Microinteractions are more user focused and we use them in this book to help us explore interactive possibilities more generally. Behaviors are more production and development focused, and we use them to detail the precise action and response characteristics of our system.

10.3 MICROINTERACTIONS AND THE DESIGN PROCESS

Traditionally, microinteractions are designed last in an interactive product (Saffer, 2014, p. 6), but we feel that doing so imposes serious limitations on what could be done with them.

Although it may likely turn out that most interactions in our system will be effectively handled by common interaction design patterns, we could have a handful of interactions which are signature moments that distinguish our product from our competition (Saffer, 2014, p. 19). Consider the swipe left, swipe right of Tinder or the character limit of Twitter. These are the microinteractions that define the entire product. In this way, a single, well-considered microinteraction can be worth billions.

By introducing them in the phase where we are still somewhat exploring interactions from the micro level to the macro, albeit in a more limited fashion than in earlier phases, allows microinteractions to influence the entire system's structure. So, as we clarify how to design them, we need to keep our good climbing habits intact by considering the best microinteraction for the component and challenge the rest of the entire structure of the interface as well as the system if need be. This is exactly the reason why we've been using wireframes for our structural explorations and keeping that separate from our aesthetic effort: So that the design can flex if we make discoveries that require it to flex.

10.4 THE WORK PRODUCT

Shortly, we will discuss what to keep in mind when considering microinteractions, but, before we do, we need to address what our work product should be at this stage. Up to this point, we've been exploring our system through wireframes. We will continue this effort, but drill down deeper by illustrating the dynamics of the microinteractions of our interface: How users act on it and how it responds.

Initially, our thoughts can be captured roughly as ideations in our design journal. As you read through this chapter, consider your primary use case and the possible microinteractions along that path. Keep your journal active and strive to capture ideas for your microinteractions as they come. At certain points, you may feel that a particular microinteraction needs more formal exploration, which is when you should clean up your ideation into sketches of their behavior (Figure 10.1).

Finally, when we believe we have a set of interactions along our primary use case that address the considerations discussed below, we can refine our sketches into a wireframe flow that depicts how our user interacts with the system along the primary

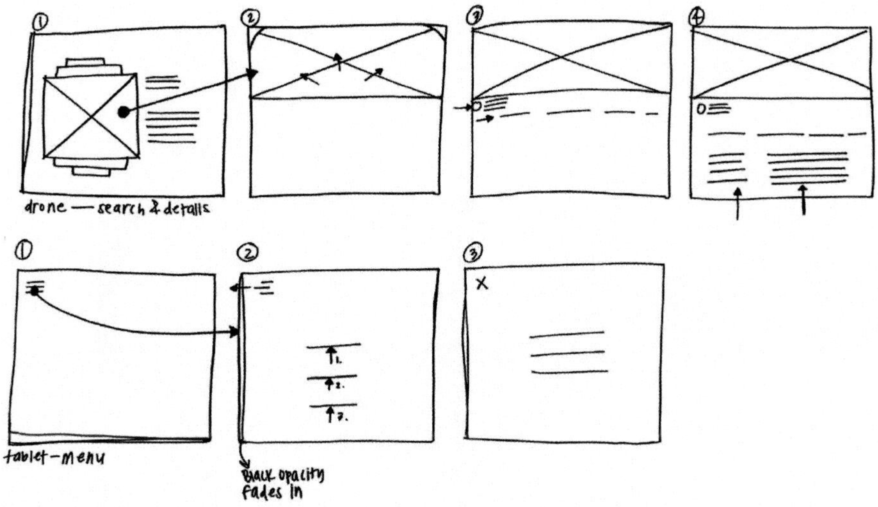

Figure 10.1
Storyboard sketches of microinteraction behaviour (from The Making, by Hanna Yi, used by kind permission of Hanna Yi).

path (Figure 10.2). We use schematics of the microinteraction's behavior to depict this. Look at the schematics depicting the transitions in the red-line (Figure 10.3). If we've progressed enough to have distilled our interactions into a refined set, we can schematize their behavior and accompany our user flow with a legend that describes our refined interactions—our interaction language (Figure 10.4). A wire-frame flow of our primary use case, depicting our refined microinteractions and accompanied by a legend is the final work product we're striving for at this stage.

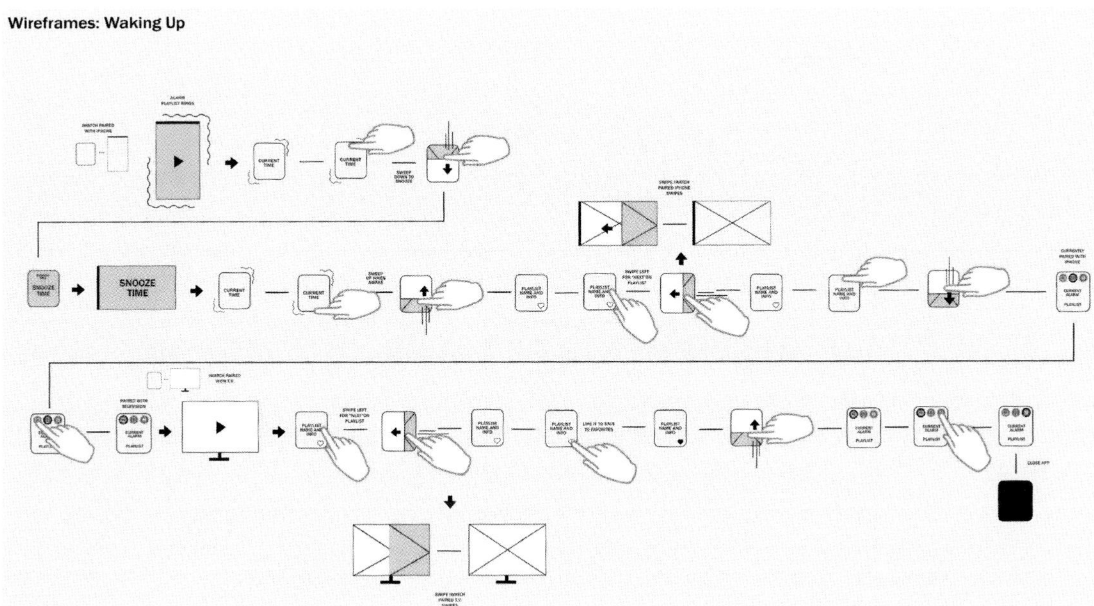

Figure 10.2
Refine microinteraction sketches into user flows (from Inliven, by Elbert Tao, used by kind permission of Elbert Tao).

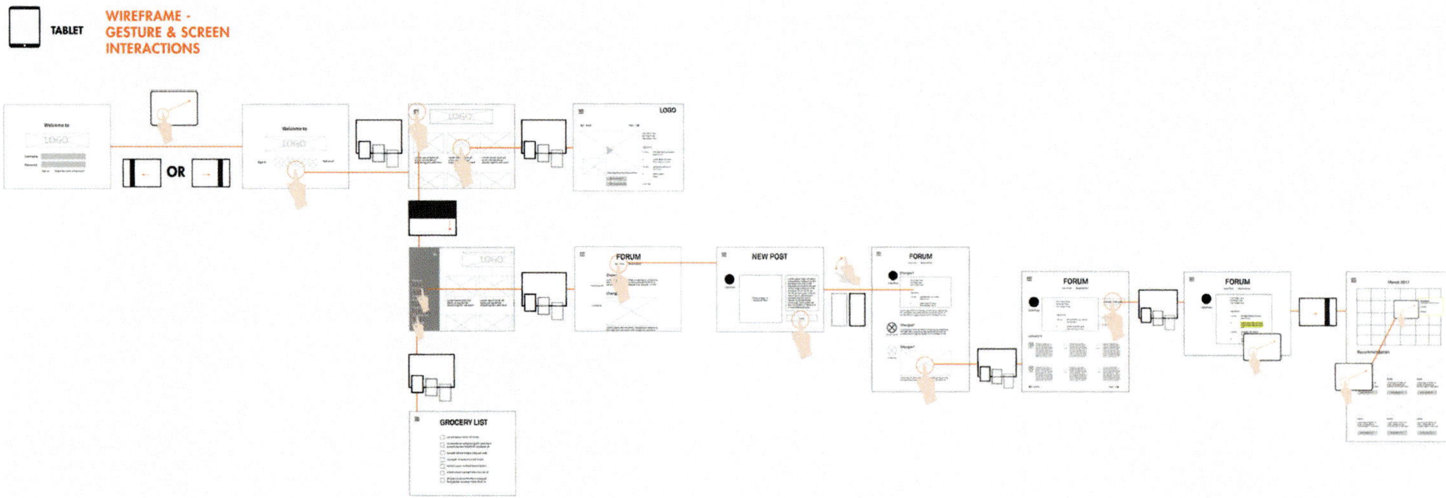

Figure 10.3
User flows depicting behavior through schematics (from The Making, by Hanna Yi, used by kind permission of Hanna Yi).

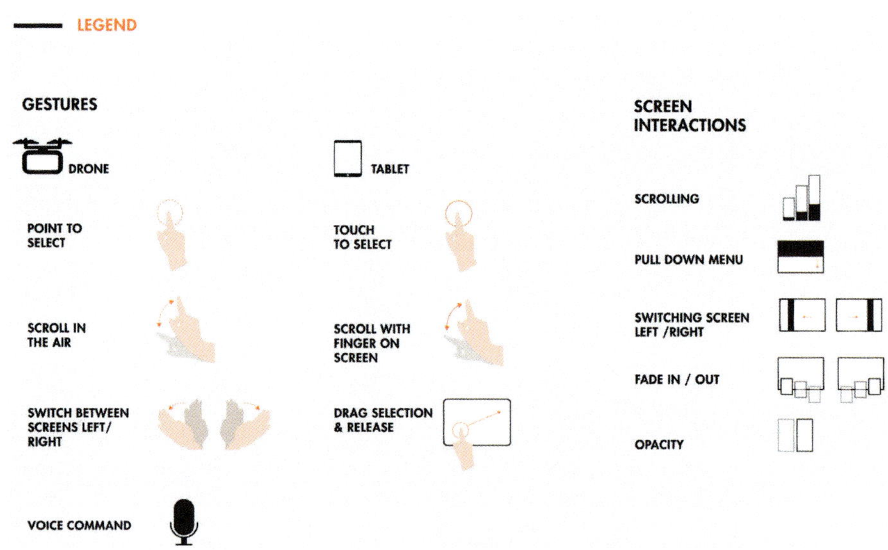

Figure 10.4
Behavior schematics in a legend illustrating an interaction language (from The Making, by Hanna Yi, used by kind permission of Hanna Yi).

10.5 THE ELEMENTS OF A MICROINTERACTION

Saffer points out that microinteractions comprise triggers, rules, and feedback (Saffer, 2014, p. 14). Triggers are what initiate the microinteraction, rules are how it behaves, and feedback is how the microinteraction communicates back to the user. He uses the elements of a microinteraction—triggers, rules, and feedback—to organize certain things we need to consider that guide us in making microinteractions well designed (Saffer, 2014).[1] To help us with our exploration, let's review these and add a few more of our own.

10.6 TRIGGERS

Triggers are the actions the user employs to control a component. For a light, it's flicking the switch either up or down. For a dimmer, it's turning the dial. They are either user controlled, like our switch or dimmer, or initiated by other means, such as clock alarms or heat sensors. When considering the triggers of our microinteractions, it's advantageous to keep the following principles in mind, especially for those that are user controlled.

10.6.1 Affordances

Users need cues. The affordance is a visual or physical "hint" that gives the user cues about how to use a thing, in this case, an interactive component (Norman, 1988). A button raised on the screen giving the impression that it should be pushed; an indentation on a knob indicating where a thumb should rest; a door handle positioned in just such a way to indicate you are to rotate it to open the door; a slice of content on the side of the screen indicating there is more over there that the user can see if they swipe to it.

Use affordances to communicate how to interact with a trigger.

10.6.2 Look

A trigger needs to communicate that it is indeed a trigger. Beyond this, it should strive to present affordances that provide the audience some insight into how to use it. Links in a body of text look different to the surrounding non-controllable text around it. Buttons in Google's Material design patterns have drop shadows that make them look raised, ready to be pressed. These elements look different than other content to indicate that we can act on them.

Make triggers look like triggers

10.6.3 Context

If we're designing a button to eject a ticket in a parking garage, many users—drivers in cars entering the garage—may be seeing that interface for the first time. Additionally, the driver needs to act quickly so as not to create a traffic jam behind them. In this context, the button needs to scream "I'm a button" as loudly as possible. It requires a clear call to action (a "CTA" in Interaction Design speak) and should be so present as to almost take cues from Staple's classic Easy Button campaign (Levere, 2008).

Conversely, though, if we have a link that appears in a body of text, we want to distinguish that link, but do so with care. We don't want to throw our audience out of the flow of reading with a bunch of fluorescent colored links peppered throughout the text. Subtle distinction is key in this context.

Make CTA's clear, yet context is critical to how we make our triggers look.

10.6.4 Discoverability and Importance

Related to context is the principle that triggers should not only be discoverable, but the presentation of the trigger should agree with its importance and how often it is used (Saffer, 2014, p. 30). For CTAs that are often used or important, they should distinguish themselves. For those that are used moderately or are less important, they should distinguish themselves more subtly.

A trigger's discoverability should agree with its importance.

10.6.5 What They Want, When They Want It

Triggers should provide users what they want, where they want it, and when they want it. Most often, we want to be able to turn lights on or off when we enter and leave rooms. Unless there are other reasons, the switch is best placed by the entrance at a height reachable by a normal person. It will be available to users when they want it and will be placed where they will want it.

If we need a ticket upon entry into a garage, the ticket button is best placed on the driver's side of the car when the user is entering the garage. If we're looking online for a book we may want to buy, the purchase button should be at the top of the page next to the book's name or description. If a quiescent state's screen is critical to our product, such as Facebook's feed, and we want it available to our audience at all times, access to it should be constantly available as well, such as a button placed in a global menu.

Consider the experience of your user and locate your triggers accordingly. Make triggers conform to what your user wants, when they want it.

10.6.6 Consistency

The easiest triggers to use are those that look and behave the same way each time they are presented and used. We don't expect our steering wheel to change at times into a dial for the radio just because it's circular and can be rotated. Likewise, we don't expect a button, either physical or virtual, to look the same and do different things, or do the same thing and look different. If it acts the same, have it look the same, and place it in the same location. If it acts differently, it is different. It needs to look different and, if at all possible, should be positioned in a different location.

Be consistent. Like triggers should look alike, different triggers should look different.

10.6.7 Surface the Data

Triggers often convey or transform the system's information. Is there some data that we can place on the presentation of the trigger to indicate the state of the most critical bit of information? When our light switch is down, the light is off. When it's up, it's on. If the light is indeed viewable from the switch, we already know if it's on or off, but if it's away from our view, like being outdoors, that little bit of information may mean we don't have to trudge outside to look. When I copy a file from one folder to another on my computer's desktop, the icon of the file that's copying is grayed out indicating that it can't be selected yet, and there's a thermometer bar that appears to its right indicating how much more needs to be copied. These subtle indicators surface data that I really would like to know: That a light is on or a file is not copied yet and how much it still has to go.

When we pay our credit card, we are presented with a pay bill button. If, instead of the text of the button being the static "pay bill," we are presented with "Pay $655.34," we are using the opportunity of the image of the trigger to convey a little more helpful information to our user. It may be meaningless to them, or it could help them avoid a mistake as they realize they may need to shift funds around to cover the payment.

Strive to use the presentation real estate of your triggers to surface the most important data that your user may like to know.

10.6.8 Control and Effect

Switches are turned on or off like the lights they control. Dials and sliders have a range of positions and control a range of values, such as the levels of a dimmable light. A keyboard has a discrete number of keys, and controls the input of a discrete number of values, such as letters or numbers. For each of these, the device we interact with—the controller—is well matched with the values it is being used to control. In these examples, the control agrees with the effect.

Sadly, this isn't always the case. Although buttons are often used for things like volume controls, they are not the best way to input a range of values. Such is the case with my poorly designed alarm clock. We end up clicking them repeatedly to get to the volume we want, or press and hold them, always overshooting our mark. Similarly, my clothes washer has a start button that is a dial. I turn it to start, and it snaps back. There is no reason for this. It should be a button because all I'm doing is telling the machine one piece of information: to start.

The control's freedom of movement should agree with the information we want to be controlled. A binary light should have a binary switch, a dimmer light should have something that controls a range of values, and a telesurgery controller should conform to all the freedom of movement of a hand. Consider the information your microinteraction needs to convey. Does the controller match what needs to be communicated? Is it the best way to communicate it?

Control should agree with effect.

10.7 RULES AND BEHAVIOR

The rules of a microinteraction are how it behaves. We will see in the next chapter how these rules can be deconstructed into discrete behaviors, but for the level we're at now—that of exploring microinteractions—that detail will only slow us down. However, at this point, it's important to keep in mind that a particular microinteraction has a set of rules that guide how it behaves when certain events occur. Those behaviors can be triggered by several things: the user, the system, or even the environment. And, just as effective triggers need to conform to certain principles, the behavior of microinteractions need to do so, too.

10.7.1 Know the Goals

Know the goals that your users are trying to achieve with the behavior. We used goals as the means by which we started our structural design, so the goals should be intrinsic to our microinteractions. But, at this point, we may have lost sight of our user's goals. Make sure they are at the forefront of your mind when you are designing your microinteractions.

Know the goals of the microinteraction and design its behavior to conform to those goals.

10.7.2 Know the Constraints

Know the constraint or limitations of the behavior. What are the extremes? For a dimmer light, the extremes are full on, and off (we will go into this example more in depth in the next chapter). Our control should behave in such a way as to work within these extremes: It should stop turning clockwise at full, and click and stop turning counter-clockwise at off. The physical design of the dimmer imposes a rule that arrests its motion when it reaches an extreme.

Consider extremes and how they should be handled.

10.7.3 Know the Context

Let's gain insight again from our posture studies. What physical actions or gestures seem to be most appropriate for our audience in the posture they're in? For example, if we're in a meeting where we need to convey that we are giving the speaker our undivided attention, it's rude for the screen on our phone to light up and for us to start reading the text. It would be much better if the device could give us a subtle nudge that we could either accept or dismiss without drawing undue attention to it. A wristband or ring that would tighten and an interface where we could squeeze it to give a quick response would be much more appropriate (Figure 10.5).

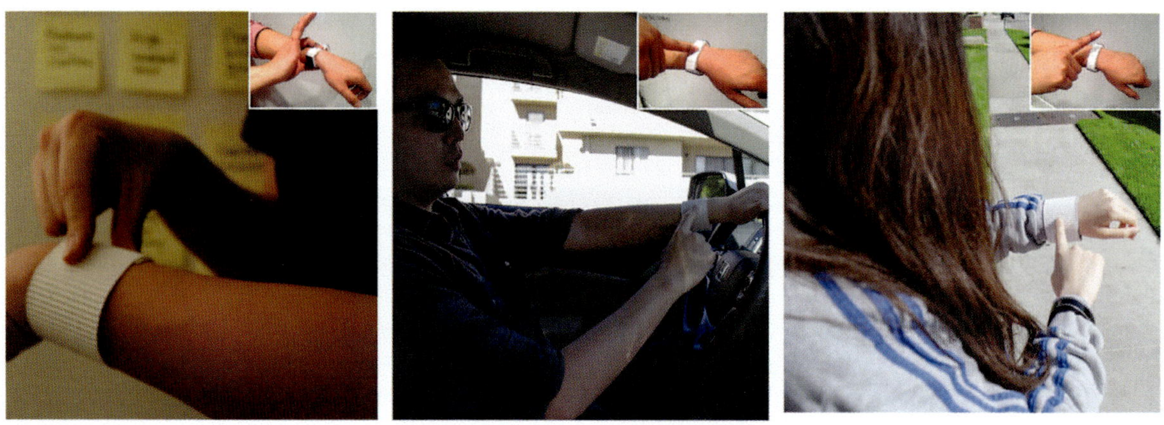

—
If Mike has free time, he can call her right back. but if he is busy he can: send a quick nudge back which means,"I'm good mom, I'll call you back" OR send a quick pinch which means,"I'm not too good right now, and I'll call you soon".

—
It's the end of the day. Mike's driving back home. He lives with his girlfriend, and he sends a nudge in order let her know he's on his way.

—
She's out walking the dog, she taps on her outer wrist three times in order to let him know what she's doing.

Figure 10.5
Action exploration of a discrete messaging device (from Nudge, by Team Nudge, used by kind permission of Michael Noh and Sean Whelan).

Understanding precisely our user's context can lead to possibilities that other competitors may have missed and components that could distinguish our system in the marketplace. As mentioned early in this book, it could be claimed that one of the most important things that made Apple's iPhone so successful was iOS's abandonment of the stylus as an interactive device, and the complete embrace of touch interactions. They went so far as to develop an entirely new operating system based on a gesture language and an interface style based on the finger.

This is an example where being acutely sensitive to a user's context—that it's often annoying to have to pull out and use a stylus—triggered innovation. Not only that, stylus interactions require two-handed interactions, while there are a whole class of touch gestures (clicks, swipes, etc.) that can be done with just a single thumb, allowing for single-handed interactions.

Know the external context and optimize for it.

10.7.4 Assist

A well-formed behavior doesn't just respond to user actions; it assists them in doing those actions to achieve the user's goal. When we type terms in Google's search bar, it helps us by providing possibilities that we can select from. When we misspell in Word, it provides us possible ways of correcting our error. These assists make the interaction more of a pleasure to perform.

Strive to have components assist users whenever possible.

10.7.5 Smart Defaults

A corollary of the principle of assistance is to use smart defaults. If a field or interaction has a most likely input, provide that as a default. When saving a Word document, we are provided the possibility of naming it with the first few words our document contains. It assumes that the most likely name of the document is the one on the title page, and title pages are often the first page in the text. We may change it, and likely do, but this isn't a bad default. Yelp assumes that we most likely want to find restaurants near us, so it provides that as the first set of items when we click on restaurants. Often the default is not exactly what we want, but these assumptions are polite and demonstrate that the system understands us and cares about what we may want.

Pre-load components with smart defaults when possible.

10.7.6 Absorb Complexity

When we steer our car, we get the feeling our steering wheel is directly connected to our wheels. But as we've previously discussed, this is not the case at all. We don't need to know what's going on behind the scenes, though. And, in fact, if we did it would make our driving much more dangerous. The inner workings of our microinteractions may be complex and confusing, but there's no reason to reveal that complexity to our users. Hide them and allow the audience to retain a simple mental model of what's going on.

Behaviors should absorb complexity and promote simple and accurate mental models.

10.7.7 Perceived Simplicity and Operational Simplicity

Our variable light attached to a dimmer can be turned on or off, or varied to a certain light level. The dimmer dial switch performs both of these actions: It can both turn the light on and off and can vary its level. We could consider another type of switch where there is a slider for the dimmer function, and an on/off switch for the power. We turn on the power with the on/off switch and control the light level with the slider.

The dial combines the two kinds of controls, power and light level, and maps them to one switch. The designers of this device have made our perception of the control simple by using just a dial. The slider separates the two, thereby isolating the controls of power and level. This simplifies the way we can control the light but makes the control more complex.

Leverage perceived simplicity over operational simplicity, unless precise control is required.

10.7.8 Prevent Errors

Humans are imperfect creatures. We are prone to errors. A polite behavior realizes this and attempts to catch our errors. If the system requires a precise selection of city names, for example, we should provide our users with a selection list as they type instead of forcing them to type the entire name out. This will ensure that the name that is input is not misspelled.

There are extremes to this, though. Being provided a country selection list organized alphabetically will not make people from Zimbabwe happy. Nor am I very happy that, as I grow older, it gets harder and harder to scroll down to my birth year when I'm filling out insurance forms. We should provide ways to prevent errors, but we should also be cognizant of the difficulties we may be making for our users. Find a happy medium.

Design behaviors to prevent errors, but do so in a way that's simple and efficient.

10.7.9 Age Gracefully

If we perform a microinteraction over and over again, it would be polite if it learned our behavior and began to supply us defaults that we most likely employ. Behaviors not only have a micro lifetime that exists during the microinteraction itself, but they may have a macro lifetime that evolves over repeated use. Consider that macro lifetime and how to make the interaction easier to use as it ages.

Behaviors should age gracefully.

10.7.10 Behavioral Orchestration

Most of our behavior considerations have been about a single microinteraction itself. But microinteractions have to work in concert with each other. As Alan Cooper advises, "It is vital that all the elements in an interface work together coherently toward a single goal" (Cooper, 2015, p. 250). Those goals are the user's goals and our microinteractions' behaviors need to work together to achieve those goals. How they work with each other is referred to as orchestration.

Often, when we break things down into finer and finer bits, we lose sight of the big picture. We lose sight of the orchestration of things. Strive to keep the big picture in mind, because microinteractions need to work in concert. The user should flow from one microinteraction to the next without facing abrupt discontinuities, moments of confusion, times where what they want is not provided, and behaviors that work against each other.

Examples of discontinuities are as simple as a cancel button that is at the top of the screen for videos, yet at the bottom of the screen for pictures. Or when we're about to check out with our shopping cart and the system asks if we want to sign up for a service. With each of these, our flow has been disturbed and we are thrown out of the moment. Good user experience analysis and use case studies should avoid this, but it's still something to look out for.

Moments of confusion occur when we are asked something that we cannot immediately respond to, such as a sinister dialog box that says, "You will lose all your changes." And it finishes the dialog off with an "OK" button. No, that's definitely not okay. We also face moments of confusion in much more subtle ways, such as when we are asked to provide input but have no idea how to start. An example of this when we are offered a list of options on a voice phone menu and none of them matches what we want. At that point, we scream for a human and wait 20 minutes in a call line.

We often face moments in the thick of a system where what we want is not provided. The phone menu example above is a common one. Another is when we may want to select multiple photos for a post, but we photographed them months apart and now have to scan thousands of photos to select each. Or we would like to copy a photo into an app, but we are not even provided the functionality of a simple cut and paste. These are failures of the designer not knowing the audience well enough to know what they would want, and failing to provide it to them.

Finally, and I believe most egregiously—because these are so simple to detect—are cases where microinteractions work at counter purposes. The best example I have of this is the scroll within a scroll that is so pervasive on mobile versions of responsive websites. When I must scroll down a screen to see content, there should not also be an area within that screen that requires a scroll down as well. This happens most often on maps contained within scrollable screens. I will get stuck at the map, and my scroll only affects the map, not the screen. I can't scroll any further, making it impossible for me to click the reservation button at the bottom.

Having a scrollable area within a scrollable area on a small screen that I'm trying to navigate with my thick fingers should be grounds for termination for any who consider themselves interaction designers. Yes, I'm looking at you, most state park camping reservation sites. We might forgive these because they were probably built on a shoestring budget, but as of this writing iTunes does this too. When I need to scroll down to my apps, I also need to scroll down within that screen to add or remove content. A scroll window within a scroll window. Exceptionally poor design. Apple isn't the only big digital company with orchestration issues. Word and Excel have annoying orchestration issues too, such as when the clean-up broom appears on a cell of data in Excel obscuring the information underneath. Get out of there! You are being annoying, not helpful! I don't care about clean up right now, I care about seeing my data!

In designing behaviors, think about the wants and needs of the user, the presence of other interactions on the interface, the user's flow, and whether the interaction supports those things or gets in the way. If these can be resolved on a microinteraction level, we're a good way towards resolving them on a system-wide level.

In the end, behaviors should be well orchestrated.

10.7.11 Maintain User Flow

The main objective in properly orchestrating an interface is to maintain that fragile thing called flow. Flow, according to Mihaly Csikszentmihalyi, is that state of mind "in which people are so involved in an activity that nothing else seems to matter" (Csikszentmihalyi, 1990, p. 4). We like to think of ourselves as sentient beings, so why is it good to lull our audience into a state where they aren't thinking about a bunch of things? Because that's when we are most productive, creative, and most satisfied.

Things that throw our audience out of flow force them to think and give them discomfort. If I want to go back to the previous screen, I want to click something on the top left of my screen—something possibly with a left-pointing arrow. Without thinking, I reach up for it, and if it's not there, I'm frustrated. Now I have to hunt, and I'm not happy. I am not in the app to pay attention to the interface; I'm there to pay attention to the content and control. Allowing our audience to remain in flow while navigating may be humbling to the designer of the navigation system, but it is the appropriate objective to enhance the user's experience.

Is the interaction we are designing supposed to help the user maintain a state of flow? If so, make it humble and fit in with expectations. If you want it to make an impression, then go ahead and make it a signature interaction by designing it to be unique and distinctive, just don't do this too often or you risk scaring away your audience.

Behaviors should support user flow, not act against it.

10.7.12 Action Language Cohesion

Previously, we've pointed out that when we interact with a system, we are having a conversation with it. In this sense, we can consider Interaction Design as the creation of a language through which our audience can converse with a device or set of devices that comprise a dynamic system.

Our users speak to the system through a set of actions, be they gestures on a screen or in the air, be they via manipulating interactive components such as a mouse, trackpad, or buttons and toggles, or through the spoken word itself. The system then responds to those actions through myriad ways, such as graphics on a screen, through lights and indicators, through physical effects, such as opening curtains or doors, or even through words.

Languages work because they are based on patterns, and we have a shared understanding of what those patterns mean. When we say "action language" we mean a pattern of actions that, when used throughout the system, act in similar ways. When presented with a button, we use our finger to press it. When presented with a list, we swipe to scroll through it. It is this structured consistency that allows us to take what could be a grab-bag of random actions and turn them into an interaction language, much like how the structured consistency of a spoken language allows us to take a bunch of sounds and turn them into a shared understanding (Figures 10.6 and 10.7).

Think of your user's actions as a language. Use ideation to explore approaches to that language. It should make sense with their experience in the real world, or

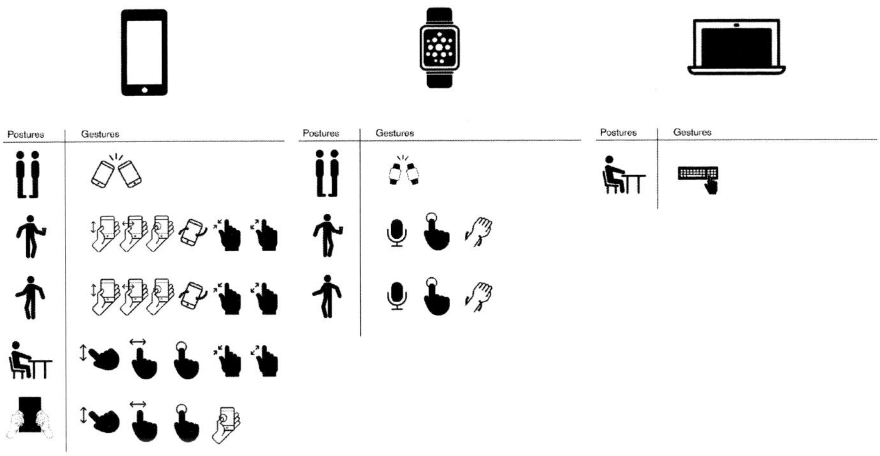

Figure 10.6
A schematic depiction of a system's interaction language (from Keepintouch, by Amber Wang, used by kind permission of Amber Wang).

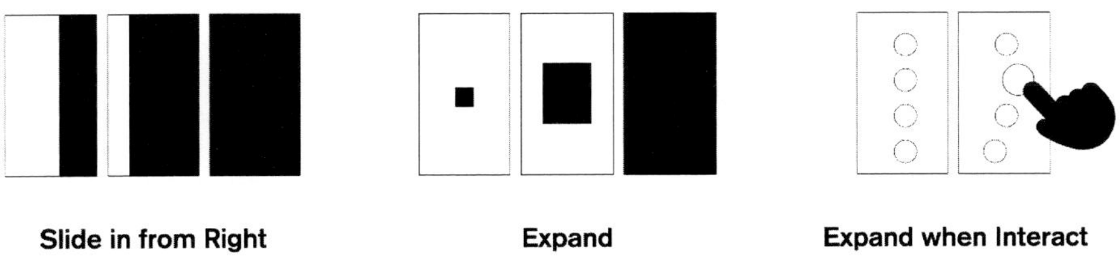

Figure 10.7
Schematizing microinteraction feedback (from Keepintouch, by Amber Wang, used by kind permission of Amber Wang).

at least be consistent. What are the actions that make up the language? Do they make sense with the user's posture? Are they ergonomic? Can you break down your user's actions to a small set that is used the same way throughout your system? How can you ensure consistency not only within the interactions in one context, but across your entire system? How can you use metaphors and affordances to help users understand how to use your interaction language? How can you to refine and simplify the language to reduce its complexity? (Figures 10.8 and 10.9.)

A system's action language needs to be consistent, cohesive, and efficient.

10.7.13 Responsiveness

The action–response couplet described above is referred to as a feedback loop and can be either as instantaneous as the shutter on a high-speed camera or as long as the commands that are sent to satellites in deep space that take hours to elicit feedback. The speed of the feedback loop is considered to be the responsiveness of the system. For the most part, we strive to make the system as responsive as possible. A high degree of responsiveness provides the user with a feeling that they are directly manipulating the system.

For example, when we are using a swipe gesture on a touchscreen, if there is any delay in the responsiveness of the system, we don't feel that our thumb is doing

Figure 10.8
Original gestures for a drone and tablet interactions (from The Making, by Hanna Yi, used by kind permission of Hanna Yi).

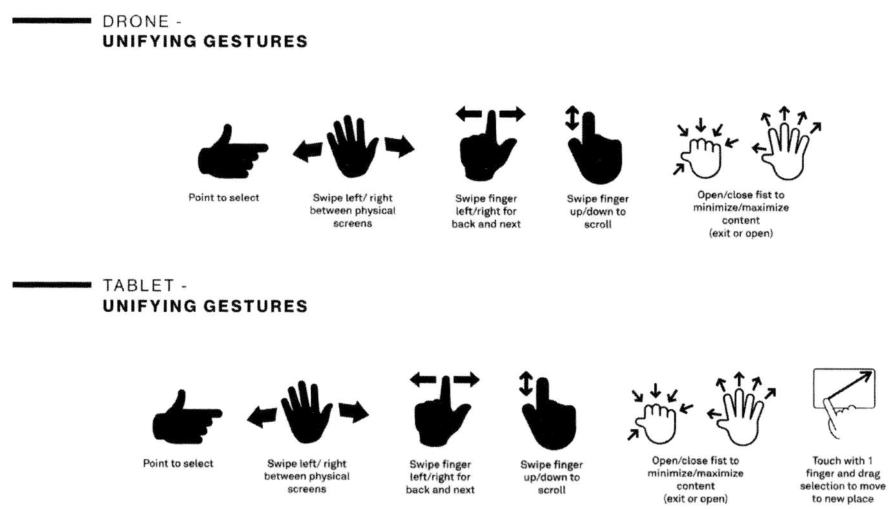

Figure 10.9
Refined gestures for the drone and tablet (from The Making, by Hanna Yi, used by kind permission of Hanna Yi).

the swiping but feel we are performing a swipe action and the system is doing the swiping. Our cause and its effect become separated. In fact, this is what is really happening, but we don't want the user to feel that way. We'd prefer that the responsiveness of the system is so fast that when the user swipes, they get the feeling that they are moving virtual items themselves, like swiping a physical slider. When we manipulate physical objects, we rarely think about how they move, we just move them. Likewise, when the system's responsiveness is tight, the user doesn't think about how the system is moving the screen, they just think about the result. This is exactly where we want their focus to be.

Tight responsiveness allows the user to transport themselves into a state of flow with the system.

10.7.14 Flow and Sense

Another thing that can allow our user to reach a state of flow is if the actions they are using make inherent sense. For example, pinching to zoom or swiping right to scroll across seem to makes physical sense. We experience things like this in the real world when we are swiping a piece of paper across the surface of a table or stretching an elastic material between our thumb and our forefinger. A pinch to swipe, or swiping right to move the screen up, doesn't make much logical sense because they don't match our experience in the real world. These will most likely throw our audience out of their state of flow.

These are action metaphors and are as useful as visual metaphors. In fact, coupling visual metaphors on the screen with appropriate action metaphors is a good way to help our users understand how to interact with the system even though it may be new to them. For example, Google's Material Design uses a metaphor of paper cards floating in layers in front of the user. Drop shadows give the impression that the cards are floating (Google, 2017). A card that is more important floats in front of other cards.

If we want to get rid of a card, we swipe it away, just as we would a physical card floating in front of us. If we'd like to provide our user with a selection to choose from, we'd place it on a card-like set of buttons that visually seems to float closer to the user than everything else. The user touches their selection, the button visually presses in, and the selection is made. The card structure of the interface and the user's actions of swipes and button presses make sense in this virtual world of cards. The actions and the interface are a coherent whole.

We don't even need to develop a metaphorical relationship with the real world as long as our action language is consistent. We can rely completely on idioms. For example, many apps use a strategy of swiping right to drill down into detail. Although there is not a physical thing we commonly use that acts in this way, we quickly understand what's going on simply by manipulating the system.

Strive to design interactions that behave consistently and make logical sense.

10.7.15 The Brand Experience

The gestures we choose and the behaviors we design can have a certain feeling. If we use only clicks, our interface seems simple and rather distant. If we employ more swipes and pinches, we are giving our audience the feeling that they are directly moving the objects on the screen and they may come away with the sense that they are more intimate with the objects that form the interface. Not only actions and gestures have feel, but how the system responds can have feeling as well. Is the response immediate and direct? Then it gives the feeling of being more professional or performance oriented. If it's bouncy, it's more playful and fun. If it's measured and deliberate, that can convey a sense of calm and serenity.

As we ideate interactions, we need to keep our brand values in mind. Use them as well as our target persona as litmus tests for whether our creation is on track or not. If we do, we can rest assured that our designs will be well founded on the objectives we set out to achieve.

Responses and behaviors should feel like your brand.

10.8 FEEDBACK CONSIDERATIONS

Feedback is how the behavior talks back to the user; it is the system's response to the user's action. Both states and transitions exhibit feedback and need to be addressed when we consider it. States most commonly exhibit either a static or cyclical form of feedback, while transitions usually have a beginning and an end, like little movies. For example, the cabin lights to my car are usually on or off, but when turned on, they transition from off to on through a graceful fade up. Likewise, when they are turned off, they fade down. In the states, the lights are either statically on or off while the fade up and down transitions have a start and an end. Care was taken to make the on/off experience elegant, thereby improving my perception of the quality of my car.

Our system's feedback is arguably the most powerful tool Interaction Design has in its arsenal of communicating to the user. It can reinforce mental models, convey brand feel, and guide users to do what they need to do next. As such we have several things we need to keep in mind when we design feedback.

10.8.1 Appropriate Mapping

Appropriate mapping is the quality of associating interactions with responses in such a way that the responses are an expected result (Cooper, 2015, p. 290). An example of proper mapping is that when I turn the wheel of my car to the right, I expect my car to turn right, and it does. If we lean forward on a Segway, it moves forward. When we perform these actions, we expect these results naturally. On the other hand, poor mapping is like the trash can icon on the Mac. If you drag a disk into it, you would expect the entire disk to be thrown in the trash. But it isn't, it is merely ejected. This way of ejecting or unmounting disks has caused a great deal of consternation ever since the Mac was invented.

Proper mapping improves usability because things work as expected. Bad mapping slows us down because of the cognitive dissonance of experiencing a result that does not match our expectation. There are also mapping problems that have to do with plain old physics. Push handle doors have good mapping because we push them to unlatch the door and the same push opens the door. Now consider if you had to pull the bar to unlatch it. We'd pull to unlatch, but have to push it to open. Not only bad mapping, but tough to do. Proper mapping not only should provide expected results, but work well with what's physically going on. Stay in tune with your posture studies to make sure this is happening.

Feedback should map well with actions.

10.8.2 Illuminate Behavior, Yet Don't Over-Inform

Feedback needs to communicate that the behavior is working, and, to some degree, how it's working. If we click on a "pay bill" button, we have no idea if we paid the bill unless we are given feedback. The appropriate response should be an indication that the button was indeed clicked, and if the procedure takes some time, the interface should also tell us that the payment is being processed. It should also provide us some means of determining how long we have until the processing is over.

We don't need to overburden the user with indicators that reveal exactly what's going on behind the scenes. We should absorb complexity, reinforce the user's mental model of what's going on, and provide them only what they need to know. In the case of our payment, this is that the pay bill action has been initiated and that they need to wait a bit while things are working behind the scenes.

Feedback should illuminate behavior, yet not over-inform.

10.8.3 Inform at the Right Time

Not only is it vital for us to inform our audience, but we must also do it at the appropriate time. We should inform when the user has done something, such as immediately after they click a button, or when the system does something, such as finishing a process. We should also inform the user during critical stages in a process that the user needs to know, such as how long it will take for a file to be copied or when a bill payment will be posted.

Finally, we should inform a user when they cannot do something, such as clicking on the back button while a payment is being posted to avoid it being posted twice. A better solution to relying on just a message to handle this possible error would be to make the back button temporarily unavailable and tell the audience if they try to use it why they can't. But if this functionality is not possible (i.e., a website cannot control the presentation and operation of the browser's back button), a message must suffice.

Feedback should inform, and inform at the right time.

10.8.4 Make Microcopy Clear

Microcopy is a term promoted by Saffer to indicate text that may be associated with microinteractions (Saffer, 2014, p. 76). These include labels and bits of text that may appear in response to user actions. A button's label is microcopy, as is a ribbon of text that may appear when we roll over it. Microcopy should be clear, concise, and use natural language, as if someone is saying it out loud. Also, Saffer advises, "Never use instructional copy when a label will suffice. Tap Next to Continue is unnecessary if there is a button labeled Next or Continue" (Saffer, 2014, p. 77).

Take advantage of microcopy, and make that microcopy clear.

10.8.5 Don't Be Arbitrary

How an element of feedback is presented to a user should provide some indication of the action that was performed. If a user presses a power-up button, the resulting audio should sound like something is powering up. If the user is dragging and dropping an item into another item, the response animation of the item being dropped should look like it's going into that other item. We should not be arbitrary with the communication of our feedback. We not only have an opportunity to reinforce mental models with responses, but we have a responsibility to do so as well.

Don't be arbitrary. Feedback should reflect the action.

10.8.6 Be Considerate

Take measures to make sure the system's feedback is considerate. As previously mentioned, users make mistakes. The appropriate mindset for a designer is that mistakes are not the fault of the user, but the fault of the designer. The user is merely doing what they think makes sense. When mistakes happen, and errors occur, the feedback response should keep this in mind and take responsibility for the problem, not blame it on the user.

We use the term "considerate" as opposed to "polite" because, as Alan Cooper points out, being polite can be construed as a matter of manners and protocol with little else that is helpful. Being considerate means being concerned with the needs of others (Cooper, 2015, p. 180). It requires being empathetic. Understanding our user's situation allows us to understand how to help them get out of it.

Place yourself in the shoes of the user and design feedback to be considerate.

10.8.7 Less Is More

Many of our principles relate to informing the user, but take care not to over-inform. Absorbing complexity, reinforcing mental models, making microcopy concise, and leveraging perceived simplicity all relate to making things as simple as possible, but no simpler. These all come back to the idea that less is more, which can be governed by asking two questions of the feedback: Is it necessary to communicate to our user? Is it sufficient to communicate what we need to? Or simply, is it necessary and sufficient? This should simplify our interface by guiding us in reducing feedback to that which is critical, and making sure it is what it needs to be.

Feedback should inform what is necessary, but no more.

10.8.8 Use the Overlooked

Interfaces contain several components necessary for their operation: Menus, buttons, sliders, lists, just to name a few. Consider these as opportunities to communicate with the user. We are not suggesting adding items to the interface; we are suggesting using the ones that are already there to communicate to our audience more effectively. Consider microcopy or simple animations associated with these often-forgotten features that can underscore things that are happening or reinforce mental models.

Consider the overlooked for your feedback.

10.8.9 Personality

We've claimed that less is more and all feedback communication should be necessary and sufficient. What we don't want to remove, though, is a healthy respect for our system's look and feel, its personality. We've placed a great deal of effort so far in establishing that personality through our brand values. Feedback is where we can put those values to use.

All communication has an emotional component; even a system that is focused on functionality has a personality—most likely one that is "direct". To ignore a system's personality is tantamount to making that personality arbitrary. It's the designer's responsibility to make sure they are in control of the entire communication, both functional and emotional. And we can do that by considering our brand values or guidewords with every element of feedback we deliver to our user.

For example, if we're designing a system to customize shoes for Nike, every animation, every microcopy, every response should have some consideration as to the feel of the brand. On the flip side, if we are designing a medical device, we will most likely need to exercise restraint, simplicity, and directness. Although we strive for simplicity, personality is one of those things that is necessary to communicate. Feedback should convey personality, not avoid it. But don't go overboard. If an animation or microcopy is sufficient to communicate personality, that's it. Don't go any further.

Feedback should deliver the personality of your brand.

10.8.10 Agee with Context

Consider the situation in which the feedback will be presented. This is where referring to your posture studies will come in handy. Is the user on the go? Are they indoors, outdoors, or at night? The presentation of the feedback should consider these situations and adapt accordingly. Things that can be controlled are the intensity of the feedback (loud or soft, high contrast or low, distinct or subtle), the duration (long or short), and whether it repeats or not. This all comes down to the severity of the communication as well as the context of its presentation. We don't want our feedback to cry "fire" all the time, but when it needs to it had better stand out. Most of the time subtle cues are sufficient. It's advisable to err on the side of the most subtle that delivers the desired result.

Feedback should work well within the context.

10.9 FORMS OF FEEDBACK

There are several forms of feedback, visual, auditory, and tactile. Each has their own set of issues to consider. Let's look into these.

10.9.1 Indicators

The most basic form of feedback is the indicator. In its simplest form, it is either on or off and signals whether something is in a particular state or not. A charging light on a remote phone tells us whether the device is charging normally or not. More complicated versions can signal multiple states such as off, good (green), warning (yellow), or danger (red). Other notable multi-state indicators are things like the Macintosh power indicator that also signals "thinking" (solid on) and sleeping ("breathing" pulses). The signal strength bars of a cell phone is another example of a multi-state indicator.

The benefit of indicators is that they are simple and direct, the drawback is that their users need to learn what they mean. If the device provides the user with some other effect tied to the states of the indicator, such as our phone call breaking up if the signal is weak, we will learn its meaning by use. We will also learn it (and very quickly) if the indicator itself guides our use such as a signal gate on a train track: If we go against that indicator and drive through it, we'll cause damage to it and our car—not to mention what could happen when the train comes.

For example, I have a personal cell tower with a set of indicators that illuminate as icons. Two of them I understand, they indicate power and signal strength, while two others confuse me: One is shaped like Saturn, and the other looks like a satellite. The satellite may have something to do with the signal I'm receiving, but there is no satellite connection with this device. And the Saturn indicator is completely vague. What does Saturn have to do with my cell phone?

These indicators are not learnable. There is nothing I can discern as a user that tells me anything about what they mean. I am completely reliant on the visual to understand them. Power and signal strength have feedback I recognize from using other devices. To understand the other two, I must break out the user's manual. When our users have to reach for a manual, we are in the realm of skilled systems, not consumer devices. Indicators succeed or fail based on whether the user understands them, and their comprehensibility should agree with the posture you're designing for, which includes not only its physical and cognitive posture, but the posture of its intended skill level as well.

Indicators should be clear, or, at the very least, learnable.

10.9.2 Text

When we were describing our feedback considerations, above, we introduced the term microcopy. Microcopy is essentially textual feedback from a microinteraction. This not only includes button labels or text that may appear during the course of interacting with a device, but physical labels printed on the surface of a device as well. Returning once more to our personal cell tower example, its indicators have no microcopy describing what the lights mean.

However, right next to my personal cell tower is my router. On it is a set of lights and associated labels: power, Ethernet, phone, broadband, and service. The first three seem clear, but what's the difference between broadband and service? Isn't my service broadband? What happens if broadband is off and service is on? Am I getting narrowband service? I don't know because the labels, the microcopy, are vague.

Text indicators delivered by microcopy need to be both concise and clear to the user.

10.9.3 Image-based Feedback

Image-based feedback requires more visual real estate than a simple light or icon, but that real estate can allow us to understand the feedback better. We can get meaning and emotion such as through emojis, or see profile photos of whom we are conversing with. The more visual real estate, the more information can be conveyed, but here, too, clarity is critical. Just because we have more pixels doesn't mean we should be any less clear than with indicators or microcopy. If our goal is to convey to users how good the food is at a restaurant, the images should indicate more than just what the bowl of ramen contains. It should clearly indicate that the dish is enticing.

Make sure images convey the correct information and the correct feel. They should be driven not only by design criteria, but your brand values as well. This is true not only for photographs, but illustrations and icons, too.

Images should inform, and do so with the appropriate look and feel.

10.9.4 Animated Feedback

Animated feedback provides an interface with life and vitality. It is also very powerful in communicating to the user what's happening in the system, or, more accurately, what we want them to think is happening: The mental model we want to reinforce. For example, when we "shrink" a window on a Mac, we are provided an animation of it shrinking down and flowing into the dock. The animation reinforces the mental model that the dock now "contains" the window, and to retrieve it we will find it in the dock.

Animated feedback is robust in the sense that it not only conveys that something is happening, but is an opportunity to convey how it happens. However, animation is also very "present" and must be used with care. Animation for animation's sake is deadly (Saffer, 2014, p. 99). When thinking about the failures of animation, I reflect back on Microsoft's Clippy character, which was supposed to provide friendly help to its Office products but became a source of ridicule (Gentilviso, 2010). The problem was that it jiggled and danced, annoying the user while they were focused on writing or number crunching. Additionally, it had nothing to do with Office's brand values. It was silly and playful, which, in a children's world, is not a bad thing, but for working professionals was the wrong note. Professionals may want help, but the means by which they get it should underscore professionalism.

For animated feedback, strive to make it meaningful. Don't animate for animation's sake. Have it solidify mental models, indicate the relationships between objects in the interface, and have its feel deliver on brand values.

Enrich your system with animated feedback, yet do not do so arbitrarily. Make it meaningful.

10.9.5 Auditory Feedback

Like imagery, auditory feedback comes in many forms: Earcons, words, speech, and ambience, just to name a few. Earcons are like icons or indicators; in fact, they are sometimes tied to indicators. They are brief bits of sound that communicate a state of a system or component. Sometimes they are a single beep, telling us that something has turned on, or a whoosh, telling us that our email has been sent. Our computer and phone's sound palette is fairly extensive, and they obey laws in a similar way to indicators and icons. If they are learnable, we can learn them. If they're not, we won't. Just as icons should provide us with insight into what the indicator means, if possible, earcons should strive to sound like the thing that is happening.

Words and speech are similar to text and image in that they need to be clear and concise as feedback responses. Wordy and confusing auditory responses are arguably more problematic than displayed text, in that we hear them once and they're gone. We don't have the opportunity to read and re-read them to understand them better.

Speech can deliver a more precise meaning than the ambiguity of an image, so it can back up animated feedback to provide more information about the state of things. But again, take care not to be too wordy. Speech can also present a great opportunity to provide personality. This is most commonly governed by the sound and tone of voice, but is also delivered by the content of the response as well. For example, when we ask Apple's Siri what she looks like, she doesn't respond with "I don't understand," but with "Let's just say multi-dimensional." This humor gives her personality that goes beyond her voice.

Ambience is made up of environmental sounds most often used to convey a sense of place. For example, a babbling brook, crickets, crowd noise, or sirens. They are employed to great effect in movies and environments, are almost subliminal, and, as such, play effectively on our unconscious emotions. They appear out of place within interfaces such as our laptops or mobile devices, but will be used more readily as digitally enhanced environments become more pervasive. Certainly, we need to know our context if we are considering ambience. The other thing to keep in mind is that to keep ambience in the background, transitions need to be smooth so as not to call attention to them. There's nothing like an abrupt transition to have a sound call attention to itself.

Finally, it's important to understand that while we can handle a great deal of imagery from a diverse number of sources, we are very sensitive to the presence of audio. For example, I personally can only concentrate on one person talking at a time (my wife seems to be able to handle many), and, in fact, if two people are talking at once, I can't understand either of them. In visual contexts, users should be provided the opportunity to turn audio off and rely solely on visuals. And since it can be turned off, audio should only convey further information, not information that is critical.

Of course, for non-visual interfaces such as those that may rely on both touch and sound, this consideration is not applicable. For example, the ding that occurs on a bus when we have pressed the stop request strip is critical because we may have few other ways of determining if our press indeed requested a stop.

Know your context and use sound appropriately. Be sensitive to the fact that audio may be intrusive in some contexts and may be turned off by the user.

10.9.6 Tactile and Somatosensory Feedback

Tactile feedback is that which we feel with our sense of touch and is often connected to the physical aspects of our interface. But touch is not all we use when we are interacting with a physical system. We use our complete somatosensory system to delineate objects and controls. These are the things we sense if we close our eyes and ears—and should be plugging our nose and closing our mouths as well. This certainly includes touch, but also reach, placement, and our sense of physical form.

To get a sense of the aspects of a somatosensory interface, it's instructive to close our eyes and sit in our car. What do we sense? What do we feel? What can we control without opening our eyes? I can certainly grasp my steering wheel, turn the car on, control the brake and accelerator, turn on the blinkers, lights, brights, and windshield wipers. Beyond that, I start having problems. I need my eyes to see what gear I'm in (if I drove a stick, I probably wouldn't). I certainly need them to determine how to control the HVAC, my audio system, and place and receive a phone call. This seems appropriate since the things I can do without my eyes are all the things that directly affect the safety of my car. The HVAC, stereo, and phone are nice, but not critical.

When performing this exercise, we should get a sense of how we are identifying the controls without our eyes. My reach determines where they are in space. Their form (a wheel, a knob on a stick) and texture (rough, smooth, raised lines to indicate settings) allow me to grasp the correct knobs and controls. Their freedom of movement, their detents, and how they feel when I control them usually determines the state I place them in. These all contribute to my understanding of the tactile interface. If we need to design for a tactile interface, think back to this blind cockpit experience to consider what is important and what is not in distinguishing physical controls.

The cockpit example relies on the physical construct of the system. We can also simulate physical feedback through haptics. Although haptics itself means the sense of touch, the term is commonly used in the context of interaction to refer to the simulation of tactile feedback. When our cell phone vibrates, that's haptics, as is the prospect of the sensation of texture in the further miniaturization of micro solenoids, and minuscule force feedback in telesurgery systems.

As of this writing, haptics is still in its infancy, but it possesses the potential of changing the way we perform physical work. Regardless of the stage we are in, if we integrate haptics into our system, there are a few things we need to consider. First of all, the haptic palette currently available to us is rather limited. Bumps and vibrations are pretty common, but beyond that, haptic feedback gets expensive. For now, if we are considering consumer-based systems, this means simplicity.

This simplicity implies that haptic responses function similarly to indicators or beeps, in that they can convey one or two things. Using them to provide instant feedback if a critical item has been selected is a common application. But like anything, moderation is key. The last thing we want is to feel a bump every time we interact with something on an interface. In this way, haptics can be approached like beeps: They should be short and can accentuate critical interactions, but it's not advisable that they be the only feedback for a critical action. This is not the case with physical interactions, however. When I set a physical dial on my dryer, for example, it's the only indicator I have, so it had better be correct.

Consider how touch and physical feel can be used in your system. Use it wisely. Don't abuse it.

10.9.7 Multi-modal Feedback

Multi-modal feedback is the aspect where more than one feedback mechanism is employed, such as a visual indicator and a beep or a haptic bump, or a whoosh and an animation. The benefit of multi-modal feedback is that coupled modes reinforce each other. Using the bus stop request as an example, when we press the strip we should see a visual indicator such as a sign lighting up that says "Stop Requested". In case the bus is crowded, and the sign is obscured, it's nice to have a bell ding. The bell is also a way that others on the bus can realize that a stop has been requested: The sign is a small part of their visual field and may be missed.

But what if the bus were crowded and was also noisy to the point where we cannot hear the bell? This happens fairly frequently, so I'd suggest using yet another mode of feedback, a physical component. If we had a system where the rider pressed a button, the bell rang, a sign lit up in front of the bus, and the button stayed pressed and possibly displayed an indicator announcing that a stop had been requested, we'd cover all cases of loud and crowded buses and would be much more confident that our request had been submitted.

Most interactions don't need this level of checks and balances. And with the case of physical interactions, our devices have limited real estate. We can easily overwhelm the audience with buttons and indicators.

Rely on multi-modal feedback for critical functions; the rest can be mapped to our primary feedback form. Make sure the feedback modes cut through environmental challenges.

10.10 HIGH-FIDELITY WIREFRAMES

Considering microinteractions focuses our design effort on the most detailed aspects of our system. Our wireframes need to reflect this level of detail. This role is assumed by high-fidelity wireframes (Figure 10.10), which not only represent the structure of our information in detail, but also allow us an opportunity to explore aspects of typographic structure, layout, iconography, and possibly color structure if it's relevant. If, for example, we are considering a typeface for our system, we can use high fidelity wireframes to determine if that typeface has all the characteristics we need. The same is true for other structural components. High-fidelity wireframes are a balancing act. They should be detailed informationally, but not so much that they cannot be iterated.

We can also add our microinteraction schematics to our user flows and red-lines. This will allow us to assess the orchestration of the interactions in our system more clearly. Revisit the user stories, the resultant user flows, and red-lines of the previous chapter and update them based on the results from our microinteraction considerations. Indicate how a user travels from one quiescent state to the next through the use of interaction schematics and a legend (Figure 10.11).

10.11 PHYSICAL REFINEMENT

If we're designing custom devices for our system, as we consider microinteractions we also need to push further into considering their physical details. Given each of our sub-target's postures and tasks, what kinds of physical interactive controls would be most convenient? (Figure 10.12.) How should they be shaped to provide

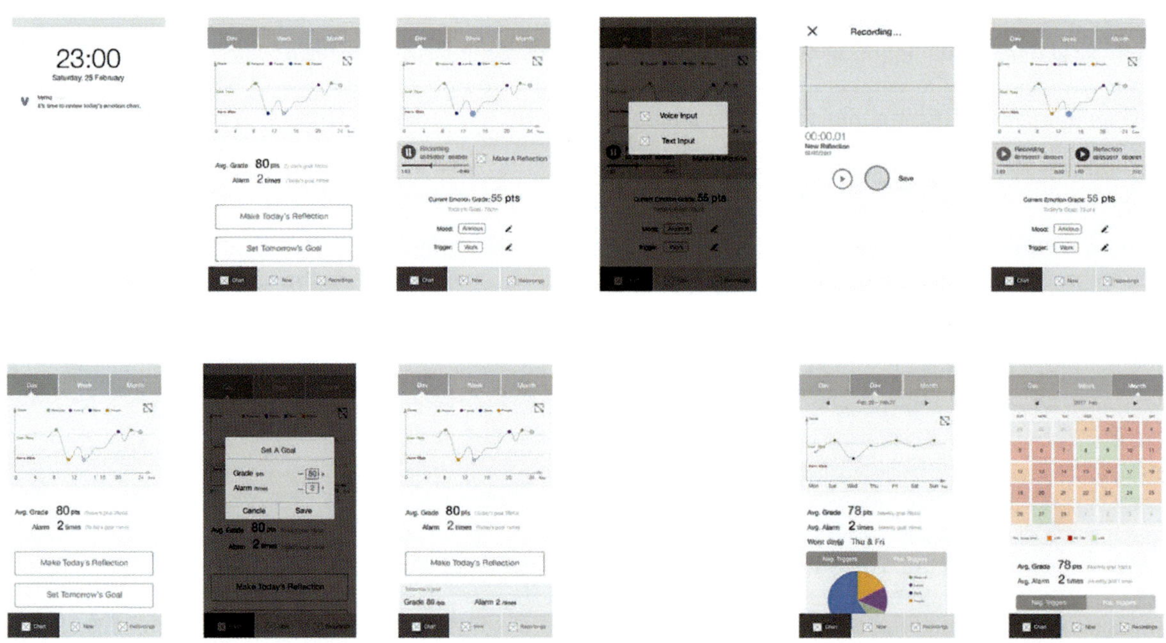

Figure 10.10
High-fidelity wireframes of the mobile context of a mood management system (from Odmo, by Hui Ye, used by kind permission of Hui Ye).

the best experience? How large or small should they be? How should they feel in the hand? See Figure 6.3 or Figure 7.15 for guidance.

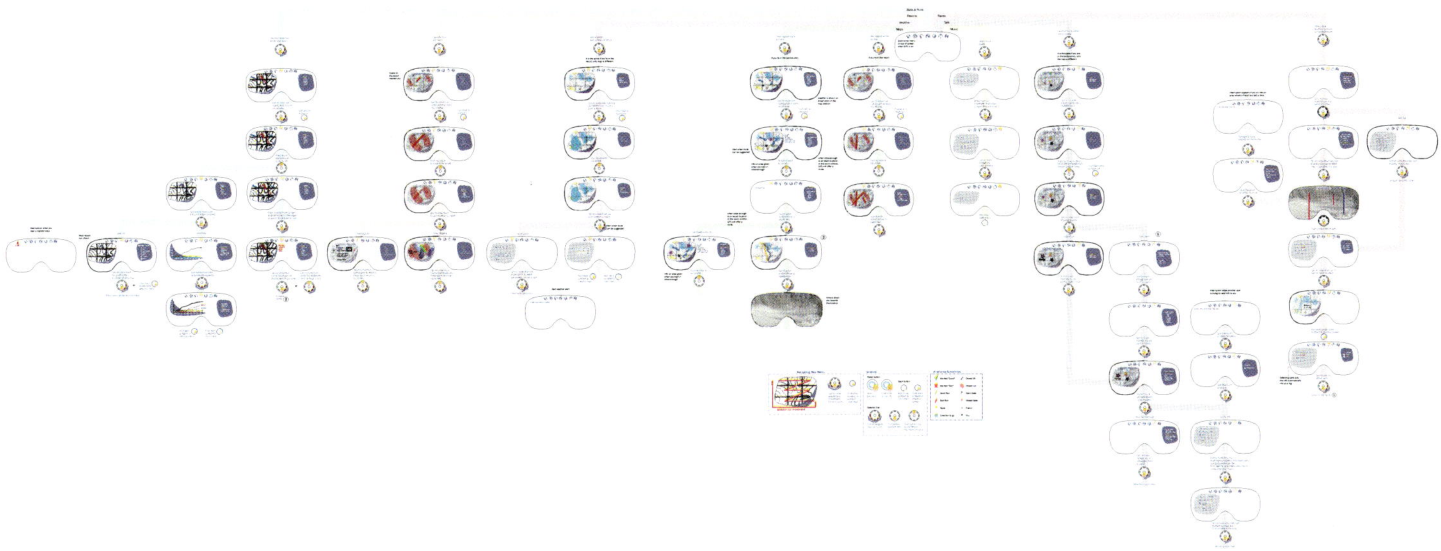

Figure 10.11
An interaction flowboard for an HUD wayfinding helmet for skiers, including a legend (from Traverse GPS, by Katy Dill, used by kind permission of Katy Dill).

Even if we're not designing custom devices, we still need to consider the physicality of our system. Is our interface convenient to use when the user is in their various postures? Are the elements of the interface—the type, iconography, and amount of information—in agreement with the user's posture and their respective physical and cognitive limitations?

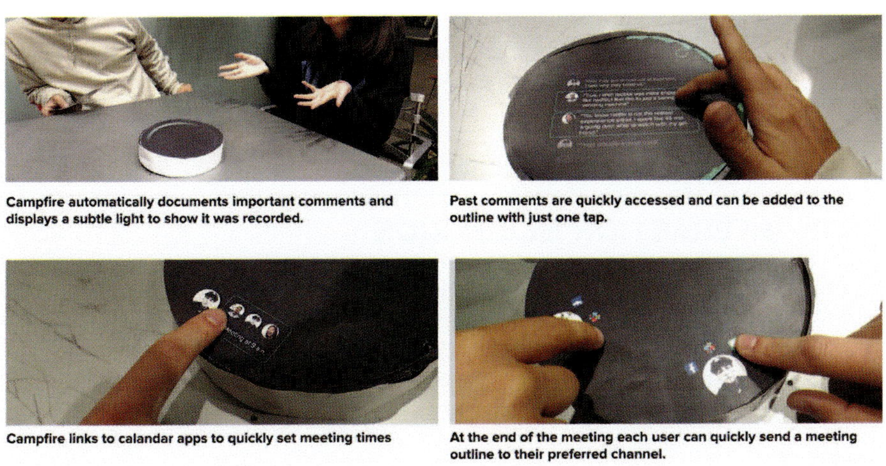

Figure 10.12
A sketch interface on mocked-up device for a natural language note taking system (from Campfire, by Team Seamrippers, used by kind permission of Matthew Benkert, Derling Chen, Ian Liao, and Mike Rito).

10.12 SPOT PROTOTYPING

When we began exploring our interface in the mid-fidelity phase, we were concerned whether our quiescent states contained the right information, and page-based prototyping tools were fine for this. Now we need to begin using tools or frameworks that can simulate complex interactions within each screen, such as drag–drop, scrolls, or touch gestures. As of this writing, there is currently an explosion of prototyping frameworks that attempt to do this. Our expectation is that, over time, competition will weed out the worst and leave an effective and ubiquitous few, most likely just one or two.

Assess prototyping tools that have captured your interest and see which can fill your needs and which can't. Look for whether a tool can create the patterns and behaviors you want, be played on the devices you are considering, how stable it is, whether it will be around in the future, and how easy it is to iterate through a set of revisions. You may think ease of learning should also be a critical feature, but if it takes a while to learn, that's a drop in the bucket to the amount of time you may be spending on revisions. A tool that may take an hour to learn but a week to revise your designs is no match for a tool that takes a week to learn but an hour to revise.

If nothing seems satisfactory, or you're dealing with a context that has no applicable prototyping framework, then you have two options: Either start honing your coding and electrical engineering chops, or simulate things using mock-ups and animation. Considering the animation/mock-up approach, all you may need to learn is some AfterEffects and possibly a 3D animation tool, projection systems, and be fond of working in wood or foam core. As for the coding/electronics approach, the code you do as an interaction designer is focused on the front end and is usually simple and straightforward. You do not need to delve into the back end complexities and system architectures that allow developers to earn their keep. All you care about is the front end and how it behaves. Additionally, there's a wealth of kits out there that make electronics simple and fun.

Whether you use a prototyping framework to create your prototypes, you code them, or you animate them, at this stage you don't have to build the whole thing. All you need to do is test how your microinteractions behave so you can make decisions about whether they work or not. This can be done through a method of using your wireframes to create small bits of an interface—possibly no more than just the specific interaction you're are addressing—and determining if it works. We call these spot prototypes, or spot animations. Keep things tightly scoped and keep them sketchy. Becoming quick and adept at this will lead to designs that are better considered.

10.13 INTERACTION SCENARIOS

Our microinteraction schematics and spot prototypes tell us how components work individually, but how do they orchestrate together as the user flows through the experience of our system? We can address this experience by creating an interaction scenario. This is essentially the design scenarios we've been working with, yet the difference being that now we are armed with the knowledge we've gained from the consideration of our microinteractions. Identify the gestures in your interface along your primary use case. Create spot prototypes for them and cut them into your scenario and *voila*! You have an interaction scenario. See the gesture schematics in Figure 9.12 for example.

10.14 CONTINUING THE AESTHETIC EFFORT

In the previous few chapters, we've explored interface possibilities through a series of comps. The result may have provided us with a selection of possible approaches, but then again, maybe not. We must be sensitive to the fact that achieving good aesthetics is not simply about whether you have talent or not; it often comes down to whether you put the work into it or not. Arriving at a distinctive solution is a process, and, as we mentioned earlier, often one that is highly non-linear. It's filled with successes and failures, and it takes effort to get through.

One of the issues we often face at this stage is a propensity for creating interfaces in such a way as we think interfaces should be designed. Or we rely too heavily on our wireframes as a source for our aesthetic designs, applying just a little color here, a different typeface there, and calling it a day. In other words, at this stage, there is usually a preponderance of interface clichés and mediocre aesthetic effort.

It's not that *clichés* are inherently bad—in fact, using common design approaches may make our interface extremely usable—they just usually result in us turning our creative brain off and producing results that have nothing that is either distinctive or inspired. We gravitate towards them, impose them on our design without much thought, and terminate our aesthetic reasoning in the process. As designers, we need to question everything (Krause, 2015, p. 180). This does not mean throwing out all ideas that others use—that top menu bar or three column grid may be just what we need—but we should use ideas with conscience, not just use them because everyone else does.

With a review of our collection of exploratory comps, we can see if we have uninspired designs or not. Do they achieve the same level of finesse as the other designs on our inspiration board? If not, it's appropriate to shake up our aesthetic design process. Even if we have some results of value at this stage, it's a good idea not to get too attached to them just yet. Let's explore some possibilities. The way around this is to consider other possible design approaches.

10.15 AESTHETIC DISRUPTION

Often, during the design process, we run into roadblocks, or just want to get the creative process stimulated. A seasoned designer usually knows how to deal with this, but sometimes we all need help. When we find ourselves in this situation, we suggest shaking things up through either inspiration or methodology. We need to disrupt the aesthetic process and embrace the thought that good aesthetic solutions come not from thinking, but from making. We need to roll up our sleeves and dive in.

Design directors and veteran designers all have their approaches for shaking things up, but, if you're feeling a little lost, we are particularly fond of the following methods, with a gracious nod to Ellen Lupton's book *Graphic Design Thinking* (Lupton, 2011). Within, she and her team of designers created a kind of instruction manual for getting designers out of their comfort zone. If your interface is seeming tired and derivative, explore some of the following techniques, but remember, we are performing these exercises to generate possible design directions. Regardless of the subsequent disruptive methods we choose, we are striving to create *viable* solutions. If not, these efforts have no purpose.

How do we make them viable? Use not only the information in your wireframes, but your guidewords, moodboards, inspiration boards, and your design criteria as guides. We suggest you review these considerations, identify several that you feel may result in something useful, and then use possibly your high traffic screen to comp out each of your selected approaches. Viability of feeling is important for this exercise, yet viability of structure is not. In fact, viability of structure is probably just that thing that needs to be turned on its head to break through the monotony. Don't overthink things. Embrace the following challenges, and use your hands, not your brain.

10.15.1 Reduce

Sometimes our interface suffers because we've added too much. What if your interface were only type? Can that work? What would you have to do to make it work? What if it were only iconographic? What if you only used three colors, black, white, and something else? What would that color be? How would your interface look? Try not to reduce the content, but reduce the amount of visual clutter. Try using only negative space to separate elements. What if you only had one weight and one style of type? Can you make something snap with that?

10.15.2 Switch Aesthetics

If your interface looks like everything else, it probably means you're applying a "web design" or "app design" aesthetic—and what we mean by aesthetic here is a particular style. Unbeknown to you, you have absorbed what you think an interface *should* be in these contexts and you're doing yours in that style. Change it. Identify a style from another medium or another era. What if it were done in a Bauhaus style, like that of Laslo Moholy-Nagy or Jan Tschichold? What if you approached your design in an international style, such as Hans Neuburg or Josef Muller-Brockmann? Or a 1960s New York aesthetic, such as Milton Glaser? How about a little Deconstructivism in the guise of April Greiman or David Cason? Explore eras, get inspired by masters, see what you can do to that interface.

10.15.3 Master Copy

In drawing, the master copy is a process where illustrators study the works of master draughtsman, such as da Vinci, Michelangelo, Greuze, Tiepolo, or Schiele, and strive to execute drawings in the same likeness. They consider the drawing's arrangement of forms, its composition, shading, and the application of each line. The effort allows the student to arrive at a profound understanding of how a master performed their art. For those who are having challenges arriving at an aesthetic approach that seems to work, we suggest something similar in order to break free from the endless cycle of producing sub-standard designs.

Before continuing with a description of this exercise, it's critical to note its dangers. Some may claim that it promotes designs that are derivative, or, even worse, copying and plagiarism. But note that this is an exercise. It serves a particular purpose in the design process to get an effort that may be going off track back on the road to success. The takeaways never should be the results of the exercise itself, but, rather, the things that are learned from it. In the same way, an illustrator does not intend to promote a master copy as an original piece of work, just a means of developing skills learned from it. Our goal is to take the learnings from the master copy effort, and create enticing original designs of our own.

To start, we prompt our designers to revisit their style analyses in section 9.8, where we created style guides for designs from our inspiration board that we thought conveyed our guidewords well. Identify those that are both usable and promote originality in their design. In other words, they're fairly successful in avoiding common *clichés*. They effectively stand out and fit in.

We are trying not only to learn techniques that allow us to execute a high degree of aesthetics, but also to break free of tired approaches. Indeed, it may seem rather ironic that we are striving to explore originality by performing an effort that is fundamentally derivative, but we've noticed that once a designer who may be locked into *clichés* explores a few distinctive and successful master copies and then returns to the effort of exploring their own designs, those designs become a great deal more original. The key is to select the masters we are copying appropriately: those that are at once useable and distinctive.

Using the style analysis you made of your inspiration previously (see Figure 9.13), apply that style to your critical interfaces. Use the information in your wireframes, yet strive to be as true as possible to your inspiration's style as if you were doing your interfaces as an extension of that style. What does this tell you about how that designer approached their design? How can you incorporate this into the design of your interfaces?

10.15.4 Be Dramatic

The final aesthetic disruption we like to suggest is to be dramatic. Create drama. Often, we get so tied up with making things usable that we place restrictions on ourselves that make our work tedious and boring. What can you do to your screen that creates drama? Can you give your type a greater dynamic range, make your headings big and "in your face", while making your captions or body copy delicate and small? Can you use bright accent colors against neutrals for things to snap out better? What if you went against the grain and used small type for a header, but surrounded it with an unusually generous amount of negative space? Whatever you decide to do, play with the extremes and see what happens.

10.16 REFINE YOUR DISRUPTIONS

Hopefully, the methods mentioned above will yield some results that, if tweaked a little, can be both distinctive and usable. Bring a second pair of eyes into the mix and have a chat about what's working and what's not. What has potential and what doesn't? Refine those that you think are most successful to a point where they can reasonably sit on your inspiration board and not seem out of place in terms of feel and quality.

10.17 ICON REFINEMENT

At this point, you should have a family, or a few families, of icons that convey their ideas well, deliver your system's brand feel, and work well together as a family. If not, strive to get to this point with a set or two—again, just focusing on three icons or so. If you've arrived at this point, expand your set of icons beyond the three you've been focused on. Try to choose those that may present the most challenge so you can assess if an approach will work or not. Eventually, you should have an iconographic style that is consistent, and delivers ideas and brand feel. Try to integrate your iconography into your comp explorations to see how they work.

Note

1 These principles appear throughout Saffer's work. We've referred to some of his ideas as a foundation, added a few of our own, and made them into a concise list here for efficacy. He also describes loops and modes, but we feel these aspects are adequately covered by the concepts of triggers, rules, and feedback.

11 Behavior

In the previous chapter, we described how microinteractions can be broken down into triggers, rules, and feedback. We used ideation, interaction sketches, and wireframes to illustrate how they worked. But the strict definition of microinteractions are that they revolve around a single use case. However, we often face interactive components that do more. These can include a drawer that may open to receive an item we may be dragging into it, yet retreat if we do not drop it there. Or a button that may fly open when we swipe, revealing other controls inside, and close when we swipe back. Or items that may behave one way if we click on them, and another way if we click and hold, and yet even another way if we drag. We may consider these to be microinteractions, but they aren't in the truest sense of the term because they have more than one use case. They behave in interactively complex ways. Whether they are microinteractions or not is an exercise in semantics, but what is important for us as designers is that they exhibit complex behavior, and that behavior needs to be clearly designed. That's the focus of this chapter.

11.1 CONSIDERING COMPLEX BEHAVIORS

How we interact with a system may be through a set of microinteractions, but those things we interact with are objects. We've been referring to these objects as interactive components, such as buttons, sliders, twirlies, et cetera, but, if we were to ask a developer, they would call them objects, and objects have certain characteristics that go well beyond our single use case definition of microinteractions.

We will go into detail about the most important of these aspects below, but, for now, suffice it to say that these objects—our interactive components—can have multiple outcomes, multiple states, complex behaviors, complex relationships to each other, and can even encapsulate each other, much like folders on our desktop can contain not only documents but folders as well. For example, a list is an object that we can scroll up and down, but it can contain other objects, such as a set of list items that can have behaviors all their own. When we begin to consider interactive components with a level of complexity such as this, suddenly the sketches we used to indicate microinteractions begin to seem woefully inadequate. We need a more robust toolset to describe them.

We could code them to demonstrate how our intended behaviors are supposed to work, or we could flowchart them. But we've found it most useful to use a methodology called state diagrams. State diagrams are easy to conceptualize, they are robust in that they can describe almost any behavior, they are implementation independent in that they don't rely on a certain programming language or platform, and they provide us clear visual referents for the things that interest us as interaction designers: triggers, rules, and feedback. They also provide an indication of the complexity of a system and a means for identifying production assets necessary to build the components contained within it. Let's see how they work.

11.2 IDENTIFY OBJECTS

We begin the process of describing behaviors through state diagrams by first identifying objects we want to design. For a simple button, this is fairly straightforward, but for something more complex, such as a scrollable list, this may be a little more difficult. If a list contains interactive items, do we include them within the specific behavior we are designing? Where does the behavior of the list object stop and the behavior of the content of the list—the list item—begin?

This is up to the designer's discretion. We could create a state diagram for the list that contains items within it, or we could separate the two and create a state diagram for the list, and another state diagram for the behavior of a particular item. The best rule to follow here, though, is to make our state diagrams as simple as possible, which implies that the best depiction of our list and list item is that they should be represented as separate objects. We will demonstrate this example later, but, for our purposes here, it's best that we look at an interface as a collection of objects with rather simple behaviors.

Is it necessary to design the behavior in detail every little component that we present in our interface? Certainly not. As we have seen in our consideration of microinteractions, visual illustrations work quite well and can get us by most of the time.

11.3 IDENTIFY OPPORTUNITIES

Most interactions in a system rely on classic patterns: a button click, a scroll bar drag, a finger swipe. As discussed previously, common patterns increase usability because our audience is familiar with them. They can approach our interface with a pre-existing understanding of how to use the components that comprise it. Although we can certainly use behavior design to clarify these components, why should we bother if they work exactly like something that is out there already? It's much more expeditious to identify the pattern and allow the examples of the pattern explain to the development team how the behavior should work.

What about unique signature interactions, though? Here, we have spotted an opportunity for detailed behavior design because these must work well and, therefore, need to be designed in detail. Or how about an interaction that is not necessarily "signature" but is different from anything else out there? This is another opportunity for us to design in detail its behavior.

Say we want to adopt a classic interaction and alter it. For example, maybe we want a scrollbar for navigating a document, but while we're scrolling, we would like it to diverge from the classic implementation by displaying a microtext of the page we are on. This is a detail that may or may not help our users, but it is certainly distinct from the classic implementation of a scroll and may need more detail as well. This is probably a case where we would spend the time necessary to detail its behavior in a state diagram.

The bottom line is that designing behaviors in detail takes time. Spend that time wisely on unique and important interactions, don't waste it on designing simple components or those that rely on common patterns.

11.4 IDENTIFY GOALS

Once we have identified critical behaviors to design, we need to begin by identifying our user's goals with the interaction (Saffer, 2014, p. 52). Using an example of a light in a room, our goal would be to be able to turn it off and on. We would then look at those goals and determine an interactive component that would work to fulfill those goals. For the light, that would be the switch. But the switch could have several possible arrangements that would work: Up and down, side to side, a button for "on" and a button for "off," just to name a few. What's important to note is that the control matches what we want to do with it: Remember, control must agree with effect. There are two states to the light; the controller should allow us to go from one to the other efficiently.

We say "efficiently" because we could certainly consider a controller that was more difficult: We could rotate a handle on a flywheel and spin it one hundred times, thereby turning the light on. But this is not efficient for a light that we would like to use in our house. However, if we were in a science museum and we were trying to have our user experience the amount of power a light used, we may consider having them turn a flywheel to generate that power. Control should agree not only with the effect, but the goal as well.

11.5 INSTRUCTIONIZE THE BEHAVIOR

The next step is to describe the behavior. Shortly, we will present how state diagrams work as descriptors, but, before we do, it's instructive just to use words and pictures to get a better understanding of the behaviour (Saffer, 2014, p. 59). For pictures, refer to the microinteraction ideation in Figure 10.1 in the previous chapter. It's instructive to ideate a few possibilities of the interaction in storyboard form before proceeding to a more rigorous means of describing it. After we've gotten a sense of how we may want it to work, we should transition to describing it in words. For word descriptors, think of describing it as a brief set of instructions. For a simple light, we flick the switch up to turn it on and flick it down to turn it off.

Notice the formulation of these commands: "Flick up to turn on", "Flick down to turn off". They are precisely the imperative action–result formulation we discussed in chapter 6 when we were describing tasks. It is a task language. These are the commands we are issuing to the system, and if we can "instructionize" them by describing them in terms of actions and results, we are laying the groundwork for their design.

A control object, such as a light, can have more than one behavior. Consider the dimmer light we discussed in the last chapter. Let's say that it has a dimmer dial. Turning it all the way counter-clockwise turns the light completely off. Turning it from that state to slightly clockwise provides a haptic "click" and turns the current of the light on, although it's still dimmed down. Turning it further clockwise increases the current and brightens the light. Turning it counter-clockwise dims it. How do we instructionize this behavior?

Almost the same way we did with the simple on/off switch. Start with the initial state, "off". Then describe how we get out of that state: "Turn dial clockwise to click on." Describe what we can do when it's on: "Turn clockwise to brighten or turn counter-clockwise to dim." Indicate that there is a limit to that behavior: "Turn all the way clockwise to full on." And then describe how to return to the initial state: "Turn all the way counter-clockwise to click off." This covers all the states with the dimmable light and all the actions necessary to control it. We are left with the following descriptors:

1. Start in "Off"
2. Turn dial clockwise to click on
3. Turn clockwise to brighten or turn counter-clockwise to dim
4. Turn all the way clockwise to full on
5. Turn all the way counter-clockwise to click off

It reads somewhat like an instruction manual for a dimmer switch, and, in essence, it is. Instruction manuals are guides to how someone uses a device. When instructions are done well, they are descriptions of how a user controls a device or system. Next time you build a shelf from Ikea, think about this. The instructions they provide are just descriptions of the interface we use to build the shelf. If we write an instruction manual for our interactive components, we are instructionizing them by describing their behavior in the imperative language of action–response

11.6 DIAGRAMMING BEHAVIORS

This text description of the behavior gets us started. Next, we describe it using a state diagram. The state diagram for a simple on/off light switch is like that shown in Figure 11.1). There are two states, indicated by ovals, and two arrows representing the ways of transitioning from one state to the next. The descriptions associated with the transitions are the events that trigger the state changes. The only way out of the "off" state is by flicking the switch up. The way out of "on" is to flick the switch down.

Now, let's see how diagrams work for the more complex dimmer. Let's take this step by step, as if we were designing it. We use the interaction storyboards we ideated and the instructionized text descriptions as guides. We begin by indicating our initial state. For the switch, it could be off or on, and we can start with either, but most naturally we would consider that it starts in the off position (Figure 11.2). Then add how to get out of that state "Turn dial clockwise to click on," or for brevity's sake, we could say simply: "Clockwise to click" (Figure 11.3). We also add the state it goes to: "On".

Figure 11.1
State diagram of simple on/off switch.

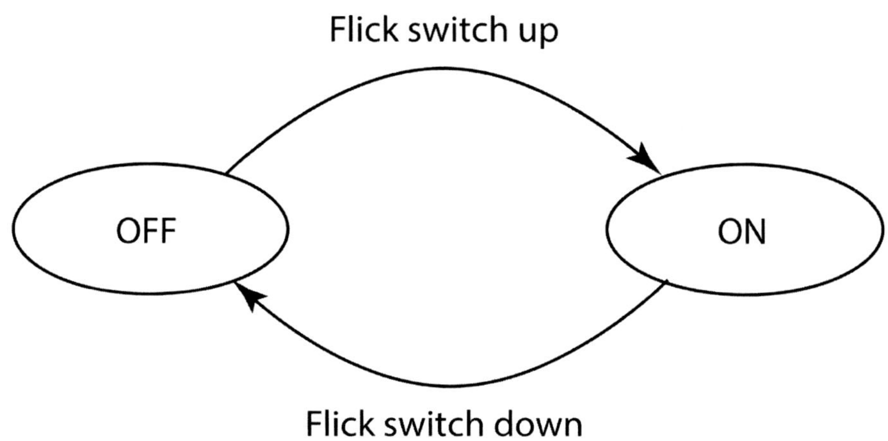

Figure 11.2
A node representing the off state.

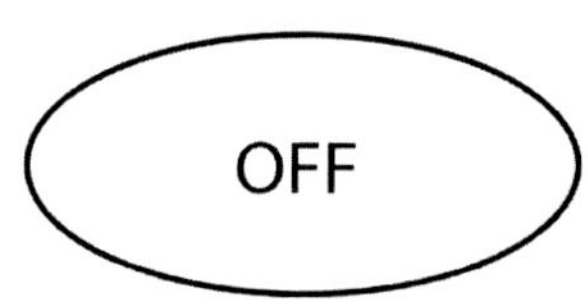

The "On" state is a little more complex than the "On" of our simple light switch. Referring to our text description of the dimmer, we indicated, "Turn clockwise to brighten or turn counter-clockwise to dim." These are two different events, turning the dial clockwise and turning it counter-clockwise. Additionally, if we don't turn it

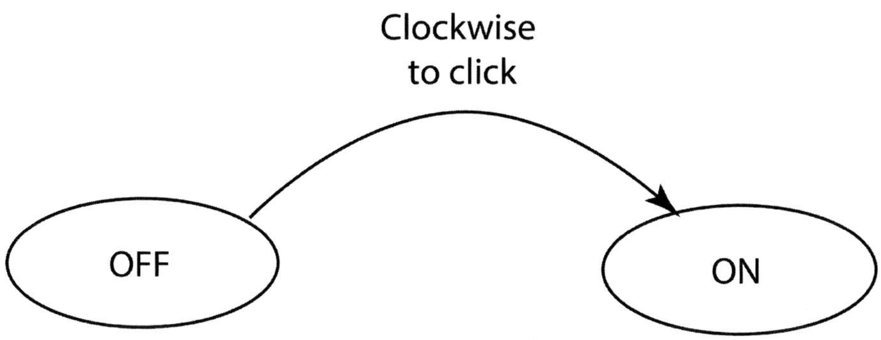

Figure 11.3
Adding the on state and the event which turns it on.

all the way to full on, we can still do "clockwise to brighten" or "counter-clockwise to dim." This is the very definition of the "On" state, so when we perform these actions we are executing transitions, but transitions that return us to the "On" state. We diagram this as Figure 11.4.

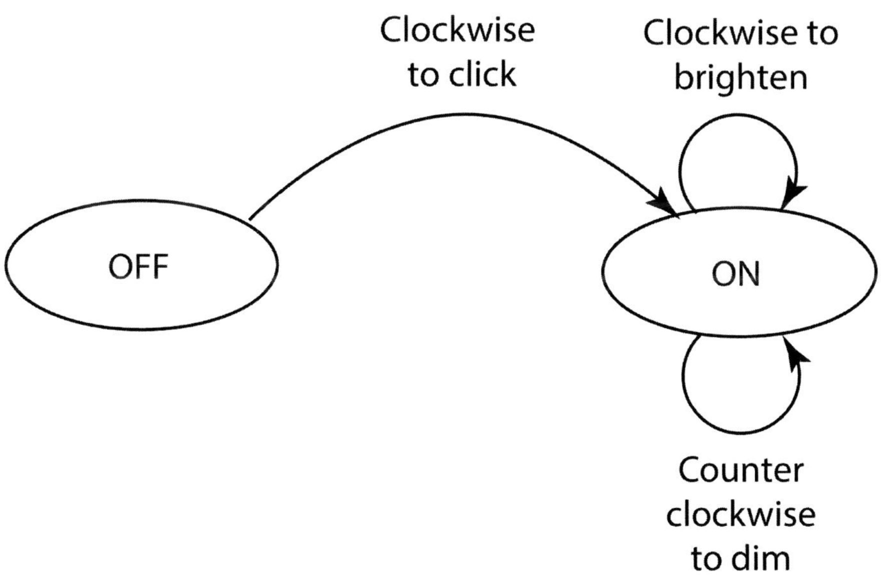

Figure 11.4
Adding the dimmer behavior.

The extreme limit of turning it on is "Turn all the way clockwise to full on." We can also describe how to get out of the "Full on" state: any time we turn the dial counter-clockwise (Figure 11.5). Finally, let's add the transition that takes us back to "Off" (Figure 11.6), and we've completed our diagram.

This process may seem very detailed, but details ". . . aren't just the details; They are the design" (Saffer, 2014, p. 2). When we use state diagrams to describe our behaviors, they force us to consider not only the broad strokes of the interaction, as we did with the storyboards that represented our microinteractions, but every aspect of the behavior as well. It is exactly this granular breakdown that designers sometimes glaze over, yet developers consider each day. What we are doing with

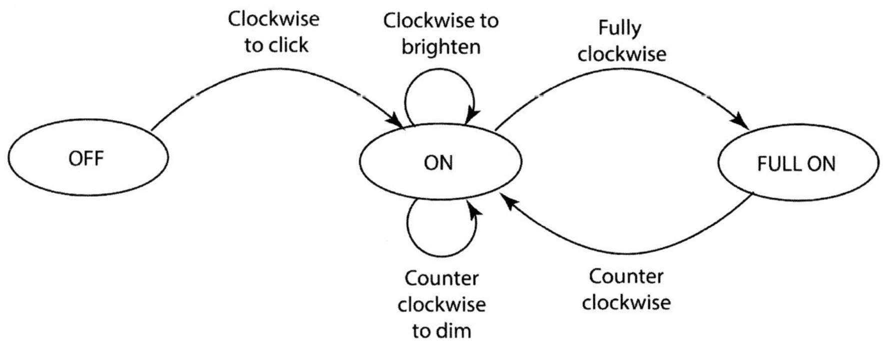

Figure 11.5
Adding the full on state and its related events.

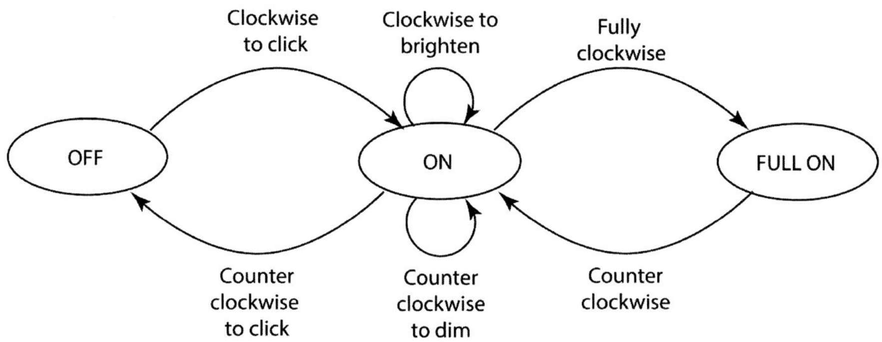

Figure 11.6
The complete dimmer switch behaviour.

state diagramming the design of our behaviors is making these decisions as a conscious part of the design process, rather than throwing them over the wall for the developer to figure out.

11.7 DIAGRAMMING COMPLEX BEHAVIORS

Apple has produced many a magical product, but also its fair share of software with questionable design (iTunes, post debacle Final Cut Pro). But its email app on the iPhone is fairly successful. In fact, I've found it so effective that I'm often drawn to my iPhone to manage my emails even when I'm on my laptop with my email application open. There is admittedly some confusion on its mobile implementation when I'm dealing with an email thread (what's the most recent email? What am I responding to?), but navigating through the email list, selecting email items, and managing those items works well for the most part.

Using the app to manage emails, we can select an item, fling open a drawer of buttons to manage the email with a swipe, or completely throw the email away with a harder swipe. It has great user feedback and is largely delightful to perform, except for one glaring flaw that we'll discuss later. When our finger is pulling open the drawer, the buttons cleverly unfurl from the right side, making them feel somewhat card-like and elastic. Refer to the wireframe of this behavior shown in Figure 11.7). On the surface, this activity seems simple because it's so natural, but, as we'll see, it's fairly complicated.

Diagramming this behavior will allow us to see more of the features of state diagrams, so let's use the email list item interaction as an example and take things step by step. First off, the initial state of the email list item is a brief description of the email with the subject, sender, date, and a few lines of the email itself. See section A of Figure 11.7. Let's call this object the "email item".

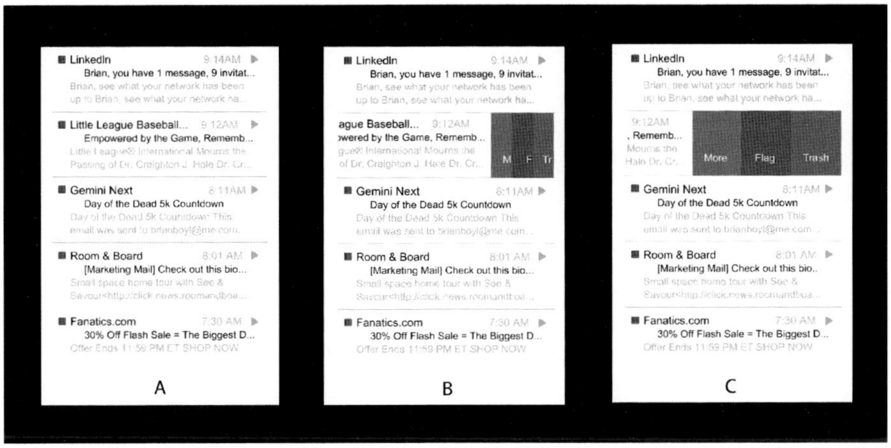

Figure 11.7
Wireframe mock-up of the iOS email item behavior: "A", initial state; "B" buttons beginning to unfurl; "C" buttons fully revealed.

The item appears in the inbox list with other email items, but we're less interested in the behavior of the list than we are of the email item itself. This is the first thing we need to consider when designing behaviors: What precisely is the object we're trying to describe? What is its scope? For this example, it's the email as represented by the email item within the inbox list. Although it is contained within the inbox, we are not describing the behavior of the inbox. That would be represented by another diagram.

With our object well scoped, we begin by creating a state node for our initial state. This is the state when we first see the email item (see Figure 11.7, section A). In fact, let's call this state "item," to clarify that we are referring to an item in the list. We also indicate this first item with a state transition arrow and a "start" label (Figure 11.8).

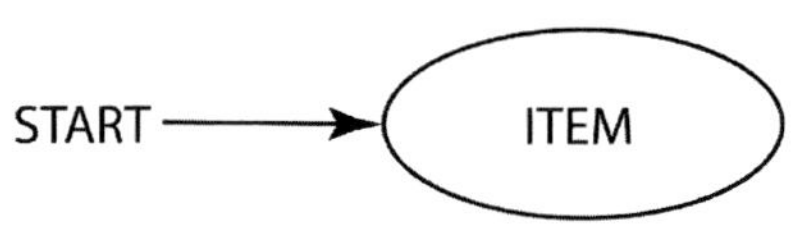

Figure 11.8
Initializing the email item behavior.

When we slide the email item partially to the left (see section B in Figure 11.7), we can fan it out and back by dragging our finger right or left. Let's call this the "FAN" state and the event that takes us there is "swipe partially left" (Figure 11.9).

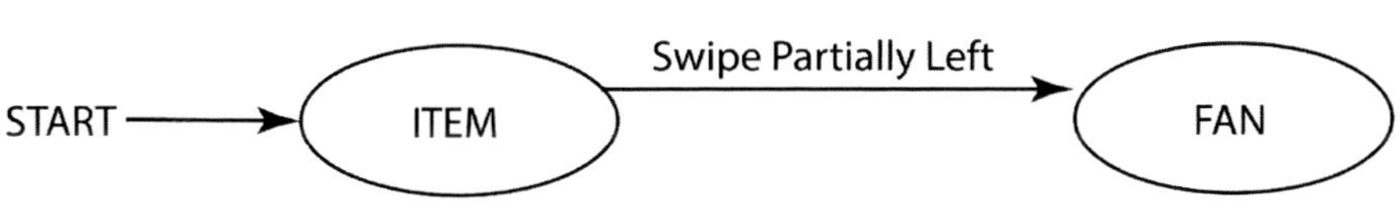

Figure 11.9
Adding the "FAN" state.

If we let go near the right side of the screen, the buttons will snap back. We can indicate this by a transition going back to the item state (Figure 11.10). If we swipe a little further to the left and let go, we fan out the buttons entirely (see section C in Figure 11.7). We can indicate this as the "buttons" state (Figure 11.11). We can return to the fan state by placing our finger back on the item and dragging it back to the right. (Figure 11.12). In sum, the behavior of the fan state is that if we let go far to the left, it will go to the buttons state, if we let go near the left, it will go back to the initial state: item.

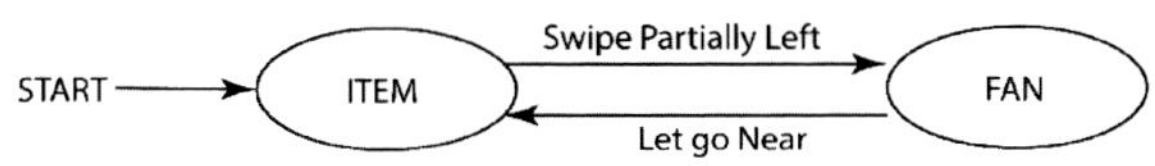

Figure 11.10
Adding the return transition from the "FAN" state.

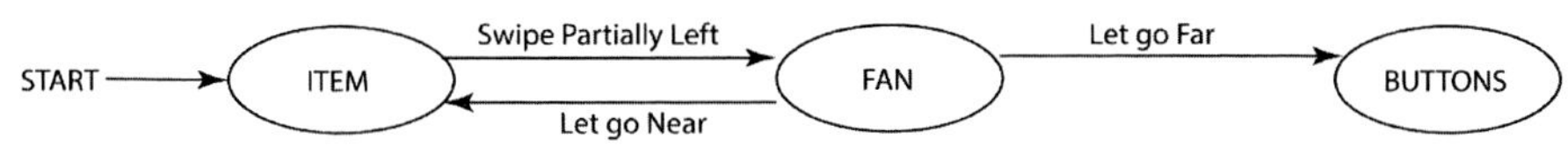

Figure 11.11
Adding the "BUTTONS" state.

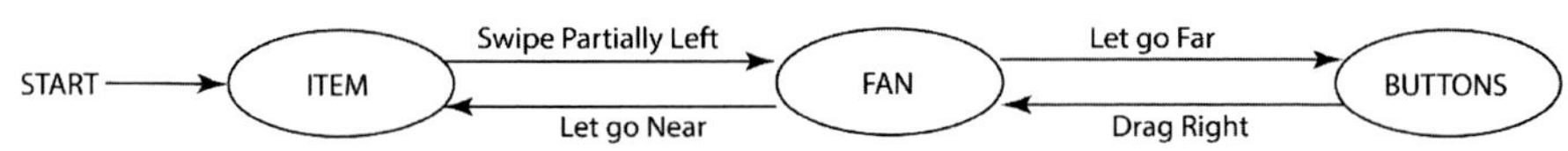

Figure 11.12
Adding the return transition from the "BUTTONS" state.

There's one more action to consider. If we are in any of these states, item, fan, or button, and we swipe all the way to the left, we throw the email item into the trash (Figure 11.13). This is diagrammed as in Figure 11.14. Trash gets rid of the item from the list, so it's considered a "terminal" state. To indicate a state as being terminal, its surrounding oval should be rendered in double lines.

Figure 11.13
Wireframe of the "TRASH" state.

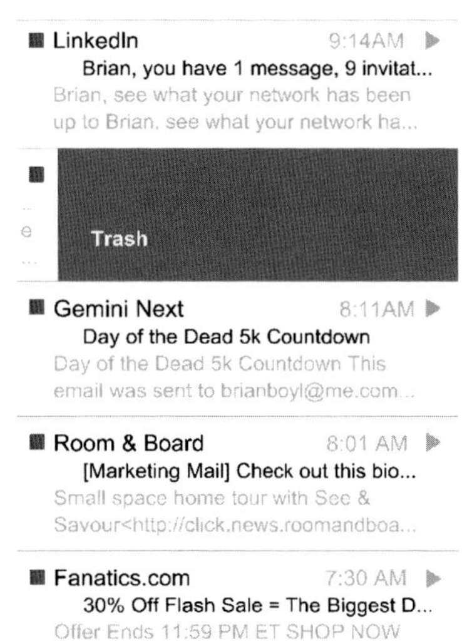

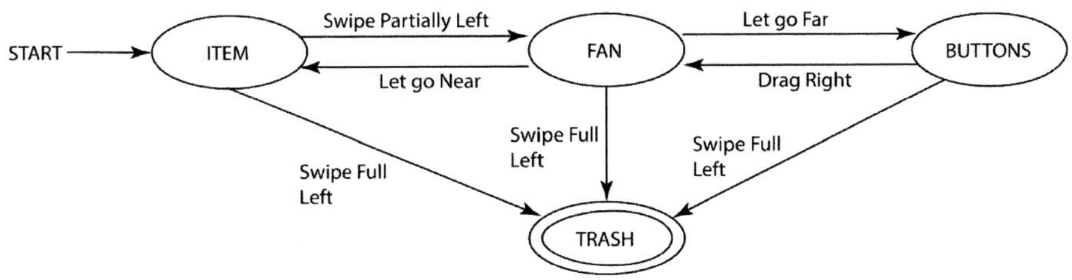

Figure 11.14
Adding the "TRASH" state to the diagram.

This is the glaring flaw that I noted above. The behavior of transitioning to the "trash" state is an interaction problem that the designer did not resolve very well: If we wish to open the buttons by sliding our thumb to the "buttons" state, it's quite possible to go too far and trash the item. They placed a dangerous result near a casual interaction, thereby increasing the chances of error. Fortunately, we can undo the action, but that's an annoying point of friction. The beauty of using state diagrams for behavior design is that we can isolate the microinteractions that are problematic and consider how to design them better.

Returning to our diagram, let's consider what happens when our user interacts with the buttons in the buttons state (see Figure 11.7, section C). If we click on trash, it trashes the item just as if we swiped it fully left. But it's a different event, so it's indicated by a different transition arrow (Figure 11.15). When we click on the flag button, it flags the item and closes the button drawer to return to the item state (see Figure 11.7, section A) (Figure 11.16). Notice that the outgoing transition from

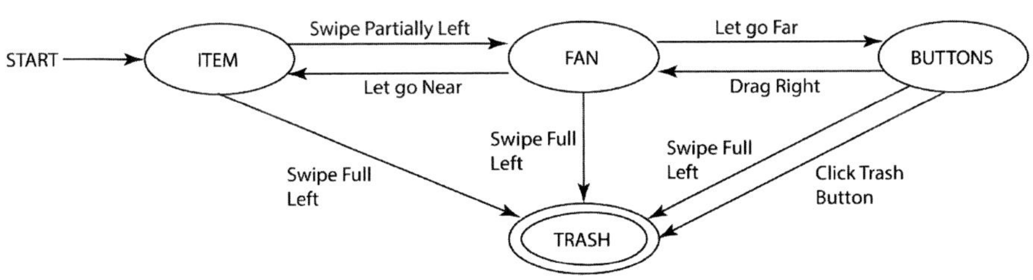

Figure 11.15
Adding the click trash button event.

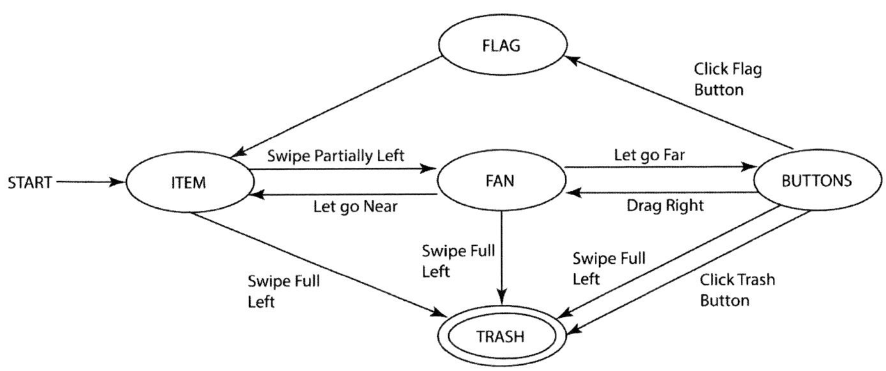

Figure 11.16
Adding the "FLAG" state.

the flag state does not have an event associated with it. That is because the component goes back to the item state directly—upon completion of flagging the email item—without any user-initiated events. Additionally, the flag state operates in two ways: If the item is flagged, the button unflags it. If it is unflagged, the button flags it. In other words, the flag operation is a toggle. We can clarify this in the diagram or further descriptions of the state, so we won't add this complexity to the diagram. For this example, we'll choose to do it in the descriptions.

When we click on the "more" button, we are taken to a separate menu of several things we can do with the email (Figure 11.17): Reply, Forward, Mark, Notify Me, Move Message, and Cancel (Figure 11.18). Several of these bring us to yet another level of menus. This is where things get complicated and tedious. Complicated because of the numerous menus and selections; tedious because there's nothing interesting at all about these interactions: They are simply menu selections. Since we strategize our detailed behavior design effort towards unique and critical behaviors, there's no reason to put effort into diagramming a standard hierarchical menu set. We know how that works. If you face this in your design, you may wish to push further to see if there's a way to make mundane interactions like the more menu enticing, but, if not, you may wish to do what I have done here: simply stub it out as in Figure 11.17.

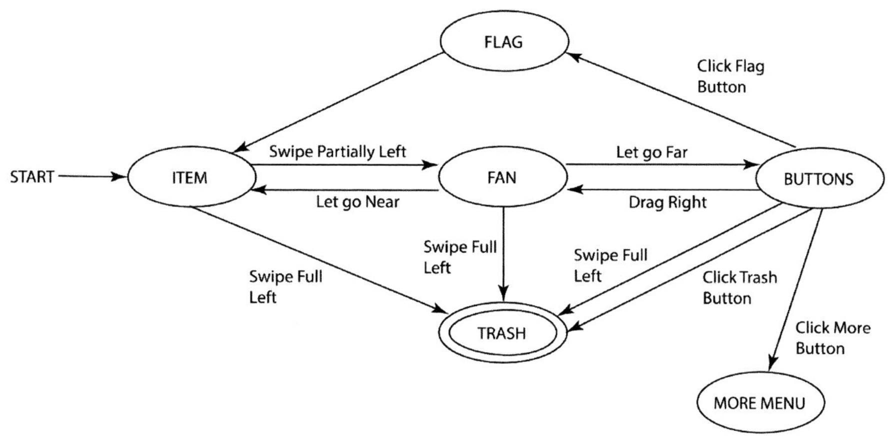

Figure 11.17
Adding the "MORE MENU" state.

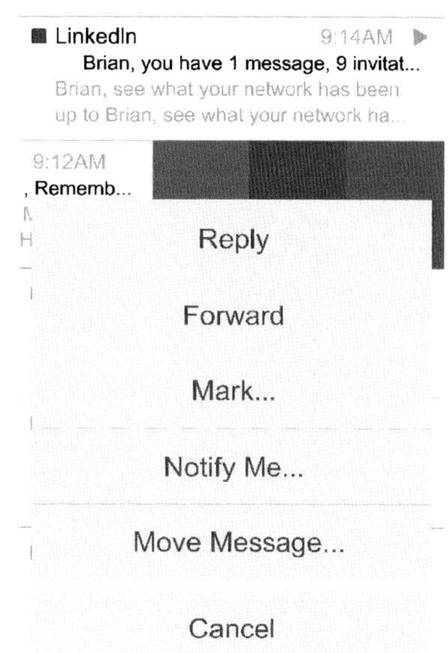

Figure 11.18
Wireframe of the "MORE MENU" state.

Finally, we saved the easiest interaction with the email item for last: Just simply clicking on the item—no swipes or anything. We held back on diagramming this because it's not a normal transition in the sense that it takes us from state to state within the interactive component. It transitions us to an entirely new quiescent state: that of displaying the detailed content of the email. The component sends a message to the system telling it to transition to the email detail screen. We diagram it as is shown in Figure 11.19. The squiggly line indicates that a message is sent to another object, in this case, the system.

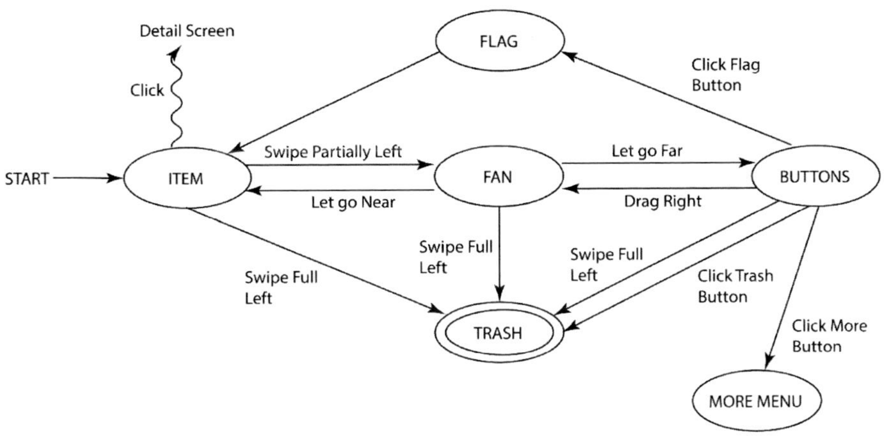

Figure 11.19
Sending a message to the system to transition to the detail screen.

Figure 11.19 represents a full description of the email item (*sans* the "More" menu), and, as we can see, it collects several microinteractions together: the fan behavior, the button selections, flagging and trashing. It looks complex, but when we interact with the item, it seems very simple. If you're not familiar with coding, you're probably surprised at how something that seems so simple is not. If you've coded before, you're probably not the least bit surprised.

If you've ever wondered why it takes developers time to build things that seem easy on the surface, this is your answer. This dichotomy between simple behavior and complex diagram indicates another value of state diagrams: Not only can they accurately describe the behavior of an interactive object, but they are also a pretty good indicator of the complexity of a system. The more objects, states, and transitions a system contains, the more complex it is, and the more time it will take to build.

11.8 DESIGNING FROM SCRATCH

Our analysis of the behavior of the email item is all well and good when we face an object that has already been built, but what about those we are designing from scratch? How do we use this methodology to define the behaviors of things in the system we're designing?

The best approach is to do things similarly to what we did above. First, identify the object we wish to design and consider all that we may want the user to be able to do with that object. Identify the user goals. Then, using our journal, we begin to sketch out thumbnail storyboards of how we may want it to behave. When we've explored possibilities and have something that we think works, instructionize it using our action–response type of grammar, that is, language such as "swipe far left to unfurl buttons."

When we start diagramming, we should detail the easiest first. Although we diagrammed the easiest interaction in our previous example last—clicking on the email item—we did so for pedagogical reasons. We would normally have diagrammed it first. At least this aspect of the interaction represents the application of good design principles: The easiest and most direct interaction, the click, takes us to the thing we want to do most often, which is to read the email.

The second easiest gestures should execute the next most important operations. For the email item, this is the swipe far left and swipe right, reserved for "trash" and "mark as read" respectively. Try to thumbnail ways that your primary gestures can be reserved for your primary operations, and your secondary gestures are reserved for the secondary operations.

For operations that follow your secondary set, you may have to get clever. The designers of the email item certainly did with the fan and button states. But as you load up your objects with functionality, you need to take more care. Complex objects have a way of becoming error-prone and unusable. Although for the most part I appreciate the interaction of the email item, the swipe far left to delete is a glaring error, and when we get to the "more" menu, the interaction becomes tedious and complicated. Be careful not to overload your objects with so much functionality that your user begins to make mistakes and loses sight of what they are interacting with. Also, be careful not to overload them with interactions that are used by other objects in the quiescent state: For example, it's fine for the email item to use swipe left and right, but it can't use swipe up and down because that's reserved for scrolling the email list up and down. Practice good orchestration.

Finally, at this stage, you may use a gesture for one interactive object only to find out later that when you begin designing another, the gesture is much more appropriate for the new one. You may need to go back to the drawing board on the first and reconsider how it works. This happens constantly and is so common that we strongly advise you to sketch out your interactions in thumbnail form first before you detail them in a state diagram. In fact, discovering these possibilities is why we diagram these in the first place: So, our interactions are well considered when we build them. It's a substantial waste to dump a lot of time into minute details of behavior just to have it thrown away because it doesn't orchestrate well.

11.9 BEHAVIOR CONSIDERATIONS

When we design behaviors in detail, we also need to keep in mind the considerations we outlined for microinteractions. We need to make sure the display of the interactive object looks like a trigger if the user needs to trigger it; it is something the user wants when they want it; and that the control agrees with the effect. We also need to make sure it makes sense in context, that we are consistent with its display, and see if we can surface any critical data for that display.

In considering the rules that form the behavior—how it transitions from one state to the next—we need to keep in mind the goals of the user, the constraints of the system, and whether we can assist the user or employ smart defaults. The component needs to absorb complexity such that it's easy to use and should strive to prevent user error. It needs to age gracefully, be well orchestrated within the context of other interactive components on the interface, and support good user flow. Finally, and probably most importantly, its responses need to be well mapped to the user's actions, and they should feel like your brand.

The feedback should be concise and clear. It needs to be delivered at the right time and should not be arbitrary. Look for opportunities for feedback that may currently be overlooked, strive for a personality that matches the brand, and make sure any feedback agrees with the context within which it is delivered. Finally, make sure the form of its feedback is appropriate for what needs to be communicated.

There are a few more considerations that will help improve the design that have not been previously mentioned. To aid in minimizing user error, behaviors that may have significant consequences should confirm if the user wants to perform them (Lidwell et al., 2010, p. 54). If a user is about to delete their entire hard drive, we'd better confirm that they want to do it. On the other hand, confirmation is annoying for small things. For my swimming chronometer, I have to confirm that I want to save my workout without heart rate information and I need to confirm it not once, but twice. First off, as of this writing, heart rate devices in the water are rare, so it's more than likely that I don't have one (which is the case). Second, I am not telling the device to delete my workout, just save it without heart rate information. What's the big fuss? This interaction is clumsy and annoying and reflects poorly on the product. Consider confirmation, but don't use it on things that aren't critical.

Related to helping our users avoid errors is the concept of forgiveness, where we should ". . . minimize the consequences of errors when they do occur" (Lidwell et al., 2010, p. 104). For example, consider how an action can be reversible. In other words, how can we employ undo? We should also provide a safety net that ". . . minimizes the negative consequences of a catastrophic error or failure," such as a way to rebuild a file that may have been mistakenly thrown away. Confirmation, as described above, also helps with forgiveness, as well as appropriate warnings and user help. The less consequential the action, the less these are necessary.

Forgiveness is what happens after an action is taken. But many problems can be averted before they are started. For example, well-designed physical affordances that indicate how to properly use an interactive component may steer the audience away from problems in the first place. For the display of an interactive component, there should be features in its form that indicate how to use it properly, such as a drop shadow on a button in Google's Material Design that indicates that it's floating and that it can be "pressed".

Also, make sure the behavior supports user input that's well within the difference threshold of their actions. For example, if I need to select an item, it had better be far enough away from another that I can individually select it. Likewise, if I have to drag an item onto a target, the target should be large enough to be dragged onto and far enough away from other targets that the item can be placed there. Or, if an object responds to a hard press, the difference between a hard press and a normal press should not be so fine as to be impossible for the user to execute one over the other.

As is common in nature, humans gravitate to the path of least resistance. Given a choice between behavior that is easy and one that is more complicated, we are attracted to the easier path. We may be more attracted to the easier path even if the more complicated one is more powerful. An additional click may seem like a little thing, but it's the removal and simplification of any of these unnecessary actions that make interactions more direct and enjoyable. Reduce your interactions to the absolute minimum and consider ways of making them easier and more direct.

Use state diagrams as a form of "wireframing" behaviors to arrive at interactions that adhere as much as possible to the principles of good design.

11.10 BLACK BOXING

The task of orchestrating interactions is inherently complex and to be poring through a bunch of complicated state diagrams could make a tough task even tougher. You may wish to hide some of the behavioral complexity of your objects, yet leave those features apparent that affect the state of the screen or system. We can do this by "black boxing" our state diagrams.

For example, the email item has a bunch of states and transitions that make up its behavior, but, from the point of view of other objects in the system, all they care about are the outcomes. They don't care about the fan behavior or whether the button state appears or not. To them, what we diagrammed in the email item looks like this: Figure 11.20. Pretty simple. We've gone from a diagram with a complicated set of states and transitions (Figure 11.19) down to an object with only three outcomes. We certainly need to keep the detailed state diagram to clarify the behavior of the item, but, at the quiescent state level, we can look at things much more simply.

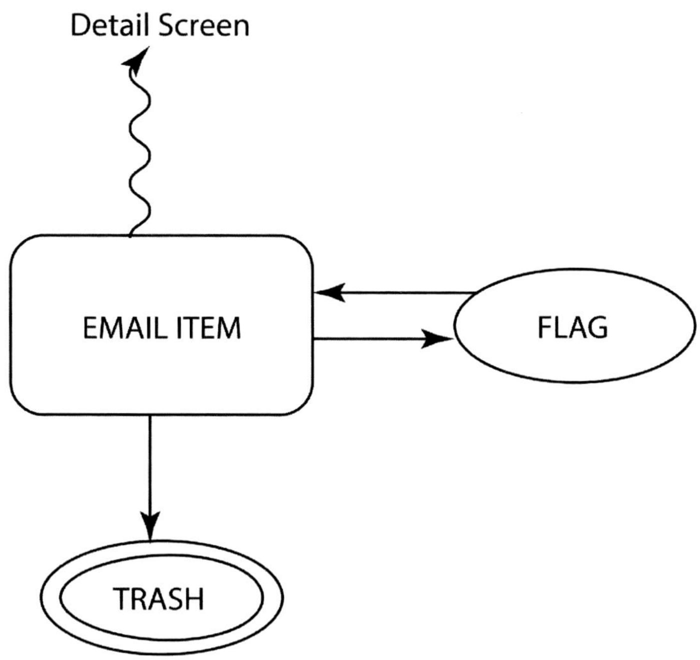

Figure 11.20
What other objects see.

So, how would this quiescent state level look as a state diagram? We would essentially have a set of interactive objects that communicate with each other, communicate with the system, and are organized in such a way as to reflect how they behave relative to each other. Before we diagram this, we need to explore what we mean by "how they behave relative to each other."

The email item is a single object that communicates with other objects. But it is contained within the inbox list. We can scroll up and down this list, and our email item and all the other email items scroll with each other. By interacting with it, we get the sense that the inbox "contains" the set of email items. Like folders on a desktop, interactive components can contain other interactive components: They can be hierarchal.

The inbox sits at a level of hierarchy above the email item and controls its display—its position on the screen. If we were to diagram the inbox, it might look something like Figure 11.21. Yet, if we open the inbox to see what it contains, it would look something like Figure 11.22. The inbox contains and encapsulates the behaviors of the email item. In fact, the quiescent state itself, the entire inbox screen, is a container for all the interactive components within it. It sits at a hierarchical level above the email list and all the links and buttons on the screen. But, since we target our detailed behavior design effort at the most critical interactions, we probably will not have to concern ourselves much with encapsulation upon

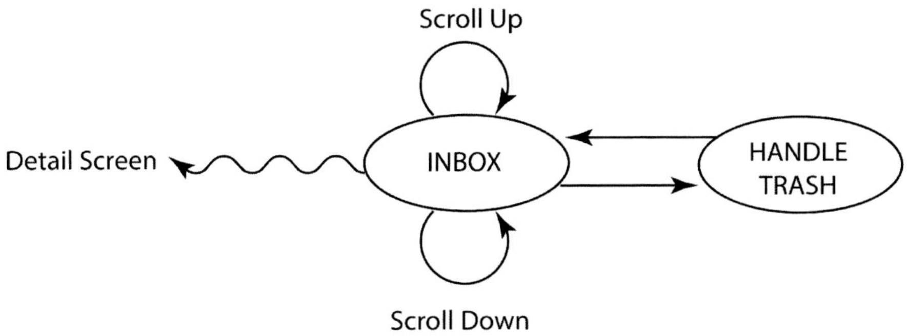

Figure 11.21
State diagram for the inbox object.

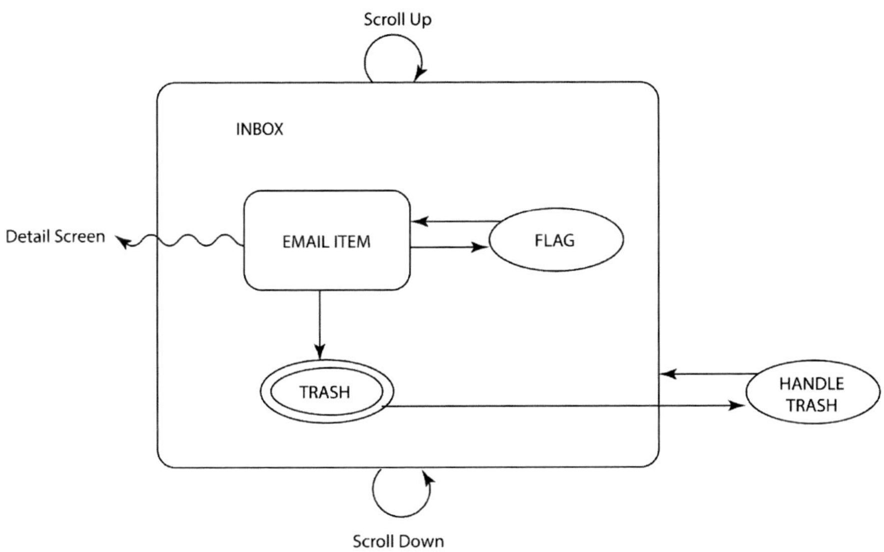

Figure 11.22
The email item behavior encapsulated inside the inbox object.

encapsulation. But if we do, we will most likely need to black box our diagrams to make things simpler and clearer.

At the quiescent state level, a much more useful way to describe things than an encapsulated set of behavior diagrams is a hierarchical user flow that includes user actions. Guess what? We've done this already. It's our user flow. (See Figure 9.4.) This depicts how the objects on the screen work together and is a more digestible indication of the behavior of the screen as a whole than encapsulated states. Design the details using state diagrams, then consider how those interactions play out at the level of a user flow.

At the user flow level, we can study questions such as how do our objects work with each other, how they are orchestrated, and whether we've overloaded them. Our user flow allows us to see those issues more clearly.

11.11 STATE TABLES

State diagrams depict the behavior of an interactive component. They allow us to see how it transitions from one state to the next and the relationship between the states. But what do the states do, and how do we build them? If we list all the states and transitions and describe them, we'll have a better understanding of these questions. This is what's done in a state table.

A state table is a structured formulation of the information provided in a state diagram; it is simply a different presentation of the same information. As we will see, state tables not only tell us what happens in an interactive component, but also provide a roadmap as to how to code them. To create them, we make a table of the states in the system and all outgoing transitions from each state. For the "item" and "fan" states in our email item diagram, (see Figure 11.19), it would look something like the table in Figure 11.23. In general, the table is structured with the rows indicating states and their subsequent outgoing transitions (the arrows coming out of each state), and the columns representing information necessary to describe each state. There is only one outgoing transition per row. The "From State" column indicates the state name, and is only filled in on the row indicating the first outgoing transition from that state. For any subsequent outgoing transitions from that state, this information would be the same as the first, so, instead of being redundant, it is simply left blank.

FROM STATE	BEHAVIOR	EXAMPLE	EVENT	BEHAVIOR	EXAMPLE	TO STATE
ITEM	Display email item in inbox list.	Image of email item in inbox.	Swipe Partially Left	Start opening of unfurling button drawer.	Animation of button drawer starting to unfurl left.	FAN
			Click on email item	Message system to transition to the email detail screen for this email.	Transition animation to email detail screen.	
FAN	Follow finger drag in swipe to open or close unfurling button drawer. Open is left, close is right.	Animation of unfurling button drawer opening and closing.	Let go Far	Transition to button drawer open.	Animation of transition to BUTTONS state.	BUTTONS
			Let go Near	Transiton to button drawer closed.	Animation of transition to ITEM state.	ITEM

Figure 11.23
A state table for the "ITEM" and "FAN" states.

The "Behavior" column describes the behavior associated with that state, and the following "Example" column describes how to depict that behavior if we were to prototype or animate it. The "Event" column is the first bit of information about the outgoing transition and it describes the event that triggers the transition. In the language of microinteractions, this is the trigger. The "Behavior" column indicates how the transition should behave, and the "Example" column describes how the transition should be depicted. Note that the "Example" column here is similar to the first "Example" column, but the difference is that the first describes how to depict the state, and this one describes how to depict the transition. The final column, "To State", indicates the state the transition takes the object to.

Let's describe the table in detail (Figure 11.23). Remember, this table does not describe the entire behavior schematically depicted in Figure 11.19, simply the behavior of two of the states: "ITEM" and "FAN". In the top row, our "From

State" is "ITEM" and it displays the email item in the inbox. If we were to create an example of this, it would be an image of the item in the inbox, like one of the items in Figure 11.7, section A. Referring to Figure 11.19, there are two arrows going out of the state: A straight arrow indicating a normal transition and a squiggly one indicating a message being sent to the system. Therefore, the "ITEM" state has two rows indicating each transition: The transition associated with the "Swipe Partially Left" event, and the transition associated with the "Click on Email Item" event.

Let's consider the first row, that which describes the behavior of the "ITEM" state itself and the "Swipe Partially Left" transition. Look at the "ITEM" state in Figure 11.19. The top row in our state table refers to the straight arrow going right, labelled as "Swipe Partially Left". The table indicates that, in the "ITEM" state, the object merely displays the item in the inbox list. It can be depicted in a prototype or animation by an image of the item in the inbox. If a "Swipe Partially Left" event is detected, the object responds by opening up the unfurling button drawer as indicated in the transition's "Behavior" column. To create an example of it, we would make a spot animation of the drawer unfurling left. The transition ends by going to the "FAN" state, which is indicated in the last column of the table.

The next row below is that which describes the second transition from the "ITEM" state: the transition triggered by a click. As we previously mentioned, we did not fill in the columns "from state", "from state behavior", or "from state example", since they are the same as the row above and would be redundant. We need only to describe the behavior of a state once, and we do so with the first transition. With all subsequent transitions, we need only to fill in the final four columns: "Event", "Behavior", "Example", and "To State".

When the user clicks on the email item, the interface transitions to the email detail screen. We illustrated it in Figure 11.19 with our squiggly line indicating that the transition sends a message to the system to go to the email detail screen. An example of this would be an animation of the transition, depicting the detail screen sliding from the right. This is noted under the "Example" column. There is no "to state" because we would no longer be on the inbox screen and the email item no longer appears. This table describes only the email item object, and if that object no longer exists, there is no state to go to. We could, however, choose to fill the "To State" column with the object to be transitioned to and the state within that object, such as the initial state in the email detail screen (see Figure 11.19), but we've left it blank here for simplicity.

Below the click transition, we have the "FAN" state. In that row, we see that its behavior is to follow the finger drag of the swipe to open or close the button drawer, with a drag right being to open and a drag left being to close. To exemplify it, we would create an animation depicting that behavior. Since two arrows lead out of the fan state in the diagram (see Figure 11.19), we have two associated transitions in the table: Let Go Near and Let Go Far.

Although, with our prior analysis of the "ITEM" state, you can probably see what's going on in "FAN", let's break this down as well to ensure that we've got it. The first row of the "FAN" state is the transition triggered by the "Let Go Far" event, and it behaves by transitioning to the drawer being opened and then going to the "BUTTONS" state. Compare that row with the "Let Go Far" arrow in Figure 11.19. We would make an example of this by creating an animation of that transition. The next transition listed is the one associated with the "Let Go Near" event. In this, the drawer snaps closed and it transitions to the item state. Again, notice that we left off the "From State" information associated with this row: It's already indicated in the row above it describing the "Let Go Far" transition and, hence, would be redundant.

What about the incoming transitions? The arrows coming into a state such as "Let Go Near" for "ITEM" and "Let Go Far" for "FAN"? We don't care about them in our state table because if we describe all states and their outgoing transitions, we will have captured all incoming transitions as well.

This table describes two of the six states in Figure 11.19, "ITEM" and "FAN". In fact, it is only a partial description of "FAN," since we did not describe the "Swipe Full Left" transition. To have a complete description of the email item behavior, we would have six states and a row for each arrow in Figure 11.19. There would be thirteen rows to completely describe the behavior of the object.

The complexity of this is likely to be shocking to you for such a simple behavior, and you may question why would we want to break things down into this level of detail. But remember, to make this behavior work, your developer has to do this anyway. If you don't break it down for them and consider each possibility, they will do it for you. Since you are the designer and have an intimate knowledge of how the behavior should work in order to have the correct impact on your user, you should be the one doing this. Now, recall that we do not propose doing this on every object. If an object has a fairly standard behavior that you feel has no need of custom nuances, by all means have your developer do it for you. But if you want absolute control over the behavioral design of an object, state diagrams and state tables are a robust set of tools to do so. In addition, they also create a "to do" list for every component that can be used in several ways, not only to help the developer, but also to help us prototype the behavior or describe it with spot animations.

11.12 PROTOTYPING BEHAVIOR

Our state table lists each state, each transition, and indicates examples we can use to describe what happens in them. This is, in essence, a small production list for the object, and if we create these examples either by animating them or coding them, we will have depicted exactly what we mean by these behaviors. This allows the designer to be in explicit control of the details of the interaction and provides invaluable examples to our developers that reduces confusion and speeds the development process.

To animate them, we start with a depiction of the "From State" and use Adobe After Effects, or some other animation tool to show how the behavior moves. We can either create single spot animations of the behavior or longer ones depicting a user flow through the system. We prefer a method where we start with simple spot animations depicting each behavior and transition. We present them for discussion and then move on to connecting them together to depict user flows. These animations may seem like minute details—and they are—but, as Saffer pointed out, design is the details.

Not only can we use state tables to guide us in animating spots or larger user flows, but we can also use them to guide us in coding interactive components. For example, for each object we could create a function for each state that behaves in the way described in the table. Then we add a set of conditionals for each transition within our states. The conditionals would contain the transition behaviors. For our "ITEM" state, it would look something like this in pseudo code:

```
function emailItem.item() {
      Display the image of this email item in the inbox list;
      Get events;
      if (event == "Swipe Partially Left") {
          Start opening the unfurling button drawer;
          }
      else if (event == "Click on email item") {
          Message system to transition to the detail screen for this email;
          // the system will handle the transition to the detail screen
          }
      }
```

We will need to translate this pseudo code into real code, and, depending on the implementation, there will be nuanced alterations, but the above is essentially the code structure for the item state. By extension, we can do this for every state in the component and all components in any quiescent state.

This approach is a method of programming called state machines or automata, and has a rich history in software development (Hopcroft, Motwani, & Ullman, 2007, p. v). The "If" statement formulation is just one of many ways of expressing them (and probably the simplest to comprehend). Other cleaner and more robust implementations include case statements, functions as variables, and multidimensional arrays (jakesgordon, n.d.), but all have the benefit of directly reflecting the behavioral descriptions in our state diagrams and tables, and they distil complex functionality into bite-sized bits of code that often lead to easier debugging. In fact, state machines are so prevalent that there are libraries available to make coding in this way extremely easy (ifandelse, 2017).

Whatever means by which you decide to depict your behaviors—either by animation, code, or both—by doing so you will be assuming your full responsibility as a designer in that you have precisely detailed how things work and behave.

11.13 WORKING PROTOTYPES

Working prototypes are quite simply prototypes that actually work. They've been built, coded, or otherwise put together in such a way as to simulate the functionality of an aspect of the system (Figure 11.24). Keep in mind these are simulations of the real thing, not the real thing itself, so working prototypes need to be clearly scoped as to what they do and what they don't do. Often, they focus on a small part of the interface to test a particular concern or present a particular aspect. Our spot prototypes were a form of working prototype that was very tightly scoped. We need to take care that, when we prototype, we keep the objective of the prototype in mind. We don't want to find ourselves building an entire working system. That's the job of our developer.

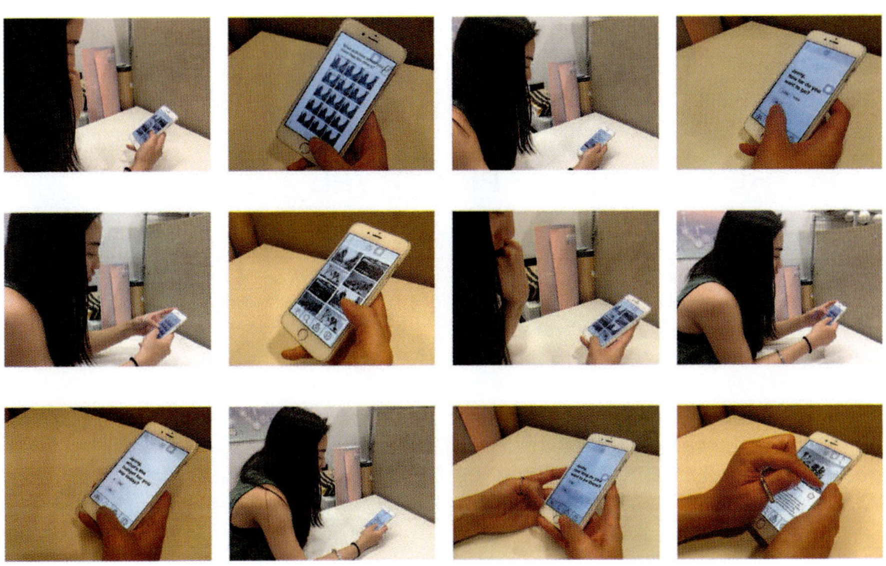

Figure 11.24
Mid-fidelity user testing (from Lastmin, by Chufan Huang, used by kind permission of Chufan Huang).

Most standard interactive devices have rapid prototyping tools available, but custom devices often don't. Becoming familiar with simple coding languages such as Python, JavaScript, or Processing in combination with digital kits that connect to the physical world, such as Arduino, Raspberry Pie, or Particle Photon, designers can construct a wealth of non-standard interaction components (Figure 11.25). You might even be able to get to where you want by taking apart a children's toy and repurposing it for your own use.

Figure 11.25
Using digital kits to build custom devices (from Culina Metra, by Team Culina Metra, used by kind permission of Katrina Hercules and Neal Smith).

Being adept at these allows us to build components quickly and experience their effectiveness in context. Keep in mind, though, that these are prototypes, so they are made to iterate. Don't cherish them too deeply, because we should be building them, using them, reflecting on their use and how to improve them, throwing them away, and building them again. Just as with wireframes, our experience prototypes are sketches that should lead us to a better design. They should be disposable.

It's critical to manage your level of effort in creating a working prototype at this stage. Designers are not developers, so we are engaging in this not to make something bulletproof, but to determine if our designs work in context. Pouring a great deal of effort into a prototype beyond this is usually counterproductive. Strive for off the shelf software and hardware, and consider if the methods you employed to create your structural or behavioral prototype can be used for your experience prototype. If not, are there other easy methods that can be used? It's best to have the prototype be interactive, but if it's too complicated to reach that point, consider creating an experience prototype or an "ozed" prototype. Let's discuss these.

11.14 THE EXPERIENCE PROTOTYPE

When we experience a prototype in context, we see things that may have eluded us when they were just interfaces on a computer screen. But if we're designing for a custom or non-standard device, we may not have the tools available to build a prototype quickly. There are ways around this, so let's spend a moment exploring ways of creating a prototype for custom systems.

We refer to a prototype that reflects a system's use in context as an experience prototype. These should be familiar to us. We were building experience prototypes when we were performing our blob and sketch scenarios. We even did it with our paper prototypes. But these explorations were not dynamic. Now that we are addressing higher fidelities, we need to determine if our dynamic spot prototypes can work in context. As mentioned previously, if we're designing for a standard device, such as a tablet or mobile, we have a vast range of prototyping tools available that allow us to put a prototype together with a great deal of behavioral accuracy with little effort.

Yet, with the explosion of smart devices and different screen shapes—almost every device in any environment can be smart—it's a lot to expect that there will be prototyping tools available for all of these. To get around this, we often use standard devices and either mask them off or otherwise reconfigure them to reflect a custom device in context. Need a screen on a fridge? Use a tablet or cell phone. Need a circular interface? Use a cell phone again, but place it behind paper or cardboard with a circle cut out. Need a navigation system for your car? Use a tablet. Need a hologram or to test AR? Angle a sheet of acetate above a screen and turn off the lights (Figure 11.26). There may be physical or virtual inconsistencies with these approaches, but they allow us to focus on the nuances of context, revealing issues that may have escaped us otherwise.

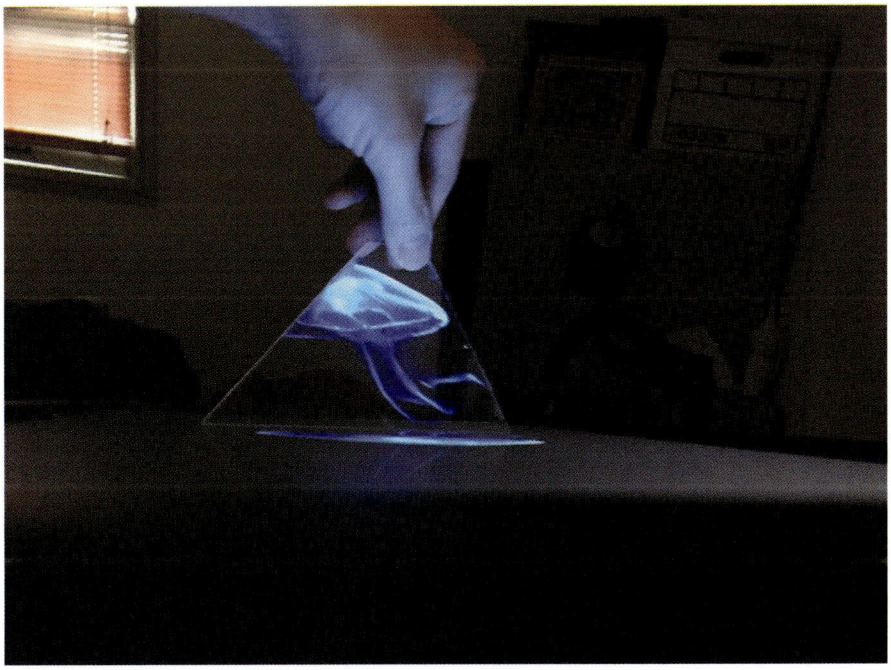

Figure 11.26
An experience prototype simulating a holographic presentation (from Knoq, by Team Cheeseburger, used by kind permission of James Chu, Chloe Kim, Juno Park, and Yidan Zhang).

Experience prototypes are useful for testing a particular aspect of the interface, but it would be disingenuous if we were to deny they don't have a significant impact on our ability to communicate our design: They carry wow factor. Say the same system were presented in two different ways: One reliant on a scenario and static artwork and the other with these, but an experience prototype as well. Which would create a more indelible impression on our audience? Clearly, the one with the experience prototype. And the closer the prototype resembles the real thing, the better the impression.

11.15 OZING

"Ozed" prototypes are experience prototypes that communicate context and how something should work, but they don't really work at all. They are performed. To create them, we animate the precise dynamics of our interface along a particular use case, the primary, for example. We create animation in, say, AfterEffects, have actors memorize the flow, and perform actions or gestures on the interface giving the impression that the system is actually working. This allows us to communicate an experience prototype without having to build it.

The technique is called "ozing", in reference to the scene in the Wizard of Oz where the wizard pulls levers behind the curtain to simulate magic. In its most surreptitious form, an ozed prototype looks like a fully functioning digital system, yet behind the scenes it's either animated or operated by simple clicks by a human (Gothelf & Seiden, 2016, p. 85). You simulate your magic by animating the interface and perform the interactions in sync with the prototype. Take care to practice your performance enough so that Toto doesn't discover you!

Ozed prototypes differ from working prototypes in that they cannot be handed to our audience to get their feedback about the interface. In this way, they are more of a presentation framework rather than one that can be used for assessment. However, if all we really care about is getting feedback on whether our system makes sense in the real world, they can often be enough.

Whether our prototype is a working prototype, an experience prototype, or is ozed, it should be well scoped, present the interface of our system within that scope, allow our audience to consider how well it works within that scope, and make an impression on them.

11.16 BEHAVIOR TESTING AND FEEDBACK

As we get further along in our design and the interactions become more specific, we get into a realm where user testing and feedback becomes simultaneously more challenging and more important. The problem is that to get appropriate information as to whether our solutions are working or not, the interface needs to behave just like we specified, and it's best to do so on the actual device (Figure 11.27). Using a click to simulate a swipe is no longer appropriate when we get into details, and assessing the performance of a wall-based physical gesture system with a trackpad on our laptop, for example, doesn't cut it either.

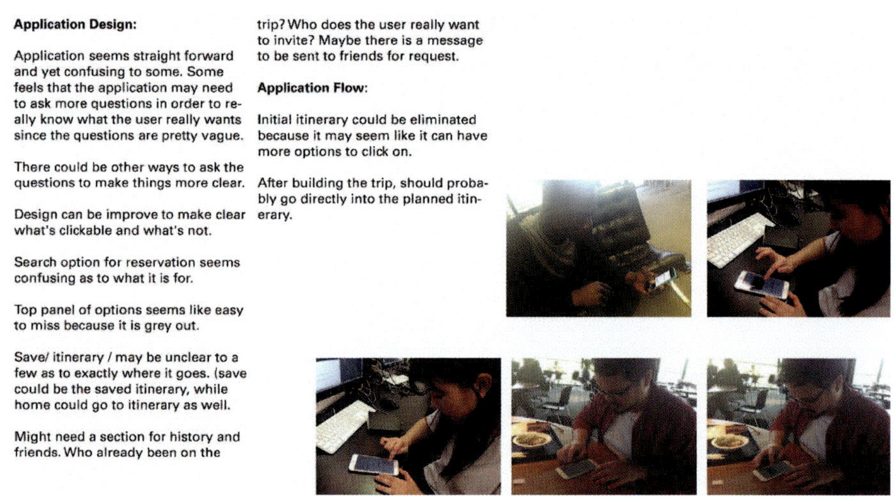

Figure 11.27
Mid-fidelity user feedback (from Sponture, by Christine Lai, used by kind permission of Christine Lai).

Unless our system can be prototyped exactly with a robust prototyping tool, if we haven't gotten there already it's starting to get to a point where we need to code. If you're not a unicorn designer who can both design and code, it may be time to get a technologist or front-end developer involved, especially one who is skilled at several systems and thrilled with the prospect of tackling new ones.

What are we looking to verify with our testing at this point? First and foremost is usability. Are the interactions we designed usable by the target audience in all our proposed contexts? If this is the first time testing the behaviors in detail, chances are that the interaction is chock full of problems. If it isn't, we probably aren't looking hard enough. When we user test, try to see if our audience understands how to use the interface without our help. Can they figure out how it works without us showing them? What do they think would make it clearer?

We should be bouncing our prototype off numerous people. Most should be our target, but others as well. Identify those problems that begin to show up consistently. Those are the ones we need to work on first. Take the designs back to the drawing board if need be; back to our interaction sketches and state diagrams; back to our information architecture if we need to, and to mid-fidelity prototypes if we have to. Keep an exploratory mindset and sweat the details. We should make sure that our system structure and interactions work before we move on, because here on out we will be pouring that structural, behavioral, and aesthetic concrete that will make things much harder to change.

12 Aesthetics

Up to this point in our design process, we've been focused on primarily on structure and behavior. We've been exploring aesthetics for the last several chapters, but the topic has played somewhat of a bit part. With our structure and behavior largely addressed, it's no longer appropriate to be exploratory with aesthetics. It needs the acute precision of focus necessary to make our designs as strong as possible. It's time we gave aesthetics center stage.

When we introduced the topic of aesthetics previously, we said that, for the purposes of this book, it refers to those things we can directly sense: How things look on a screen, how they feel in our hand, how far away something is when we reach for it, how things sound, how they could taste or smell. When we worked on our wireframes and mock-ups, arranging the elements and importance of content in our quiescent states, we were laying the groundwork for their aesthetic design. But those wireframes and mock-ups were not designs—they were depictions of structural organization. Now let's consider the aesthetics of those structures: How to communicate hierarchy, how to separate content and control, how to associate similar elements, and how to allow our audience to better flow through that content and improve their ability to affect control.

12.1 THE WORK PRODUCT

As with our chapters on interface design and microinteractions, I feel aesthetic guidance is best communicated through principles and considerations. For this chapter, continue to focus your aesthetic effort on your critical interfaces. Review the principles put forth and use them to critique your designs. If you arrive at a principle or two that illuminates a particular weakness in your approach, put this text aside and work on one or two of your critical interfaces to address it. Don't fear throwing out a particular approach and starting over. It's only one interface, your wireframes should still be valid, and sometimes (in fact, often) it's better to start over than to tweak what is already there.

Return to the chapter after your exploration, and when you arrive at other problems, address these as well. The point is to act on these considerations immediately, while they are in the forefront of your mind. Don't wait until you've read the entire chapter and attempt to keep them in your head. Read a little, work a little. You'll have much more fruitful results. Then, when you're done, review your effort. Take further those designs that you think are most successful. Can they be considered favorably in terms of quality and feel to the interfaces you have in your inspiration board? If not, continue to refine them (Figure 12.1). Don't accept mediocrity. When you've arrived at a point where you believe they compare favorably to your inspiration, apply your approach to all your critical interfaces and strive to solve all the challenges they present. With this as our process, let's address the considerations of aesthetics.

12.2 TYPOGRAPHY

If we are designing an information system based on the word, such as most websites and apps, we start with typography. When we speak of typography, we are not only speaking of typefaces; we are, more importantly, speaking of typographic structure.

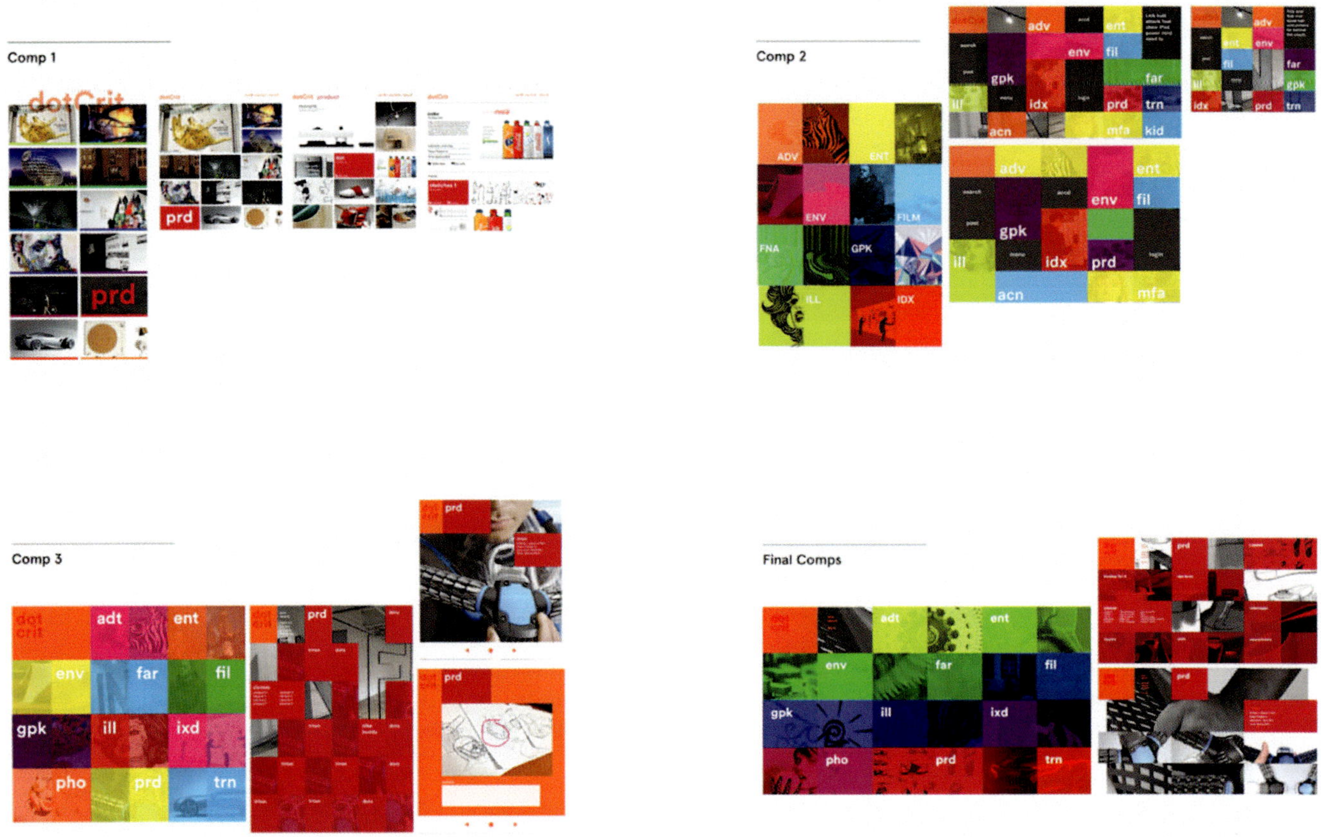

Figure 12.1
Iterating an aesthetic approach for an online gallery (from Dotcrit, by Angela Chu, used by kind permission of Angela Chu).

Our eyes need structure and organization to chunk the content of a screen into constituent elements, thus making them easily digestible. Typography is one of the most powerful tools at our disposal to do this.

At one end of the spectrum, if the type on an interface has but one typeface set at one size, one weight, and one style, we have limited ourselves mainly to position (layout) to communicate the structure of the information. We will have removed one of the most potent tools for communicating a hierarchy of importance: levels of type. As designers, we are responsible for communicating this prioritization and organization, and if we say that everything is important, then nothing is. If we say everything should stand on its own, then nothing does.

At the other end of the spectrum, if we use a different typeface, size, weight, and style for every little thing, then our interface will be sloppy, noisy, and confused. We've essentially given our audience no help in determining the organization of our information because everything is different. It's the same as doing nothing, and probably worse, because our interface may look as if it was designed by someone who may be on the verge of losing touch with reality.

The best approach for the most effective conveyance of information is somewhere between these two extremes. Strive for a low number of typefaces. One or two is best, three if we have a very good reason. (A logotype is not considered a separate typeface; it's more of a visual impression.) One of these should be our primary typeface that performs most of the organizational heavy lifting, and, as such, it should contain a robust set of weights and styles. Each of our typefaces should contrast with, yet complement, each other. In this way, they can have a harmonious relationship, yet do the job of differentiating typographic elements.

Similar items should have similar typographic effects. Headers should be treated the same way, as should sub-heads, captions, body text, and footers. Identify all the uses that we intend for our type, and strive to consistently treat each role the same way. We need to discover the appropriate organization and application of typographic attributes to our content elements. Our information-rich critical interface is ideal for developing our approach to this structure.

The physical organization of type is critical to its legibility. It is designed to flow left to right and in columns down the page. The length of a line, called its measure, should not be so short as to force the eye to be continually jumping down to the next line, nor be too long so as to make it difficult to find and grab the start of the line below it. Sixty-six characters across is often considered ideal, although, depending on the role of the line, it can be more or less (Bringhurst, 2004, p. 26). A left justified, ragged right alignment is generally considered the most legible (Bringhurst, 2004, p. 27), and should be considered your default arrangement for most typefaces. Titles and headings can be centered, but body copy likes to be left aligned. Centering type for more than a few lines—especially for body copy—should be avoided.

Type is rectilinear in nature and often does not like to sit on arcs and diagonals. These arrangements are hard to read and appear clumsy. Vertically lettered words and other novel arrangements are not very legible either and should be avoided. Type makes its own organizational blocks and often does not need the help of boxes and frames to help arrange it on the screen. If we find ourselves using framing devices such as rules between blocks of type, frames surrounding them, or background rectangles to block them, see what happens when we remove these elements. If we have a good typographic layout, likely we'll find that they weren't necessary. If we feel that our typographic sections are still blending together, maybe what we need is more separation (negative space, or blank space) between our typographic blocks, not the addition of some other element. Less is more is a good design principle in general, but especially when dealing with type.

Because of its rectilinear nature, type loves grids. They provide a guide to organize the textual information and allow the eye to flow down and across an interface easily. We should be creating tools such as grid systems and typographic structure diagrams so that our screens have a consistent approach typographically (Figure 12.2). It would be a shame to have spent so much time on the high-level organization of our information just to see it go to waste at the interface level. Good interaction

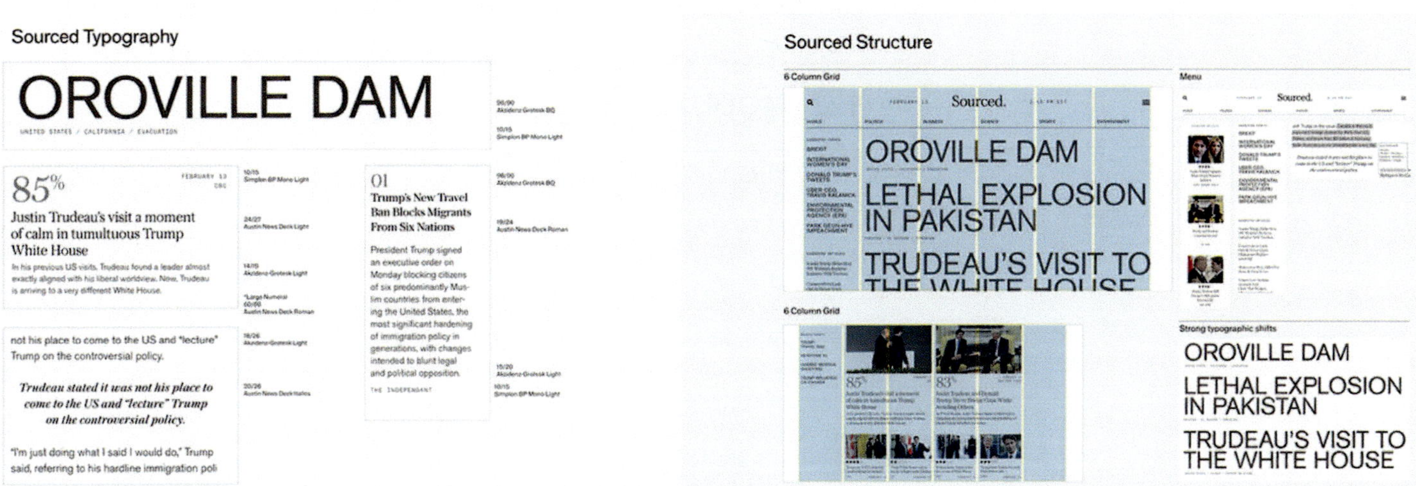

Figure 12.2
Typographic structure of a news aggregator (from Sourced, by Jonathan Nishida, used by kind permission of Jonathan Nishida).

design is often based on good information design, and good typography is the most obvious manifestation of good information design.

Finally, like all design principles, these rules are made to be broken. But use caution: Break one or two, and we may have an interesting solution, break all and we'll have a mess. Solutions can both stand out and fit in, but they need to make sense and be strategic.

Type is not just about choosing typefaces; it's about typographic structure. Intentionally design that structure when you're designing your interface.

12.3 PICTURE AND TEXT

When considering the function of content, bear in mind that we remember pictures better than words. The ease with which images are recognized and recalled is called the picture superiority effect (Lidwell et al. 2010, p. 184). A content element we are considering may be best expressed as an image rather than text. But there is a limit to this: Pictures may be more quickly identified, remembered, and more efficiently convey feeling, but they are imprecise. A complex concept or idea may be impossible to depict clearly and concisely in an image. A picture may be worth a thousand words, but if your ideas require a thousand pictures, you may be better off going with the words.

Be sensitive to the role of pictures vs. the role of words. Pictures are easily remembered, but imprecise.

12.4 ICONOGRAPHY

Previously, we introduced the concept of iconography and discussed how icons are an efficient way of compressing information into a small package. Not only that, they're much more glanceable than words themselves. It's spatially much more efficient to use the symbol for windshield wipers, for example, than the words. It's also much easier for the driver to recognize that symbol against other symbols on our steering column, such as our lights or brights, than if they all were words.

But their downside is that if they're not clear, or there is not a universally agreed upon symbol for the concept being iconified, they have to be learned. And they are not as specific as words. We may have to supply microtext to describe them, in which case why not go with just the words themselves?

Use icons for efficiency, but if they aren't shared or learnable, they may introduce confusion.

12.5 MODULARITY

Modularity is the principle ". . . that involves dividing large systems into smaller, self-contained subsystems" Lidwell et al., 2010, p. 160). To be precise, we've been engaged in the process of modularizing our system from the very beginning when we were considering how to organize its content and functionality. But, at this stage, what we mean by modularization is that of content and functionality on each interface: the arrangement of elements on our system's physical surfaces and each quiescent state. We use modularity to help our users understand and otherwise manage the vast amount of information our system provides. It requires that we group related items together.

Modularize or "chunk" your designs so that like items are together and disparate items are separate.

12.6 SEPARATION

For us to modularize, we have to be able to separate elements. For elements to *be* separate, they have to *look* separate. This may sound like a tautology, but in fact, it's something that many designers seem to forget quite often. There's a psychological principle that is called difference threshold that establishes how much difference we can perceive between two similar elements (Pannafino, 2012, p. 29). If we haven't reached or gone beyond the difference threshold, our user will perceive little to no difference in the elements we present.

Take, for example, type of the same typeface with one sentence being set at 12 point, and the other at 14. There is a difference between them, and possibly because we were the ones setting the type, we can see that difference, but someone reading a paragraph at 12 point vs. one at 14 may not be able to see much difference. For most people, the type will read like everything was set at 12. If we want to separate items, we need to make sure there is enough difference between them to separate them.

Orientation sensitivity is another visual rule related to difference threshold, yet it deals with elements positioned at angles. This concept is clarified by considering an analog clock face. By looking at the hour hand, we can certainly see the difference between the angle of the hour hand at one o'clock and two o'clock, but the difference between two-thirty and three is not as clear. This corresponds to our ability to see differences in angles of 30 degrees or more (Lidwell et al., 2010, p. 176). When we are using orientation to separate items, we will need to orient them for the most part at no less than 30 degrees for the separation to be perceived.

Apply enough difference in your separation to make things different.

12.7 FIGURE-GROUND

Separation allows us to see the "chunks" of information on a surface, but the separation between elements is not all that we have to consider. Elements also need to stand out from the background to be recognized. This is the concept of figure-ground, ". . . the human perceptual system separates stimuli into either figure elements or ground elements. Figure elements are the objects of focus, and ground elements compose an undifferentiated background" (Lidwell et al, 2010, p. 96). We can easily have a typographic strategy whereby the header distinguishes itself from the body copy because it is several points bigger. But if we set both elements on top of a textured background that obscures the type, this difference may be compromised. The same may occur if the contrast is reduced, where the type is black and the background is a dark gray.

The concept of figure-ground relationship is packaged in many ways: Signal to noise ratio (Lidwell et al., 2010, p. 224) and the data-ink ratio (Tufte, 2001, pp. 93–96) are just a few concepts closely related to the idea of figure-ground. But whatever the terminology, improving the separation of figure-ground leads to simplicity in design. Maximize those elements that convey information, and minimize distraction. And when we say "information" here, we are not talking only about text or image. We are referring to any treatment of the elements on the interface that conveys information, such as style, color, alignment, and separation.

Make sure your background is truly a background, and your foreground snaps out.

12.8 REDUCE

Given a solid understanding of our interface's information structure and the ramifications of context, we can begin to work with the arrangement of elements on the interface. When dealing with arrangement, first reduce to that which is necessary. Strive for an economy of form (Cooper, 2015, p. 172).

Keep figure-ground in mind: the principle of improving signal, and reducing noise. Be guided by Occam's Razor (discussed further below): "Given a choice between functionally equivalent designs, the simplest should be selected" (Lidwell et al., 2010, p. 172). Given two functionally equivalent displays—equal in information and readability—select the one with the fewest elements (Lidwell et al., 2010, p. 172). Evaluate each element and remove it if it does not connect to our user's goals. You may have employed reduction already in your aesthetic disruption, and, if so, you may wish to resurrect that exploration to provide you guidance.

Reduce and simplify to that which supports the achievement of the user's goals.

12.9 HIERARCHY

Separation and association allow us to chunk our information, but we also need to communicate the structure of our surface elements in the sense of what is important. This is the concept of the hierarchy of importance. On screen-based interfaces, we call this visual hierarchy. Visual hierarchy answers the question of what is the most important element on the surface. What is secondary? What is of the least importance?

When we speak of hierarchy in these terms, we are using it differently than in the context of a data structure such as a set of folders within folders. When we encapsulate items within items, we do not mean that elements of high importance need to encapsulate elements of lesser importance, just that a folder on a desktop encapsulates its sub-folders. Conversely, hierarchy of importance is the principle that, on a surface, some elements are more important than others and we need to arrange the display of those elements so they stand out.

We may claim that everything on our surface is important. We wouldn't put it there if it weren't! This certainly may be true, but not everything is as important as everything else. If everything is important, nothing is. As designers, we need to make hard choices as to what's most important, and what is not. What should be seen first? What should be seen second? Our users don't read the content on our interface as they would read a book—from beginning to end, savoring every moment. News flash, all: They scan our content they don't read it (Pannafino, 2012, p. 69), and a hierarchy of importance allows them to identify and differentiate elements that they may be interested in while allowing them to flow past those they aren't.

In a way, information hierarchy is a form of navigation: Users scan our hierarchy and select elements they're interested in, just as they may select a menu item that takes them to a separate quiescent state focused on that item. This is one of the reasons why we feel it's important to approach Interaction Design holistically: The aesthetic structure should support the information structure at the most fundamental level of design.

Hierarchy supports another design consideration: the Pareto Principle or the 80–20 rule (Lidwell et al., 2010, p.14; Pannafino, 2012, p. 61) which states that ". . . approximately 80 percent of the effects generated by any large system are caused by 20 percent of the variables in that system." Well, then, why don't we just simplify things and get rid of the 80 percent that isn't used? The problem is that often we don't know which 80 percent is used and which isn't. And even if we did, we would likely be getting rid of very important things people still need every once and a while. I rarely need to pull something out of the trash on my computer's desktop, but when I do, I'm certainly glad my operating system didn't just directly delete it. A well-considered hierarchy of importance allows the user to scan and select the 20 percent they're interested in and spend a little less time with that other 80 percent.

Ask what is most important and what is less so. Use clear indicators to express this level of importance.

12.10 NEGATIVE SPACE

We may feel that the importance of an item is proportional to its size and scale: the bigger the object, the more important. But the same role can be performed by negative space. When I think of this, I am always drawn to the poster Warner Brothers Animation created when the renowned voice artist Mel Blac died (Warner Communications, 1989). It has the Looney Tunes characters, including Bugs Bunny and Daffy Duck, poised on the left, and a microphone standing empty and alone on the right. It is the lonely mic that is the most important element of the image, symbolizing the missing Mel Blanc. The use of negative space is so impactful that it brings tears to one's eyes. When you add more and more content to an interface and feel you need to make something really large to grab an audience's attention, remember this Warner image, reduce content and inject negative space.

Use negative space as an active element in your design.

12.11 PROXIMITY

Separation allows us to divide our content and control into chunks, but we also need tools that allow us to associate things together. If negative space separates items, then it's counterpart, proximity, associates them. When we see a caption under a photo, we don't think that the caption refers to an image twenty pages before it. We think that it refers to the image right above it. Likewise, a control positioned next to a content element leads us to believe that the control is associated with that element.

Just as negative space is one of the most powerful tools in our kit to communicate separation and distinction, proximity is one of the most powerful tools for association (Lidwell et al., 2010, p. 196). Consider whether elements you wish to be related are too separate from each other. If it is more proximal to another unrelated element, it may confuse your audience into thinking it's related to that instead. Use separation in combination with proximity to improve the chunking of your information.

If using proximity to associate items, make sure they're close enough together to look associated.

12.12 ALIGNMENT

Elements that are aligned either vertically or horizontally reflect an association with each other. This is the visual principle called good continuation (Lidwell et al., 2010, p. 116) and can reflect direct relationships, such as a caption aligned with the image to which it directly refers, or to a headline, dateline, and body copy that are associated with it as well. Or, these can be relationships of class, such as menu items aligned horizontally, items in a list, or sub-sections of an outline that fall vertically down the same line. The elements of the list or outline may be separate, but their alignment allows us to perceive them as related. In this way, negative space or proximity can be used to separate these items from each other, but alignment can associate them as having a relationship to each other (Lidwell et al., 2010, p. 24).

Alignment strategies for typography have several different forms such as left justified, centered, right justified, bottom, top, baseline, diagonal, x-height, and by area (Lidwell et al., 2010, p. 30). As designers, we are at liberty to select the strategy that makes the most sense—that both organizes the content, improves legibility, and activates the surface, but the important thing to remember is that the strategy you choose needs to be clear and consistent, or it becomes simply noise.

Use alignment as a way to associate items. It can be used as an additional dimension of separation or association in conjunction with elements such as proximity, style, or scale.

12.13 LAYOUT IN GENERAL

Layout is the spatial organization of elements, and well-designed layouts allow us to associate some elements on a surface and separate them from others. They make it easier for our audience to absorb the information in their field of view.

The physical aspect and arrangement of objects on a screen or physical surface tells our audience a great deal about how we want them to absorb the information we are providing them. Consider your layout carefully. Develop multiple possibilities and see which provide the best expression of the way in which you wish you users to perceive your information (Figure 12.3).

Figure 12.3
Exploring various arrangements of interface elements (from Munio, by Team Wolf Pack, used by kind permission of Judy Chu, Tina Ou, Jane Park, and Jade Tsao).

Use layout to enhance comprehension.

12.14 GRID

Grids, or gridding, is a special case of layout, important enough to be teased out as its own discussion. Grids and grid systems are ubiquitous because content is often conveyed by type, and as we stated before, type loves grids. Rectangular images, like photos, love grids, too. "The benefits of working with a grid are simple: clarity, efficiency, economy, and continuity" (Samara, 2002, p. 22).

There are only a few components of a grid, but they can be arranged and rearranged in several ways. Most importantly, grids are shaped by columns that span the surface vertically. Columns are often evenly spaced. Rows, or flowlines, run horizontally, and they are usually evenly spaced as well. Between each column and row are the margins: the empty spaces that allow for the separation of content. Margins flow around the boundaries of the surface and provide a frame of negative space that allows the content to breathe. Modules are the cells or the rectangular blocks formed by the cross-hatching of the columns and rows.

In editorial layout there are four basic grid forms: manuscript, columnar, modular, and hierarchical (Samara, 2002, p. 28). The manuscript grid is what is primarily used in books, and provides one column of content. The columnar grid provides for several columns of content. It's what we see in a book with several columns of text on a page. The modular grid is one of the most prevalent and is based on the modular rectangles formed by the columns and rows. Content can flow through and be broken up by each rectangular module. Think of the layout of a newspaper.

The hierarchical grid is common to websites where emphasis and importance are given to a few elements, and the rest of the content flows around them. In our experience, the hierarchical grid is a form of modular grid, where the columns, rows, margins, and modules still exist that form the grid, but it's been formulated based on the desired scale of the important elements (Samara, 2002, pp. 26–29). All these can be mixed and matched, and sometimes even broken for effect.

The most robust examples of gridding are found in newspapers and magazines. These forms of communication pack a great deal of content on a limited surface by using a grid system that is consistent page by page. Each column of the grid contains the flow of a story or content. Sometimes content spans multiple columns, but in a rigid grid system, it fills the horizontal span of each module fully, never part way. On the other hand, the vertical aspect of a grid can often be partially filled with content, but the remainder is filled with negative space: We do not begin a new section of content partially through a module.

There are also sections at the top of a magazine article, newspaper, or even websites reserved for headers and at the bottom for footers that may operate differently than the central content. Special columns such as those to the right or left may be reserved for other features, such as a menu or ad placement.

Since interfaces deal with the delivery of a great deal of information on a limited surface, grids are common in websites and apps. A scrolling list of items may have pictures on the far-left side and text content to their right. A grid system is employed to keep all pictures and text content from each list item aligned with the item below it. This helps our users to flow through the system and absorb the content quickly.

Grids allow typographic content to be justified, aligned, associated, and modularized (Figure 12.4). Grids that span across several surfaces, screens, or pages are

Grid Structure

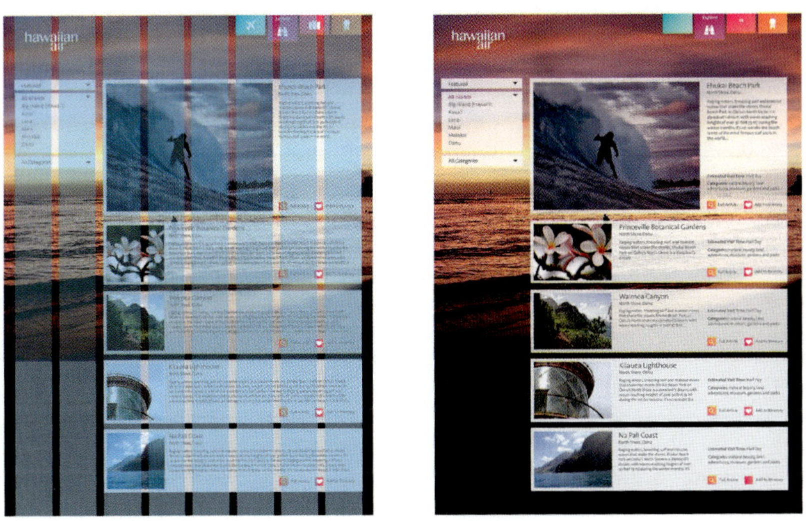

Figure 12.4
The underlying grid of a vacation travel system (from Hawaiian Airlines, by Oliver Lo, used by kind permission of Oliver Lo).

called master grids. They establish a baseline grid for your entire system and can be expanded or otherwise altered for each screen. The master grid ensures flow throughout the system; the individual grid ensures flow throughout that page.

Use grids to enhance the organization and comprehension of your interface.

12.15 LIQUID LAYOUTS

Liquidity is the aspect that a display can be changed by the user, such as scaling the window of a web browser on a desktop or switching between landscape and portrait by rotating our mobile device. How should we deal with these changes? One approach is to identify a set of design targets: When the browser is *x* width, the content should be displayed in configuration A, when it is at width *y*, it should be displayed in configuration B, and so on. This technique can also be used for landscape and portrait swaps when our user turns their mobile device from vertical to horizontal.

The screen target strategy is effective in many cases, but only goes so far. Say we're designing for mobile and we'd like to have our interface look good on many of the top-selling devices. Having display targets for each, as well as their landscape and portrait possibilities, would be challenging based on the number of devices out there and the continual release of new ones. In this situation, it's good to start with display targets, but then consider how the content expands or contracts based on the dimensions of a particular screen. Should a set of elements be attached to the top, sides, or bottom of the display, or should they float in the middle? It's often useful to identify areas of negative space that can be expanded or contracted without disturbing the overall visual impression. Developing these liquid layout rules will allow designs to be well considered across several interface orientations without having to design for each specifically.

If your context is liquid, develop a liquid layout strategy that considers both the fixed and liquid aspects of the interface.

12.16 DESIGN RESPONSIVELY

Responsive designs introduce yet another challenge to our already complex liquid layouts. The main goal of responsive designs is to adapt content to several different devices, screen shapes, and sizes. We can start with display targets and liquid layouts, but it's more likely that we will recognize that the extreme differences between contexts will lead us to completely different designs for each. And this approach makes a great deal of sense: How we use mobile and how we use the web through a browser is different.

On the other hand, we should be able to see a website on a mobile browser and have it be sensitive to the limitations of the device. Because of this, our responsive display strategy may include not only liquid layouts, but liquid content as well: The identification of rules for hiding or revealing content elements that may work for one context, yet not for the other.

Liquid content strategies may not only include rules for elements within a particular quiescent state but could also include a rearrangement of the quiescent states themselves. There may be entire sections of content that we may reveal or hide, based on context. If the effects on the arrangement of content due to a responsive design are small, we may be able to handle it within the quiescent states we have. As the differences become large, we may need to consider it as an entirely new context. Where exactly is that breakpoint? That's often not clear, so we need to make that determination on a context-by-context basis.

Design responsively, but consider that a new context may mean an entirely new design.

12.17 CONSIDER USE

When we consider liquid layouts and responsiveness, we are considering the various contexts in our system. How are those contexts or devices to be used? What are their ergonomics? Let's once again return to our posture studies, but from an aesthetic point of view. If we are designing for a mobile device, we need to keep touch target areas in mind: the minimum area in which a finger or thumb can select an item without selecting another item (Pannafino, 2012, p. 78). These place a minimum limit on the size of interactive components, requiring that they be fairly large to handle the size of a finger. More area taken up by buttons often means less area taken up by content. Content on mobile is squeezed by both the small dimensions of the interface and the large dimensions required by the touch targets as well. We can be much more precise with a cursor on a desktop, allowing for smaller controls and more content.

The size of a touch target is also affected by other things such as the skill of the user, the amount of concentration they can provide, their level of dexterity, and the amount of jiggle of the device in their hand. If this sounds somewhat familiar, it should be: Many of these are things we considered in our posture studies. The less skill, the less concentration, the less dexterity, and the more jiggle, the bigger the information and the touch targets should be. Dust off your posture studies and see what they tell you.

We should consider other physical aspects required by the interface as well. For example, if our audience needs margins on the sides of the displayed content to allow for thumb placement for holding the device, or whether we expect our audience to use one-handed or two-handed gestures. Reflect on these considerations, refer to your posture and ergonomic studies for guidance, then determine how these affect the interface. When we are conducting our aesthetic designs, we need to keep a firm focus on these characteristics of the display and how our user experiences it. If we ignore that work now, we are essentially throwing all that careful consideration away.

Consider use. Use your posture studies. Aesthetics should agree with posture.

12.18 CONTEXT

Print designers have it easy: They are almost universally guaranteed to know the exact dimensions of the thing they are designing. They are given the tabloid spread of a book or the dimensions of a poster, and they can count on those dimensions being fixed. Digital designers have none of that. The browser window can be scaled dramatically by the user. Mobile devices have myriad different scales and sizes as well. Responsive sites must handle both trackpads and multi-touch gestures.

How do we handle all this when considering aesthetics? The trick is to know our primary contexts well, design for them, and strive to adjust for secondary contexts. If we face contextual conflicts that challenge our primary approach, consider possible solutions that may make both perform better, and, if that can't be achieved, prioritize the primary.

With all this flexibility, to know our context means we need to know the display factors of that context (Pannafino, 2012, p. 31). These factors include the size and scale of the display area, the various screen components of the display, whether our designs need to be fixed or liquid, and, if they are liquid, how do they change. Finally, we need to know the ergonomic characteristics of the display. The best way to understand display factors is not for me to waste precious ink here providing you with some pixel dimension that will be outdated the day after this book is in print—and is fictitious anyway, since it ascribes some erroneous fixed ratio to a display characteristic that is not fixed—but for me to provide you the means of figuring that out yourself.

Perform a search on screen sizes or screen resolutions. In the results, look for a dependable source that indicates recent data for various screens and their popularity.[1] Identify a popular target set of sizes for the contexts in your ecosystem that agrees with your target user. Next, consider the components of the system that are displayed within those frames, such as system information, menu bars, browser window components, scroll bars, and footers. It's best to create a screen capture of these components and identify the pixel dimensions of the content display window itself.

Know your contexts. Research their configurations. Prioritize your primary.

12.19 TACTILITY

How should your device feel to the touch? How should it be held? What should be its weight and balance? How should tactility convey your brand values: hard, soft, spongy, rubbery? (Figure 12.5.) How should its physical interface feel? Should components have hard clicks for their detents, or should things more gradually slide into place? What are the physical limitations of your target audience? Are the movements you are asking them to perform too frictive? Do they move too easily, making them difficult to control? Consider the tactile feedback of your physical designs in the context of your brand values. They have an emotional component just as any other aesthetic aspect.

Figure 12.5
Tactile aesthetics for a system connecting those in distant relationships (from Sync and Harmony, by Team ABC, used by kind permission of Ofir Atia, Calvin Lien, Serena Jorif, and Alice Yu).

12.20 ARRANGE CONTROL APPROPRIATELY—FITT'S LAW

When arranging our interface, we not only need to keep in mind the flow of the eye in absorbing content, we also need to pay attention to where we place control as well as its scale and size. Fitt's Law tells us that the time it takes for us to move to a target in order to interact with it is a function of the target's size and our initial distance from it (Lidwell et al., 2010, p. 98). For example, if we want to interact with a button with our cursor, if that button is large and near where our cursor already is, the interaction will be quick. If it's small and far away, it will take longer. Interfaces are more usable when like functionality is grouped and large.

But when we consider Fitt's Law, we yet again we run into issues based on our audience's relationship with the interface. If it's one that they use casually and infrequently, it's best that interactive elements be larger. But the larger the size, the fewer the elements we can present on a given surface. If it's an interface on which our users spend eight hours a day in the context of their professional practice, the importance of size gives way to having more control available at their fingertips. In both cases, though, logically grouping functionality together that has a high degree of connectivity is best for both the casual user as well as the professional.

Group connected interactive elements together. Their size is a reflection of the user's level of skill.

12.21 ASSOCIATION AND COMPARISON OF CONTENT AND CONTROL

Consider the content on an interface. What is the relative connectivity between elements? Is there a high or low degree of association? Will our audience be using some elements together and not others? If there is a high degree of connectivity between elements, according to Fitt's Law we should be grouping or modularizing them together. If they are disparate, they need to separate.

When was the last time you walked into a grocery store and found it to be organized alphabetically? How about by color? I would hazard to guess you never have. That's because grocers strive to place like items together so we can find things that are related to each other and improve the chances of purchasing them. There certainly are exceptions, such as staples like bread, eggs, milk, and butter being strategically distributed across the store so that we pass by more stuff, increasing the probability of more purchases. But, for the most part, produce is together, breakfast items are with breakfast stuff, and lunch items are with lunch stuff.

Other than that, stores are organized by placing like items next to each other. This allows us to consider an item and compare it with another like item on the shelf. This comparison shopping technique allows us to choose, providing us the sense of selectivity that, in turn, increases consumption.

For some surprising reason, the digital world has difficulty embracing the concept of comparison. When we shop online, we certainly fall into areas such as shirts or shorts that collect those items together, but, with a few notable exceptions, as of this writing it's rare when we are presented the opportunity to compare items directly. REI's comparison shopping tool is one of those notable exceptions. We can load up a set of tents, say, and compare them against each other by price, size, weight, and style. We can do the same for sleeping bags, where warmth is another parameter to be considered. The interface to do this is rather clumsy, but at least users can consider their needs, and purchase exactly the product that fits best.

The upshot is that we need to consider the relative connectivity of items and associate them on the surface of our interface accordingly. In addition, there may be situations where a direct comparison may be useful. If that's the case, consider ways of marking and selecting items to be compared and offer information and interaction methods to compare them. Your audience will be grateful.

The arrangement of content should agree with connectivity between elements. Offer comparison if useful.

12.22 AFFORDANCES

Previously, we introduced the concept of affordances, which are those aspects of the form of a component indicating how to use it (Lidwell et al., 2010, p. 22). Affordances can be both physical and virtual. The classic example of a physical affordance is the well-designed door-knob which indicates that the knob must be turned and pulled to open the door. Virtual affordances are common as well. Window components, such as scroll bars and corner pull areas, used to be indicated with friction pads—three or four lines that looked like raised bumps—indicating that the item should be "grabbed and pulled." Friction, of course, is a complete fiction on a virtual interface, but friction pads were used so commonly that we came to understand them as being applied to things that could be dragged. In more modern window-based interfaces, these have largely disappeared. Whatever the aspect of the affordance—tabs, arrows, nubs, drop shadows, etc.—pay attention to the form of these indicators and strive to make them a conscious part of the design. They need to be both consistent across your system and accurately reflect the user's mental model of how the interactive component should be used.

Use affordances to communicate to users how to interact with objects they may be unfamiliar with.

12.23 CALL TO ACTION

Calls to action (CTAs) are clear indicators that prompt our user to act. Consider the Amazon interface. The purchase buttons indicate what to do: Either add to cart or purchase using one click. The text tells us exactly what the actions are, and the fill of the buttons makes them stand out from everything else. We have a clear CTA: The visual treatment of the button is the call, and the text tells us the action.

When you want your audience to do something above all else, prime them and make clear CTAs.

12.24 ORCHESTRATION AND FLOW

We've discussed the concept of orchestration and flow several times. For the most part, these discussions have been about the user's flow through the system. But let's look a little more closely at these flows—these use cases. When we walk through these paths, do the aesthetic elements hold up? Is the hierarchy clear, type legible, does color convey the brand values well? Do the dynamics carry the experience along from one state to the next while communicating the structure and the feeling? Flowing through the system may not be how we designed it, but it certainly is how users experience it. What can you do about the flow of the system that makes it more aesthetically delightful? Refer to the flows in Figures 9.7, 10.2, and 10.3, yet swap your wireframes for your completed designs. Assess how that experience feels and polish your designs if necessary.

Carefully consider how the system appears when a user flows through it, because that's how they experience it.

12.25 CONSISTENCY

Consistency is the quality whereby elements that appear a certain way in one place of the system appear logically the same way in another. When we walk into a Target store, their logo and their brand color are applied consistently throughout, from signage, to price tags, to shopping carts, to the interior design of the store itself. Every opportunity where red and the target logo can logically appear, it does, even on patterns on the store's walls. No surface is left untouched. As an interface example, Strava consistently uses its brand color, orange, to call attention to critical interactive elements on its interface, thereby providing insight into how to use their system; a consistent application of surprising usability.

Consistency is an aspect of uniform connectedness in that "Elements that are connected by uniform visual properties . . . are perceived to be more related" than those that aren't (Lidwell et al., 2010, p. 246). We want our entire system to feel as one; therefore, we should strive to connect those elements to achieve that oneness. This not only enhances the brand, but also enhances usability (Lidwell et al., 2010, p. 56). When similar elements are expressed in similar ways, our audience doesn't have to learn them anew. They can rely on what they've learned already.

Consistency also appears in interactions. The behavior iOS uses in the email item we analyzed in the previous chapter appears consistently throughout several standard-issue iOS apps. In Notes, we can swipe left on a note item and the functions "Move" and "Delete" appear. Same goes for items in the Reminders app as well. There are many benefits to consistency in this case. When users understand how to interact with an item from one app, they know how to interact with others. Learn once, use many: The reason why design patterns are effective.

There is also a production benefit to consistency: Developers usually build systems based on objects that have certain behaviors. If the behavior is the same between any two objects, they can leverage the code that is already written. Applying the same interaction patterns throughout promotes code reuse and cuts down development time. Write once, use many. Design patterns rely on consistency to enhance usability. If we've used a scroll bar on one application, we know how to use it on another, thereby improving the learning curve by reducing the number of new things that have to be learned.

Are there elements of your design that could be made consistent throughout (Figures 12.6 and 12.7)? What would you need to do to those elements to bring them in line with each other? Does this make sense with each of the elements, or does one become rather odd when forced into being consistent with others? Look

Figure 12.6
Consistent visual elements across interfaces for an online gallery (from Dotcrit, by Angela Chu, used by kind permission of Angela Chu).

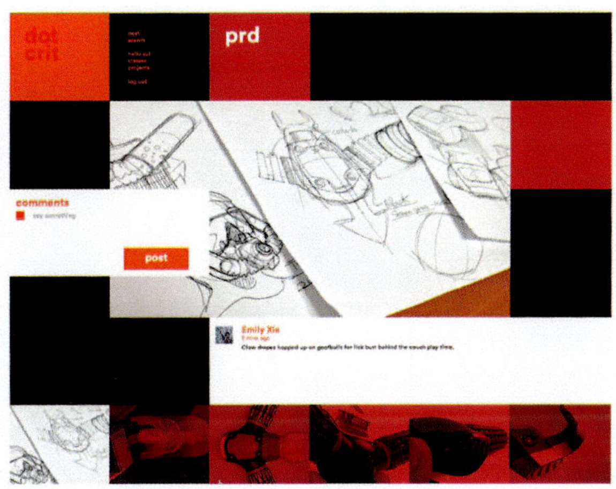

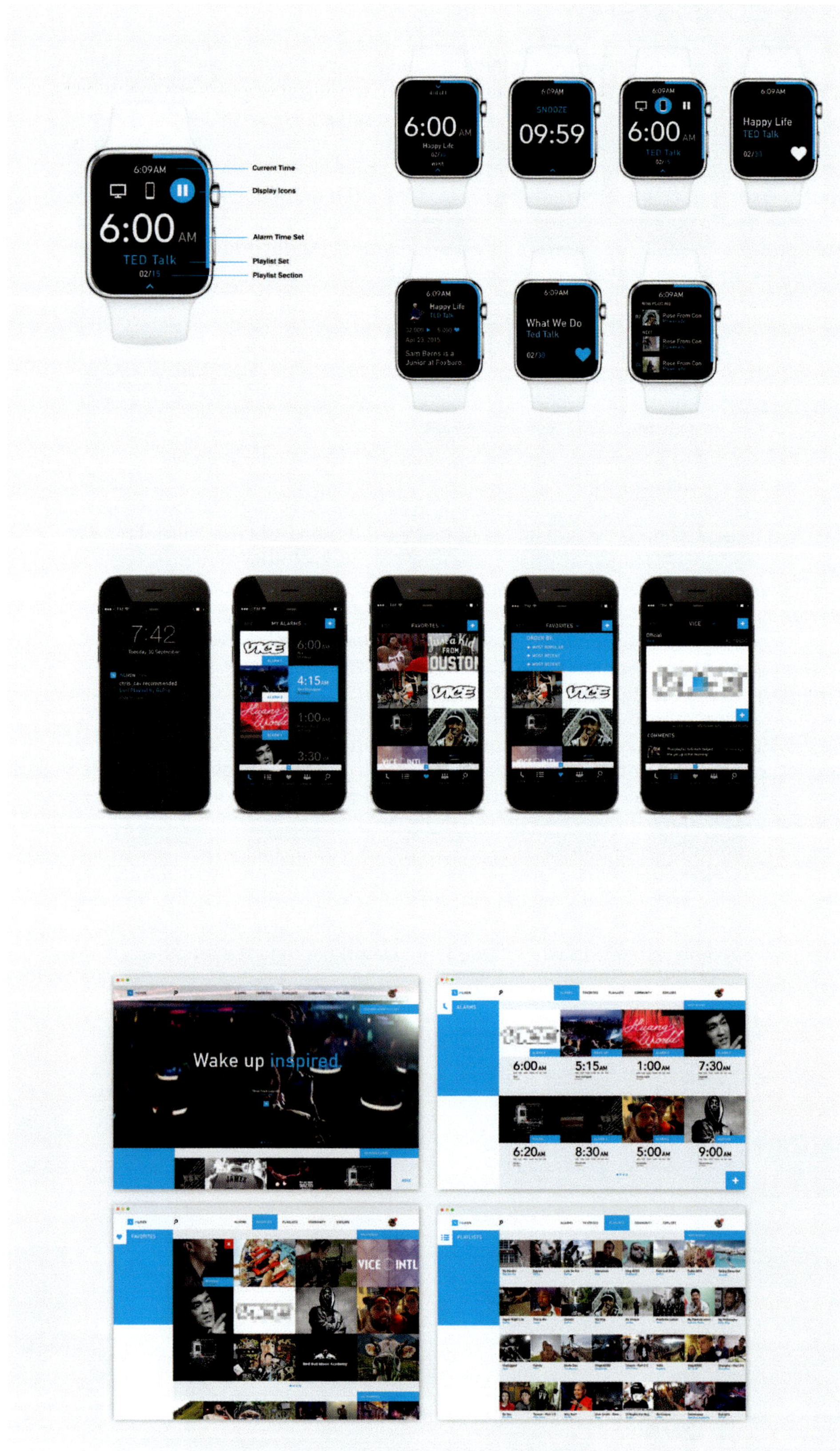

Figure 12.7
Consistency across an entertainment based wakeup system (from Inliven, by Elbert Tao, used by kind permission of Elbert Tao).

for similarities and differences. Strive for consistency, but don't shoehorn something into being consistent when it really should not be.

Strive for consistency across the system. Use it to associate similar elements.

12.26 COLOR

Color is a fascinating tool in our design kit. It can affect us emotionally as well as provide us with another channel of communication for structure. Color, as a structuring device, works similarly to scale and size in the sense that it can associate elements across the surface of the interface irrespective of its location (Figure 12.8). For example, if we wish to identify a certain element as the headline to a story, we could use type size or we could use color. For either choice, it matters less where the headline appears, but that all headlines are treated the same way.

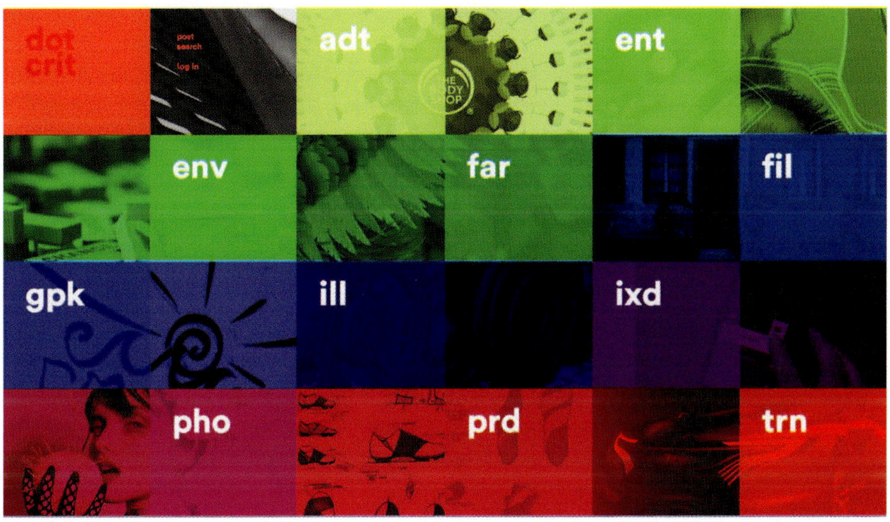

Figure 12.8
Color design for an online gallery (from Dotcrit, by Angela Chu, used by kind permission of Angela Chu).

But color is not size. It may have similar characteristics in the sense that it is another means of separating and associating elements, but while an interface may have several scales of type and still remain quite legible, the more colors we introduce, the noisier our interface gets. When color is used, it must be done with a high degree of strategic intent, especially if it is to be used to communicate structure. For example, if we use a color to indicate that an element is interactive, we will be confusing our audience if we also use that color for elements that are not interactive. Consistency of application is critical.

Strava's use of orange presents a good example of this level of consideration. They chose one color, orange, as their brand color. Often the logo and logotype are set in orange against a neutral background (black or white), or the background is orange, and the logo is reversed out as white. The bright orange communicates the energy and vibrancy of the brand. And when we get into the interface, the orange that so effectively conveyed Strava's brand values is used structurally to indicate that an element is interactive. Color can be used not only for emotion, but information as well.

But this works only because the designers of Strava were controlled in their application of the color. If it were applied haphazardly, we wouldn't associate it with interactive elements, and it wouldn't be effective. Also, bear in mind that orange isn't used for every interactive element in the Strava interface. For example, there is a "legal" link on their web interface that is interactive, yet not orange. This is a rarely used element, so to call it out with orange would have been giving it too much emphasis. Likewise, throughout the rest of the system on other screens, the orange is used sparingly. If it were used too much, the screen would look cluttered. They wisely reserved it for the most important interactive elements.

Consider color as a structuring tool. To use it effectively, it needs to be controlled and consistently applied.

12.27 COLOR, MATERIAL, FINISH

Color, materials, and finish, otherwise known as CMF, is an aspect of industrial design that considers the final surface details of a product or product line. Combined, these three can both communicate a brand yet distinguish the various products in the line from each other. In a way, this is similar to the standout and fit in characteristics of iconography. The configuration of a color or material or finish employed by a product serves to make items unique but still work as a family. Well branded car lines, fashion lines, fashion accessories, and product line families are all examples of this.

To illustrate, how many versions of Apple Watch are there? People buy different ones as an extension of their own identity, so the CMF is orchestrated to reach a particular segment of their target population. There are the colorful, less expensive ones attractive to those who want a more playful or sporty feel, and then there are the metallic and more neutral ones that strive to target a feeling of elegance or professionalism.

Although the surface details of the various Apple Watch lines are different, there is a unity as well. There are only fairly flat colors and smooth surfaces—no gaudy patterns or materials. Everything is clean and simple. Users can certainly buy bands with zebra prints or rhinestones, but none come off the line from Apple. The surface materials and colors are applied in the same way, yet are different in color, material, or finish. CMF brings both consistency and distinction to the line.

What are the feelings you wish to convey with your physical devices? You have a target market, but are there sub-markets within that target that you wish to reach as well? Who are they? How are they separate from each other, yet comprise the whole of your entire target? How can you use CMF to reach them and make them feel a level of individuality when they purchase your devices? Even if you don't have a collection of sub-targets, how can the CMF of your devices convey your sense of brand identity just as type or color would (Figure 12.9)?

Figure 12.9
CMF for a digital wearable (from Emma, by Team Delta, used by kind permission of Devin Montes, Naomi Tirronen, Joshua Woo, Angela Dong, and Jenny Kim).

12.28 DIMENSIONAL COHERENCE

Dimensional coherence is an aspect of a system where both its physical and virtual presence work well with each other. Traditionally, product design and screen-based interface design were developed as separate efforts. The device a system was run on was designed by one group, and the interface was done by a completely separate group often in a completely different country. The hardware would be designed and "thrown over the wall" to the interface group. The two would rarely mesh or coordinate.

This still happens today, but, fortunately, organizations are beginning to see the benefit of improving their brand impression by unifying hardware and software (Cooper, 2015, p. 557). Consistent branding and identity attributes are a clear way to bring them together, but this is the low hanging fruit. More powerful solutions also bring interactions and behaviors into the mix. The Nest thermostat is an excellent current example of this. Its circular design stems from the traditional circular thermostat of yesteryear, but that circularity is applied not only to the form but the screen as well. Not only that, the way we interact with it by dialing a circular ring carries that aspect all the way into its interaction.

As screens break out of their traditional rectangles, we have a wealth of opportunity to explore interface forms that support physical forms. As users become more comfortable with interactions beyond pointing and clicking on screens, we will be able to consider behaviors that are more integrated with these novel forms as well. Challenge yourself to break out of the box of tradition, and the literal screen-based box itself, to see what possibilities you can discover that improve the dimensional coherence of your system (Figures 12.10 and 12.11).

Consider consistency not only through the virtual aspects of the system, but through all aspects that impact the senses, visual, tactile, spatial, auditory, flavorful, and aromatic.

Figure 12.10
Dimensional coherence on an airport wayfinding column: the form of the interface and that of the column work hand in hand (from Xeno, by Team HA+CH, used by kind permission of Cindy Hu, Andrew Lee, Harry Teng, and Harmonie Tsai).

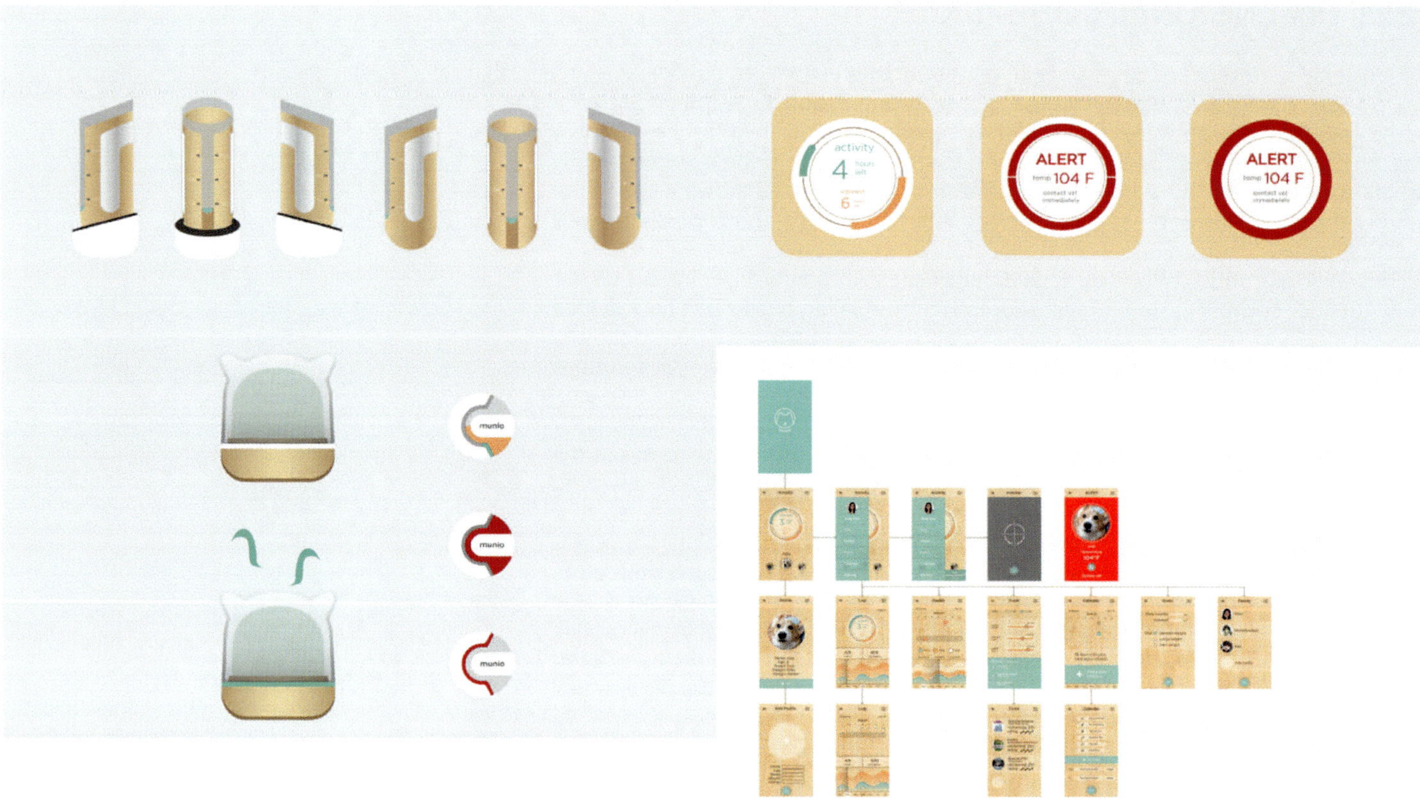

Figure 12.11
Unified look of a pet care system through dimensional coherence: food scoop, wall display, scent indicator, collar clasp, and app (from Munio, by Team Wolf Pack, used by kind permission of Judy Chu, Tina Ou, Jane Park, and Jade Tsao).

12.29 STANDING OUT AND FITTING IN

Drama has its place in design and conformance has its place as well. As is true with most design disciplines, Interaction Design is a balancing act of standing out and fitting in. When we use previously established design patterns, we tend to improve usability by fitting in, but at the expense of originality. Originality aids distinction and allows our designs to stand out from a crowd. The von Restorff effect underscores the reason why this is useful in that ". . . noticeably different things are more likely to be recalled than common things" (Lidwell et al., 2010, p. 254). But novel interfaces are often a challenge to learn and use. Both standing out and fitting in have good aspects and bad, and the trick is to be strategic with how we stand out and how we fit in.

To fit in means to look, perform, and otherwise feel as expected. To stand out means to have a look, style, performance, or feeling that distinguishes it from others. Companies such as Nike, Apple, Target, Disney, and Porsche apply a great deal of their resources into standing out from their competitors. From a design perspective, these organizations seem exciting and may lead us into thinking that everything should have this level of distinction. But if you strive for your designs to stand out in everything, then nothing works as expected and you will most likely frustrate your audience. Even though these brands have unique elements that distinguish themselves, they still have advertising, stores, graphics, and products that work as expected. Even these aspirational brands both stand out and fit in.

How these companies pull it off is that they are highly strategic with what stands out vs. what fits in. Like any other company, they need ads to promote their products, packaging to contain them, and a place to sell them, but the style of the type, color, imagery, materials, and form of those elements do not have to be like the rest. In fact, they should be distinctive to allow the brand to be distinctive.

What should you do? First off, understand the goals of your system. If it's intended as an experience where the main goal is promotional, then by all means be aggressive with standing out. If, on the other hand, its main goal is to work well as a tool, then fitting in probably takes precedence. A product's style is a good place to be distinctive, but the question of standing out gets rather dicey when we are considering how something works. If the interactions you design are always novel, they may be fun and exciting for you as the designer but will frustrate your audience because they won't be able to rely on their prior knowledge.

We may have a few signature interactions that are aspirational and are more about feel than substance, but the rest of the functionality should be delivering on expectations. On the other hand, it is our user's aspirations manifested in our guidewords that drive our aesthetics. Yet, even with aesthetics, we should take care. Originality of everything is originality of nothing. Just as heavily branded companies are strategic about where they stand out, you need to be strategic as well. You may wish to err on the side of comfort and usability with your aesthetics or may wish to push the boundaries of distinction. This needs to be a conscious decision on your part so that everyone on your team buys into the approach.

Most often, though, we strive for both standing out and fitting in. We do this by identifying elements that should stand out. Those become our signature elements. We may insist on a consistency of function, yet originality or subtle imperfections of form such as a Wabi-Sabi effect, where those imperfections may allow for a deeper, more meaningful aesthetic (Lidwell et al., 2010, p. 256). As long as our elements work well and don't frustrate our audience, usability issues will be manageable. For the rest, it's okay to fit in. This will allow our audience a level of comfort that will keep them satisfied and coming back. Consider your aesthetic explorations and signature interactions in light of this balancing act of standing out and fitting in. What things should be distinctive, and what should deliver on expectations?

Don't let the dominance of usability completely eliminate the possibility of elements of distinction. Balance familiarity against distinction appropriately.

12.30 BRAND COHERENCE

Brand coherence is the consistent application of the impression of the brand throughout all touchpoints. The example of Target, described previously, is an excellent illustration of this. They seemingly spare no surface in the application of the brand, and they do so in vibrant and creative ways. In our case, the touchpoints of interest are those that are not only in the system itself, but also those things that prompt users to begin to interact with our system. How well do those touchpoints—those both internal and external to the system—adhere to the brand? When we consider this, we are not just considering how it presents the logo or uses the brand color; we are also considering all the aesthetic aspects of how it adheres to the brand values. Even though the term "brand coherence" may be new to us, our use of guidewords have baked brand coherence into our design since our earliest forays into aesthetics. Simply review if we've done so effectively and whether there are opportunities we haven't considered.

Let's look again to Strava as an example of brand coherence. Everything about it promotes action. It starts with its name, a combination of "strive" and "va" (to go). It's brand color, orange, is fiery and hot, promoting the energy of an active lifestyle. Its logo uses the "v" from its name and forms it in such a way as to signify mountains and valleys, reminiscent of the challenges a cyclist faces on the road or trail. I found out about it by listening to cycle mechanics in a bike shop talk about their performance on Strava segments—testimonials that focused on performance.

When we visit the app store to download it, the sample screens are the performance feedback screen and the segment screen. This gives us an impression that Strava is about my performance and how it stacks up with others.

Launching the app, the first thing we see is people doing endurance athletics, riding, running, and swimming. It shows us Strava people being active in a Strava way. We want to be part of the crowd, so we do stuff, too, by launching the record screen and starting to ride or run. During the activity, we see our performance and how we're performing on segments—action promoted by competition. When we finish, we see our results stacked up against others, providing us with a desire to continue to be active to do better.

Strava delivers. From its name, through its logo, through its ads, through its use is all about action motivated by friendly competition. All of its touchpoints are about action. Its entry points into the product delivers it, and its continued use delivers it as well.

Consider your primary use case and consider your onboarding process. If those use cases don't already, extend out a bit from your system itself and consider how your user is first seduced into your system. Do those external touchpoints that prompt the entry into the system have good brand coherence (Figure 12.12)? When users enter your system, does it deliver on its brand values? Does the design of each quiescent state, content element, control element, behavior, and dynamic response carry those values? This is the perspective from which we need to consider if an element should stand out and fit in. A few distinctive signature elements and interactions strategically placed in a largely expected set of patterns will provide both wow and comfort.

The elements in the system should cohere to the look and feel of the brand.

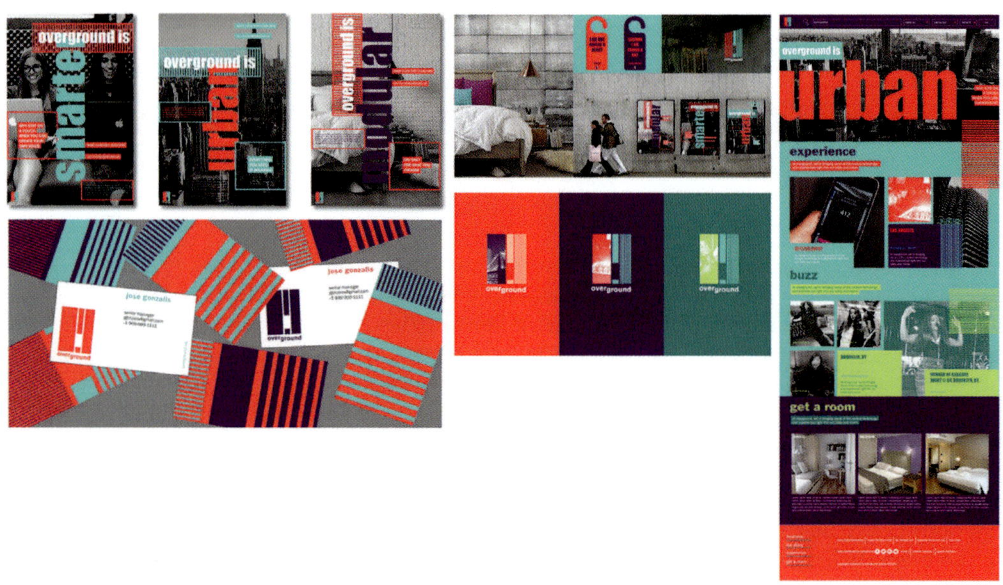

Figure 12.12
Brand coherence across media forms for a hotel: Posters, business cards, door hangers, website (from Overground, by Sana Desai, used by kind permission of Sana Desai).

12.31 STRUCTURAL AESTHETICS AND DYNAMIC RANGE

My experience has been that the aspects that are the most bland with a designer's work at this point usually revolve around a lack of hierarchy and separation. These are related in the sense that if elements do not have a great deal of separation, it's very difficult to express hierarchy with any degree of visual impact. If the negative space between elements is conservative and similar, we've removed that as a tool in our toolbox to express importance. Likewise, if our type is pretty much at the same size, we've eliminated typographic scale as well. Injecting a dynamic range into the tools we use to communicate separation and hierarchy often leads to better impact.

But establishing a greater dynamic range is not always that easy. We need to decide what is important, and what is less so. We may be minimizing the range of these elements because we are confused about this, but we really shouldn't be. Each interface has a purpose, and with all the information design we've done, we should have a very clear idea what that purpose is. We should be able to itemize the elements on the interface and place them in order of importance. In fact, it's a good idea to do so.

When we develop a prioritized list of elements, we may be led to the conclusion that the top three to five of these are about at the same level of hierarchy, so they should be pretty much at the same level, yes? The answer to this is a very definite "maybe" verging on "no". (I have an overwhelming urge to put a smiley here, if it weren't unacceptable in academic writing.) In a brand rich interface, this is usually not the case. Take the Apple website, for example. At any one time, Apple sells hundreds of products, yet, when we visit its landing page, the first we see is one. It's big, and it's right at the top. At any one time, Apple is acutely aware of the product they are promoting as their hero. As we scroll down, we see other products, and, at the very bottom, we see a collection of lesser sections to the website. Those sections may be important, but they are less so in the sense of what Apple wants to promote.

On the other hand, if our interface is more information-rich, this distinction may be a great deal more subtle. When I visit Strava's activity feed, certainly the most important element is the most current activity of the athletes I follow. But if we treated this information as if it was the landing page of the Apple website—in that we featured this element almost exclusively—our interface would be a failure. We may be most likely interested in the most recent post, but we are probably interested in many other aspects as well. We signify this importance by placing it at the top of the list, but we don't use extremes of hierarchy and separation in terms of scale and negative space to promote this element exclusively. It's the same size as everything else; it's just at the top.

Compare these examples with flattening the hierarchy to the furthest extreme, to that, say, of an application such as Illustrator. In this case, we are presented several tools exemplified by the contents of its tool palettes that are more or less the same size on the screen. Scale, as an element that communicates importance, is almost entirely removed. Arrangement is used for importance instead, and it's very subtle. For example, the selection tool is on the top, but all the tool icons are the same size.

The aspects Adobe employs to signify a hierarchy of importance is more aligned with hiding and revealing functionality. Those elements that are more commonly used are more present, those that are not are more hidden. The object selection cursor is present all the time, and the lesser used effects features are buried in pull-down menus. None of them is too far away, though, because those that are important do not take up that much real estate. If they did, we would most likely have to bury lesser functions even more. The Illustrator interface is boring, and that's all right because the "fun" is not contained in the presentation of the interface, it's in what is done with it.

If we strive for emotion and brand impact, we should be aggressive with the dynamic range of the aspects we are using for distinction (recall Figure 12.2). If our interface is more about functionality, we should be more subtle. It may be useful to consider each interface as a manifestation of the content triangle described earlier in this book: If an interface is more about information or control, its dynamic range is subtle. If it's more about emotion, its dynamic range may be more aggressive. Consider where your interfaces reside on a content triangle and approach their dynamic range accordingly. Take care, though; if you find that all your interfaces end up being on the side of information and control, you may be devaluing the importance of emotional impact in the aesthetics of your system.

12.32 SURPRISING USABILITY

We may rationalize our way to mediocrity in our design by claiming that our interface needs to be usable, so we better not push things too far. Ignore that. Push your aesthetic design to achieve greater aesthetic impact. It's always easier to pull back once we've seen how far we can go. It's important to see the possibility of a Maserati so that we can integrate the right touches in our Nissan. Certainly, our interfaces must be usable, but that doesn't mean they must be mundane. Disney Hall is far from mundane, but it also is one of the most beautifully sounding concert halls in the world. It is an inspiring integration of form and function.

Throughout this book, we have been hammering on the notion that form should follow function, but that's not entirely correct. Agreed, if we've achieved good form and fail on function, our system will fail. Recall my alarm clock. If we achieve function but fail on form, our system will still work, but be uninspiring. We must set a high bar for both usability and aesthetics so that our system achieves a beautiful integration of both form and function (Figure 12.13). It needs to be an example of what we like to call surprising usability: It must be both usable and distinctive.

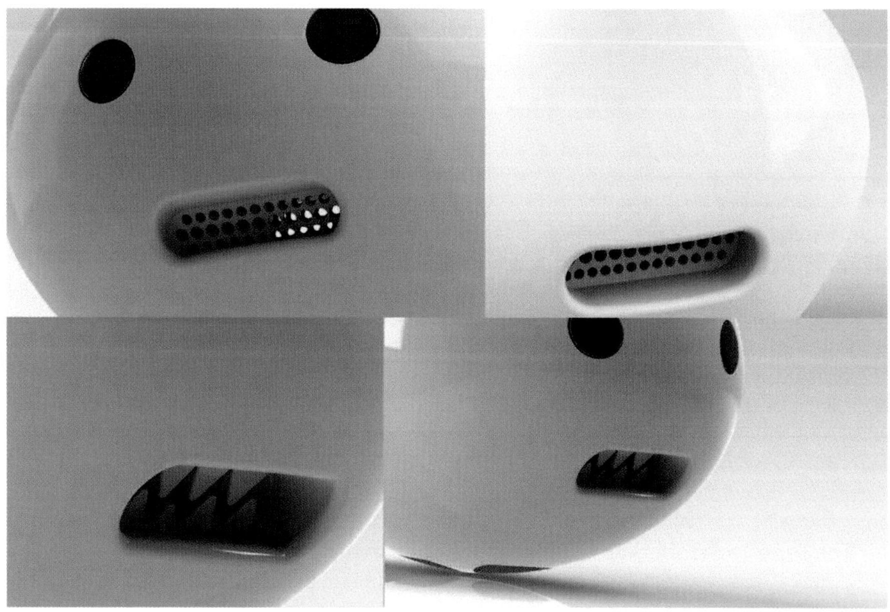

Figure 12.13
Subtle adjustments of form for a toy swim drone (from Fino, by Steve Wang, used by kind permission of Steve Wang).

12.33 OCCAM'S RAZOR

With the presentation of all the above considerations, you may get the idea that we are promoting the inclusion of all of them. That's entirely not the case. In the end, we should keep in mind Occam's razor: that the best design is usually the simplest (Lidwell et al., 2010, p. 172). Too many elements introduce noise and make our interfaces unusable. We've seen that, after a few iterations of an aesthetic approach, it's often better to reduce elements than to add them. You may consider revisiting the aesthetic disruption method of reduction again if your design seems to be getting complex. And, of course, when we reduce, we are forced to make difficult decisions about what to eliminate and what to keep. Those choices are the tough part of design, but also necessary.

Reduce to only what is necessary.

12.34 INTERFACE GUIDELINES, AGAIN

At this stage in our design process, we should have familiarized ourselves with any rules and approaches that guide our design, be they from we ourselves, our organization, or a third party, such as the manufacturers of the devices in our ecosystem. Use them liberally as a resource for your aesthetic solutions, but keep in mind that, in so doing, your interface may tend to look like everything else. They're great for having your work fit in, but you may need to break with them from time to time to handle novel interactive situations or provide an air of distinction to your system.

Guidelines are a useful resource. Use them to fit in, but be prepared to break with them if you have a good reason.

12.35 ACCESSIBILITY GUIDELINES

It's also important to keep your eye on accessibility concerns. For example, if we need big type because our audience has poor eyesight, that will have a dramatic effect on the amount of information a screen can hold. Likewise, if we are designing for an audience with a high probability of having arthritis, our gesture language, behaviors, and the size of our touch targets will certainly be affected.

During the course of interviewing and becoming familiar with your audience, you may have conducted research that led to a set of rules or standards. Recall the stipulations made in Figure 8.7 for example. These guidelines should be clear, actionable, and precise. They should briefly explain why they're important and provide specific instructions to allow project stakeholders to determine if the guidelines are being met. They should be followed not only in your structural design as we have been applying them so far, but in your aesthetic approach as well.

Keep in mind the accessibility issues for your audience. Use them to increase the inclusivity of your design.

12.36 AESTHETIC REFINEMENT

Aesthetics is where we can gain the most traction in making our system consistent across contexts and use cases. Let's start by harvesting the best results from our aesthetic disruptions. During that process, we engaged in various efforts, the goal of which was to break through design *clichés* that may have been collecting in our comp explorations. If we were sufficiently exploratory, we should have a wealth of fresh ideas.

To determine which to take further, let's look to our guideposts—our guidewords, moodboards, and inspiration boards—to see those approaches that have the most merit. Study these guideposts again carefully. What are the words that we used? What are the images that we have selected? What results from our disruptive explorations best match those values? Are there any executions that could be comfortably placed on our comprehensive inspiration board in terms of feeling? How about in terms of quality? If there are no complete executions that you think achieve this level, are there elements that have promise? These are the things that we should take forward.

If you have been working on only an interface or two to explore your aesthetic approach, now is the time to return the full set of our critical interfaces: high traffic, info rich, and brand impact. Not only that, now we should expand our aesthetic effort across our entire system by working on the critical interfaces of all the contexts within our ecosystem. Consider all artifacts within the system as well, such as physical designs, environmental designs, auditory styles, and even marketing communication. Apply the aesthetic considerations in this chapter to all of these in order for them work in concert to formulate a unified systemic aesthetic approach.

Figure 12.14
Screen designs and style boards communicate our final aesthetic approach (from Sourced, by Jonathan Nishida, used by kind permission of Jonathan Nishida).

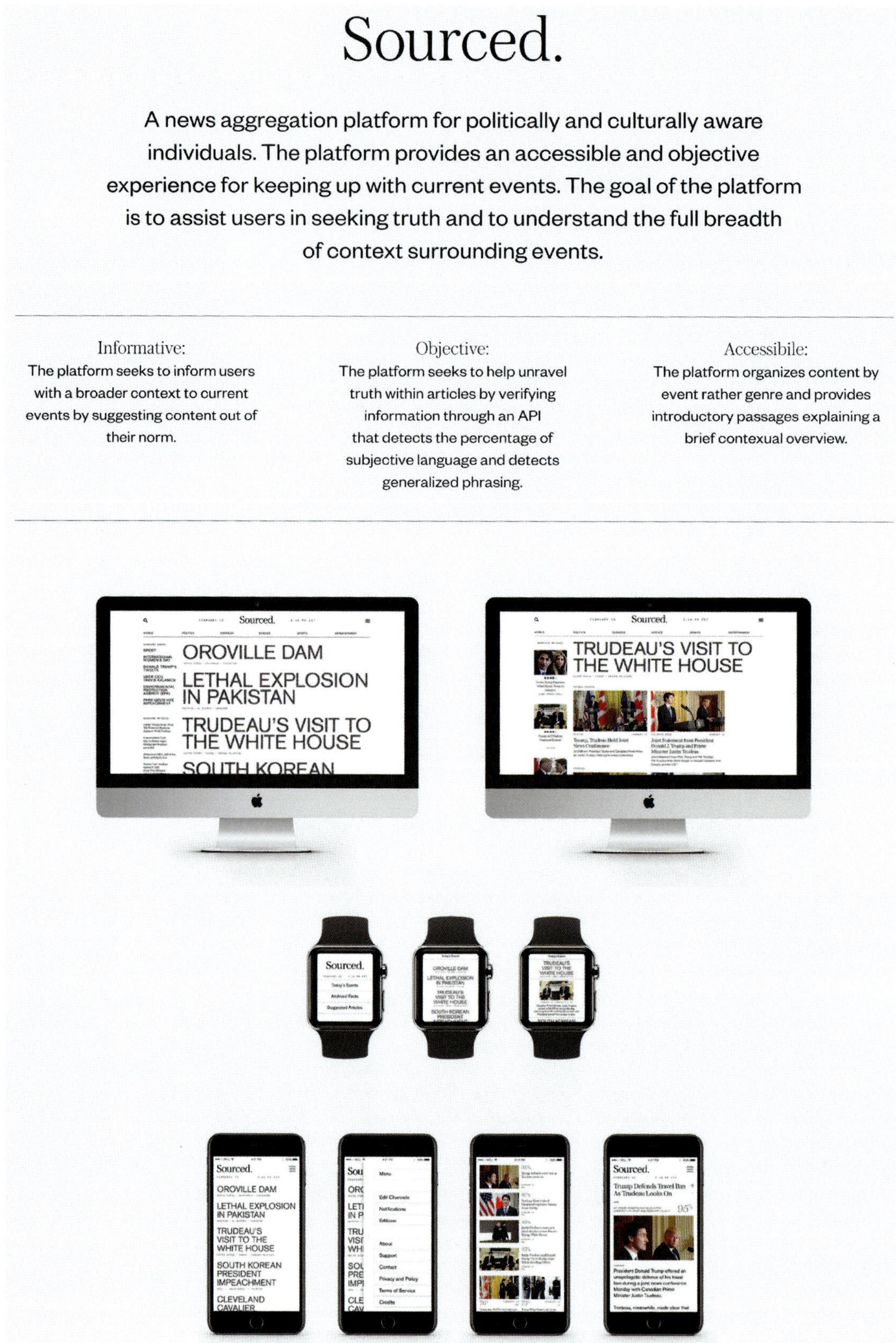

12.37 STYLE FRAMES

Remember, if our comps do not yet reach the level where we can place them on our inspiration boards, and they carry that very same level of polish, we are not yet done with our aesthetic designs. Work on them until they either reach or surpass this level.

If you and others on your design team believe you've achieved that level, lay out your comps on a board for presentation. We refer to your comps as style frames, and the presentation board as a style frame board (Figure 12.14). The board should contain three to five style frames for each critical context.

12.38 STYLE GUIDES

Once we've achieved a strong unity of structural aesthetics across our critical interfaces, then we can create a style guide. This allows us to interpret the style we've developed as a set of design elements: color palette, typographic strategy, iconography, navigation, and other interface elements, imagery and image strategy, grid and layout, and other design elements. (Figure 12.15).

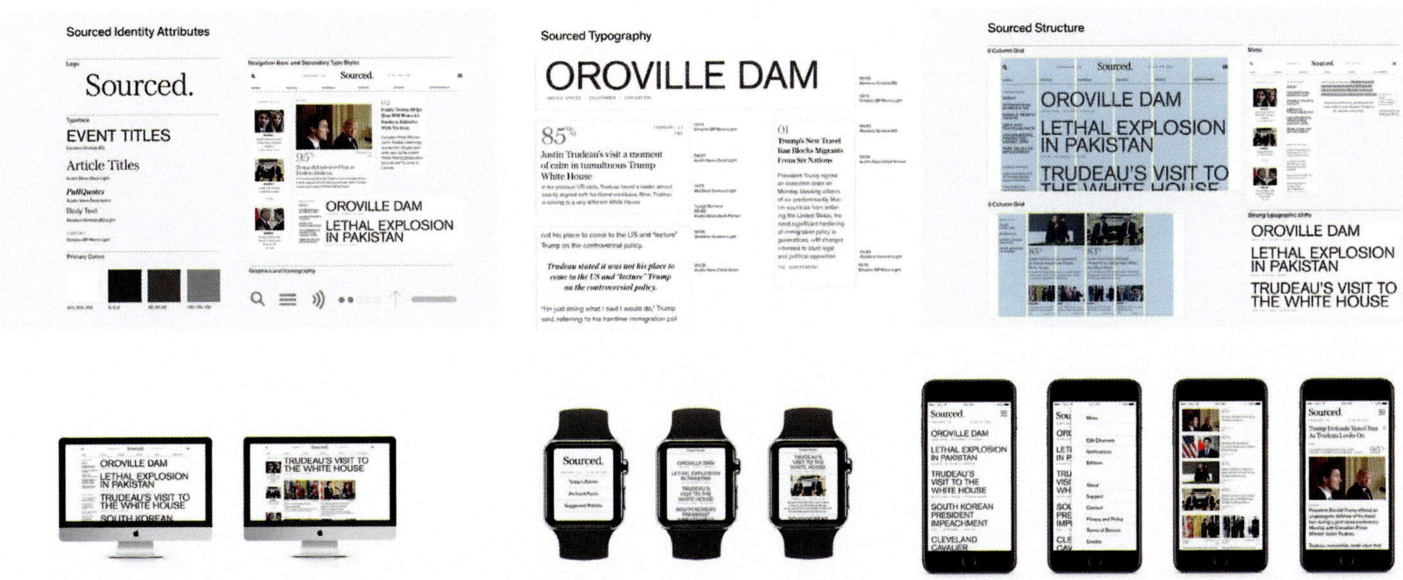

Figure 12.15
Style guide and sample screens for a news aggregator (from Sourced, by Jonathan Nishida, used by kind permission of Jonathan Nishida).

Note

1 As of this writing, (Typecode 2017) is a decent resource for this information.

13 Expanding Scope

Up to this point, we've considered the structure of our system from its highest level all the way down to the lowest, but we've refrained from considering its full breadth. We've been looking at our primary use case, mainly on our primary context, with a few excursions into the critical alternate cases of onboarding or advanced features. To design a system fully, we must expand our horizons. In this chapter, we will be expanding our scope and looking at the use cases that encompass our system in its entirety.

Do not let the brevity of this chapter fool you. The amount of time spent on the work within it could easily be the lion's share of the time you spend on your project. Many of its basic concepts have been discussed previously but are simply applied to uncharted branches of the system. This chapter is one of our shortest because there is no need to be redundant, so we use shorthand to explain what to do, expecting that you will revisit earlier topics if you need a little review.

13.1 WHY NOW?

Wait! We've explored interfaces in detail and dove down deeply into microinteractions, and we are just now thinking about other use cases that are critical to our system? Why haven't we addressed this earlier?

There are many appropriate approaches to the process of designing a system; for example, we could complete our structural design—our wireframing—before we even begin considering our aesthetic design. This is not only possible, but quite common. Instead, within these pages, we threaded aesthetics into our structural development so that each had a chance of playing off the other and the effort kept our aesthetic sensitivities active.

We've held off considering other use cases for specific reasons as well. We wanted our primary use case—our MVP—to be the focus of our effort up to this point to ensure its experience was uncompromised. We also wanted to introduce interface and behavior before our information design was fully resolved, so that the structure of our information could be more strongly influenced by our context ecosystem and microinteractions.

If we are designing a website with a great deal of content using only simple buttons and links for interaction, the arrangement of that content would be its complexity, not control. For these systems interactions are simple, and interfaces are layout problems more than anything else. It would make complete sense to address our information architecture in its entirety first, since it is the primary driver of the design. But the wealth of interactions involved in gesture systems, physical interfaces, and even natural language systems are much more complex than a simple point and click. The interrelationship between information, interface, and interaction is much tighter, so we advanced the latter two phases of design—interface and interaction—in the process so they could be better positioned to influence information organization. For any project, it's a good idea to identify where the critical complexity lies, and advance that in the design process so that it influences the more simple aspects. Here, we advanced interface and interaction and are now beginning to consider the full scope of the content.

13.2 THE WORK PRODUCT

When we expand our scope to the design of the system, we will certainly be increasing our consideration of users from intermediate to both novice and expert, and will be extending from our primary context to all contexts that we think are relevant to our ecosystem. Yet, in addition, we will be broadening the scope from the routine use of our product to other possible applications as well. Throughout this process, we will be performing activities similar to those done with our primary use case, yet we will be considering how every aspect affects the whole.

As with our primary use case, we begin by looking at the physical situations our audience will most likely be in and their limitations within those situations by using our posture studies. We should weigh the role that each situation plays in our ecosystem, identify the goals our users have in each, break those down into the features that support them, and the tasks necessary for our users to complete to achieve them. Then, we should identify the contexts or devices used to execute those tasks, specify the information and control elements necessary to provide our users to complete them within those contexts, consider what the interface and behaviour should be for that information and control, and, finally, how that interface should look and feel aesthetically. We should be employing think maps, sticky note walls, scenarios, structure maps, wireframes and prototypes at various fidelities, user flows, behavior diagrams, our system's style guide, and interface comps to reveal how our audience experiences our system while striving to achieve specific goals.

We should engage our good climbing skills to zoom out to the big picture of a structure map to see how quiescent states are best organized across the system, and zoom in to the minutiae of microinteractions and behaviour to see how our users engage in interactions that get things done. We will add detail to our structure map to transform it into a wireframe flowboard for each context, and refine that even further to depict an interaction flowboard, illustrating not only the mid-fidelity wireframes, but also the gesture language needed to navigate between quiescent states.

The ultimate goal of our scope expansion is to arrive at a final structure of our system across all contexts depicting the organization of the information and control it provides, and representing how our user experiences it. As we will see, mid-fidelity wireframe interaction flowboards do just that. The well-considered creation of these is the goal of this chapter.

While we are progressing through this effort, we should also expand our scope aesthetically. As with our primary use case, we should be exploring the look and feel of each context and how it delivers on the brand as a whole. Although your structural design may not be fully complete for a particular use case, don't get wrapped up in the perception that you must wait until all the structural design is done to work on aesthetics. To keep all aspects of your design team engaged, use the best information you can and continue to develop the approach to your interfaces structurally, behaviorally, and aesthetically.

In terms of our structural design, it's fine, but not critical, to integrate what's resulting from our aesthetic effort as long as it doesn't bog us down. For example, incorporating the typeface and typographic strategy we now have for our system could have minimal negative impact on the efficiency of building wireframes, and, in fact, could make that effort faster. The same may be true with an approach to a general layout or grid system. However, getting obsessive about pixel perfection will slow down our wireframing and structural design. Remember, the main point of wireframes: to be able to execute and iterate approaches quickly.

Recall, however, that if we intend to present our wireframes to clients who may improperly interpret them as aesthetically polished, we may have to consciously avoid integrating any aesthetics at all. If this is the case, our wireframes don't have to be ugly, but it should be clear that these are not aesthetically designed through the use of common yet robust typefaces, such as Helvetica or Univers, possibly grayscale colors, and functional yet uninspired layouts. Let the realities of your particular situation guide you.

13.3 FACTORIAL ITERATION

Since we're engaged in fleshing out aspects of our system we haven't previously considered, we need to take a step or two back in the fidelity we've been brought to in the preceding chapters. Because we may be dealing with these use cases for the first time, it's not advisable to jump right into mid-fidelity wireframes and their respective microinteractions. We need to start with the same things we started with when considering our primary use case—our user's goals—and we need to explore a little.

What are the goals of our novice? What are the goals of our expert? Identify them, consider what features are necessary to achieve their goals, create user stories, and break them down into tasks. Conduct posture studies on each use case and assign tasks to contexts. Then break these tasks down further to identify the information necessary to complete those tasks.

Sketch lo-fi wireframes that organize that information into interfaces and user test them to see which of several approaches are best. Then we can create mid-fidelity wireframes, scenarios, user flows, behavior designs, and microinteractions for these cases. We've gone through these stages already in previous chapters, so there's no need to waste ink going over them again. Simply perform the same activities on these cases that we already performed on the primary.

When we peel back a layer of our design onion, we often must return to earlier methodologies magic moments, (task breakdowns and lo-fi wireframes, for example) to address that new layer. This should happen not only with different user types, novices and experts, for example, but also when we consider other contexts in our ecosystem, such as a TV or watch, or other use cases that we will address below. We call this factorial iteration because, just as when a factorial adds a new number we must multiply all the numbers before it, when we add a new use case, we must go through the design process from the start for that case and consider all the use cases before it. Factorial iteration may seem like a lot of work, but it's essential to consider how everything affects the whole to arrive at the best system. You will find that the speed and efficiency with which you go through these iterations becomes faster and more efficient as you do them.

13.4 CONTEXT SCOPING

Just as we have previously been focusing on our primary use case, we also may have been limiting ourselves to our primary context. We did this for the same reasons we limited our scope to our primary use case: It allowed us to focus on that context so that its interface and interaction could have the greatest influence on the design of the system as a whole. However, systems that allow our users to flow from device to device gracefully are a joy to experience, so if we aren't considering our systemic use cases already, we need to do so now. How our user flows through our device ecosystem is essential to making that multi-device experience joyful. We need to broaden the scope of our devices and contexts in the same way we needed to broaden our user scope.

What devices and contexts can we leverage to take full advantage of our user's experiences? Recall the day in the life and journey map of our users. Recall their postures throughout their day. What did we specify as being our device ecosystem? Consider those other devices or contexts. For a particular context, first ask what type of user goal or set of goals it is good for. A watch is excellent for quick glanceable notifications, but poor for the detailed analysis of a wealth of information. That's usually the role taken by a website.

Just because we're at a point of mid- or high-fidelity wireframes and microinteraction schematics with our primary use case, it does not mean that we are at that level for these new use cases. Apply good factorial iteration and return to magic moments and lo-fi sketches until you're confident with your approach to each user role within each context. And refrain from being confident about a particular approach until you've determined how well it orchestrates with those you've already designed.

13.5 ALTERNATE CASES

Beyond the primary use case and critical alternates are the alternate cases. Alternate cases are not critical—your system could survive without them—but they achieve user goals and offer features that are "nice to have." These may come from lower priority must-haves, or the "could do" section of our MUSCOW chart. Are there non-critical yet helpful things your system can do based on what it does already? If we can inject these into the system without disrupting the primary use case or critical alternates, then consider how users can flow through them if they wish to achieve these goals.

To think of alternate cases, try to think of ways the system can be used that may differ from the way it's intended (Figure 13.1). If we intend our system to be used by students in a classroom, consider how it could be used outdoors. What if it were

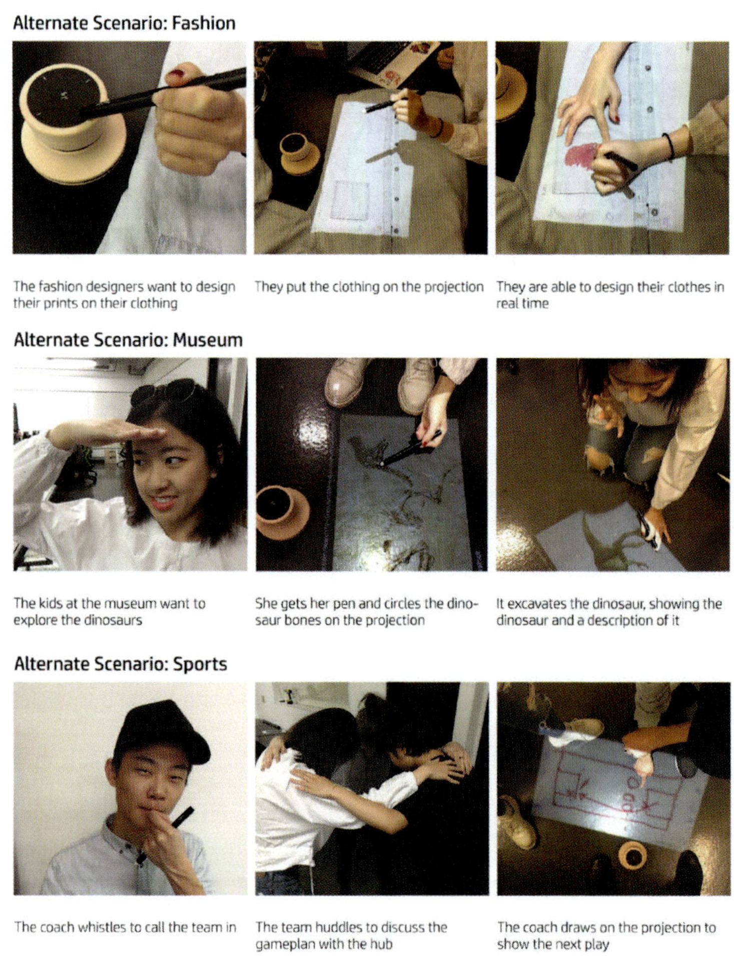

Figure 13.1
Alternate applications for an idea brainstorming system for the workplace (from Cosmos, by Team Laundry, used by kind permission of Asli Akdemir, Lynn Lei, Nathan Lu, and Yozei Wu).

used by players on a sports team? How about construction workers, or actors in a play? If the system is for a video conference between two people or just a few, how could it handle a conference of twenty? Asking these questions expands our scope, challenges the robustness of our system, and broadens its intended use.

Alternates are useful in making our system robust, but be careful! We should not be modifying our system to satisfy these cases at the expense of our primary or secondary cases (our critical alternates). If we find ourselves changing things because of a less important case, we need to assess whether that change at best improves our primary and secondary cases, or, at the very least, does not inhibit them. If they are negatively affected in any way, we may have to abandon it. Be sensitive to the fact that even the simple addition of a single piece of information or the addition of one more step in a task could have a profound adverse effect on usability. Alternates should strengthen and make our critical cases more usable.

Wireframe the interfaces and information that these alternate flows should contain. Do they enhance or detract from the critical cases? If they detract, what could be done that would make them enhance the primary and secondaries?

13.6 INFRASTRUCTURE USERS

Let's expand our scope further by looking at yet another user type: the infrastructure user. An infrastructure user is one whose primary task is to create, maintain, or add to the infrastructure of the system beyond that of the intermediate or expert consumer. This includes individuals who add or edit stories on a news site, maintain the inventory on a product site, or a real estate agent when they're gathering new listings for their clients. These are not consumers of the information they deal with, but are the managers of that information.

Does your system require infrastructure users? If so, consider their level of technical skill. For example, those who maintain inventory systems would probably be hired with a specific set of skills to be able to operate that system. On the other hand, a real estate agent is not going to spend their time learning your system when they could be working on sales leads. The presentation of the interface for the inventory specialist would be focused more on function, while the one for the real estate agent would still have function, but be simplified and have a greater emphasis on form.

As we can see with users such as the real estate agent, it may be unclear whether they are an expert user or an infrastructure user. Dispense with getting all wrapped up in the nuance between the two. The importance of the concept of the infrastructure user is to prompt us to consider who else is necessary for the system to run besides our primary target, and asking whether we should be designing interfaces specifically for them.

What are the infrastructure features that need to keep your system running? What is the information necessary for those features and the goals of the users who supply or maintain that information? In the same way we developed design approaches for our primary use case and critical alternates, do this for your infrastructure users as well.

In terms of the wireframe flowboard, we usually depict infrastructure users on a separate board than that for our consumers. Often the system looks very different from their perspective, so we capture it in its own board as if it were a different system. Although infrastructure users may have a more professional posture with respect to our system than a consumer, they are people too, so we should considerately apply our aesthetic to them as well. However, it will probably be more reserved and more targeted at a skilled professional user. The aesthetics should hark back to our brand values, but may be a more professional extension of it.

13.7 CONSUMER STAKEHOLDERS

Let's expand our consideration yet again to include not just those who are our users, but those who may be affected by it as well. These are our consumer stakeholders (Figure 13.2). It's clear that the user's wants and needs are critical to the system, but why should we consider anyone else? Because our user's behavior may be affected by these people. As the main user, I may love to use Apple Pay, but I can only use it at stores that adopt it. If the store owner doesn't want it, it doesn't matter how much I like it, I won't be able to use it. Consumer stakeholders are important in this sense.

Figure 13.2
Stakeholder personas for airport wayfinding system (from Xeno, by Team HA+CH, used by kind permission of Cindy Hu, Andrew Lee, Harry Teng, and Harmonie Tsai).

Who are your consumer stakeholders? What is their role with respect to your target user or your system? How do they affect your target user? Are they system users as well? If so, what is their experience with the system? Our analysis of stakeholders allows us to consider possible entry points into our system that may not have been considered if we merely looked at its primary target audience. If these are users as well, we must treat them as such by identifying a set of goals for them and a resultant set of features. If they are not, but are affected by the use of the system, we don't need to go to that extent, but we will need to keep these individuals in our minds as we set about the process of design. Regardless of the role they play, it's essential to make their characteristics quickly readable by supplying an image, role name, and description for each as shown in Figure 13.2). Giving them a little personality as well will make them more realistic and memorable.

What are our stakeholder's scenarios? How do they fit into our picture? These scenarios may not have the same depth as a complete user scenario—in fact, they may look more like magic moments—but building scenarios for them allows us to become empathetic with them. They need to be considered, too, especially if the success of our system relies upon their involvement or favorable impression of it.

13.8 EXTREME CASES

We tend to consider alternate cases where our system is functioning well. What about times when it's not? These are your error, extreme, or fringe cases (Cooper, 2015, p. 257). They push our system into extreme situations. What happens when a navigation system has no GPS signal? What happens when the social network can't reach the internet? What happens when the power shuts down on our primary device while a user is editing information?

We like to think that our systems work as expected all the time. But rarely is that the case. Users do odd things. They don't click on buttons in the order we'd like, or they pound on them several times in succession out of frustration. Users don't read instructions. They go down paths we hadn't expected. How do we gracefully catch them and lead them back to where they should go, or design our system to not break when something happens unexpectedly?

We've all experienced people who can't figure out an interface: They may be an older member of our family, a child, or simply someone who is insecure with the basic interaction behaviors of a particular device or context. People who have a difficult time with technology often feel stupid when they don't interact with a system in a way the designers expect. As we've previously mentioned, we designers should flip this perception: If an inexperienced user has trouble with our system, it's not their fault, but ours.

Think of the myriad ways users can get lost. When they do, let's not berate them, but design a considerate way that gracefully catches them and gets them back on track (Cooper, 2015, p. 180). In this way, it's instructive to show our interface designs to someone who has trouble with technology. I consider these people experts in usability: They will show us problems with our interface quicker than any digital native ever could. Even though they may not be our target audience, see how a senior uses your system, or a child. They are experts at showing us what doesn't work.

Recall the toddler test we referred to earlier in the book: Toddlers have an uncanny ability to discover ways of using things that we would never imagine. Adults are too well educated in the world so that even the clumsiest user carries with them at least a little knowledge of the way things work. If a toddler knows how to use it, everyone will.

How do we depict these fringe cases presented by errors or non-standard users? We use our wireframe flowboard, but these cases often do not easily conform to the graceful flow of our system. For example, losing a GPS signal can happen anywhere at any time, an insecure user can hammer on a button several times, or a toddler can put one of our devices into their mouths. To use a developer term, we call these interrupts: events that interrupt the normal operation of the system. We usually list the flows associated with these error or fringe cases on the bottom of the flowboard, disconnected to anything else. We clarify the events that trigger them, and then depict the use case resultant from that trigger. These may be a simple dialog box or a more complicated user flow.

13.9 HANDLE EXTREMES WITH GRACE

After considering extreme uses of your system and the events that trigger them, we should weigh whether effort needs to be placed into creating specific designs for that extreme. Indeed, fix the low hanging fruit: Those situations that either improve or have little or no adverse effect on our critical cases while being very inexpensive to implement. For more expensive adjustments—either in terms of effort or design complexity—we should consider whether creating a custom solution for that extreme case is worth the additional expense. If the problem will trip up many users, design for it. If not, let's consider a standard way of catching the error and leading users back to a correct path.

An example of gracefully handling error cases is Google Maps. When we're traveling, it's often the case that we'll lose our data connection. This means that we lose the ability to update the map we're using. Archaic systems used to solve this by having users purchase or download maps within an area manually. This required the device to store a lot of unused map information covering areas where users may never go as well as opening up the possibility that there would be only a blank screen if the user went outside of that area. Neither of these was very user-friendly.

Google Maps allows downloads, too, but, in addition to that, it makes intelligent decisions about where we are and where we may want to go, and it downloads map details for those areas in the background, so we don't know that it's even doing it. It makes these predictions based on places that we've built routes for, searched for, or looked at in detail. In addition to this, if we try to use it for an area that it hasn't downloaded, it at least uses overview data to provide us a pixellated version of the place. It doesn't just stop and give us a blank screen.

In sum, Google's system is smart, or is as smart as it can be given the circumstances. It makes intelligent predictions. Creating this intelligence certainly did not come for free. I'm quite sure they employed several developers to solve this, but they did so because they assessed that travelers run into data connection problems constantly when they're on the go. And that is precisely the time we need a map. Paper maps are always "on"—they don't disappear when you move from spot to spot. To compete with paper, the digital map needs always to be "on," too.

13.10 SYSTEMIC ORCHESTRATION

Since we've expanded our scope, let's look at how these cases all work together as a system, in other words, let's look at their orchestration. All elements of a system—user types, devices, contexts, and their manifested interfaces—need to achieve three things: They need to be consistent, complementary, and continuous (Levin, 2014, p. 4). When we say consistent, we do not mean identical. We mean that there are elements within them that are shared and provide the user the impression that they are within the same system (Levin, 2014, p. 23).

Since functionality changes from context to context, consistency is often not achievable through functionality. We may have arrived, though, at a signature interaction that is consistent across all contexts. This takes a great deal of consideration to make it work while not feeling stilted or forced. It's tough, but entirely possible. Beyond signature interactions, consistency is most commonly achieved through aesthetics. A unified look and feel is necessary to achieve consistency, and is quite often completely sufficient.

What we mean by being complementary is that we need to recognize the difference between the contexts in our ecosystem, and leverage those differences in allowing our users to achieve their goals. Contexts can complement each other "either by collaborating as a connected group, controlling each other, or both" (Levin, 2014, p. 95).

Strava, for example, does not offer GPS recording on its website. That would be ridiculous, given that laptops commonly do not have GPS, nor would we be using our laptop during a bike ride, a run, or, for heaven's sake, a swim. On the mobile app, however, the GPS recording system is central. On the flip side, however, the mobile app context does not offer the level of information analysis that the website does. This is because the screen limitations of the mobile context make it rather difficult to present detailed data. GPS recording and information analysis happen in the contexts where they make sense and avoid contexts where they don't.

However, both Strava's mobile app and website present the activities of the user's followers. This underscores the third and final thing that needs to be achieved with our system: continuity. Think of this as seamlessly "passing the baton" from one context to the next (Levin, 2014, p. 53). It isn't enough merely to look at each context in isolation; we need to look at how users go from context to context and smooth out the hiccups between them. To be seamless, we need to look at the seams.

Strava does this between website and mobile by presenting follower activities in each. This information is shared between them and provides a sense of continuity as we flow from one context to the next. Continuity often requires overlap. An even tighter impression of seamlessness is Apple's AirPlay where we can start listening to a song on our mobile and have it pick up on our speaker system when we go into the living room. This is not only overlapping information, but is also overlapping functionality.

User flows that travel from one context to the next are excellent at exposing these hiccups and provide us a framework within which to solve them. If you've been focusing on a single context, extend beyond it and demonstrate how your intermediate user can achieve their goals by flowing through all the critical contexts of your system and engaging in their most important complementary features. Previously, we introduced the concept of the "systemic" primary use case. This is what we mean here. Again, look at the systemic user flow in Figure 9. 7. This depicts a primary use case flow across several contexts, which allows us to consider the "seams" between contexts to smooth them out and inspire delightful ways of going from one context to the next. We want our system to be as "seamless" as possible. We do that by refining the seams, or handoffs.

When considering other use cases, respect the solutions we developed for the primary use case. One of the reasons we detailed this case first was to be able to apply what we learned to other areas of the system. Are there examples that can be drawn from our original primary use case that can be applied to our other cases? Can we use our work on our primary to arrive at signature interactions that seem natural to each context, yet consistent across them? It's all right if we can't—certainly don't force this—but it's an appropriate question to explore at this stage. Indeed, taxonomies, copy, tone, branding, and aesthetics will be consistent, but it's interesting to consider whether certain interactions, behaviors, and functionality can be shared as well.

13.11 INTERACTION FLOWBOARDS

The presentation framework that best depicts the structure of our system is a flowboard. It can highlight the main user flows of the system, the primary and secondary cases, as well as alternates and extremes. It can also depict error or fringe cases as interrupts. When we expanded our system from our primary use case to consider critical alternates, simple alternates, and extremes, we should also have been considering the microinteractions along these paths. Previously, when we added microinteraction detail to our primary use case, we schematicized these behaviors and added them to the primary user flow. We should be doing the same for the newly considered flows along our expanded scope. Integrating these into our flowboard results in what we call an interaction flowboard (Figure 13.3). These mid-fidelity wireframes in turn lead to more polished designs within flowboards such as that depicted in Figure 10.11.

To properly create an interaction flowboard, consider and refine the user flow along the primary use case first, then consider the microinteractions along the secondary cases, the alternates, and then the extremes. Use this order to prioritize the importance of the ease of use of each of the flows. In addition, make sure that emergency cases are well thought out: those that rarely if ever happen, but when they're needed they need to work. Finally, balance the microinteractions to arrive at a proper orchestration, prioritizing those that are most critical, and then

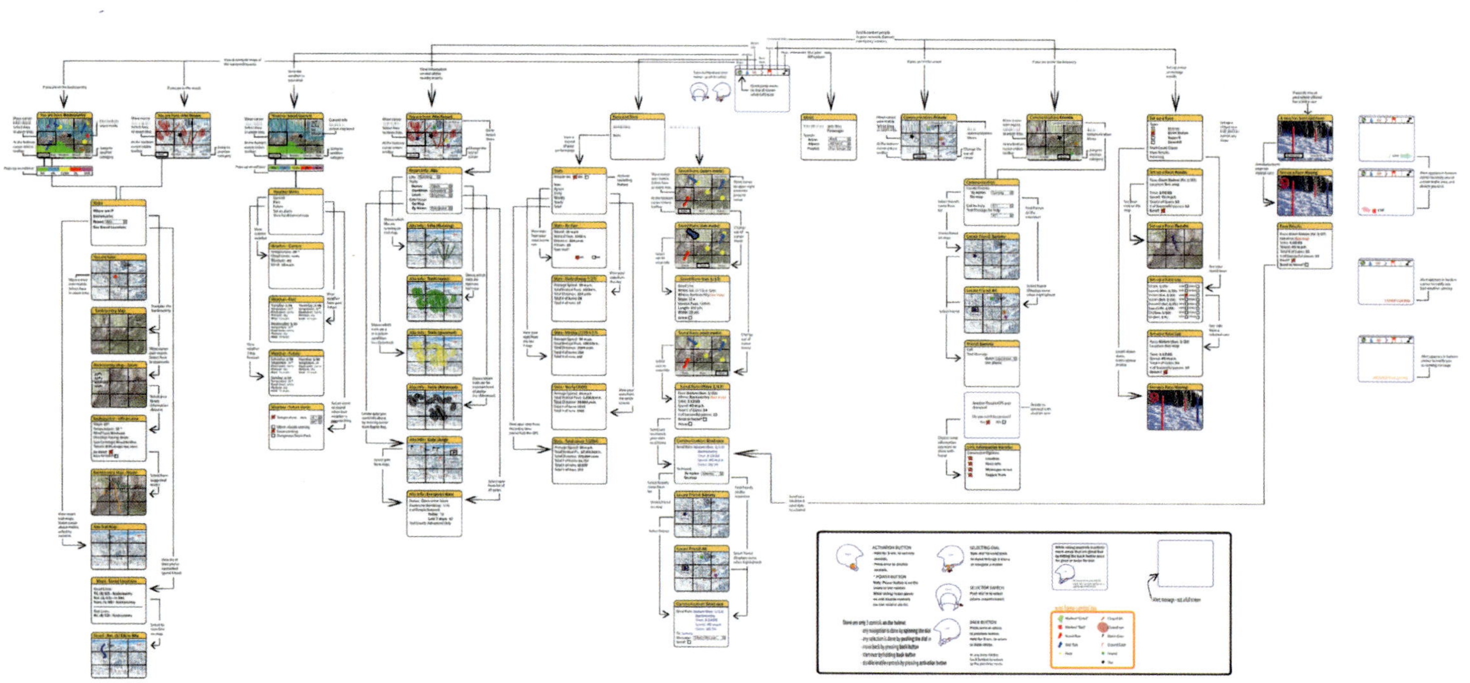

Figure 13.3
From Traverse GPS, by Katy Dill, used by kind permission of Katy Dill.

lay out the quiescent states and their associated microinteractions onto an interaction flowboard. There should be one flowboard for each context and each conceptually distinct target user, such as our primary user vs. an infrastructure user.

Use appropriate factorial iteration when doing the above process. Don't expect to get it right the first time with high-fidelity wireframes. Explore first with lo-fidelity interfaces; consider returning to 3 x 5 cards and a big surface to arrange things, such as a wall or floor. The cards can contain not only interfaces, but microinteraction schematics as well. Consider how each user flow affects, and can be orchestrated with, the others. Refine them, and arrange them into interaction flowboards. Then increase the fidelity and consider them further. Your ultimate goal is to eventually arrive at the interaction flowboards for each context and user type that covers the main flows of your system. The process of scope expansion works hand in hand with agile methods where your team identifies aspects of the system to extend, designs it, develops it, releases it, and assesses its use. Becoming familiar with the agile process should help your scope expansion efforts tremendously.

This effort is time consuming, requires a great deal of creativity and brain power, and is often fraught with frustration when we see that a particular interaction on which we've spent a great deal of time may not work. But this should also be thrilling, because what you are doing is the essence of Interaction Design. Spend the time to make it right, and enjoy the process.

13.12 AESTHETIC EXPANSION

As we expand our scope, we should also expand our aesthetic effort. You may be tasked with the responsibility of doing this now, or may need to do it in the context of an agile sprint several months from now, but, in either case, we should be well equipped for this effort. We created a set of style frames and a style guide just for this purpose. Yourself, or any capable aesthetic designer, should be able to take these and apply that look and feel to the rest of the interfaces in the system.

13.13 USE CASE PROTOTYPING

Just as when we were prototyping our primary use case, it's also an integral part of the process to prototype our expanded use cases. But don't jump right into high fidelity use case prototypes or animations immediately. Use proper factorial iteration techniques by developing low-fidelity explorations first, then mid-fidelity. Start with paper prototypes and scratch assets. Then move on to structural prototypes to test things further. Finally, when you have weeded out most of the fundamental problems, then consider creating spot prototypes of your microinteractions and begin using tools where you can prototype their behavior and dynamics. Finally, test your most important use cases by creating prototypes or animations of entire use cases: primary, secondary, alternates, extremes, errors, and emergencies.

14 Communication

We've covered hundreds of pages of process. At the end of it all, we need to deliver and present our work, but there's more to it than just delivering and presenting. We need to show that our design satisfies the objectives that launched the project in the first place. And to help convince people that our design has quality, our final presentation needs to have quality, too. It should be slick, clear, and succinct.

The final presentation is not the time to discuss in detail our design process and every feature we developed along the way. If questions and concerns arise that we considered, certainly discuss them, but stay focused that your presentation is about the final results. Our audience wants to know the final design. Give them the big picture first, and if they would like further detail, they will more than likely bring up a litany of questions at the end of the presentation.

Recall that, at the very beginning of this project, we had the design brief. It outlined what the project team was being tasked to do. We brainstormed concepts related to that brief and arrived at a handful that we researched further. That research led to the identification of a market position and a target market, which, in turn, led to a strategic vision for the project. We verified our hypotheses by researching potential users and allowed that investigation to further our understanding of the design challenge we faced. That vision steered the creation of an approach which was the foundation of our system architecture, our device ecosystem, our interface design, its branding, behavior, and aesthetic design. In a nutshell, this is what we've done, and this is essentially what our final presentation needs to deliver.

We could spend hours talking about this, but our audience most likely has only minutes. We need to be simple, clear, direct, and engaging about how we went from brief to design. We need to show how everything conceptually links up, ties together, and points back to the design brief that kicked everything off.

The structure is fairly straightforward: Allow for a brief framing of the design challenge and the requirements, and then give the stage to the scenario which helps our audience understand the context of our solution. After that, we can present other features and details that may not have been contained in our scenario, and conclude by clarifying how our solution ultimately satisfied the project objectives. We'll see ways of doing this in this chapter.

14.1 FRAMING THE CHALLENGE

We should start our presentation by framing the challenge we faced. There are undeniably several ways to do this, but we have seen the most success with a presentation method that includes the following set of steps:

1. State the important points about the design brief: those with the greatest impact on the final design. These are the themes that should have been reflected throughout the entire process.
2. Present the most important findings of the research process. These are usually the positioning matrix, our top findings from the user research, and the definition of the target market. Briefly state how these were determined based on the research, and point out the most important findings that had an impact on the final design.

3. Present how the research led to the project's strategy. Specifically, how it motivated the expression of the project's mission, how it led to the identification of the goals it should satisfy for the target, and, most importantly, how it led to the design criteria.
4. Briefly clarify the overall approach to the solution in terms of its most high-level features and contexts, and how this approach satisfied the project's mission, user goals, and criteria.

Bear in mind that framing the challenge should be quick: five minutes max and two minutes is better. And it should be backed up with visuals. We've made all these visuals along the way; they just need a unified look to tie them together.

In our design process, we did a plethora of things that led from our approach into a final design, but avoid going into detail about these nuances at this point in the presentation. The best way to communicate our design is to show it. Do not belabor framing the design any longer. We've framed it. Now deliver the design.

14.2 DELIVER THE DESIGN

Often, when designers talk about their designs, they talk about the design's features. It does this thing or that thing, and this stuff over here does this tricky maneuver. Aren't I smart and clever? No, you're not. If this is a final presentation, you're blowing it.

Show the design. If we're smart and clever, it will be right there in front of us. The best way to show the design? We've been doing it throughout the entire process, so there's no reason to stop now: the scenario. It allows our audience to enter the details of the design from the perspective of human experience, allowing them to connect with the system's intricacies quickly.

But this is no longer the detailed design scenario we've been using to tease out the elements of the design. We must transform our design scenario into a pitch scenario, the goal of which is to communicate the system's most salient experiences and provide context. Pitch scenarios are concise and engaging, yet infused with enough detail to provide a sense that we've been comprehensive and our audience can see clearly how it could fit into the user's life.

If we are presenting this in the flesh, often the most impressive way to communicate the scenario is to perform it, especially if our experience prototypes are somewhat functional. One of the drawbacks of this is the audience's inability to see interface details, but this is often mitigated with projections or alternative displays.

High-quality scenario videos of the primary use case are also effective, and with good cinematics. Rely on one image, one idea, cause and effect, use establishing shots, over-the-shoulders, and especially close-ups. A scenario video is also advisable if we are presenting solo: It's tough to play all the characters of a performance all at once. But keep in mind that videos can be cold and sterile when shown in a physical presentation. A lively presentation that then shifts to a monitor for several minutes kills the energy we've established. A way to avoid this is to remove any captioning from the video and narrate it live. This injects our humanity back into what would have been a cold and sterile video presentation.

If you do choose to narrate a video live, take measures to control the timing. Often, the time it takes us to describe something, and the time it takes to show it are vastly different. Descriptions are often longer, leading to situations where the presenter is playing catchup with the video. We have witnessed many an excellent design destroyed by bad timing. Pausing the video to finish what we're saying is a possible solution, but better is to shave up the video into short yet complete ideas, placing the segments into a presentation stack, such as Keynote or PowerPoint, and clicking through them as we speak. This allows the video to stop automatically at points we've prepared in advance, avoids having us reach for the pause button while we're talking, and allows us to use a presentation remote so we can move about the stage.

Regardless of the method we decide to use—a performance or a video presentation—a pitch scenario video should be a required delivery. It may not be shown in the final presentation, but invariably the project leadership will want something to take away that they can show others. A scenario video is just that thing.

Remember, this is a pitch scenario, so a detailed depiction of every microinteraction is not necessary. A few to provide verisimilitude is ample. People lose interest in only a few minutes so set a time limit of only five minutes or less for delivering the scenario. At the risk of being redundant, remember that the pitch scenario is not a design scenario; it's about delivering the big picture of the system's features and contexts.

14.3 DESIGN DETAILS

After the scenario has been presented, we have now provided the introduction of our solution necessary to communicate the system's features and details. The reason why it's bad form to go into design details before the scenario is that our audience needs context before they see details. Otherwise, they will become lost and confused. The scenario gives them that context.

Additional features and system details can be given as a collection of short scenarios or even magic moments. Our audience should know contextually what is going on at this point, so it's acceptable to show interface details without going into a full-blown scenario. Use cases and user flows could be sufficient for this. Take care, however: if context is critical and still somewhat unclear, a short scenario may still be necessary.

We will most likely not have time to present every nuance and detail, so we should focus on those that directly satisfy the features leading back to our approach and our design criteria. These should be the ones the primary stakeholders are most interested in. We can certainly integrate others but keep an eye trained on the time. Show them if time allows, leave them for the question and answer period if not.

Possible features to highlight at this stage are the overall organization of the system, its signature interactions, gesture languages, and how well these are considered for our user's primary postures; we spent a great deal of time in our design process developing our aesthetic approach so it's important to discuss how we developed our brand values and how our aesthetic approach satisfies those values. Certainly, feel free to present other aspects of note if time allows. Yes, if there ever is a point in the presentation where we can show how smart and clever the design is, this is it.

14.4 CONCLUSIONS

We should not just stop our presentation dead in its tracks at the end. We should take the opportunity to conclude it gracefully. Often, we are at a loss for what to say at the end, but if we consider what we are striving to do with our presentation, it should come into focus: We are communicating how our design satisfies what we were tasked to do in the first place. We may think that the audience can see how our framing of the problem, our scenario, and our presentation of the design details satisfied this, but that's being lazy. Draw the connections for them. A little clarity never hurts anyone.

Our framing of the design challenge initiated the connection between our design criteria and the project brief through our research, strategy, and approach.

But what our audience didn't have at that point were the details of our solution. Now they do. In our conclusion, we should repeat the connection between the brief and our design criteria, and clarify explicitly how aspects of our design deliver on that criteria. It's up to them to determine if our assertions are true or not, but at least we've made the best case we can.

As you can see, the lynchpin of this approach is the design criteria. If the framing of the challenge at the beginning of our presentation created a clear connection between the project brief, our mission, and the criteria, what we need to do in conclusion is draw a connection between the features of our design and those criteria. This should tie everything up into a nice package for our audience.

14.5 INSTALLATIONS

Invariably, our audience will have questions, and there are important materials to present that are not best delivered in a brief final presentation. This is where installations come in. After concluding the presentation, it's effective to retire to an environment that stages the presentation materials and adds those that we weren't able to present, such as our wireframe flowboard, our journey map, our style guide, and a full complement of our aesthetic designs. This is also a good place to stage a video loop of our pitch scenario followed by a video presentation of our design details.

Although we may be present at our installation to field questions and remarks, it's best to design it with the assumption that we may not be there. It should communicate those important aspects of the design on its own. This means that we need to ensure that the flow of the communication across the installation is clear and the message is well orchestrated. Deliver your message by considering how someone approaches your installation: Some images are effective at a distance to draw us in. They can provide us an overview at about five to ten meters out. Then there are those presentation frameworks that require us to be close up. These are the ones that deliver the details.

Since we should be designing our installation to be stand-alone, any videos being presented should reflect this and be stand-alone as well. They should also work well with the audio off. This means the story should be communicated visually, and captioned with only brief phrases that describe the action. If we created our pitch scenario to show and not tell—as if it were a silent movie—it should do this already with a few brief title cards inserted here and there for clarity.

Let's address audio a little more. It can be used for the installation, but it should be of an ambient nature that enhances, and not distracts, from the real star: the design. Please bear in mind that audio may repeat over and over and over and may make your audience, your neighbors, and you go completely crazy. This will not serve anyone's purpose very well. Having an extremely long ambient track or playlist that doesn't repeat may allow people to retain their sanity. Also, take care about using any music with a vocal track. Vocals are distracting and add a layer of meaning to the installation that may have unintended consequences. We advise avoiding vocals altogether.

The installation should attract from a distance, yet also be an effective environment to answer questions and deliver the fine details of the design. It should be able to stand on its own without us. Take care to recognize that the installation itself is not the hero. Our design is. Anything that overwhelms that message is a distraction. The environmental design of the installation should sit in the background and serve up the design as the foreground.

14.6 FINAL PRESENTATION DEVELOPMENT

The above states what we are trying to achieve with our final presentation, but getting there doesn't happen overnight. It takes a great deal of hard work and solid focus to achieve a high caliber design presentation. Give it the attention it deserves: The final presentation should be considered a design in and of itself. It needs good concept, exploration, preparation, production, exquisite presentation, and should be coupled with a well-organized final delivery. Yet, just as our design's interface shouldn't draw attention to itself, but serve up the content of our system, so, too, the design of our presentation shouldn't draw attention to itself but serve up our design. Now that we have a broad picture as to how our presentation is to be structured, let's discuss in a little detail issues and concerns that relate to the materials we create for it.

14.6.1 Presentation Preproduction

One of the most time-consuming items to produce for your final presentation is also the thing that has the greatest impact: the pitch scenario. As previously mentioned, the pitch scenario is based on, yet is different from, the primary use case scenario we've been using to design our system. Certainly, one of the differences is that it uses final assets in the way of final interfaces, device designs, and high-quality visuals, but also it's a version of our primary use case that may only touch upon some of the interaction details, but not all. It is not a deep dive into every click and drag of the system. Show that detail briefly, then get out of it. This is because the final pitch is usually a brief affair. If the project stakeholders agree with our design, then we will have more than enough time to deliver the details. If we've put them to sleep or scared them with complexity, we may not even see approval.

14.6.2 Pitch Scenario

Put your primary use case scenario on a slight diet. Reduce it down to the essentials of the user's experience. Introduce some interaction detail, but then quickly get back to the human level. Show a few of the most clever features, but don't wax encyclopedic. To make things quick, sketch or photograph a storyboard of the new "scenario on a diet": the pitch scenario (Figure 14.1).

In preparation for the production of our pitch scenario, we should consider the kind of style we'd like it to have. We should conduct research that leads us to the visual inspiration that can guide us. This, in turn, should lead us to explore a set of possibilities for its style. We should execute a few frames from our scenario in our chosen style to test that we know how to achieve that look (Figure 14.2).

Figure 14.1
Excerpt of a photographed pitch scenario storyboard (from Cosmos, by Team Laundry, used by kind permission of Asli Akdemir, Lynn Lei, Nathan Lu, and Yozei Wu).

Figure 14.2
Various styles for pitch scenarios by teams Face It, Remora, Aura, Rytm, Cora, and Respire (Face It: Leah Demeter, Yenju Lai, and Fred Tsai; Remora: Shane Li, Victoria Lin, Peter Santos, and Kuan Yu; Aura: Margo Dunlap and Vanessa Gu; Rytm: Kim Chow, Sherry Chen, and Kenneth Tay; Cora: Christina Hsu, Andy Cooper, and Rachel Goldinger; Respire: Wendy Wang and Katarzyna Burzynska. Used by kind permission of the creators).

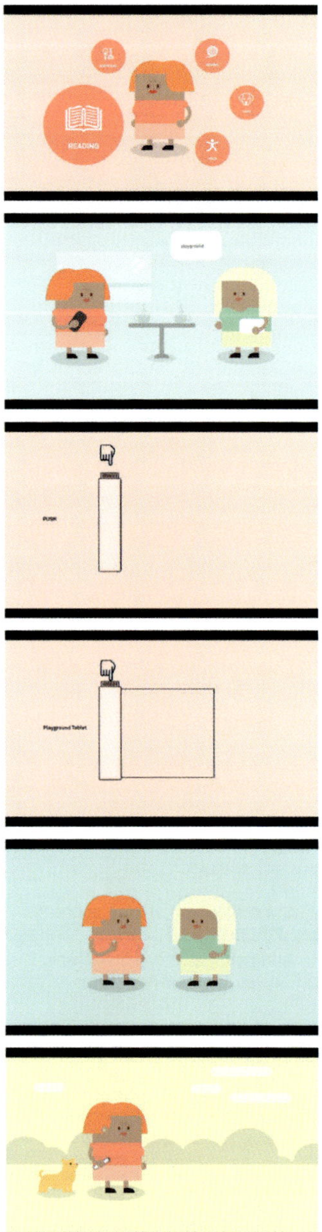

Figure 14.3
Commercial breaks should be distinct, yet supportive of the theme of the pitch (from Playground by Team WeeFee, used by kind permission of Caitlin Conlen, Cindy Hu, and Chase Morrison).

14.6.3 Commercial Breaks

There may be moments where we will need to break away from the main narrative of the scenario to explain a feature in a little more depth. We should not belabor these moments, but we should make them distinctive so as not to mar the flow of the story. We should approach these sections of a pitch scenario with a different "voice" than that of our main scenario. We affectionately call these "commercial breaks" since they act like a commercial in the middle of a TV show: They're different in style from the show, offer a different message, and allow the show to resume where it left off. Strive for these moments to be complementary: distinct, yet supportive of the main theme (Figure 14.3).

14.6.4 Pitch Scenario Script

The most successful scenarios rely as much as they can on image: The main storyline should be understood with the audio turned off. Yet, there are moments where we may need additional information to convey the narrative of our interaction. In these instances, it's appropriate to rely on a script.

Commonly, writing the script precedes the development of the storyboard, but, to accentuate the importance of image in telling the story, we advise that the script is written after the storyboard. If the story makes sense visually, then the script can be used to make it more concise or to add another layer of information. There are formatting formalisms in script writing, yet in Interaction Design we don't get too wound up about that—interaction designers are not filmmakers—whatever indicates what needs to be said is usually sufficient (Figure 14.4).

FINAL SCENARIO SCRIPT

Meet Frank.
Frank is a 37-year-old successful business man...

who has sacrificed his health and well being for money and progress.

Frank is at early high risk for heart disease. So his doctor recommends Effi.

Effi is a health monitoring system that can easily build Frank's health database and share it with his care team.

In the morning Effi's LifeBand notifies Frank that blood test testing is needed

Using his Effi Home Frank easily tests his blood in the com comfort of his PJs.

Once the test completes Effi Home sends Frank's results...

up to the Effi Cloud where they're securely stored.

Frank can then access his health database and view his results anytime of the day using his Effi's app.

As Frank moves about his day Effi's LifeBand tracks import important information to build a better overall picture of his health.

If Frank's vitals spike in an abnormal way Effi' is there to notify him

And when Frank has a health issue arise...

Effi Diagnosis can help Frank figure out what's going on...

through a series of questions and photos.

Effi cloud determines the severity of the diagnosis by using aggregated patient data to cross check against Franks health history and symptoms, and then determines if and who on Franks Care Team needs to be involved.

Using Effi Doc App Frank's care team specialist can access his information and determine the most effective treatment plan...

to send back to Frank

Frank can then follow the recommended treatment plan to get back in good health.

With Effi's guidance

Frank can begin making better informed decisions about his life...

and everything that affects his health.

With Effi, Frank has a new lease on life, and becomes one less health statistic

To get your own Effi talk with your doctor today.

Figure 14.4
Script development for a pitch scenario (from Effi, by Team Effi, used by kind permission of Wendy Wang, Java Amilari, and Quinton Larson).

Be careful, however, of what we call "the hegemony of the script." Just as we are not filmmakers, many of us are not actors either. If we're doing a live presentation, having to deliver a tightly detailed script where every word is precisely chosen may lead to a presentation crash and burn if our lines get flummoxed. Memorize the key points, and allow yourself the flexibility to say it in your terms. Flustering yourself during a presentation by turning pages while you're clicking through your scenario, and losing your place in a detailed script is a recipe for disaster. Use the script to design what you're going to say, memorize it by getting the gist of it, then as actors say, get off book: Throw the script away and proceed by memory or cue cards.

14.6.5 Final Storyboard, Slideshows, and Animatics

With a sketch scenario storyboard, a selected style (including a style for the commercial breaks), and a script, we may think we are ready for production. Slow down. The first thing we should do is create a storyboard of the entire pitch scenario in the final look. If we're engaging a filmmaker or animator, we should ask them to do this as well. We can use sketches to get the story down, but if it's to be animated, you should require a final storyboard that looks exactly like the final creation (Figure 14.5).

This final storyboard performs several essential functions: It tests whether the person doing the animation can execute the look throughout the movie; it provides a guide as to how long it takes to create an image that we can use for scheduling; and if the production of the movie misses the deadline of the pitch, by creating a slideshow of the storyboard we have a communication tool we can fall back on if the animator fails to deliver.

And don't disparage a slideshow as opposed to a fully animated scenario anyway. It may not have the wow factor of an animated or filmed sequence, but if the goal is to communicate the user experience and interaction to those unfamiliar with it, slideshows are completely effective. And they require a small percentage of the resources to produce than that of a fully animated movie.

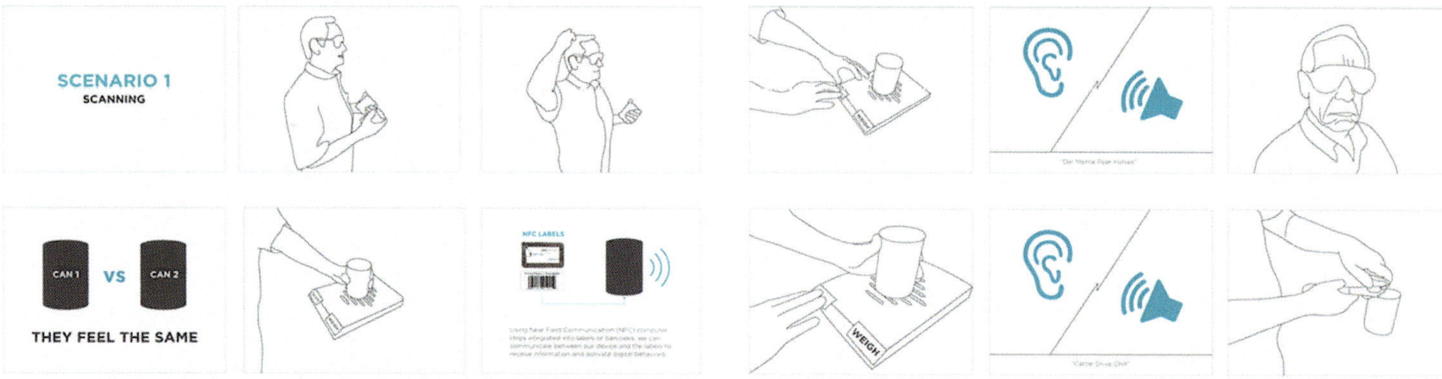

Figure 14.5

Excerpt of a final storyboard (from Culina Metra, by Team Culina Metra, used by kind permission of Katrina Hercules and Neal Smith).

Filmmakers and animators use storyboards to guide their work, so there's no reason to avoid them. They should be part of the process of creating the movie in the first place. We additionally suggest that designers create the slideshow of their storyboard anyway. In fact, in animation slideshows are made into movies themselves during the production process and are called animatics, and when animated sequences come in from the production team, they are inserted into the slideshow. The animatic becomes an important means of tracking the completion of the movie. There is no reason why interaction designers shouldn't be doing this too.

14.6.6 Installation Layout and Wall Art

If we are physically there to present our system, we should orchestrate how that is to be done. Explore installation possibilities by sketching a set of layouts (Figure 14.6). These explorations should take into account the allotted space, dimensions of the installation, and the various components that need to be there—such as a video, appearance models, interface comps, various forms of communication in wall art,

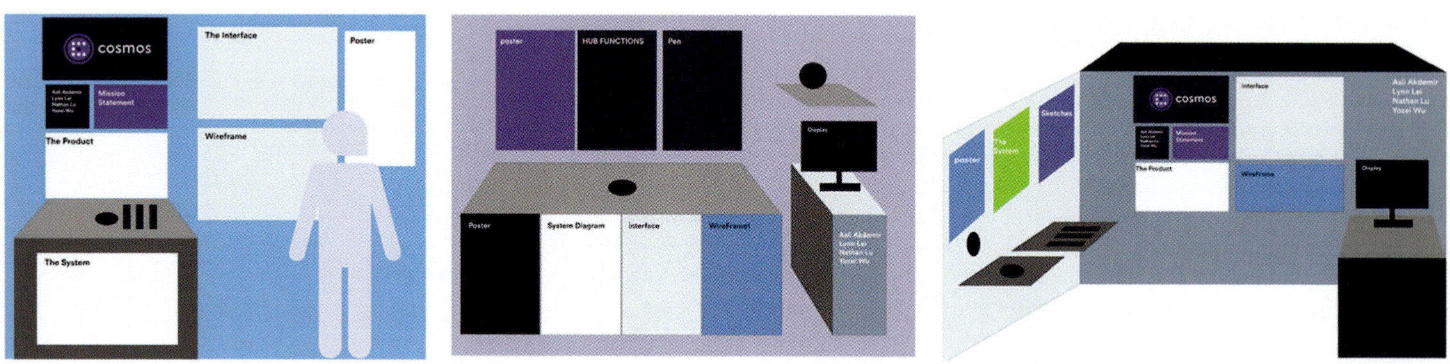

Figure 14.6

Installation layout approaches (from Cosmos, by Team Laundry, used by kind permission of Asli Akdemir, Lynn Lei, Nathan Lu, and Yozei Wu).

and possibly experience prototypes. Include guides like a human silhouette to indicate scale. Also consider the viewpoint of your audience: What draws them in from far away? What keeps them coming closer when they're near? What provides them the precise information they need when they're close? How can we use scale, hierarchy, emotion, and information to achieve these goals?

In the same way that we addressed the style of our final scenario, we should address the style of our wall art. Explore possibilities and make sure they are symbiotic with other presentation elements. Once an installation approach or set of approaches is selected, and some of the assets we are presenting begin to take form, it's useful to insert these into our sketch layouts to see if they're working.

14.6.7 Final Flowboard

A challenging piece of wall art is the final flowboard. For some stakeholders, this provides essential information as to the structure and aesthetic design of the system. To others, it may cause information overload. Additionally, because of the amount of information it presents, flowboards are usually big, often dwarfing other pieces on the wall. To manage their impact, we suggest exploring methods of hiding the flowboard and revealing it when needed: Maybe it's on the back side of another piece of wall art that can be turned around, maybe it's on the back of a set of doors that display it when opened, and display something else when closed. Whatever the solution, be aware that presentation of the flowboard needs to be well considered with respect to your audience's wants and needs.

14.6.8 Production

Throughout our design process, we often explored a possibility, reflected on it, and revised it. Reflection was an integral part of the process, yet that is less the case now. Production is the time when we put our collective heads down and make it happen, whether it be for executing the detailed design, creating final interfaces from our style guide, or for creating the final communication. Take the approach that's been established, and turn the draft into the final product. There will certainly be moments where we will confront something we haven't encountered before, and we must explore a little and reflect on its solution, but not like before. We've done our thinking. This is about cranking it out.

The experience prototype must work and be functional within its role in the final communication for all relevant contexts that are presented (Figure 14.7). All assets

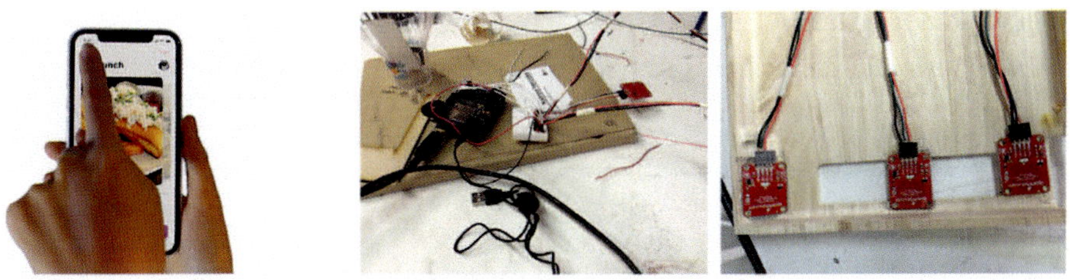

Figure 14.7
Experience prototypes: A virtual prototype and the electronics for one that is physical (from Subi, by James Chu, used by kind permission of James Chu).

need to be created, and sequences need to be shot (Figures 14.8 and 14.9). Final appearance models must be built, as well as the installation for the pitch presentation (Figures 14.10 and 14.11).

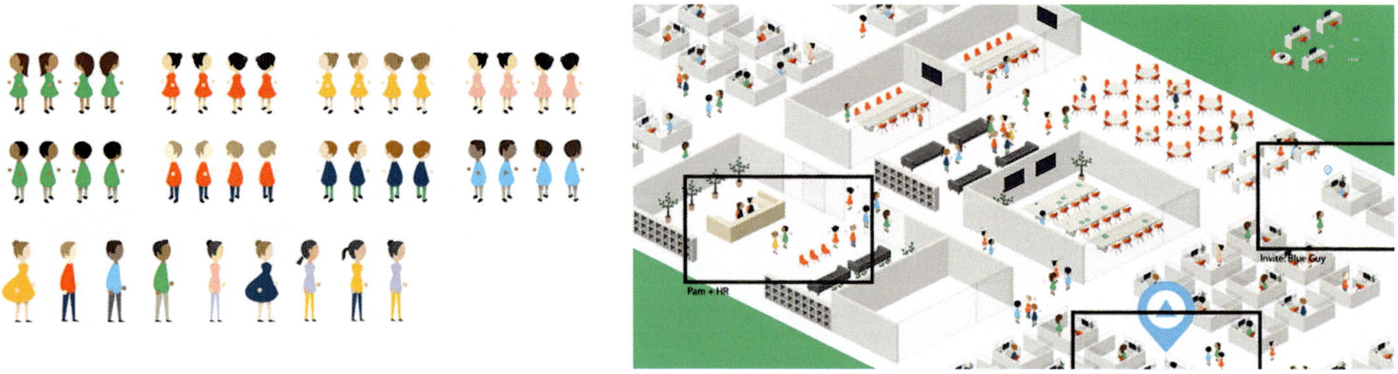

Figure 14.8
Production assets for an animated scenario (from Tink, by Team Brown, used by kind permission of Justin Babakian, Dennis Dang, Joe Tsao, and Ben Kasum).

Figure 14.9
Video production for a pitch scenario (from Knoq, by Team Cheeseburger, used by kind permission of James Chu, Chloe Kim, Juno Park, and Yidan Zhang).

Production takes time, so allow time for it. This is usually not something that happens overnight. Depending on the depth of the presentation, its sophistication, the number and skill of the production team, this could more often be in the realm of a few weeks as opposed to a few days. It happens consciously, methodically, and with planning and care. Let's now look into the role of each piece of our pitch.

14.7 ROLE OF THE INSTALLATION

The installation should frame the message, work on many levels of information delivery, and present the designs with as little confusion as possible (Figure 14.12). The best installations are clean frames for the system's design. Communicate the design, not your installation.

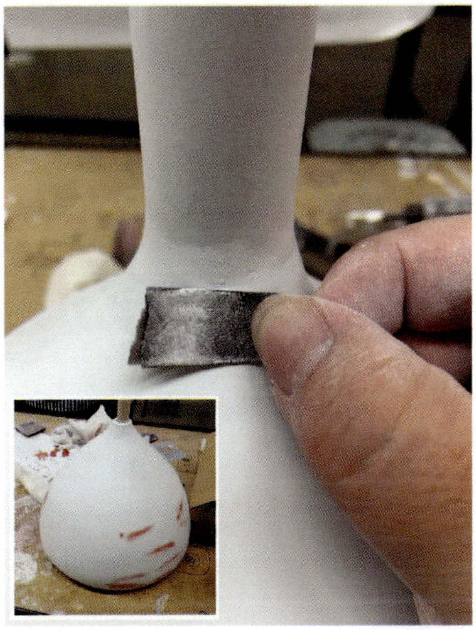

Figure 14.10
Making appearance models for the pitch installation (from Berry, by Team Porkbun, used by kind permission of Justin Nam and Daniel Smitasin).

Figure 14.11
Pitch installation construction (from Munio, by Team Wolf Pack, used by kind permission of Judy Chu, Tina Ou, Jane Park, and Jade Tsao).

Figure 14.12
Clean installation (from Effi, by Team Effi, used by kind permission of Wendy Wang, Java Amilari, and Quinton Larson).

14.8 ROLE OF THE WALL ART

The wall art should both attract from a distance and deliver detail when the audience is close up. We approach this from many different levels. Something more abstract and less informational can work to grab the eye from across a room (Figure 14.13). As our audience gets closer, they'd like to see what all the fuss is about. This is the role of the hero poster that depicts the system in use in its most salient fashion (Figure 14.14).

Figure 4.13
Artwork for distance communication should grab the eye (from Xeno, by Team HA+CH, used by kind permission of Cindy Hu, Andrew Lee, Harry Teng, and Harmonie Tsai).

Figure 4.14
The hero poster should inspire, yet also provide a sense of use (from Cosmos, by Team Laundry, used by kind permission of Asli Akdemir, Lynn Lei, Nathan Lu, Yozei Wu).

The next level may be taken by strategic imagery such as a concept board that illustrates the foundation of our strategic pyramid: What it is, who it's for, why they want to use it, and how it is used (Figure 14.15). This role can also be played to some extent by an ecosystem diagram (Figure 14.16). We can also supply a board underscoring our research findings if demonstrating a market is critical to our presentation (Figure 14.17).

Eventually, we present the designs themselves (Figures 14.18 and 14.19). Depending on the structure and goal of our presentation, we can lead with these, or lead with the more strategic imagery listed above. If we need to make the case as to why the system is needed, the strategic imagery may take precedence; if that case has already been made to our stakeholders, then the designs should be front and center.

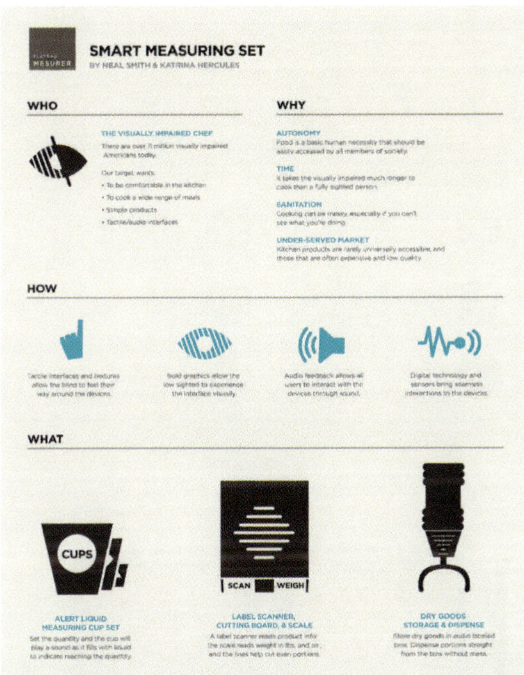

Figure 14.15
The concept board is for a closer read and delivers finer detail (from Culina Metra, by Team Culina Metra, used by kind permission of Katrina Hercules and Neal Smith).

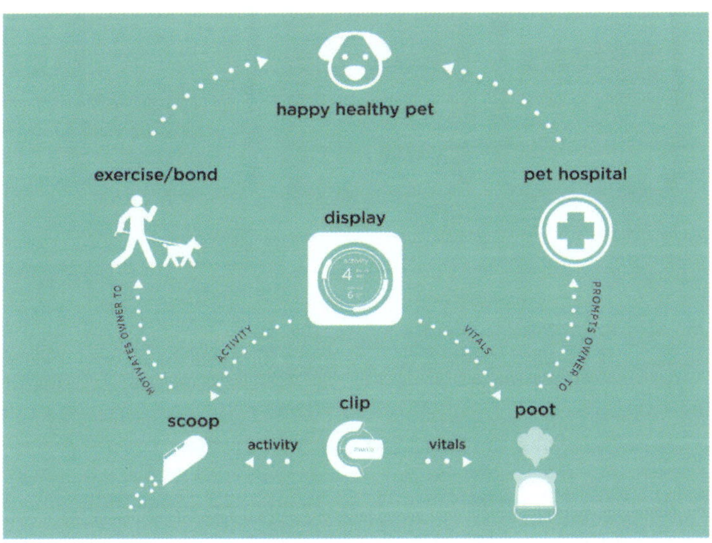

Figure 14.16
The ecosystem diagram provides a sense of the system's structure (from Munio, by Team Wolf Pack, used by kind permission of Judy Chu, Tina Ou, Jane Park, and Jade Tsao).

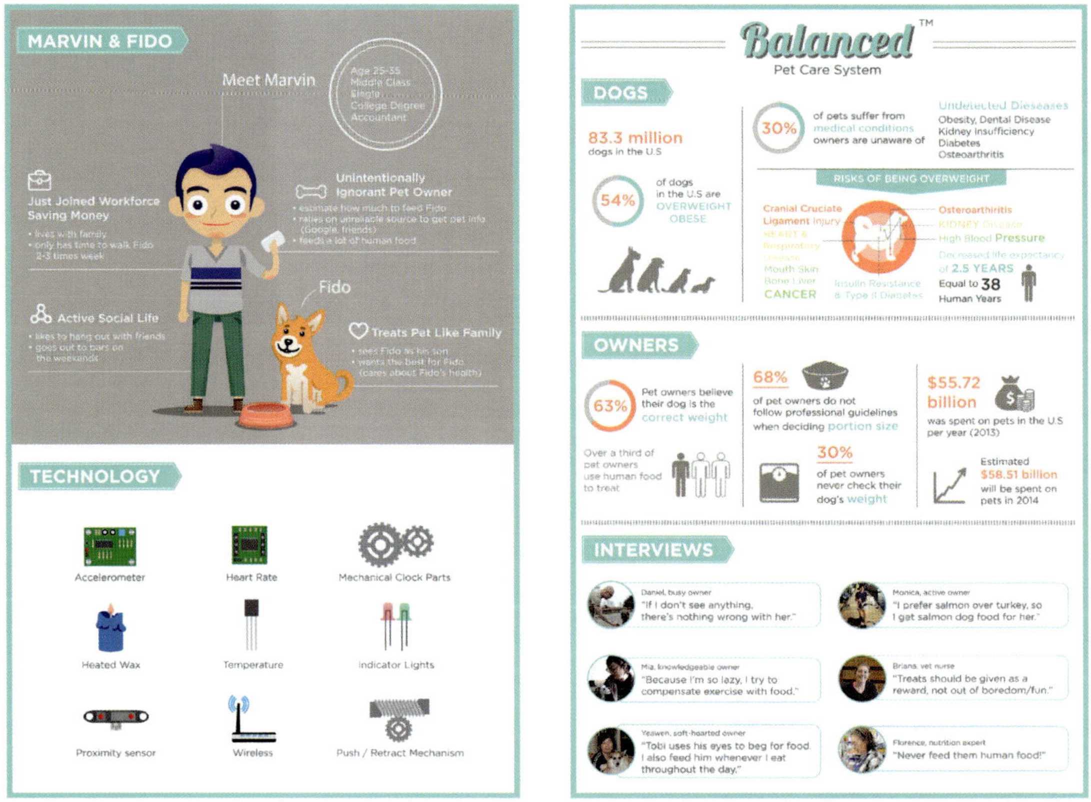

Figure 4.17
Research presentation for a pet care system (from Munio, by Team Wolf Pack, used by kind permission of Judy Chu, Tina Ou, Jane Park, and Jade Tsao).

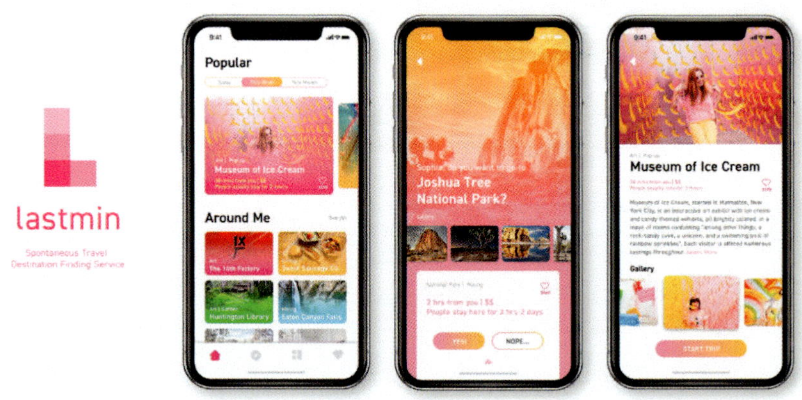

Figure 14.18
Using critical interfaces to present the design (from Lastmin, by Chufan Huang, used by kind permission of Chufan Huang).

The finest level of informational granularity in wall art is taken by either the flowboard or a storyboard presentation of the scenario (Figures 14.20 and 14.21). For wall art, the scenario could be simplified to the bare essentials, as long as it's backed up with a detailed video or slideshow within the presentation itself (Figure 14.22). These both require time and engagement on the part of the audience to fully understand, so that audience must be a motivated group: They want to know how it works and how it fits together. If we also have a screen depicting a stand-alone scenario, the scenario board may be superfluous.

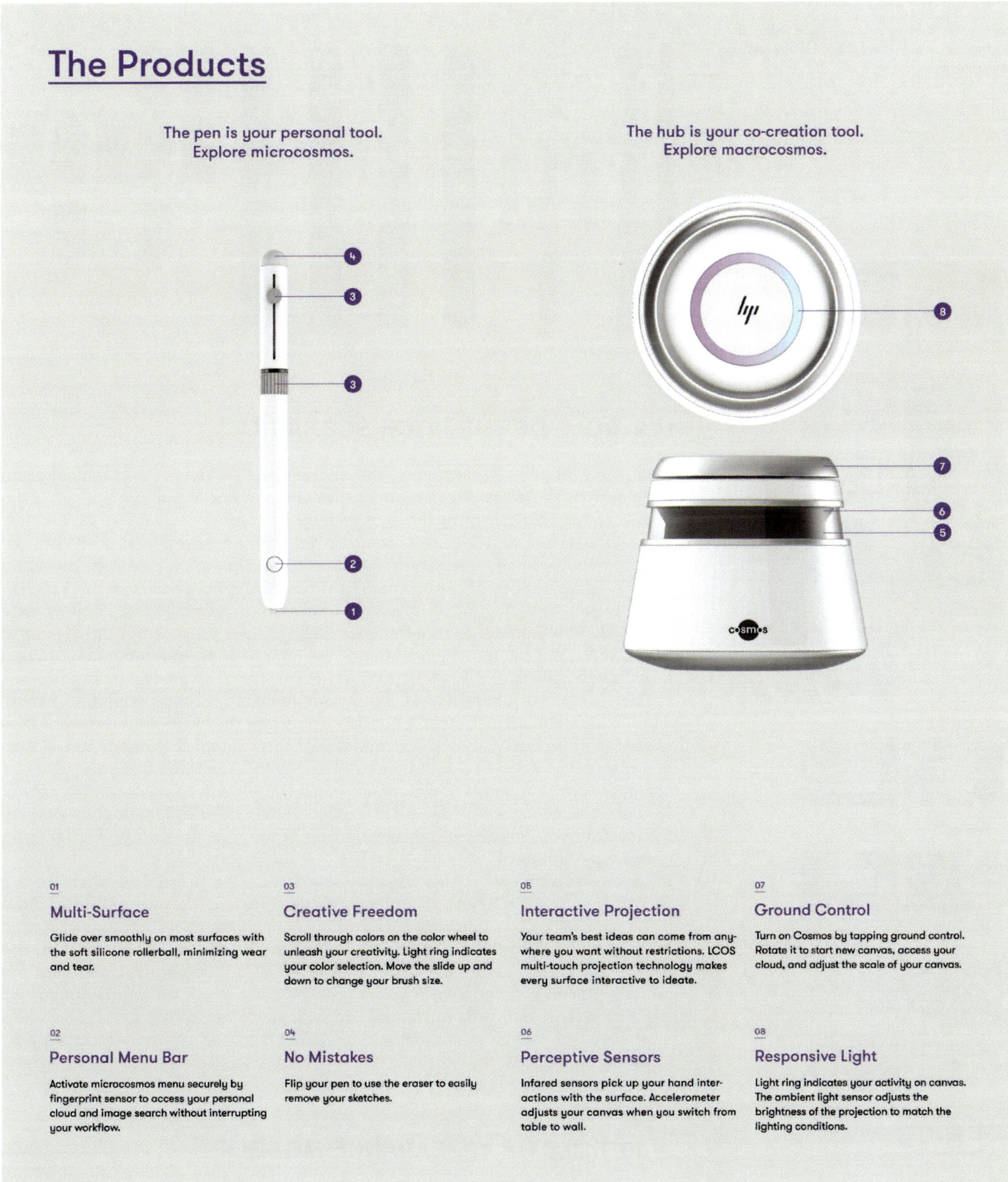

Figure 14.19
A product board indicates the aesthetics and features of the physical products (from Cosmos, by Team Laundry, used by kind permission of Asli Akdemir, Lynn Lei, Nathan Lu, and Yozei Wu).

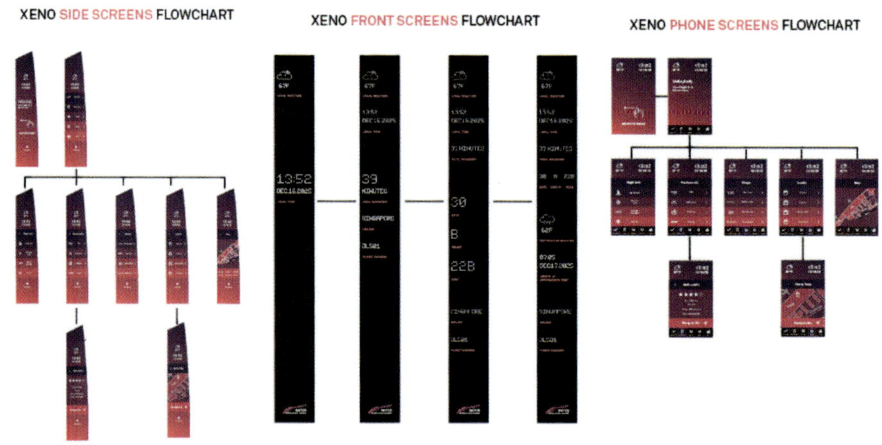

Figure 14.20
A final flowboard depicts the interface structure (from Xeno, by Team HA+CH, used by kind permission of Cindy Hu, Andrew Lee, Harry Teng, and Harmonie Tsai).

14.9 ROLE OF THE PITCH SCENARIO

While, for a physical presentation, the installation can frame the communication of the system as well as providing design details and ancillary information, it is the pitch scenario that performs the heavy lifting of communicating the experience. As mentioned before, the pitch scenario is not a design scenario. It does not contain the minute detail necessary to consider for design. It's a means of providing the uninitiated a sense of context as well as how the system solves its central challenge. Details are included to give an expression of verisimilitude, communicate any signature features, and give the impression that we've done our due diligence as designers, but pitch scenarios are not the time to show the entire breadth and depth of our design.

They can just as effectively be illustrated, animated, photographed, or filmed, yet their style should be carefully considered so that they work with the rest of the presentation, as well as being appropriate for the content that needs to be communicated. If you don't have the time or budget for your pitch scenario to be in a cinematic form (animated or filmed), it's much better for it to be photographed or be illustrated stills at a high degree of execution than to be cinematic at lower quality. Consider your resources, time being one of the most important, and execute accordingly (Figure 14.23).

There are often two types of pitch scenarios: One presented when we are there giving the pitch, and the other presented when we are not. They differ in the sense that the one presented when we are not there needs to be able to stand-alone. Recall that the stand-alone video needs to deliver the message clearly without our assistance. This usually implies captioning. Yet, this captioning is distracting during our physical presentation, so it's best to produce two scenario videos, one with captioning on, and the other with it off. This clarifies another reason why scenarios should be visual first, and rely on text as support only. The more visual the scenario, the less difference between the two, and the easier the creation of both.

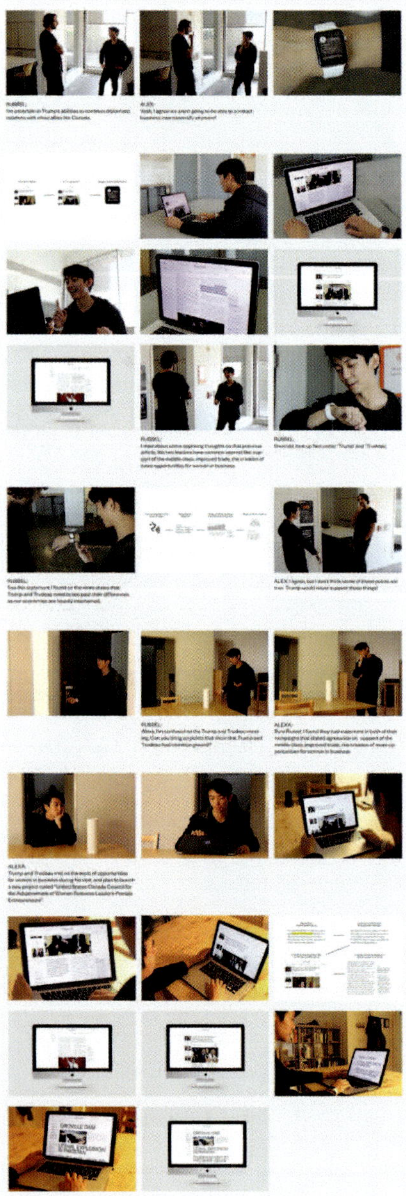

Figure 14.21
A scenario board presenting the final pitch scenario (from Sourced, by Jonathan Nishida, used by kind permission of Jonathan Nishida).

14.10 ROLE OF APPEARANCE MODELS

For device based solutions, appearance models hold a special place of importance. They provide an audience with a sense of dimensionality and reality that cannot be conveyed in pictures alone. We can observe the product in three dimensions; get a sense of color, material, and form; and feel what its size and

Figure 14.22
Use a reduced scenario for wall art, the full scenario should be in the presentation (from Munio, by Team Wolf Pack, used by kind permission of Judy Chu, Tina Ou, Jane Park, and Jade Tsao).

Figure 14.23
The final scenario should be of high quality, and use good cinematics—especially the principle of show, don't tell (from Sync and Harmony, by Team ABC, used by kind permission of Serena Jorif, Calvin Lien, and Ofir Atia).

scale may be like. The drawback with appearance models is that they are often static sculptures that don't articulate or behave like the product—if they were, we'd have the product itself! Static appearance models can be relied upon as the primary design communication medium for products with limited dynamics, such as a chair or a shoe, or even a bicycle. But digital devices are often just a frame for the interactive experience within. Consider the smartphone, for example: The physical features are simple and reduced, while the real complexity is what is happening on the interface.

This does not mean that appearance models are no longer important. We still need a sense of what the device will be in the real world, but our appearance model is no longer front and center. To clarify, it needs to be delivered with a scenario: The thing that communicates its use. Consider point of sale marketing: Without a display telling us how to use something like Amazon's Echo, it's just a black cylinder with some texture and branding. Regardless of their lessened status in the communication of a product, appearance models are still effective and need to be executed with the same kind of care they have been in prior eras. But now consider things that we may wrap around the product so that it not only communicates realistic form, but hints at dynamics as well (Figure 14.24).

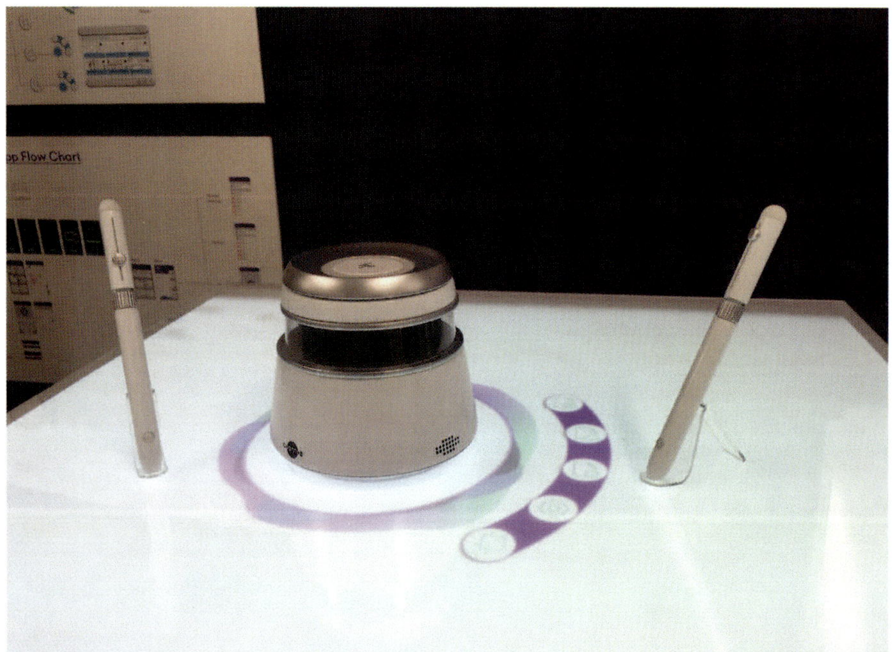

Figure 14.24
Appearance models deliver the final aesthetics of the physical devices (from Cosmos, by Team Laundry, used by kind permission of Asli Akdemir, Lynn Lei, Nathan Lu, and Yozei Wu).

14.11 ROLE OF THE PRESENTATION PROTOTYPE

Beyond the appearance model is the presentation prototype. While the appearance model focuses on what the device looks like, the presentation prototype focuses on what it's like to experience the system. It is the culmination of the work we've done on the various prototypes that we have built up to this point. It strives to present the essence of context delivered by our experience prototype, the dynamics and behavior of our behavioral prototype, to some degree the organization of our structural prototype, and the polish and sophistication of our final interface. Context, behavior, organization, interface.

The presentation prototype is the dynamic and interactive analog to the appearance model: Just as the appearance model simulates the look of a device, the presentation prototype simulates the experience of the system. Yet, they differ from

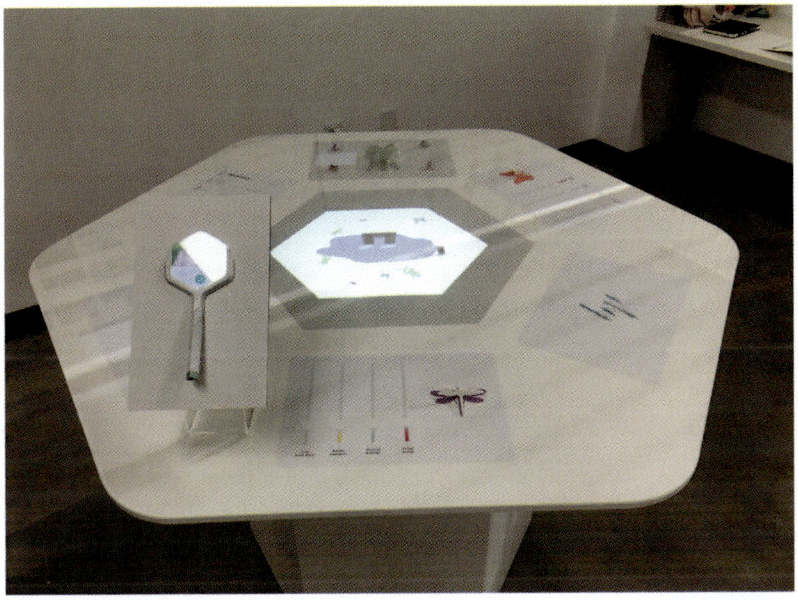

Figure 14.25
The experience prototype communicates use in context (from Sandbox, by Team O2, used by kind permission of Gen Hur, Ryan Van Noy, and Charlie Hodges).

each other as well: While the appearance model is focused on indicating form, the experience prototype is focused on indicating behavior in context. Form is often less important for an experience prototype. It's an added benefit if it can be achieved, but it's not as necessary as it is to communicate how things work. So, if you feel a time crunch in creating a prototype, focus less on what it looks like, since that's handled by appearance models and screen designs; focus more on what it does and how it acts in an external context (Figure 14.25).

The presentation prototype can vary in fidelity, with the ultimate being a working prototype with a coded front-end of an interface playing on the target device that we can place in the hands of a user, and it operates exactly as expected. Or it could be a lower fidelity mock-up, using off the shelf technology where the interface is animated linearly, and that we oz in a presentation to simulate the experience.

If it is coded to be a working prototype, it's usually not necessary to include the bullet-proofing required by released products, such as backend technologies, security, and sophisticated error checking. This allows it to be much simpler and faster to build than a released system. If, on the other hand, we go with a lower fidelity prototype, we can do something that is mocked up and ozed: It can be as simple as having a person secretly clicking through a slideshow while we simulate the interaction on a linearly playing movie. Whatever the fidelity, the emphasis for a presentation prototype is on communicating the physicality of the experience of the system in the real world. Making it seem real, even though it is not.

14.12 THE PITCH PRESENTATION

The component that ties all these elements together is the pitch presentation itself: The presentation slideshow that we use to deliver the communication. As we mentioned previously, like all other elements in our solution, this needs to be designed as well. Yet, not over-designed. It should complement the type, image, and color themes that support our design, yet it shouldn't overwhelm our design.

Bear in mind that a presentation slideshow has similar characteristics to a pitch scenario in that when we are physically there to present it we should be the ones telling the story, not captions in the slideshow. If we find ourselves simply reading the text on our slides, we need to rethink our presentation. The slides should enhance the presentation with visuals, not *be* the communication. On the other hand, if the slideshow is stand-alone, it needs to deliver the entirety of the pitch, so text and captions are necessary. It should also orchestrate well with the stand-alone pitch scenario video.

Please don't think that you will do a perfect presentation the first time, unrehearsed. Professional actors put a great deal of time into rehearsal, and they perform all the time. What makes you think you can execute flawlessly without rehearsal yourself? You can't. Rehearse what you need to say, how it all flows, and try to get "off book" (memorize the script). Work on cues and handoffs if you're doing a team presentation. Rehearse until you feel you've worked out all the kinks (Figure 14.26).

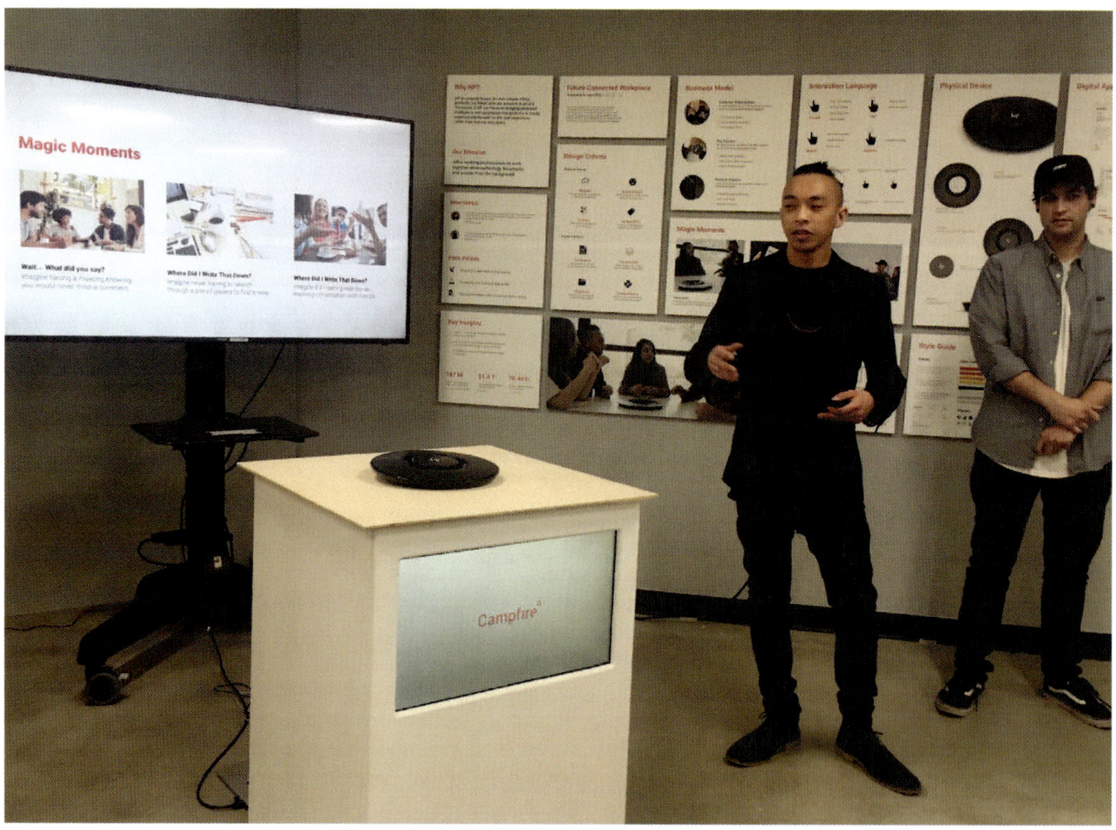

Figure 14.26

Rehearse your presentation until it runs smoothly (presentation of Campfire, by Team Seamrippers, used by kind permission of Matthew Benkert and Ian Liao).

14.13 TAKEAWAYS

We mentioned earlier in the chapter that our audience will most likely desire to take something away that exemplifies the design, to either consider on their own or show to others. An effective way to deliver this is through a website that presents the design. It can draw from the elements of the presentation and the installation, but be aware that the audience of a website is not a captive one like that of a presentation. If it takes too long for a visitor to get to the essence of the design, they're gone. This means the framing of the challenge needs to be extremely short, and possibly the scenario needs to be quite brief as well. Site visitors can always drill down for more information if it is provided, but if they face a long drawn-out introduction and video, they will quickly lose interest.

At the physical presentation, it's advisable to offer the audience some form of material that they can take with them. Classically, this has been a brochure, and, through tradeshow culture, this has evolved into swag. But many of these things get thrown away right after the audience leaves the building. An effective takeaway is something that someone keeps that reminds them of our project. If we're going to put time into takeaways, they should be effective. This implies they should be unique and cherishable. Almost by definition, they should be custom.

They should be intriguing, relevant in some way to the design, and deliver the website link or a place to go for further information. Artifacts and enclosures can be effective ways of doing this, but care must be taken that they don't smack of cheesy swag or they will be disposed of. They need to reflect the quality that we put into our design and firmly deliver on our brand values. In fact, this is a good rule of thumb not just for artifacts, but for any takeaway, including the website.

14.14 FINAL DELIVERY

Speaking of delivery, we should not drop the ball when we finally hand off our designs. Whatever the delivery specifications are, ensure that they are adhered to diligently. A clumsy delivery indicates a lack of care on the part of the deliverer. If a client receives a sloppy delivery, that tips them off that your design may not be trusted since your attention to detail is lacking. You may end up squandering weeks, if not months, of diligent work. A few hours of careful organization will promote trust in you as an attentive professional.

14.15 FURTHER QUESTIONS AND RESPONSES

Expect additional questions and responses from the client after the presentation and delivery have been made. These may be points of clarification or suggestions of further refinement. If the client has been involved throughout the process, these will most likely be minimal. If they haven't, they may uncover issues that have not yet been addressed. Be responsible and responsive to them, but also make sure the issues fall within the scope of the design brief. If there are significant alterations, discuss with your project stakeholders how to address them.

14.16 PITCH ORCHESTRATION

In the end, all the elements of the final presentation need to work as a seamless whole. The installation captures attention and teases an audience in; wall art frames the issues; the scenario and pitch presentation outline the context and experience;

the presentation prototype, interface designs, and appearance models communicate detail and how the system will live in the real world; and the flowboard, high-fidelity prototypes, and scenario storyboard can function as support for detailed question and answer sessions. Consider how your presentation operates on all these levels and achieves the goal of selling the design you worked on so diligently. Don't sell yourself short: Allow the epic work you've done the greatest opportunity to be enthusiastically accepted.

Conclusion

We have covered the process of Interaction Design from initial brief to final delivery, with pitstops that included concept, research, strategy, approach, exploration, detail design, aesthetics, and communication. As you can see, this discipline is vast. It touches upon and integrates several topics that are rich disciplines in their own right. These include not only the expected topics, such as interface, user experience, interaction, prototyping, and information architecture, but also topics such as design innovation, business strategy, design research, branding, cinematics, product design, and graphic design, just to name a few. Although it has taken us hundreds of pages to get through this, due to the profound scope of Interaction Design, you may still feel that we've only touched upon things in a very cursory fashion. To be honest, we share this feeling as well.

Our goal has been to provide you with a basic structure of the process that you can customize for your own needs and take further. If you're curious about any of the topics probed here and wish to dive into them further, we've done our job. We've included a robust bibliography just for this purpose and you can also consult the website InteractionForDesigners.com.

As mentioned in the introduction yet may be important to remind you here, we also recognize that the process within these pages is our particular process, although it has been born out of literally hundreds of cases combined with extensive tuning. The process that leverages your skills, within the environment of your organization, facing the issues of your particular project objectives may be something entirely different. We hope, however, that sharing our process has helped you consider effective ways of getting things done. Take what we have given you, adapt it for your needs, and make it better.

Above all, we hope that what we've given you here provides direction, fills you with inspiration, and allows you to make things that people love.

References

Alexander, C., Jacobson, M., Silverstein, M., Ishiwaka, S., Fiksdahl-King, I., & Shlomo, A. (1977). *A Pattern Language: Towns, Buildings, Construction.* Oxford, UK: Oxford University Press.

Apple. (2017, October 13). Design: Apple. Retrieved from https://developer.apple.com/design/

Berners-Lee, T. (1989). *The Original Proposal of the WWW.* Retrieved from W3c.org: https://www.w3.org/History/1989/proposal.html

Brewer, J. (2000). *Ethnography: Understanding Social Research.* London, UK: Open University Press.

Bringhurst, R. (2004). *The Elements of Typographic Style.* Vancouver, Canada: Hartley & Marks.

Canaan, D. (2003). Research to Fuel the Creative Process. In B. Laurel (Ed.), *Design Research Methods and Perspectives.* Cambridge, MA: MIT Press.

Carroll, J. (2000). *Making Use: Scenario-Based Design of Human Computer Interactions.* Cambridge, MA: MIT Press.

Cooper, A. (2015). *About Face* (4th ed.). Indianapolis, IN: Wiley.

Crouch, S., & Housden, M. (2003). *Marketing Research for Managers.* Oxford, UK: Butterworth-Heinemann.

Csikszentmihalyi, M. (1990). *Flow.* New York: Harper & Row.

Don, A., & Petrick, J. (2003). User Requirements. In B. Laurel (Ed.), *Design Research Methods and Perspectives* (pp. 70–81). Cambridge, MA: MIT Press.

Elmer-DeWitt, P. (2011, June 22). The Final Cut Pro X Debacle. *Fortune.*

Garrett, J. (2003). *The Elements of User Experience.* San Francisco, CA: New Riders.

Gentilviso, C. (2010, May 27th). The 50 Worst Inventions: Clippy. *Time.*

Google. (2017, 12 29). Page Ranking. Retrieved from www.google.com: www.google.com/search/howsearchworks/

Google. (2017, October 13). Guidelines: Material.io. Retrieved from https://material.io/guidelines/

Gothelf, J., & Seiden, J. (2016). *Lean UX: Designing Great Products with Agile Teams.* Sebastopol, CA: O'Reilly.

Hammerstein, O., & Rodgers, R. (1965). Do-Re-Mi [Recorded by J. Andrews]. On *Sound of Music.*

Hopcroft, J., Motwani, R., & Ullman, J. (2007). *Introduction to Automata Theory, Languages, and Computation.* San Francisco, CA: Pearson.

ifandelse. (2017, October 28th). Machina.js – Finite State Machines. Retrieved from http://machina-js.org/

IDEO. (2003). *IDEO Method Cards: 51 Ways to Inspire Design.* William Stout.

International Institute of Business Analysis. (2009). MoSCoW Analysis. In *A Guide to the Business Analysis Body of Knowledge* (2nd ed.). Toronto, Canada: International Institute of Business Analysis.

jakesgordon. (n.d.). javascript-state-machine: jakesgordon. Retrieved October 28th, 2017, from Github: https://github.com/jakesgordon/javascript-state-machine

Johnson, J. (2010). *Designing with the Mind in Mind: Simple Guide to Understanding User Interface Design Rules.* Burlington, MA: Morgan Kaufmann.

Karjaluoto, E. (2014). *The Design Method: A Philosophy and Process for Functional Visual Communication.* San Francisco, CA: New Riders.

Kolko, J. (2011). *Exposing the Magic of Design: A Practitioner's Guide to the Methods and Theory of Synthesis.* New York: Oxford University Press.

Krause, J. (2015). *Visual Design*. San Francisco, CA: New Riders.
Krug, S. (2014). *Don't Make Me Think*. San Francisco, CA: New Riders.
Levere, J. (2008, July 21). Press a Button and Your Worries Are Gone. Retrieved October 24, 2017, from *New York Times*: http://www.nytimes.com/2008/07/21/business/media/21Adnewsletter1.html
Levin, M. (2014). *Designing Multi-Device Experiences*. Sebastopol, CA: O'Reilly.
Lidwell, W., Holden, K., & Butler, J. (2010). *Universal Principles of Design*. Beverly, MA: Rockport.
Lupton, E. (2011). *Graphic Design Thinking: Beyond Brainstorming*. Hudson, NY: Princeton Architectural Press.
McCauley-Bush, P. (2012). *Ergonomics: Foundational Principles, Applications, and Technologies*. Boca Raton, FL: CRC Press.
Microsoft. (2018). Microsoft Design. Retrieved January 12, 2018, from Microsoft.com: https://developer.microsoft.com/en-us/windows/desktop/design
Morville, P., & Rosenfeld, L. (2007). *Information Architecture*. Sebastopol, CA: O'Reilly.
Neil, T. (2014). *Mobile Design Pattern Gallery: UI Patterns for Smartphone Apps* (2nd ed.). Sebastopol, CA: O'Reilly Media.
Nielson, J., & Genter, D. (1996). The Anti-Mac Interface. *Communications of the ACM, 39*, 70–82.
Norman, D. (1988). *The Design of Everyday Things*. New York: Basic Books.
OXO. (2017, September 25). Retrieved from www.oxo.com
Pannafino, J. (2012). *Interdisciplinary Interaction Design*. Assiduous.
Pascale, B. (2014). *Provincial Letters*, T. M'Crie (Trans.). Adelaide, Australia: University of Adelaide.
Portigal, S. (2008, Jan/Feb). Portigal-Consulting-White-Paper-Persona-Non-Grata.pdf. Retrieved September 16, 2017, from http://www.portigal.com/: http://www.portigal.com/wp-content/uploads/2008/01/Portigal-Consulting-White-Paper-Persona-Non-Grata.pdf
Quesenbery, W., & Brooks, K. (2010). *Storytelling for User Experience: Crafting Stories for Better Design*. Brooklin, NY: Rosenfeld Media.
Ries, A., & Trout, J. (2001). *Positioning: The Battle for Your Mind*. New York: McGraw Hill.
Saffer, D. (2010). *Designing for Interaction*. Berkeley, CA: New Riders.
Saffer, D. (2014). *Microinteractions: Designing with Details*. Sebastopol, CA: O'Reilly.
Samara, T. (2002). *Making and Breaking the Grid*. Beverly, MA: Rockport.
Skok, M. (2013, June 14). 4 Steps to Building a Compelling Value Proposition. *Forbes*.
Strava. (2017, September 2). Retrieved from strava.com
Tidwell, J. (2006). *Designing Interfaces: Patterns for Effective Interaction Design*. Sebastopol, CA: O'Reilly.
Tilley, A. (2002). *The Measure of Man and Woman: Human Factors in Design*. New York: John Wiley.
Traufetter, G. (2010, February 25). Death in the Atlantic: The Last Four Minutes of Air France Flight 447. *Der Spiegel*.
Tufte, E. (2001). *The Visual Display of Quantitative Information*. Cheshire, CT: Graphics Press.
Typecode. (2017, November 8). *Screen Sizes*. Retrieved from http://screensiz.es/
UI Patterns. (2017, October 16). *Patterns*. Retrieved from ui-patterns.com: http://ui-patterns.com/patterns
Unger, R., & Chandler, C. (2009). *A Project Guide to UX Design*. Berkeley, CA: New Riders.
Van Dijck, P. (2003). *Information Architecture for Designers: Structuring Websites for Business Success*. Mies, Switzerland: RotoVision SA.
Van Welie, M. (2017, October 16). Patterns. Retrieved from Welie.com: http://www.welie.com/patterns/
Warner Communications. (1989). *Speechless* (Poster). Warner Bros.
WC3. (2017, October 15). Web Accessibility Tutorials. Retrieved from https://www.w3.org/WAI/tutorials/
Zaki Warfel, T. (2009). *Prototyping: A Practitioner's Guide*. Rosenfeld Media.

Index

Note: Page numbers in *italic* refer to figures.